CICS APPLICATION AND SYSTEM PROGRAMMING

Books from QED

Database

Managing IMS Databases
Building the Data Warehouse
Migrating to DB2
DB2: The Complete Guide to Implementation
  and Use
DB2 Design Review Guidelines
DB2: Maximizing Performance of Online
  Production Systems
Embedded SQL for DB2
SQL for DB2 and SQL/DS Application
  Developers
How to Use ORACLE SQL*PLUS
ORACLE: Building High Performance Online
  Systems
ORACLE Design Review Guidelines
Developing Client/Server Applications in an
  Architected Environment

Systems Engineering

From Mainframe to Workstations: Offloading
  Application Development
Software Configuration Management
On Time, Within Budget: Software Project
  Management Practices and Techniques
Information Systems Architecture:
  Development in the 90's
Quality Assurance for Information Systems
User-Interface Screen Design: Workstations,
  PC's, Mainframes
Managing Software Projects
The Complete Guide to Software Testing
A Structured Approach to Systems Testing
Rapid Application Prototyping
The Software Factory
Data Architecture: The Information Paradigm
Software Engineering with Formal Metrics
Using CASE Tools for Practical Management

Management

Enterprise Architecture Planning: Developing a
  Blueprint for Data, Applications, and
  Technology
Introduction to Data Security and Controls
How to Automate Your Computer Center
Controlling the Future
The UNIX Industry
Mind Your Business

IBM OS/2 Series

OS/2 Presentation Manager Programming for
  COBOL Programmers
Micro Focus Workbench for the Application
  Developer
OS/2 2.0: The Workplace Shell—A User's
  Guide and Tutorial

IBM Mainframe Series

VSE/SP and VSE/ESA: A Guide to
  Performance Tuning
CICS: A Guide to Application Debugging
CICS Application and System Programming
CICS: A Guide To Performance Tuning
MVS COBOL II Power Programmer's Desk
  Reference
VSE JCL and Subroutines for Application
  Programmers
VSE COBOL II Power Programmer's Desk
  Reference
Introduction to Cross System Product
Cross System Product Application Development
The MVS Primer
MVS/VSAM for the Application Programmer
TSO/E CLISTs: The Complete Tutorial and
  Desk Reference
CICS: A How-To for COBOL Programmers
QMF: How to Use Query Management Facility
  with DB2 and SQL/DS
DOS/VSE JCL: Mastering Job Control
  Language
DOS/VSE: CICS Systems Programming
VSAM: Guide to Optimization and Design
MVS/JCL: Mastering Job Control Language
MVS/TSO: Mastering CLISTs
MVS/TSO: Mastering Native Mode and ISPF
REXX in the TSO Environment, 2nd Edition

Technical

Rdb/VMS: Developing the Data Warehouse
AS/400 Architecture and Planning
C Language for Programmers
AS/400: A Practical Guide to Programming and
  Operations
Bean's Index to OSF/Motif, Xt Intrinsics, and
  Xlib Documentation for OSF/Motif
  Application Programmers
VAX/VMS: Mastering DCL Commands and
  Utilities
The PC Data Handbook
UNIX C Shell Desk Reference
Designing and Implementing Ethernet Networks
The Handbook for Microcomputer Technicians
Open Systems

This is Only a Partial Listing. For Additional Information or a Free Catalog contact
QED Information Sciences, Inc. • P. O. Box 812070 • Wellesley, MA 02181-0013
Telephone: 800-343-4848 or 617-237-5656 or fax 617-235-0826

CICS APPLICATION AND SYSTEM PROGRAMMING

Tools and Techniques

Barry K. Nirmal

QED Technical Publishing Group
Boston • Toronto • London

© 1992 QED Information Sciences, Inc.
P.O. Box 82-181
Wellesley, MA 02181

QED Technical Publishing Group is a division of QED Information Sciences, Inc.

Library of Congress Catalog Number: 91-26380
International Standard Book Number: 0-89435-393-4

Printed in the United States of America
    93 94 10 9 8 7 6 5 4 3 2

Library of Congress Cataloging-in-Publication Data

Nirmal, Barry K., 1949–
    CICS application and system development / Barry K. Nirmal.
        p.   cm.
    Includes index.
    ISBN 0-89435-393-4
    1. CICS (Computer system)   I. Title.
QA76.76.T45N57   1991
005.4'3—dc20   91-26380
                                                                          CIP

Contents

Preface

For many years, I have wanted to write two books, one on CICS and another on IBM assembler language programming. I have been fascinated with both these subjects for a long time. Since 1975 I have been working with CICS in both applications and system programming, and since 1972 I have been programming in Assembler, after learning this language at the University of Nebraska at Lincoln. (This is not to say that this book only has programs in Assembler. In fact, there are many programs here in COBOL, the most popular language among application programmers.) I have never wanted to write a book on COBOL, even though I mastered it many years ago. (My first book, published by Prentice Hall Inc., in 1986, deals with programming standards and guidelines with emphasis on COBOL programming, and my second book, published by QED Information Sciences Inc., in 1990, teaches MVS/TSO CLIST programming.) With the publication of this third book, both of my wishes have been fulfilled.

I have been fascinated with CICS because of its structure, its functionality, and the comprehensive set of tools and features it provides to the application designers and programmers for building complex on-line systems with such crucial features as recovery/restart, support for databases, etc. I have been fascinated with IBM assembler language, because unlike those who program in high-level languages, an assembler language programmer has so much power and so much control. Also, an assembler language programmer gets to understand how the machine really works.

People have asked me, "Why do you write books? Is it for money or fame or for both?" Even though I cannot deny that money and fame are of interest to me, those are not my sole motivations behind writing books. In fact, the desire to help people, especially those who are not related or personally known to me, *is* an important motivation. This is because, like most people, I consider this life temporary. It may come to an abrupt end at any moment. and the worse thing, to me, is not knowing where I will go after my life ends. I find it difficult to accept that this life was created without any purpose. Whatever the answer to this question, I feel the main purpose of human life cannot be the seeking of happiness for oneself and one's family. A human being must spend at least part of his or her life doing things for others, especially those unknown to him or her. In fact, a person who spends his time helping others selflessly is indeed a person to be envied.

So, I thought that I would live and die peacefully if I knew that I spent my life not only seeking happiness for myself and my family but also for others. Writing books that teach computer programming in CICS, assembler, COBOL, or MVS/TSO CLISTs is my way of helping others. Even though it is true that one who reproduces never dies, it is a definite fact that should I die tomorrow all my knowledge of CICS and other subjects will also die with me unless I share my knowledge through books and articles. So, publication of this book on CICS gives me consolation that all my knowledge of CICS will not go unused should I die tomorrow.

Acknowledgements

I thank all my teachers who taught me at the schools, college, and university I attended both in India and the United States of America. I also thank the authors of books, both technical and nontechnical, who have acted as indirect teachers to me. Without studying books and articles written by authors whom I have never met, I would not have been able to write this book. I am thankful to the many authors whose articles in CICS Update and MVS Update journals have been great sources of new knowledge and information for me. (These journals are published by Xephon plc, and edited by Steve Piggott, who have my gratitude for publishing these and other fine journals. Their address is: Xephon plc, 27-35 London Road, Newbury, Berkshire, RG13 1JL, England (U.K.))

I am also thankful to my wife, Gargi, for her patience and understanding while this book was being written. The researching and writing of this book cut into the time I had available to spend with my family.

I also thank SCECO East in Saudi Arabia, especially my EDP department manager, Mr. Yahya S. Al-Dhukair, for whatever they have done for me.

I would be failing in my duty if I did not thank Edwin F. Kerr, president and publisher of QED Technical Publishing Group, for accepting my proposal and acting quickly to ensure that this book arrived in the hands of the readers. The staff at QED Technical Publishing Group, in particular Beth A. Roberts deserves my appreciation for their professionalism and efficiency.

Why Should You Buy This Book?

There is a proverb that says, "Give a man a fish, and you feed him for a day. Teach a man to fish, and you feed him for a lifetime." So, you can say that this book teaches the readers how to fish, i.e., write CICS programs, rather than giving them fish to eat, i.e., programs to use. There are software vendors who give companies ready-made programs to use, many of which are similar to those in this book, undoubtedly meeting an important need of their customers. But, by not giving the companies the source code of programs, and by not explaining the programs, they create a mystique around their product and make their customers dependent on the product vendors. This book does not do that. It not only gives you tools, that is, programs, JCL, etc., that you can use with little or no change, but it also explains them so you can learn how to develop similar tools yourself.

All programs, facilities, concepts, and techniques contained in this book have been developed in the author's spare time and thoroughly tested to work on CICS test and production regions running on IBM mainframe computers.

What Releases of CICS Are Covered

The tools and techniques contained in this book should work under all versions of CICS, i.e., CICS/OS/VS, CICS/MVS, and CICS/ESA. With little or no change, they will also work under CICS/DOS/VS. They have been rigorously tested under CICS/OS/VS Version 1 Release 7. If a program does not work under a certain CICS release, slight modification will make it work.

A Request to the Reader

If you have any comments to make regarding the usefulness of this book, or have any ideas for improving it, e.g., by giving some specific programs or facilities that you have in mind or have need for, please write to me in care of QED Publishing Group, P.O. Box 812070, Wellesley, MA 02181-0013.

Barry K. Nirmal

Introduction

1.1 IS THIS BOOK FOR YOU?

As you read this introduction, you may be trying to decide if this book is for you and whether or not you should spend your own or your company's money to buy it. If you are a supervisor, administrator, or a manager of programmers and system analysts, you may be contemplating purchasing copies of this book for each member of your group, division, or department.

As the title of this book suggests, it is a "tools and techniques" book. It contains many complete utilities (consisting of BMS maps, COBOL and assembler programs, and JCLs), facilities, and systems that serve as the "tools" for CICS professionals in both application and system programming areas. There is even a complete system called Humor Storage and Retrieval Facility that can be entertaining in times of boredom. All the utilities and techniques given in this book have been successfully tested on a CICS Release 1.7 system under MVS/XA. But they should also work under other software platforms, such as other CICS releases that run under MVS or DOS/VSE.

The utilities contained in this book solve the most common types of practical problems and meet the most pressing requirements of programmers and analysts in both application and system programming. Certain utilities that perform the same functions as those in this book are available from some software vendors for hundreds and even thousands of dollars. And generally, software vendors don't provide you with source codes. For less expense, however, this book supplies source codes and installation instructions that are clear and easily understood.

The BMS maps, programs, and JCL decks—all complete—can be easily copied to your own data sets, compiled or assembled, and executed with little or no change. (Sample JCL decks for assembling BMS maps and programs and for compiling and linking CICS COBOL programs are given in Appendix

B to help in installation.) All utilities are accompanied by detailed instructions for installing and using them and include thorough explanations. A good understanding of them will enable you to either modify the utilities or write similar ones to meet your unique needs on the job. This book also contains many CICS programming examples and techniques.

If you are a programmer, a programmer/analyst, a systems analyst, or a supervisor of such groups and you work with CICS on a mainframe or a PC, this book is definitely for you. If you are a student or an instructor and use or have CICS on the computer of your school, college, or university, this book will be helpful. The complete programs and facilities written in COBOL and assembler can be used not only to perform programming jobs but also to understand how COBOL and assembler programs can be designed and constructed to serve as utilities. The utility to issue any MVS or JES command in batch can be used by system programmers or operators even if CICS is not used.

A thorough understanding of CICS is very important for anyone who supports an application system based on CICS, which is the most widely used teleprocessing monitor for developing and running on-line applications on IBM mainframes and personal computers. Because CICS runs under OS, MVS, and DOS operating systems on IBM and compatible mainframes, and under DOS and OS/2 operating systems on IBM and compatible personal computers, and because it is part of IBM's system application architecture (SAA), its importance as IBM's strategic software product of the future can not be overestimated.

That is all there is to deciding whether this book is for you. And if so, then it is worth its weight in gold. The programs and facilities contained here are both useful and practical. They can be put to immediate use, and they will give you valuable insights into the needs for which similar utilities can be written. This will hopefully inspire you to write similar utilities for your own unique needs, ones that will be suitable and relevant to your own particular environment and application.

1.2 WHAT THIS BOOK COVERS

This first chapter gives you the essential information about the entire book's content and the resources defined in CICS tables that will be referred to in subsequent chapters. It also gives you a brief overview of CICS and discusses the requirements and other issues related to running CICS on an IBM or compatible personal computer.

Chapter 2 contains useful programs and facilities that serve as the "chest of tools", especially for the application programmers. System programmers will also find some of these utilities interesting and useful to them in their jobs.

Chapter 3 answers questions that are commonly asked by the application programmers. System programmers will also find this chapter useful and interesting, because a good understanding of these topics will help them in providing technical support to the applications staff.

Chapter 4 presents problem-determination techniques for application programmers. Once again, system programmers should also learn these techniques so they can provide technical support to the application programmers and analysts.

Chapter 5 presents useful programs and facilities for system programmers. Some of these utilities, such as the program to display the actual VTAM logical nodename of a terminal, can also be used by application programmers and help desk staff.

Chapter 6 answers questions commonly asked by system programmers. Application programmers will also find some of these questions and answers interesting and useful.

Chapter 7 answers questions regarding CICS performance and tuning that are commonly asked by system programmers. The questions in Chapters 6 and 7 should also be of interest to application programmers, especially if they want to undertake system programming or study causes of poor performance or problems in CICS that affect their application systems.

Chapter 8 presents problem-determination techniques for system programmers.

Chapter 9 presents an interesting application called Humor Storage and Retrieval Facility (HSRF) that can be used to store any humor or quotation of one or more lines on a VSAM file for display on the screen. Each humor or quotation item consists of one or more lines. The humor/quotation items displayed are in random order, which makes it an interesting facility to entertain yourself with in moments of boredom. This facility is most appreciated when the file contains a large number of items, so we have included some humor/quotation items in Appendix A.

Chapter 9 also presents a simple but powerful CICS monitor that can be used to display important information about the running system. It can also display active and suspended tasks in the system and any area of virtual storage in the CICS region.

Appendix B contains the sample JCL decks for installing various programs and facilities presented in Chapters 2, 5, and 9.

In Appendix C we present subroutines, macros, and COPYLIB members that are used in one or more programs in Chapters 2, 5, and 9. These subroutines are designed to be of a general-purpose nature and are invoked by a calling program. They are not executable by themselves. This is why they have been included in this appendix.

1.3 WHAT THIS BOOK DOES *NOT* COVER

This book does not present detailed information about the various commands available for programming at the CICS command level. This information is available in the IBM publication *Application Programmer's Reference Manual (Command Level)* for CICS (manual number: SC33-0241 for CICS/OS/VS). Even though this IBM manual is the ultimate reference source for command-level programmers, beginners should not use this manual for learning CICS command-level programming. They should use one of the several excellent books published on the subject by U.S. publishers. In order to understand the CICS command-level programs in this book, one should have basic knowledge of command-level programming.

This book also does not teach the basics of COBOL and assembler language programming. So, in order to understand the COBOL programs in this book, one should have basic knowledge of COBOL, and in order to understand the assembler programs, one should have basic knowledge of the assembler language.

1.4 HOW TO BENEFIT THE MOST FROM THIS BOOK

This book is for both the experienced and the inexperienced CICS programmer, in both application and system programming areas. Because it is more of a reference book than a text, this book should not be read from cover to cover. Instead you should read what interests you. For example, if you are an application programmer, Chapters 2, 3, and 4 will be of primary interest to you, and other chapters that deal with system programming will be helpful only if you desire to move into system programming or to learn about it. If you are a system programmer, Chapters 5, 6, 7, 8, and 9 will be of primary interest to you; the chapters that deal with application programming will be of interest to you if you do not have an application programming background or if you want to reinforce your knowledge of application programming to provide technical support to the applications staff.

Everyone can appreciate the Humor Storage and Retrieval Facility in Chapter 9. There are times when you are not completely occupied with developing systems, diagnosing and solving problems, or meeting a deadline. In such moments, it is nice to have an on-line facility that refreshes you with humor and quotations.

You may ask, "How can I benefit from a utility written in assembler when I don't know assembler language?" Well, all the utilities and facilities presented in this book are accompanied by detailed instructions for installing them. They also include detailed explanations. So, if you need the function performed by a utility, follow the instructions for installing and using it and start using it. After this you can read the explanations and try to understand them. Suppose you don't know assembler programming at all. In this case you will not be able to understand the utilities written in assembler. If you know the basics of COBOL and command level programming but are not strong in them, the explanations that accompany the utilities written in command level COBOL will be helpful. This will enhance your knowledge of COBOL as well as command-level programming.

So, even if you do not particularly want to understand the utilities, the accompanying detailed instructions for installing and using them will greatly facilitate their use.

1.5 CONVENTIONS USED IN THIS BOOK

When reference is made to the CICS program processing table (PPT), the program control table (PCT), and the terminal control table (TCT), it should be understood that they refer not only to the macro-based tables but also to entries on the DFHCSD file, which is also called the resource definition on-line (RDO) file. In fact, on CICS Release 1.7 and higher systems, all programs, transactions, and terminals should be defined on the DFHCSD file using transaction CEDA. This facilitates adding a new program, transaction, or terminal dynamically, as well as altering the definitions of existing resources.

Since MVS JCL decks are coded using only upper-case characters, whenever lower-case words are used in JCL statements (see Figures B.1 and B.6 in Appendix B), the user should replace the lower-case words with appropriate, meaningful words.

The TSO commands, as well as CEMT and other CICS transactions, can be entered on the terminal in upper-case or lower-case letters. But on all commands given in this book, lower-case words should be replaced as necessary. Upper-case words should not be changed. For example, suppose the command reads

LISTC ENT ('your.vsam.file.name') ALL

Here you would replace 'your.vsam.file.name' with the complete name of your own VSAM file. Other parts of the command, including quotation marks, should *not* be changed.

1.6 RESOURCES TO BE DEFINED IN CICS TABLES IN ORDER TO RUN THE PROGRAMS IN THIS BOOK

Because this book is more of a reference than a text, programs and facilities presented in the various chapters have been made as self-contained as possible. So, in CICS tables resources to be defined to run a particular program or facility are given as part of the instructions for installing that program or facility. However, references are made throughout the book to the sample definitions given below. These definitions are valid for CICS Release 1.7 and have been rigorously tested on CICS systems in both test and production environments.

For CICS Release 1.7 and, later, the PCT, PPT, and TCT are all contained in the DFHCSD file which is a VSAM key-sequenced file. These tables are maintained using the IBM-supplied CEDA transaction, described in the Resource Definition On-Line manual. Other tables are macro-based and reside in a partitioned dataset. Tables such as FCT, DCT, and SIT are updated using TSO/ISPF and assembled and linked into a load library using assembler and linkage-editor.

All the definitions below assume that external security is not present on the CICS system. If your CICS system has external security, you will have to make suitable changes wherever necessary.

Definition of Transaction BNC1 in the Program Control Table (PCT)

```
TRANSACTION       : BNC1
GROUP             : CICSBOOK
PROGRAM           : BNPROG1
TWASIZE           : 00000
PROFILE           : TRANPROF
PARTITIONSET      :
  STATUS          : ENABLED
  PRIMEDSIZE      : 00000
REMOTE ATTRIBUTES
  REMOTESYSTEM    :
  REMOTENAME      :
  TRPROF          :
  LOCALQ          :
SCHEDULING
  PRIORITY        : 100
  TCLASS          : NO
ALIASES
  TASKREQ         :
  XTRANID         :
RECOVERY
  DTIMOUT         : 0010
  INDOUBT         : BACKOUT
  RESTART         : NO
  SPURGE          : NO
  TPURGE          : NO
  DUMP            : NO
  TRACE           : YES
SECURITY
  EXTSEC          : NO
  TRANSEC         : 01            Note 1
  RSL             : 00
  RSLC            : NO
```

Note 1. If TRANSEC is 1, the user need not first sign on to CICS using transaction CSSN before using this transaction. This makes this transaction unprotected and available to everyone.

Definition of Profile TRANPROF on the DFHCSD file

```
PROFILE      :  TRANPROF
GROUP        :  CICSBOOK
SCRNSIZE     :  DEFAULT
MODENAME     :
PRINTERCOMP  :  NO
JOURNALLING
JOURNAL      :  NO
MSGJRNL      :  NO
PROTECTION
MSGINTEG     :  NO
ONEWTE       :  NO
PROTECT      :  NO
PROTOCOLS
DVSUPRT      :  ALL
INBFMH       :  NO
RAQ          :  NO
LOGREC       :  NO
RECOVERY
NEPCLASS     :  000
RTIMOUT      :  NO
```

Definition of Program BNPROG1 in the PPT
(Program Processing Table)

```
PROGRAM      :  BNPROG1
GROUP        :  CICSBOOK
LANGUAGE     :  COBOL (OR ASSEMBLER)   Note 1
RELOAD       :  NO
RESIDENT     :  NO
RSL          :  00
STATUS       :  ENABLED
```

Note 1. Use COBOL if the program is a Command Level COBOL program. Use ASSEMBLER if the program is written in Assembler using Command or Macro level.

Definition of VSAM file (base cluster) BASCLUST in the FCT (File Control Table)

```
DFHFTC TYPE=DATASET,                                             X
  DATASET=BASCLUST,                                              X
  DISP=SHR,                                                      X
  DSNAME=full.name.of.vsam.cluster,                             X
  ACCMETH=VSAM,                                                  X
  FILSTAT=(ENABLED,CLOSED),                                      X
  JID=NO,                                                        X
  LOG=NO,                                                        X
  RECFORM=(FIXED,BLOCKED),                                       X
  SERVREQ=(READ,BROWSE,UPDATE,ADD,DELETE),                      X
  STRNO=2
```

Note the following:

1. Insert the fully qualified name of the VSAM cluster after DSNAME keyword. This file will be allocated to CICS.
2. If the VSAM file has fixed length records, use RECFORM=(FIXED, BLOCKED), or else use RECFORM=(VARIABLE,BLOCKED).
3. If you only want to read and browse a file and never modify the file through CICS programs, use SERVREQ=(READ,BROWSE). However, if you want to perform all kinds of operations on the file, then use SERVREQ= (READ,BROWSE,UPDATE,ADD,DELETE)

Definition of Path AIXPATH for an Alternate Index Cluster in the FCT

```
DFHFTC TYPE=DATASET,                                             X
  DATASET=AIXPATH,                                               X
  DISP=SHR,                                                      X
  DSNAME=full.name.of.path,                                     X
  ACCMETH=VSAM,                                                  X
  FILSTAT=(ENABLED,CLOSED),                                      X
  JID=NO,                                                        X
  LOG=NO,                                                        X
  RECFORM=(VARIABLE,BLOCKED),                                    X
  SERVREQ=(READ,BROWSE),                                         X
  STRNO=2
```

Note the following:

1. Insert the fully qualified name of the path after DSNAME keyword. This path was defined using DEFINE PATH command of IDCAMS.
2. For alternate index files, RECFORM is always (VARIABLE,BLOCKED),

and SERVREQ is always (READ,BROWSE), because it is recommended that the alternate index path be used only for reading and not updating the base cluster.

1.7 A BRIEF OVERVIEW OF CICS

Here is a brief overview of CICS, which is a complex software system. The main reason behind its complexity is that it is designed to meet the needs of all kinds of users, from the simplest to the most sophisticated. That is why CICS can support almost any kind of terminal that IBM ever produced. Some of the concepts and terms used here may be difficult to comprehend, but concepts are best understood when they are seen as applied in practice. For our purposes, it is not logical to show the application in practice of all the terms and concepts pertaining to CICS. So, we will be content with presenting the ideas on an overview level. The reader should refer to other books and IBM manuals to study in-depth concepts that might be unfamiliar to him such as multi-region operation, quasi-reenterancy, and so on.

There are many CICS products:

CICS/OS/VS Version 1 that runs under OS/VS2 MVS, MVS/XA, and OS/VS1 operating systems. IBM has decided to stabilize CICS/OS/VS Version 1

CICS/MVS Version 2 that runs under MVS

A new CICS with new code base to run in MVS/ESA environment

CICS/DOS/VS that runs under DOS/VSE

CICS/OS/2 Version 1 to run under OS/2 on IBM or compatible personal computers

Now let us discuss CICS in the mainframe environment. The next section will discuss CICS for the PC environment. CICS/VS is a table-driven system with high modularity. As mentioned before, it supports almost every kind of terminal that IBM ever produced, and their functions. It supports standard files (e.g., sequential access (SAM) files and VSAM files), its own private files, and DL/I and DB/2 databases.

A CICS system runs in a single region, where a region stands for an address space of MVS or a partition of OS/VS1 or DOS/VSE. CICS runs as a single operating system task. But CICS provides concurrent processing of multiple transactions through its own multi-tasking facility. A maximum of 999 concurrent tasks are possible.

CICS is basically a transaction driven and terminal-oriented system. When the user enters a transaction on the terminal, CICS creates a task for it, provided a CICS task and storage are available. Each transaction is initiated and executed independently from other transactions that might have the same transaction ID. The priority of each task controls its execution. Task priority is derived from terminal, transaction, and operator priorities. As application programs request access to files and databases, they are allocated to the task.

Multiple tasks share application programs in storage. This requires that the programs be quasi-reentrant. The application programs, if not already there, are brought into virtual storage by CICS program management. (CICS, being a modular system, has various components such as task management, program management, storage management, and so on.) CICS provides features that are comparable to operating system features such as program linking, storage, and timer management and enqueue/dequeue (ENQ/DEQ) of resources. This is why CICS is called a teleprocessing monitor system.

CICS tasks can be classified as conversational or pseudo-conversational. In pseudo-conversational processing, a task ends and specifies a transaction ID to be associated with the new task and, optionally, a communication area to be passed to it. When the user enters some data and presses a key on the terminal, the transaction whose transaction ID was specified by the previous task is started. In pure conversational processing, a task does not end until all conversational steps are processed.

CICS provides automatic transaction initiation (ATI) facility for asynchronous processing. This way a task can be created internally using the intrapartition transient data queue or the time-based facility using interval control. With this facility, a transaction can be initiated automatically but appear as if it had been entered from a terminal. A transaction started using the ATI facility may not be associated with a terminal, which means that its processing is not tied up with the availability of a terminal.

We noted that ATI uses transient data queue. CICS uses transient and temporary storage queues as its private files. Transient data queues are of two kinds: intrapartition data queues and extrapartition data queues. The former has a transaction trigger function, whereas the latter is a sequential file generally used for exchanging data between CICS and batch jobs. The temporary storage data queue can be either in main storage or on a DASD dataset. It is used by application programs as temporary scratch files. It is also used by the CICS system control program and by the BMS for storing data during terminal paging.

CICS provides its own exclusive control mechanisms for standard files and its own private files. There is also the implementation of the concept of recoverability of resources. DL/I data bases are always recoverable, whereas recoverability of other resources depends on the needs of the user. For example, if a VSAM file is to be recoverable, it must be specified with LOG = YES in the file control table.

The master terminal transaction can be issued from any CICS terminal including the operating system console. The CEMT transaction provides user-friendly panels including command syntax and help screens. A master terminal command can also be issued from an application program.

The security feature of CICS supports internal security which checks user authorization to execute secured transactions as well as resource level security with an external security package such as RACF, ACF2, or Top Secret.

Communication between CICS systems on different computers is accomplished by using CICS/VS intersystem communication (ISC) via SNA (System Network Architecture) LU6 (Logical Unit 6) sessions. Communication between various regions in the same host computer is accomplished using Multi-Region Operation (MRO). Multi-region operation allows the routing of transactions, sharing of terminals, and CICS function shipping between various CICS systems in the same host. MRO and ISC are transparent to terminal users who do not know which systems or regions are servicing their request. Through CICS function shipping, one can achieve transparent access by an application program to resources in other CICS systems such as standard files, CICS private files, and DL/I PSBs. So, the benefit of MRO is that it increases the parallelism of CICS processing and also increases storage isolation.

1.8   CICS ON AN IBM OR COMPATIBLE PERSONAL COMPUTER

For some time now, CICS has been available for running on a DOS machine. Now CICS OS/2 Version 1 is available for running under OS/2 Extended Edition using Presentation Manager on an IBM or compatible PC. In this section we will explore the various issues involved in running CICS OS/2 Version 1.

What are the requirements for running CICS OS/2 version 1?   You need an 80286, 80386, or higher CPU with OS/2 Extended Edition 1.1 or higher. You also need at least 1.3 megabytes of memory for CICS use, which is over and above the memory required by OS/2. You also need language compilers. CICS/OS/2 Version 1 supports Micro Focus COBOL, the IBM COBOL2 compiler, or the IBM C/2 compiler. Microsoft COBOL and C compilers may also work. The Micro Focus COBOL compiler is the best choice because it has built-in SQL support.

What are the functionalities of CICS/OS/2 version 1?   This product is not just a tool for checking application programs before running them on the mainframe. It is a real CICS product for developing and running applications in both test and production environments. Its functionality is very similar to the mainframe CICS, as we will soon see. It is so compatible to the mainframe CICS that IBM has not written an application programmer's reference manual exclusively for it. You should use the *Application Programmer's Reference Manual (Command Level)* (IBM manual number SC33-0512) for the mainframe CICS. In fact, you can download a copy of a command-level COBOL program from the mainframe to the PC, compile it, set up test files, and run the program. There should be no problems. The displays will be very much like those on a 3270-type terminal. But even though the functionalities of the CICS on the PC and the mainframe are the same, their internal structures are entirely different. This is because the platforms on which they run, the machines, and their operating systems are not the same.

But what about datasets? CICS/OS/2 uses its own VSAM file access method. The command-level interface is identical with that on the mainframe. So you can develop and test applications using VSAM on a PC and them migrate them for execution on the mainframe. The VSAM implementation is a part of CICS/OS/2 and not that of OS/2 or the COBOL compiler. CICS/OS/2 can access data on the computer's hard disk drive and data on other systems as well.

What about communications? Can I communicate with my mainframe? CICS/OS/2 supports LU2 (3270-type terminals) or LU6.2 (APPC) at the EXEC CICS level. Just as you can connect two mainframe host computers, you can connect an OS/2 machine with another OS/2 machine or a mainframe, using VTAM. You can also use the CRTE transaction on your mainframe CICS to route transactions to CICS/OS/2. IBM provides routines for ASCII to EBCDIC translation and vice versa, which helps in data transfer.

What are the advantages of running CICS/OS/2? If a company has no mainframe computer and they need the functionalities provided by CICS/OS/2, it would be advantageous to acquire one. Even if a company has a mainframe computer on which they run CICS, there are advantages in using a CICS/OS/2 machine for developing CICS applications. Programmers who know CICS command-level programming, COBOL, and VSAM can use those skills and become productive immediately on CICS/OS/2. After development and testing, applications can be migrated to the mainframe for running in production mode. Programmers do not have to wait for the VTAM network to be started, for the CICS test system to be started, and for changes to CICS tables to be made. Application programmers can assume responsibility for making changes to CICS tables on CICS/OS/2 through the RDO (Resource Definition On-line) facility. If a CICS/OS/2 system crashes, there is little harm done. It will not affect everyone else, unlike in the mainframe CICS environment. The PC system can be rebooted easily and work resumed.

On CICS/OS/2, there is better storage isolation than on mainframe CICS. If an application program or CICS/OS/2 itself tries to alter storage that does not belong to it, OS/2 displays an errors message and terminates the session.

Is it cost-effective to run CICS/OS/2? If you have CICS on your mainframe and have plenty of horsepower left, it would be more economical to connect another 3270-type terminal to it than to invest in a CICS/OS/2 system. But for reasons outlined above, in many instances it would be cost-effective to acquire and use CICS/OS/2 systems.

2

Useful Tools Especially for Application Programmers

In this chapter we will present and explain a number of programs that will serve as useful tools for the application programmer. This does not exclude system programmers since most of the programs can be useful to them as well. There is no clear line of demarcation between application programmers and system programmers. In the author's opinion, in order to become a good system programmer, a person must have sound, if not extensive, background in application programming that will give him a good appreciation for the work and needs of his colleagues in the application area.

Some of the programs presented in this chapter are in the Assembly language, which most application programmers do not know. The detailed instructions given will enable the reader to assemble and link these programs and use them. Once these Assembly language programs are being utilized, the system programming group, which has expertise in the language, can be responsible for maintaining the programs.

2.1 A ROUTINE TO PROVIDE CURRENT DATES AND TIMES IN VARIOUS FORMATS TO ITS CALLER

Figure 2.1 shows a program that you can LINK to in order to obtain current times and dates in various formats.

Procedure For Using This Program

In a CICS COBOL program, do the following:

Set up a communication area in working storage of 38 bytes. For example, you may set it up as follows:

```
01 WS-COMM-AREA.
   05 DATE-G          PIC X(8).
   05 DATE-TEXT       PIC X(22).
   05 TIME            PIC X(8).
```

In Procedure Division, LINK to program BNDATETI passing it to the 38-byte communication area, as follows:

```
EXEC CICS LINK PROGRAM ('BNDATETI') COMMAREA (WS-COMM-AREA)
LENGTH(38) END-EXEC.
```

After control comes back to your program from BNDATETI, various fields in WS-COMM-AREA contain valid values. DATE-G contains current date in the YY/MM/DD format. DATE-TEXT contains date in words, e.g. DECEMBER 02, 1992, and TIME contains current time in format HH:MM:SS.

In a GENER/OL program, you would have to follow the procedure shown by this example:

```
DATEAREA   WORK                        D1 COMMON50
           ----
           LINK      (BNDATETI),D1COMMAREA
```

After control comes back to your GENER/OL program from BNDATETI, various fields in D1COMMAREA contain valid values. The layout of work area DATEAREA, which in this example has a prefix of D1 is as follows:

FIELD NAME	STARTS AT	LENGTH	TYPE	COMMENTS
COMMAREA	1	38	C	
DATEEG	1	8		YY/MM/DD
DATETEXT	9	22	C	
TIME	31	8	C	HH:MM:SS

Note that D1COMMAREA used on the LINK command is the name of a field of 38 bytes length in work area. The names of the work area, its prefix, and the name of the fields within it given here are only for the sake of illustration. You can use some other meaningful names if you wish. But the length of the fields and their type are fixed, because they depend on the design of routine BNDATETI.

Procedure For Installing Program BNDATETI

Step 1. Enter this program in member BNDATETI of a source PDS.

Step 2. Compile and link program BNDATETI using the JCL given in Section B.1 in Appendix B. During linking, program BNDATE will be required, because

```
*******************************************************************
 1        IDENTIFICATION DIVISION.
 2        PROGRAM-ID. BNDATETI.
 3        ENVIRONMENT DIVISION.
 4     *=================================================*
 5     * THIS PROGRAM WILL GIVE YOU SYSTEM DATE AND TIME. *
 6     *=================================================*
 7     * HISTORY OF CHANGES TO THIS PROGRAM FOLLOWS:
 8     * VER.  DATE  PROGRAMMER   DESCRIPTION/MODIFICATIONS
 9     * ---   ---
10     * 0000 YY/MM/DD NIRMAL  NEW PROGRAM
11     *=================================================*
12        DATA DIVISION.
13        WORKING-STORAGE SECTION.
14        01 IN-TYPE    PIC S9(8) COMP VALUE +9.
15        01 OUT-TYPE   PIC S9(8) COMP VALUE +3.
16        01 TIME-1     PIC 9(7).
17        01 TIME-2     REDEFINES TIME-1.
18           02 FILLER   PIC X(1).
19           02 HOUR     PIC X(2).
20           02 MIN      PIC X(2).
21           02 SEC      PIC X(2).
22        01 TIME-3.
23           02 HH       PIC X(2).
24           02 COL1     PIC X(1) VALUE ':'.
25           02 MM       PIC X(2).
26           02 COL2     PIC X(1) VALUE ':'.
```

Figure 2.1. Source code of program BNDATETI

```cobol
27          02  SS        PIC X(2).
28      01  OUT-GREG-TEXT.
29          03  OUT-GREG-MONTH      PIC X(10).
30          03  OUT-GREG-DAY        PIC 99.
31          03  FILLER              PIC X(04)  VALUE ', 19'.
32          03  OUT-GREG-YEAR       PIC 99.
33      01  GREG-MONTH-TEXT.
34          05  FILLER   PIC X(10)  VALUE 'JANUARY'.
35          05  FILLER   PIC X(10)  VALUE 'FEBRUARY'.
36          05  FILLER   PIC X(10)  VALUE 'MARCH'.
37          05  FILLER   PIC X(10)  VALUE 'APRIL'.
38          05  FILLER   PIC X(10)  VALUE 'MAY'.
39          05  FILLER   PIC X(10)  VALUE 'JUNE'.
40          05  FILLER   PIC X(10)  VALUE 'JULY'.
41          05  FILLER   PIC X(10)  VALUE 'AUGUST'.
42          05  FILLER   PIC X(10)  VALUE 'SEPTEMBER'.
43          05  FILLER   PIC X(10)  VALUE 'OCTOBER'.
44          05  FILLER   PIC X(10)  VALUE 'NOVEMBER'.
45          05  FILLER   PIC X(10)  VALUE 'DECEMBER'.
46      01  FILLER REDEFINES GREG-MONTH-TEXT.
47          05  MONTH-G OCCURS 12 TIMES PIC X(10).
48      01  WS-DATE-1.
49          05  D1-MM    PIC X(2).
50          05  FILLER   PIC X(1).
51          05  D1-DD    PIC X(2).
52          05  FILLER   PIC X(1).
53          05  D1-YY    PIC X(2).
54
55      01  WS-DATE-2.
56          05  D2-YY    PIC X(2).
```

```
57        05  FILLER              PIC X(1)  VALUE '/'.
58        05  D2-MM               PIC X(2).
59        05  FILLER              PIC X(1)  VALUE '/'.
60        05  D2-DD               PIC X(2).
61    *-----------------------------------------------------------------*
62    01  LENGTH-160              PIC S9(4) COMP SYNC  VALUE +160.
63    01  WS-DATA-IN              PIC X(160).
64    01  WS-OUT-MSG-X            PIC X(160).
65    01  WS-OUT-MSG-1.
66        05  FILLER              PIC X(80) VALUE
67        'AN ERROR OF SOME KIND HAS OCCURRED IN PROGRAM BNDATETI   '.
68        05  FILLER              PIC X(80) VALUE
69        'USE CEDF TO DEBUG. NOW PRESS CLEAR KEY TO CONTINUE.      '.
70
71    01  WS-OUT-MSG-2.
72        05  FILLER              PIC X(80) VALUE
73        'COMM-AREA  PASSED TO PROGRAM BNDATETI IS NOT OF 38  BYTES '.
74        05  FILLER              PIC X(80) VALUE
75        'PROGRAM ABORTED. PRESS <CLEAR> KEY TO CONTINUE.          '.
76
77    LINKAGE SECTION.
78    01  DFHCOMMAREA.
79        05  CD-CURR-DATE-G.
80    ******* YY/MM/DD  GREGORIAN ******************************************
81            10  CD-YY-G         PIC 9(2).
82            10  FILLER          PIC X.
83            10  CD-MM-G         PIC 9(2).
84            10  FILLER          PIC X.
```

Figure 2.1. continued.

```cobol
85              10  CD-DD-G                    PIC 9(2).
86          05  CD-CURR-DATE-TEXT-G            PIC X(22).
87  ********* DECEMBER 02, 1990   *********************************
88          05  CD-CURR-TIME               PIC 99B99B99.
89  *******  HH:MM:SS             *********************************
90  PROCEDURE DIVISION.
91      EXEC CICS HANDLE CONDITION ERROR(ERROR-PROCESS) END-EXEC.
92      IF EIBCALEN = 38
93         NEXT SENTENCE
94      ELSE
95         MOVE WS-OUT-MSG-2 TO WS-OUT-MSG-X
96         GO TO SEND-MSG-END-PGM.
97      MOVE EIBTIME TO TIME-1.
98      MOVE HOUR TO HH.
99      MOVE MIN  TO MM.
100     MOVE SEC  TO SS.
101     MOVE TIME-3  TO CD-CURR-TIME.
102     PERFORM GET-CURRENT-DATE.
103     EXEC CICS RETURN END-EXEC.
104     GOBACK.
105 ERROR-PROCESS.
106     MOVE WS-OUT-MSG-1 TO WS-OUT-MSG-X.
107     GO TO SEND-MSG-END-PGM.
108
109 GET-CURRENT-DATE.
110     CALL 'BNDATE' USING IN-TYPE OUT-TYPE CD-CURR-DATE-G.
```

```
111    ** CURRENT DATE IS NOW IN CD-CURR-DATE-G
112        MOVE CD-DD-G TO OUT-GREG-DAY.
113        MOVE CD-YY-G TO OUT-GREG-YEAR.
114        MOVE MONTH-G (CD-MM-G) TO OUT-GREG-MONTH.
115        STRING OUT-GREG-MONTH DELIMITED BY ' '
116            ' ' DELIMITED BY SIZE
117            OUT-GREG-DAY    DELIMITED BY SIZE
118            ', 19'          DELIMITED BY SIZE
119            OUT-GREG-YEAR   DELIMITED BY SIZE
120            INTO CD-CURR-DATE-TEXT-G.
121
122    SEND-MSG-END-PGM.
123        EXEC CICS SEND FROM (WS-OUT-MSG-X)
124            LENGTH(160)
125            ERASE
126        END-EXEC.
127        EXEC CICS RECEIVE INTO(WS-DATA-IN)
128            LENGTH(LENGTH-160)
129        END-EXEC.
130        EXEC CICS RETURN END-EXEC.
131        GOBACK.
```

****

Figure 2.1. continued.

BNDATETI calls it using the CALL verb of COBOL. So, this program must be present in a load library which is included under DDname SYSLIB of the linkage-editor step. The code for program BNDATE, the date conversion routine, and the procedure for assembling and linking it are given in Appendix C.

This job will create load module BNDATETI in your load library. This load library must be included under DDname DFHRPL in the CICS start-up procedure or job.

Step 3. Define the following in the CICS PPT:

Definition of Program DNDATETI in the PPT

```
PROGRAM     BNDATETI
GROUP       CICSBOOK
LANGUAGE    COBOL
```

Other parameters for BNDATETI in the PPT should be the same as those for the sample program BNPROG1 given in Section 1.6.

In what way can this program be useful? Application programmers often need current dates and times to display on screens and to write as time and date stamps on files. The problem is that CICS gives us fields EIBDATE and EIBTIME, but EIBDATE is in the Julian format, which is not very user-friendly. So, your application program can easily LINK to program BNDATETI and obtain the information in more readable formats. Another point is this: It is better to display the current date on the screen as, say, November 20, 1992, rather than 11/20/92, and it is better to store the current time on file as 11:20:10, rather than 112010.

GENER/OL programmers have access to reserved word RWTIME, which gives them the time the program was invoked. If in your GENER/OL program you prompt the user for input using the INPUT command or through the MAP command, RWTIME is not changed. So, if you use RWTIME to write time stamp on a file to indicate the time the record was added, you would not be writing the exact time of record addition. You should use program BNDATETI which will give you the exact time this program executed.

Explanation of Program BNDATETI

When a calling program issues the appropriate LINK command to link to this program, control flows to the first executable statement in the procedure division (see line 91 in Figure 2.1). Here the HANDLE CONDITION command is executed to set up things so if there was an error in the execution of any CICS command, control would flow to the line with label ERROR-PROCESS in the program. Next, on line 92, a test is made if the length of the communication area passed to this program is 38 bytes. If not, control flows to label SEND-MSG-END-PGM. So, if you issued the following command to link to BNDATETI:

```
EXEC CICS LINK PROGRAM ('BNDATETI') COMMAREA (WS-COMM-AREA)
LENGTH (40) END-EXEC.
```

you would see the following message on the screen:

```
COMM-AREA PASSED TO PROGRAM BNDATETI IS NOT OF 38 BYTES
PROGRAM ABORTED. PRESS <CLEAR> KEY TO CONTINUE.
```

Next, on line 97, CICS variable EIBTIME is used to obtain current time. On line 102, the GET-CURRENT-DATE routine is performed, which calls BNDATE to obtain the current date and store it in CD-CURR-DATE-G in format YY/MM/DD. On line 103, the RETURN command of CICS is executed, which transfers control to the caller. So, control flows to that statement in the calling CICS COBOL or GENER/OL program which follows the LINK command that was used to invoke BNDATETI. At this time, the 38-byte communication area passed by the calling program to BNDATETI contains valid values.

2.2 A PROGRAM TO DISPLAY THE CURRENT DATE AND TIME IN VARIOUS FORMATS

Figure 2.2 shows the program BNDISPTI list, and Figure 2.3 shows the listing of map BNMAPTI. Program BNDISPTI, when executed, will display a screen as shown in Figure 2.4.

Procedure for Installing This Program and Map and Using It

Step 1. Enter the map shown in Figure 2.3 in a source PDS (partitioned data set) as member BNMAPTI. Enter the program shown in Figure 2.2 in the same source PDS as member BNDISPTI.

Step 2. Now assemble this map using the JCL given in Section B.4 in Appendix B. Let us suppose that the name of the load library where the load module for this map will be created is P1BKN.LOADLIB, and the name of the macro (copybook) library where the copybook for the map will be created is P1BKN.MACLIB. After you have run the job given in Section B.4, it will create load module BNMAPTI in P1BKN.LOADLIB and copybook member BNMAPTI in P1BKN.MACLIB. The load library must be included under DDname DFHRPL in the CICS start-up procedure or job.

```
*****************************************************************
 1      IDENTIFICATION DIVISION.
 2      PROGRAM-ID. BNDISPTI.
 3  *****************************************************************
 4  * THIS PROGRAM WORKS UNDER CICS. IT DISPLAYS CURRENT DATE IN
 5  * TWO FORMATS AND CURRENT TIME. IT USES MAP BNMAPTI.
 6  *****************************************************************
 7      ENVIRONMENT DIVISION.
 8      DATA DIVISION.
 9      WORKING-STORAGE SECTION.
10      01  BNMAPTII COPY BNMAPTI.
11      01  AMPM         PIC X(2) VALUE 'AM'.
12      01  TIME-1.
13          02  TIMEBUF  PIC X(7).
14      01  TIME-2 REDEFINES TIME-1.
15          02  BLNK     PIC X(1).
16          02  HOUR     PIC X(2).
17          02  HOUR-N REDEFINES HOUR PIC 9(2).
18          02  MIN      PIC X(2).
19          02  SEC      PIC X(2).
20      01  TIME-3.
21          02  T        PIC X(8).
22      01  TIME-4 REDEFINES TIME-3.
23          02  HH       PIC X(2).
24          02  COL1     PIC X(1).
25          02  MM       PIC X(2).
26          02  COL2     PIC X(1).
27          02  SS       PIC X(2).
28      01 DATE-1.
29          02  DATEBUF  PIC X(7).
30      01 DATE-2 REDEFINES DATE-1.
```

22

```
31    02  FIL          PIC X(2).
32    02  YEAR         PIC X(2).
33    02  DAYS         PIC X(3).
34  01 TYPE-INPUT            PIC 99999 COMP VALUE 4.
35  01 TYPE-OUTPUT           PIC 99999 COMP VALUE 3.
36  01 JULIAN         PIC X(6).
37  01 JUL-WITH-DOT REDEFINES JULIAN.
38    02  YY           PIC X(2).
39    02  DOT          PIC X(1).
40    02  DD           PIC X(3).
41  01 GREGORIAN       PIC X(8).
42  PROCEDURE DIVISION.
43     EXEC CICS HANDLE CONDITION ERROR(ALRIGHT) END-EXEC.
44     MOVE EIBTIME TO TIMEBUF.
45     IF HOUR-N GREATER THAN 12 THEN
46        COMPUTE HOUR-N = HOUR-N - 12
47        MOVE 'PM' TO AMPM.
48     MOVE HOUR TO HH.
49     MOVE AMPM TO INDICO.
50     MOVE MIN TO MM.
51     MOVE SEC TO SS.
52     MOVE ':' TO COL1.
53     MOVE ':' TO COL2.
54     MOVE T TO TIMEO.
55     MOVE EIBDATE TO DATEBUF.
56     MOVE DAYS TO JULO.
57     MOVE YEAR TO YY.
58     MOVE '.' TO DOT.
```

Figure 2.2. Source code of program BNDISPTI

```
59          MOVE DAYS TO DD.
60          CALL 'BNDATE' USING
61               TYPE-INPUT TYPE-OUTPUT JULIAN GREGORIAN.
62          MOVE GREGORIAN TO GREGO.
63          EXEC CICS SEND MAP('BNMAPTI') ERASE END-EXEC.
64    ALRIGHT.
65          EXEC CICS RETURN END-EXEC.
66          GOBACK.
```

****

Figure 2.2. continued.

```
***********************************************************************
     1     *====================================================*
     2     *  MAP TO DISPLAY CURRENT DATE AND TIME.  CURRENT DATE IS DISPLAYED IN
     3     *  TWO FORMATS: YY/MM/DD AND IN JULIAN.
     4     *====================================================*
     5  PASSION  DFHMSD TYPE=&SYSPARM,MODE=INOUT,CTRL=(FREEKB,FRSET),        *
     6           LANG=COBOL,TIOAPFX=YES,EXTATT=MAPONLY,COLOR=GREEN
     7  BNMAPTI  DFHMDI SIZE=(24,80)
     8           DFHMDF POS=(03,05),LENGTH=45,                              *
     9           INITIAL='****************************************'
    10           DFHMDF POS=(5,10),LENGTH=24,INITIAL='TODAY IN YY/MM/DD IS: '
    11  GREG     DFHMDF POS=(5,35),LENGTH=9,ATTRB=(BRT)
    12           DFHMDF POS=(7,10),LENGTH=24,INITIAL='CURRENT TIME IS: '
    13  TIME     DFHMDF POS=(7,35),LENGTH=8,ATTRB=(BRT)
    14  INDIC    DFHMDF POS=(7,44),LENGTH=2,ATTRB=(BRT)
    15           DFHMDF POS=(9,10),LENGTH=24,INITIAL='TODAY IN JULIAN FORMAT: '
    16  JUL      DFHMDF POS=(9,35),LENGTH=3,ATTRB=(BRT)
    17           DFHMDF POS=(11,05),LENGTH=45,                              *
    18           INITIAL='****************************************'
    19           DFHMSD TYPE=FINAL
    20           END
***********************************************************************
```

Figure 2.3. Source code of map BNMAPTI

```
*****************************************************

         TODAY IN YY/MM/DD IS:      90/11/05

         CURRENT TIME IS:           10:09:09 AM

         TODAY IN JULIAN FORMAT:    309

    *****************************************************
```

Figure 2.4. A sample screen displayed by executing program BNDISPTI

Step 3. Now compile and link program BNDISPTI using the JCL given in Section B.1 in Appendix B. During compilation, copybook BNMAPTI created in Step 2 will be included in the program. This job will create load module BNDISPTI in your load library. This load library must be included under DDname DFHRPL in the CICS start-up procedure or job.

Step 4. Define the following resources in CICS tables:

Definition of Mapset BNMAPTI in the PPT

```
MAPSET BNMAPTI
GROUP  CICSBOOK
RSL    00
STATUS ENABLED
```

Definition of Program BNDISPTI in the PPT

```
PROGRAM   BNDISPTI
GROUP     CICSBOOK
LANGUAGE  COBOL
```

Other parameters for BNDISPTI in the PPT should be the same as those for sample program BNPROG1 given in Section 1.6.

Definition of Transaction BNTI in the PCT

```
TRANSACTION BNTI
GROUP       CICSBOOK
PROGRAM     BNDISPTI
```

Other parameters for BNTI in the PCT should be the same as those for sample transaction BNC1 given in Section 1.6.

Procedure For Using This Program

Log on to CICS. On a clear screen, type BNTI and press Enter. You will receive a screen similar to the one shown in Figure 2.4.

In what way can this program be useful? This program displays current time as well as current date in two formats, YY/MM/DD and Julian. Often it is necessary to know today's date in Julian. One can always look up a calendar, or alternatively one can execute this program to receive this information. I have used this program and this map as tools for testing. After making a change to the procedure for assembling CICS maps, I would make a small change to this map, perhaps to line 9 in map BNMAPTI. I would then assemble this map and execute transaction BNTI to verify that the changed map was being displayed. Similarly, after installing a new release of CICS, I would compile and link program BNDISPTI and check whether it was successful. I would then execute this transaction to ensure that program BNDISPTI was running properly under the new release of CICS. The small size of this program and map and the fact that they are not commonly used make them good test tools for CICS programmers.

Explanation of Program BNDISPTI

This program is straightforward. When you type BNTI and press Enter, the CICS control program checks the PCT and finds that transaction BNTI is associated with program BNDISPTI. Since this is a command-level COBOL program, a copy of the working storage is made for the task, and then this program is given control. Program execution starts from the first executable statement under the Procedure Division. So, line number 43 in Figure 2.2 is the first statement executed. On line 44, EIBTIME is moved to variable TIMEBUF in the working storage. EIBTIME is a CICS supplied variable that is not defined anywhere in Figure 2.2. It is included automatically in the LINKAGE SECTION at translation time. Along with other fields in the EIB (Execute Interface Block), this field is generated at translation time. On line 60, program BNDATE is being called to convert a Julian date into Gregorian format YY/MM/DD. So, this program, which is assembled separately, must be present in a dataset that is included under DDname SYSLIB in the linkage-editor step of the job used to compile and link program BNDISPTI. Date conversion program BNDATE, which is used by many other programs presented in this book, is given in Appendix C.

Finally on line 63, through the SEND command, map BNMAPTI is sent out to the terminal. The ERASE option specifies that the screen is to be erased prior to displaying the map. After that, the RETURN command on line 65 terminates program execution and control flows to CICS control program. At this time the operator can press the Clear key to clear the screen and then enter BNTI again or some other transaction.

In this program, note that on line 63, the MAPSET option is missing. So mapset defaults to the same value as map, i.e., BNMAPTI. This means that BNMAPTI, the name of the mapset, must be present in the PPT and in the load library. Remember, it is the mapset and not the map that must be defined in the PPT and be present in the load library. Another point worth noting is that the name of the label on line 5 in BNMAPTI can be anything. Here it has been arbitrarily named PASSION.

Note also that if a mapset contains just one map (and this is recommended), you can use just one name (in this example BNMAPTI) in the load library, copybook library, PPT, and in the program. Just remember to use that same name as the label on the DFHMDI macro in the map and use any other name as the label on the DFHMSD macro, as shown in Figure 2.3.

2.3 A PROGRAM TO LOG OFF CICS COMPLETELY

Figure 2.5 lists a program that when executed will log the user off the CICS system. In other words, the result will be the same as if the user typed CSSF LOGOFF on a blank screen and pressed the Enter key.

Procedure to Install This Program on Your CICS System

Step 1. Enter this program as member LOGOFF in a source PDS.

Step 2. Now compile and link this using the JCL given in Section B.1 in Appendix B. This job will create load module LOGOFF in your load library. This load library must be included under DDname DFHRPL in the CICS start-up procedure or job.

Step 3. Define the following resources in the CICS PPT and PCT:

Definition of Program LOGOFF in the PPT

```
PROGRAM   LOGOFF
GROUP     CICSBOOK
LANGUAGE  COBOL
```

Other parameters for LOGOFF in the PPT should be the same as those for the sample program BNPROG1 given in Section 1.6.

Definition of Transaction BKN2 in the PCT

```
TRANSACTION BKN2
GROUP       CICSBOOK
PROGRAM     LOGOFF
```

```
****************************************************************
    1       IDENTIFICATION DIVISION.
    2       PROGRAM-ID.  LOGOFF.
    3      *===========================================*
    4      * THIS PROGRAM IS ASSOCIATED WITH TRANSACTION BKN2.
    5      * ON A BLANK SCREEN, JUST TYPE BKN2 AND PRESS THE
    6      * ENTER KEY. YOU WILL BE LOGGED OFF CICS. IN OTHER
    7      * WORDS, THE EFFECT WILL THE SAME AS IF YOU ISSUED:
    8      * 'CSSF LOGOFF'.
    9      *===========================================*
   10       ENVIRONMENT DIVISION.
   11       DATA DIVISION.
   12       WORKING-STORAGE SECTION.
   13       PROCEDURE DIVISION.
   14      *===========================================*
   15           EXEC CICS ISSUE DISCONNECT END-EXEC.
   16           EXEC CICS RETURN END-EXEC.
   17           GOBACK.
****************************************************************
```

Figure 2.5. Source code of program LOGOFF

29

Other parameters for BKN2 in the PCT should be the same as those for sample transaction BNC1 given in Section 1.6. Additionally, make sure the security level of BKN2 in the PCT is 1 so that all users can execute this transaction without any restriction. This transaction is harmless and need not be controlled.

Procedure to Use This Program

On a blank screen, you can type BKN2 and press the Enter key. You will be logged off CICS. In other words, the result will be the same as if you typed CSSF LOGOFF and pressed the Enter key.

You can also link to this program from a CICS or GENER/OL application program. Suppose that your program displays a menu that has the following option:

```
PF10: EXIT FROM CICS COMPLETELY AND DISPLAY COMPANY LOGO
```

So in your application program, suppose control goes to label PF10 when the user presses the PF10 key. The following code is required in a CICS COBOL program:

```
PF10.
  EXEC CICS XCTL PROGRAM('LOGOFF') END-EXEC.
```

And in a GENER/OL program, you would have:

```
PF10 XCTL    (LOGOFF)
```

In what way can this program be useful? If you want to get out of CICS, typing BKN2 and pressing the Enter key is easier than typing CSSF LOGOFF and pressing the Enter key. Another point is that this program can be invoked from any CICS application program. So, rather than asking your user to first exit from your application, clear the screen, and then type CSSF LOGOFF to log off CICS, you can place an option on your application menu so that if the user wants to log off CICS, he need only press a PF key. This is definitely easier, especially if he or she needs to log off CICS frequently in order to access other applications such as TSO or another CICS system.

Explanation of Program Logoff

This program is the simplest of all programs given in this book. When you type BKN2 and press the Enter key, CICS checks the PCT and finds that transaction BKN2 is associated with program LOGOFF. So, control is transferred to this program. Execution starts from the first executable statement in the procedure division, which is the ISSUE DISCONNECT command, as shown in Figure 2.5. This command causes CICS to disconnect your terminal from CICS. The next line has the RETURN command which causes control to flow to the CICS control program. The GOBACK statement is not really required; it is there so that the COBOL compiler will not issue a warning and the compilation step will end in condition code of zero.

A note for the system programmer: In order for this program to work on a terminal, the TYPETERM for that terminal's entry in the TCT (Terminal Control Table) must have DISCREQ=YES. This indicates that CICS is to honor a disconnection request for this VTAM device and issue a VTAM CLSDST (Close Destination) macro to terminate VTAM session with that terminal. It also means that CSSF LOGOFF from that terminal will cause disconnection. Usually the TCT definitions for all CRT type terminals have this parameter set this way, so there is no problem here, but it is an important feature to be aware of.

2.4   A PROGRAM TO ELIMINATE EXTRA BLANKS FROM DATA AREA OF ANY SIZE

Figure 2.6 shows the program COMPBLNK that can be used to eliminate extra blanks from any area.

Procedure to Use COMPBLNK in a CICS Cobol Program

Suppose you have a 60-byte contiguous field in working storage as follows:

```
JAMES  RICHARDS  P.O. BOX 649  CALGARY  CANADA
```

You want to display this field on the screen, but there is not enough room for a 60-byte field on the map. So, you have to get rid of extra blanks between data so that the content becomes:

```
JAMES RICHARDS P.O. BOX 649 CALGARY CANADA
```

The compressed data will fit in less than 60 bytes. Also it is easier for the user to read. How do you do this? Suppose in your CICS COBOL program, the 60-byte field is defined as follows:

```
01   NAME-ADDRESS.
          05 NAME-LAST      PIC X(15).
          05 NAME-FIRST     PIC X(15).
          05 ADDRESS        PIC X(15).
          05 CITY-COUNTRY   PIC X(15).
```

Then, to compress 60 bytes starting at field NAME-ADDRESS, you can simply issue this command:

```
EXEC CICS LINK PROGRAM('COMPBLNK') COMMAREA(NAME-ADDRESS)
  LENGTH(60) END-EXEC.
```

Program COMPBLNK scans the entire area passed to it and substitutes a single blank wherever it finds multiple blanks. Any data shifted to the left is replaced by blanks. No other change is made.

Procedure to Use COMPBLNK in a GENER/OL Program

Suppose in your working storage or record layout, which has a prefix of P1, you have the following:

FIELD NAME	STARTS AT	LENGTH	TYPE
ADDRESS	39	72	C

To eliminate extra blanks within the 72-byte field ADDRESS, you can issue this command in your GENER/OL program:

```
LINK (COMPBLNK),P1ADDRESS
```

Note that the starting position, length, or the name of the field can be anything. But the length of the field, which is passed to COMPBLNK on the LINK command, as defined in working storage or record layout, is significant. COMPBLNK will only change the content of the field passed to it by eliminating extra blanks.

Procedure to Install This Program on Your CICS System

Step 1. Enter this program as member COMPBLNK in a source PDS.

Step 2. Now assemble and link this program using the JCL given in Section B.2 in Appendix B. This job will create load module COMPBLNK in your load library. This load library must be included under DDname DFHRPL in the CICS start-up procedure or job.

Step 3. Define the following resources in the CICS PPT and PCT:

Definition of Program COMPBLNK in the PPT

```
PROGRAM   COMPBLNK
GROUP     CICSBOOK
LANGUAGE  ASSEMBLER
```

```
****************************************************************************
 1  *----------------------------------------------------*
 2  * PROGRAM NAME: COMPBLNK                              *
 3  * FUNCTION:    GET RID OF EXTRA BLANKS FROM THE       *
 4  *             COMMUNICATION AREA SUPPLIED BY THE CALLER. *
 5  *----------------------------------------------------*
 6  R0       EQU   0
 7  R1       EQU   1
 8  R2       EQU   2
 9  R3       EQU   3
10  R4       EQU   4
11  R5       EQU   5
12  R6       EQU   6
13  R7       EQU   7
14  R8       EQU   8
15  R9       EQU   9
16  R10      EQU   10
17  R11      EQU   11
18  R12      EQU   12
19  R13      EQU   13
20  R14      EQU   14
21  R15      EQU   15
22  COMPBLNK DFHEIENT CODEREG=(9,10),DATAREG=11,EIBREG=12
23           EXEC CICS IGNORE CONDITION LENGERR
24           EXEC CICS HANDLE CONDITION ERROR(ERROR99)
25           LH    R3,EIBCALEN    LOAD R3 WITH COMM AREA LENGTH
26           LTR   R3,R3          DOES R3 CONTAIN ZERO
```

Figure 2.6. Source code of program COMPBLNK

33

```
27           BZ    ERROR01           YES, THIS IS ERROR
28           L     4,DFHEICAP        R4 POINTS TO INPUT AREA
29           LR    5,4               R5 POINTS TO OUTPUT AREA
30           MVI   SW,C'0'           INITIALIZE SW
31  REPEAT   EQU   *
32           CLI   0(R4),X'40'       IS IT A BLANK
33           BE    YESPACE           YES, BRANCH
34           MVI   SW,C'0'           INITIALIZE SWITCH
35           CR    R4,R5             BOTH REGS. SAME?
36           BE    NEXT01            YES, BRANCH
37           MVC   0(1,R5),0(R4)     MOVE INPUT CHAR TO OUTPUT POSITION
38           MVI   0(R4),X'40'       MOVE SPACE TO INPUT POSITION
39  NEXT01   LA    R5,1(R5)          POINT TO NEXT OUTPUT POSITION
40           B     NEXTCHAR
41  YESPACE  EQU   *
42           CLI   SW,C'1'
43           BE    NEXTCHAR
44           MVI   SW,C'1'
45           MVC   0(1,R5),0(R4)     MOVE INPUT TO OUTPUT
46           LA    R5,1(R5)          INCREMENT OUTPUT POINTER
47  NEXTCHAR EQU   *
48           LA    R4,1(R4)          INCREMENT INPUT POINTER
49           BCT   R3,REPEAT         DECREMENT R3 AND BRANCH IF NEEDED
50  *--------------------------------------------------------------------
51           B     RETURN
52  ERROR01  EQU   *
53           EXEC CICS SEND FROM(ERRMSG01) LENGTH(80) ERASE
```

```
54          EXEC CICS RECEIVE INTO(DATAIN) LENGTH(LEN160)
55          B      RETURN
56  ERROR99  EQU    *
57          EXEC CICS SEND FROM(ERRMSG99) LENGTH(80) ERASE
58          EXEC CICS RECEIVE INTO(DATAIN) LENGTH(LEN160)
59          B      RETURN
60  *=========================================================
61  RETURN   EQU    *
62          EXEC CICS RETURN
63  *=========================================================
64  LEN160   DC     H'160'
65  ERRMSG01 DC     CL40'NO COMM AREA PASSED TO PROGRAM COMPBLNK.'
66          DC     CL40' NO ACTION TAKEN.'
67  ERRMSG99 DC     CL40'SERIOUS ERROR DETECTED IN PROGRAM COMPBL'
68          DC     CL40'NK. CONTACT TECH. SUPPORT- CICS TEAM.'
69  *=========================================================
70          DFHEISTG
71  *=========================================================
72  SW       DS     C
73  DATAIN   DS     CL160
74          END
```

****

Figure 2.6. continued.

35

Other parameters for COMPBLNK in the PPT should be the same as those for the sample program BNPROG1 given in Section 1.6.

Explanation of Program COMPBLNK

Line 22 in this program uses macro DFHEIENT which sets up entry logic using registers 9 and 10 to address the code, register 11 to address the data, and register 12 to address the EIB. On line 25, register 3 is loaded with the length of the communication area passed by the caller. And on line 26, we are testing if R3 contains zero. If so, control flows to line 52. So, if the calling program simply transferred control to COMPBLNK without passing it to any communication area, an error message would be displayed. So, suppose the calling program has:

```
EXEC CICS LINK PROGRAM('COMPBLNK') END-EXEC.
```

This will display the following message on the terminal:

```
NO COMM AREA PASSED TO PROGRAM COMPBLNK. NO ACTION TAKEN.
```

Suppose that the length of communication area is not zero. In this case, line 28 will get executed, which loads register 4 with the address of the communication area. And the code that follows will compress blanks in the communication area. Finally, line 51 will get executed, which sends control to line 61 where the RETURN command of CICS transfers control back to the calling program.

2.5 A PROGRAM TO MODIFY A SPECIFIED RECORD ON ANY VSAM KEY-SEQUENCED DATASET (KSDS)

In Figure 2.7 a sample program is given that can be easily changed to modify any record on any VSAM KSDS having fixed or variable length records. Let us see what this program does before we discuss how to change it. Suppose there is a file with DDname BKNFILE1 that has variable-length (or fixed-length) records. We know that a record with key = '1COMMON23XXXX' exists on this file, and it is 120 bytes long. The record key is in positions 1 through 13. We want to modify this record by changing the two bytes following the key to 11. This program will do this job. You will find that in the working storage section field WS-FILE-RECORD describes the record of interest to us. Field LEN-RECORD on line 30 must be defined as S9(4) COMP because it is used on CICS READ and REWRITE commands. When this program executes, CICS gives control to this program at line number 33. On line 34, we read the record with key = '1COMMON23XXXX'. After this read is successful, the record is present in WS-FILE-RECORD. Next we change the two bytes following the key. We then rewrite the record back to the file. After this, a confirmation message is sent to the terminal. Then, on line 49, we return to CICS. The GOBACK on line 50 is never executed; it is there merely so we don't get a diagnostic message at compile time.

Procedure to Install This Program on Your CICS System

Step 1. Enter this program as member BNMODREC in a source PDS.

Step 2. Now assemble and link this program using the JCL given in Section B.1 in Appendix B. This job will create load module BNMODREC in your load library. This load library must be included under DDname DFHRPL in the CICS start-up procedure or job.

Step 3. Define the following resources in the CICS PPT and PCT:

Definition of Program BNMODREC in the PPT

```
PROGRAM   BNMODREC
GROUP     CICSBOOK
LANGUAGE  COBOL
```

Other parameters for BNMODREC in the PPT should be the same as those for the sample program BNPROG1 given in Section 1.6.

Definition of Transaction BNVU in the PCT

```
TRANSACTION  BNVU
GROUP        CICSBOOK
PROGRAM      BNMODREC
```

Other parameters for BNVU in the PCT should be the same as those for sample transaction BNC1 given in Section 1.6.

Procedure to Use This Program

On a blank screen, type BNVU and press the Enter key. The program will do the job and end. It will send you the following message on your terminal:

```
SPECIFIED RECORD ON VSAM FILE BKNFILE1 HAS BEEN MODIFIED.
```

However, if an error occurred in the program, the task would abend and you would get an abend message at the bottom of the screen, in which case you should run this transaction again under CEDF to figure out what went wrong.

```
      *****************************************************************
    1      IDENTIFICATION DIVISION.
    2      PROGRAM-ID.      BNMODREC.
    3      AUTHOR.          BARRY NIRMAL.
      *****************************************************************
    5  *  THIS IS A COMMAND LEVEL CICS PROGRAM. IT IS ASSOCIATED WITH
    6  *  TRANSACTION BNVU. IT WILL UPDATE A SPECIFIC RECORD ON FILE
    7  *  BKNFILE1 WHICH HAS KEY LENGTH OF 13. THE RECORD WITH KEY =
    8  *  "1COMMON23XXXX" WILL BE MODIFIED BY CHANGING ITS DATA PORTION.
    9  *  THIS FILE CAN HAVE FIXED OR VARIABLE LENGTH RECORDS, BUT THE
   10  *  IMPORTANT THING IS THAT THE RECORD THAT WE WANT TO MODIFY IS
   11  *  120 BYTES LONG, AND THIS IS KNOWN TO US. WE ALSO KNOW WHAT
   12  *  WE WANT TO CHANGE IN THIS RECORD.
   13  *  THIS PROGRAM CAN BE EASILY CHANGED TO MODIFY ANY RECORD ON
   14  *  ANY VSAM FILE.
   15  *  THIS PROGRAM CAN NOT BE USED TO CHANGE THE KEY OF A RECORD.
      *****************************************************************
   17      ENVIRONMENT DIVISION.
   18      DATA DIVISION.
   19      WORKING-STORAGE SECTION.
   20      01  MSG-OK              PIC X(80) VALUE
   21          'SPECIFIED RECORD ON VSAM FILE BKNFILE1 HAS BEEN MODIFIED'.
   22      01  WS-FILE-RECORD.
   23          05 FILE-KEY      PIC X(13) VALUE '1COMMON23XXXX'.
   24          05 FILE-DATA1    PIC X(02).
   25          05 FILE-DATA2    PIC X(105).
   26  ****************
```

```
27       * CONSTANTS AND VARIABLES FOR CICS CALLS
28       **************
29       01  CICS-LENGTHS.
30           05 LEN-RECORD              PIC S9(04) COMP SYNC.
31       PROCEDURE DIVISION.
32       1000-MAINLINE.
33           MOVE +120 TO LEN-RECORD.
34           EXEC CICS READ
35               INTO (WS-FILE-RECORD)
36               DATASET ('BKNFILE1')
37               LENGTH (LEN-RECORD)
38               RIDFLD (FILE-KEY)
39               UPDATE
40           END-EXEC.
41           MOVE '11' TO FILE-DATA1.
42           MOVE +120 TO LEN-RECORD.
43           EXEC CICS REWRITE
44               FROM (WS-FILE-RECORD)
45               DATASET ('BKNFILE1')
46               LENGTH (LEN-RECORD)
47           END-EXEC.
48           EXEC CICS SEND FROM(MSG-OK) LENGTH(80) ERASE END-EXEC.
49           EXEC CICS RETURN END-EXEC.
50           GOBACK.
```

Figure 2.7. Source code of program BNMODREC

For example, if file BKNFILE1 was not defined to CICS, or was defined but not open, this program would abend when the READ command of CICS is executed. If the record with key = '1COMMON23XXXX' is not present on file or is present but is not 120 bytes long, for fixed length record file, then, also, the program would abend upon execution of the READ command.

In what way can this program be useful? This program can be used to change any specific record on any VSAM file. Suppose that in your test CICS system you have file SPCLFILE defined as a variable-length file. It is not really used; it is there for special needs. Now you have a VSAM KSDS with record length of 1200 bytes and you want to change the eight bytes in the data portion of the record in positions 50 through 57 to 'HARRY JR'. To do this, you can do the following:

> Make suitable changes to the program in Figure 2.7 so that it works on file SPCLFILE and does what it is expected to do. No new feature needs to be added to this program. Only make suitable changes to lines already in the program.
>
> Compile the program as described above.
>
> Allocate your VSAM file under DDname SPCLFILE, using the CEMT transaction.
>
> Open file SPCLFILE using the CEMT transaction.
>
> On a blank screen, type BNVU. You should get the message confirming that the record has been modified. If not, run the transaction under CEDF to figure out what went wrong.

You can see that program BNMODREC and transaction BNVU can be used as general purpose tools.

2.6 A PROGRAM TO DELETE ONE OR MORE RECORDS FROM ANY VSAM KEY-SEQUENCED DATASET (KSDS)

The listing of program BNUTL01 that is a VSAM utility is shown in Figure 2.8. It has two functions:

> To delete one or more records from any VSAM KSDS defined to CICS. The VSAM file can have fixed-length or variable-length records.
>
> To copy all records from one VSAM KSDS to another. Both files must have the same characteristics.

Procedure to Install This Program on Your CICS System

It is assumed that subprogram HEXCOMP given in Appendix C has already been assembled into the load library.

Step 1. Enter this program as member BNUTL01 in a source PDS.

Step 2. Now compile and link program BNUTL01 using the JCL given in Section B.1 in Appendix B. Since this program on line 285 (see Figure 2.8) uses the CALL verb of COBOL to call HEXCOMP, the load library containing HEXCOMP must be included under DDname SYSLIB in the linkage-editor step. This job will create load module BNUTL01 in your load library. This load library must be included under DDname DFHRPL in the CICS start-up procedure or job.

Step 3. Define the following resources in the CICS PPT and PCT:

Definition of Program BNUTL01 in the PPT

```
PROGRAM    BNUTL01
GROUP      CICSBOOK
LANGUAGE   COBOL
```

Other parameters for BNUTL01 in the PPT should be the same as those for the sample program BNPROG1 given in Section 1.6.

Definition of Transaction BNU1 in the PCT

```
TRANSACTION BNU1
GROUP       CICSBOOK
PROGRAM     BNUTL01
```

Other parameters for BNU1 in the PCT should be the same as those for sample transaction BNC1 given in Section 1.6. Additionally, make sure the security level of BNU1 in the PCT is not 1, so that only authorized users can execute this transaction. Using this transaction, one can delete all or many records from a master file, e.g., payroll/personnel master file, by mistake or intentionally. So it is clear that this transaction is very powerful and needs to be properly controlled.

Procedure to Use This Program

Let us illustrate the procedure for using this program through a couple of examples.

Example 1: Suppose you want to delete all records from file VPPY001A whose key has '11' in the first two positions. Suppose this VSAM file has key length of 8. First you must enter the following on a blank screen and then press the Enter key:

```
BNU1/H D
```

```
*****************************************************************
 1      IDENTIFICATION DIVISION.
 2      PROGRAM-ID.  BNUTL01.
 3      *===============================================*
 4      * THIS PROGRAM USES CALL VERB OF COBOL TO CALL SUBPROGRAM HEXCOMP.
 5      *===============================================*
 6      ENVIRONMENT DIVISION.
 7      DATA DIVISION.
 8      WORKING-STORAGE SECTION.
 9      01  WS-KEY-IN               PIC X(99).
10      01  WS-KEY-OUT              PIC X(99).
11      01  REC-IN.
12          05 FILLER              PIC X(9000).
13      *******************
14      * CONSTANTS AND VARIABLES FOR CICS CALLS
15      *******************
16      01  CICS-LENGTHS.
17          05 REC-IN-LEN              PIC S9(04)  COMP SYNC.
18          05 CICS-KEY-LENGTH         PIC S9(04)  COMP SYNC.
19
20      01  WS-MSG-COPY-DONE.
21          05 FILLER PIC X(80) VALUE
22          'RECORDS FROM INPUT VSAM HAVE BEEN ADDED TO OUTPUT VSAM'.
23          05 FILLER PIC X(43) VALUE
24          'TOTAL RECORDS READ FROM INPUT   VSAM FILE:  '.
25          05 CTR-REC-READ           PIC 9(5) VALUE ZERO.
26          05 FILLER                 PIC X(32) VALUE SPACES.
27          05 FILLER PIC X(43) VALUE
28          'TOTAL RECORDS WRITTEN TO OUTPUT VSAM FILE:  '.
29          05 CTR-REC-WRITTEN        PIC 9(5) VALUE ZERO.
```

42

```
30        05 FILLER                    PIC X(32) VALUE SPACES.
31        05 FILLER   PIC X(54) VALUE
32        'TOTAL RECORDS THAT WERE NOT COPIED (DUPLICATE KEYS) : '.
33        05 CTR-REC-DUP               PIC 9(5) VALUE ZERO.
34        05 FILLER                    PIC X(21) VALUE SPACES.
35
36     01 WS-MSG-LENGERR.
37        05 FILLER   PIC X(80) VALUE
38        'LENGTH ERROR CONDITION WAS DETECTED. PHONE BARRY FOR HELP'.
39
40     01 WS-MSG-STARTBR-ERR.
41        05 FILLER   PIC X(80) VALUE
42        'STARTBR HAD A PROBLEM LOCATING FIRST RECORD ON FILE'.
43
44     01 HEXCOMP-AREAS.
45        05 LENGTH-COMP               PIC S9(8) COMP SYNC.
46        05 STATUS-CODE               PIC X.
47
48     01 CICS-AREAS.
49        05 CICS-LEN-1920             PIC S9(4) COMP SYNC VALUE +1920.
50        05 CICS-LEN-80               PIC S9(4) COMP SYNC VALUE +80.
51        05 CICS-FILE-KEY             PIC X(20).
52
53     01 DEBUG-AREA.
54        05 LINE-1        PIC X(80).
55        05 LINE-2        PIC X(80).
56        05 LINE-3        PIC X(80).
```

Figure 2.8. Source code of program BNUTLO1

```
57      01  WS-DATA-IN.
58      *===========================================================*
59      * LENGTH OF WS-DATA-IN = 1920 BYTES (24 LINES X 80 BYTES)
60      *===========================================================*
61
62          05 FILLER           PIC X(1840) VALUE SPACES.
63          05 SYS-MSG           PIC X(80)   VALUE SPACES.
64
65      01  WS-DATA-IN-DEL  REDEFINES WS-DATA-IN.
66          05 FILLER           PIC X(7).
67          05 PARM-IN.
68             15 FILE-ID        PIC X(8).
69             15 DELIM3D        PIC X.
70             15 DEL-TYPE       PIC X.
71             15 DELIM4D        PIC X.
72             15 KEY-LENGTH     PIC 99.
73             15 DELIM5D        PIC X.
74             15 DATA-FORMAT    PIC X.
75             15 DELIM6D        PIC X.
76             15 DEL-KEY        PIC X(40);
77             15 FILLER         PIC X(1857).
78
79      01  WS-DATA-IN-COPY  REDEFINES WS-DATA-IN.
80          05 FILLER           PIC X(7).
81          05 PARM-IN.
82             15 FROM-DD        PIC X(8).
83             15 DELIM3C        PIC X.
84             15 TO-DD          PIC X(8).
85             15 DELIM4C        PIC X.
86
```

44

```
87   01   FILLER REDEFINES WS-DATA-IN.
88        05  FILLER                  PIC X(04).
89        05  PARM-HELP               PIC X(04).
90            88  WANTS-HELP-WITH-DELETE   VALUE '/H D'.
91            88  WANTS-HELP-WITH-COPY     VALUE '/H C'.
92
93   01   FILLER REDEFINES WS-DATA-IN.
94        05  FILLER                  PIC X(04).
95        05  PARM-WORK               PIC X(03).
96            88  WANTS-DELETE             VALUE '/D/'.
97            88  WANTS-COPY               VALUE '/C/'.
98
99   01   WS-MSG-HELP-D.
100       05  FILLER             PIC X(80) VALUE
101       'BNU1/D/DDNAME    /T/NN/F/KEY-VALUE-GENERIC-OR-FULL    '.
102       05  FILLER             PIC X(80) VALUE
103       '***** PLEASE JUST OVERTYPE ON FIRST LINE AND PRESS ENTER.  '.
104       05  FILLER             PIC X(80) VALUE
105       '     T= KEY TYPE (G= GENERIC, F = FULL)                    '.
106       05  FILLER             PIC X(80) VALUE
107       '     NN= KEY LEGTH; MUST BE ONE OF 01,02,03.....20         '.
108       05  FILLER             PIC X(80) VALUE
109       '     F= FORMAT OF DATA (C= CHARACTER, H = HEX)             '.
110       05  FILLER             PIC X(80) VALUE
111       '     KEY VALUE: IN CHAR MAX 20 BYTES; IN HEX MAX 40 BYTES  '.
112
113  01   WS-MSG-HELP-C.
114       05  FILLER             PIC X(80) VALUE
```

Figure 2.8. continued.

```
115        'BNU1/C/FROM-DD  /TO-DD   /                                      '.
116        05 FILLER         PIC X(80) VALUE
117        '***** PLEASE JUST OVERTYPE ON FIRST LINE AND PRESS ENTER.       '.
118        05 FILLER         PIC X(80) VALUE
119        '   FROM-DD = DDNAME OF INPUT VSAM KSDS                          '.
120        05 FILLER         PIC X(80) VALUE
121        '   TO-DD   = DDNAME OF OUTPUT VSAM KSDS                         '.
122        05 FILLER         PIC X(80) VALUE
123        '*************************************************************** '.
124        05 FILLER         PIC X(80) VALUE
125        'NOTE: ALL RECORDS OF INPUT FILE WILL GET COPIED TO OUTPUT       '.
126        05 FILLER         PIC X(80) VALUE
127        'FILE. RECORDS WITH DUPLICATE KEYS WILL BE IGNORED, BUT          '.
128        05 FILLER         PIC X(80) VALUE
129        'THEIR COUNT WILL BE REPORTED. IF OUTPUT FILE IS OF FIXED        '.
130        05 FILLER         PIC X(80) VALUE
131        'LENGTH, ENSURE INPUT FILE HAS ALL RECORDS OF SAME LENGTH        '.
132        05 FILLER         PIC X(80) VALUE
133        'AS OUTPUT FILE.                                                 '.
134
135        01 ERR-MSG-0      PIC X(80) VALUE
136        '??????????????????????????????????????????????????????????????'.
137        01 ERR-MSG-1      PIC X(80) VALUE
138        'YOUR REQUEST IS FOR DELETE.  ALL DELIMITERS MUST BE SLASH.      '.
139        01 ERR-MSG-1C     PIC X(80) VALUE
140        'YOUR REQUEST IS FOR COPY.    ALL DELIMITERS MUST BE SLASH.      '.
141        01 ERR-MSG-2      PIC X(80) VALUE
142        'INVALID DELETE TYPE. MUST BE G (GENERIC) OR F (FULL)            '.
143        01 ERR-MSG-3      PIC X(80) VALUE
144        'KEY LENGTH MUST BE NUMERIC, AND IN RANGE 01, 02 ....20          '.
```

```
145  01  ERR-MSG-4      PIC X(80) VALUE
146      'DATA FORMAT MUST BE C (CHAR) H (HEX).                      '.
147  01  ERR-MSG-HEXCOMP.
148      05 FILLER    PIC X(80) VALUE
149      'ERROR DETECTED WHILE COMPRESSING HEX CHARACTERS ENTERED BY'.
150      05 FILLER    PIC X(80) VALUE
151      'USER AS FILE KEY. RETURN CODE FROM HEXCOMP IS NOT S.       '.
152  01  WS-MSG-OK.
153      05 FILLER                        PIC X(80) VALUE
154      'THE RECORDS YOU REQUESTED HAVE BEEN DELETED. I GUARANTEE.  '.
155  01  WS-MSG-NOT-FOUND.
156      05 FILLER                        PIC X(80) VALUE
157      'SIR/MADAM, THE RECORDS YOU SPECIFIED ARE NOT ON FILE.      '.
158
159  01  WS-MSG-ERROR.
160      05 FILLER                        PIC X(80) VALUE
161      'AN ERROR OF SOME KIND HAS OCCURRED. CONTACT BARRY FOR HELP'.
162
163  PROCEDURE DIVISION.
164      EXEC CICS IGNORE CONDITION LENGERR
165           END-EXEC.
166      EXEC CICS HANDLE CONDITION NOTFND(NOT-FOUND)
167           ERROR(SOME-ERROR) END-EXEC.
168      EXEC CICS RECEIVE INTO(WS-DATA-IN) LENGTH(CICS-LEN-1920)
169           END-EXEC.
170      IF WANTS-HELP-WITH-DELETE
171           MOVE WS-MSG-HELP-D TO WS-DATA-IN
172           GO TO DISPLAY-MSG-END-PGM.
```

Figure 2.8. continued.

```
173          IF WANTS-HELP-WITH-COPY
174              MOVE WS-MSG-HELP-C TO WS-DATA-IN
175              GO TO DISPLAY-MSG-END-PGM.
176          IF WANTS-DELETE
177              GO TO  DEL-RTN
178          ELSE
179          IF WANTS-COPY
180              GO TO COPY-RTN
181          ELSE
182              MOVE ERR-MSG-0 TO WS-DATA-IN
183              GO TO DISPLAY-MSG-END-PGM.
184
185      COPY-RTN.
186          IF DELIM3C  NOT =  '/'  OR
187              DELIM4C  NOT =  '/'
188              MOVE ERR-MSG-1C TO SYS-MSG
189              GO TO DISPLAY-MSG-END-PGM.
190
191          EXEC CICS HANDLE CONDITION ERROR(STARTBR-ERROR)
192              LENGERR(LENGTH-ERROR)
193          END-EXEC.
194          MOVE LOW-VALUE TO WS-KEY-IN.
195          EXEC CICS STARTBR
196              DATASET(FROM-DD)
197              RIDFLD(WS-KEY-IN)
198              GTEQ
199          END-EXEC.
200          EXEC CICS HANDLE CONDITION ENDFILE(THATSALL) NOTFND(THATSALL)
201              ERROR(SOME-ERROR) DUPREC(DUPREC)
202          END-EXEC.
```

```
203   LOOP.
204       MOVE 9000 TO REC-IN-LEN.
205       EXEC CICS READNEXT
206           DATASET(FROM-DD)
207           INTO(REC-IN)
208           RIDFLD(WS-KEY-IN)
209           LENGTH(REC-IN-LEN)
210       END-EXEC.
211       ADD 1 TO CTR-REC-READ.
212       MOVE WS-KEY-IN   TO WS-KEY-OUT.
213       EXEC CICS WRITE
214           FROM (REC-IN)
215           DATASET (TO-DD)
216           RIDFLD(WS-KEY-OUT)
217           LENGTH(REC-IN-LEN)
218       END-EXEC.
219       ADD 1 TO CTR-REC-WRITTEN.
220       GO TO LOOP.
221
222   DUPREC.
223       ADD 1 TO CTR-REC-DUP.
224       GO TO LOOP.
225
226   STARTBR-ERROR.
227       MOVE WS-MSG-STARTBR-ERR TO SYS-MSG.
228       GO TO DISPLAY-MSG-END-PGM.
229
```

Figure 2.8. continued.

```
230  LENGTH-ERROR.
231      MOVE WS-MSG-LENGERR TO SYS-MSG.
232      GO TO DISPLAY-MSG-END-PGM.
233  THATSALL.
234      MOVE WS-MSG-COPY-DONE    TO WS-DATA-IN.
235      GO TO DISPLAY-MSG-END-PGM.
236
237  DEL-RTN.
238      IF DELIM3D  NOT = '/'  OR
239          DELIM4D  NOT = '/'  OR
240          DELIM5D  NOT = '/'  OR
241          DELIM6D  NOT = '/'
242          MOVE ERR-MSG-1 TO SYS-MSG
243          GO TO DISPLAY-MSG-END-PGM.
244
245      IF DEL-TYPE = 'F' OR 'G'
246          NEXT SENTENCE
247      ELSE
248          MOVE ERR-MSG-2 TO SYS-MSG
249          GO TO DISPLAY-MSG-END-PGM.
250      IF KEY-LENGTH NOT NUMERIC
251          MOVE ERR-MSG-3 TO SYS-MSG
252          GO TO DISPLAY-MSG-END-PGM.
253      IF KEY-LENGTH = 0 OR GREATER THAN 20
254          MOVE ERR-MSG-3 TO SYS-MSG
255          GO TO DISPLAY-MSG-END-PGM.
256      MOVE KEY-LENGTH TO CICS-KEY-LENGTH.
257      IF DATA-FORMAT = 'C' OR 'H'
258          NEXT SENTENCE
259      ELSE
```

```
260         MOVE ERR-MSG-4 TO SYS-MSG
261         GO TO DISPLAY-MSG-END-PGM.
262     IF DATA-FORMAT = 'H'
263         PERFORM CONVERT-HEX-DATA
264     ELSE
265         MOVE DEL-KEY TO CICS-FILE-KEY.
266
267     IF DEL-TYPE = 'G'
268         EXEC CICS DELETE
269             DATASET (FILE-ID)
270             KEYLENGTH(CICS-KEY-LENGTH)
271             GENERIC
272             RIDFLD (CICS-FILE-KEY)
273         END-EXEC
274     ELSE
275         EXEC CICS DELETE
276             DATASET (FILE-ID)
277             KEYLENGTH(CICS-KEY-LENGTH)
278             RIDFLD (CICS-FILE-KEY)
279         END-EXEC.
280     MOVE WS-MSG-OK TO SYS-MSG.
281     GO TO DISPLAY-MSG-END-PGM.
282
283 CONVERT-HEX-DATA.
284     MOVE KEY-LENGTH TO LENGTH-COMP.
285     CALL 'HEXCOMP' USING DEL-KEY, CICS-FILE-KEY, LENGTH-COMP,
286         STATUS-CODE.
```

Figure 2.8. continued.

51

```
287          IF STATUS-CODE NOT = 'S'
288              MOVE ERR-MSG-HEXCOMP TO SYS-MSG
289              GO TO DISPLAY-MSG-END-PGM.
290
291      NOT-FOUND.
292          MOVE WS-MSG-NOT-FOUND TO SYS-MSG.
293          GO TO DISPLAY-MSG-END-PGM.
294
295      SOME-ERROR.
296          MOVE WS-MSG-ERROR TO SYS-MSG.
297          GO TO DISPLAY-MSG-END-PGM.
298
299      DISPLAY-MSG-END-PGM.
300          EXEC CICS SEND FROM(WS-DATA-IN) LENGTH(1920)
301              ERASE END-EXEC.
302      GET-OUT.
303          EXEC CICS RETURN END-EXEC.
304          GOBACK.
******************************************************************
```

Figure 2.8. continued.

52

where H stands for Help, and D stands for Delete. So, you are asking for help with using the delete function of transaction BNU1. The system will display a screen as shown in Figure 2.9. On this screen, the first line is formatted for you. There are seven fields on this line, each of fixed length. The slash character is used to separate these fields. You only need to enter the relevant information on the first line. The other lines on the screen are there merely to guide you. Change the first line so it looks like this, and then press the Enter key:

```
BNU1/D/VPPY001A/G/02/C/11
```

The first field is BNU1, which is the transaction ID associated with the program in Figure 2.8. The next field is D, to indicate delete. The third field of eight characters indicates the DDname of the file from which records are to be deleted. (If the DDname of a file is less than eight characters long, the third field will have one or more spaces at the end.) Here we are using G (for generic) in the fourth field, because the key specified on the command is of 2 bytes only, which is less than the VSAM file's key length. The fifth field is 02, to indicate that the key specified on the command is of 2 bytes only. (The program will ignore any characters that follow the first two characters of the last field on the first line.) The next field has C to indicate that the key specified is in character format rather than in hexadecimal. The next field has 11 which is the value of the generic key.

The program will perform the deletion, and if there was no error, it will display the same screen, but the last line on the screen will have the following message:

```
THE RECORDS YOU REQUESTED HAVE BEEN DELETED. I GUARANTEE.
```

If file VPPY001A is not defined to CICS, or if it is defined but not open, you will get the following message on the last line:

```
AN ERROR OF SOME KIND HAS OCCURRED. CONTACT BARRY FOR HELP.
```

And if the records you specified are not on the file, you will get the following message on the last line:

```
SIR/MADAM, THE RECORDS YOU SPECIFIED ARE NOT ON FILE.
```

Example 2: Now suppose there is file CICSLOG that has key length of 5. From this file you want to delete a record whose key in hexadecimal is X'00000000FF'. So, first you must enter the following on a blank screen and press the Enter key:

```
BNU1/H D
```

The program will display a help screen as shown in Figure 2.9. On this screen, you must change the first line to the following, and then press the Enter key:

```
BNU1/D/CICSLOG /F/05/H/00000000OFF
```

If this file is defined to CICS and is open, this record will get deleted from it, and the following message will appear on line 24. All other lines will remain unchanged:

```
THE RECORDS YOU REQUESTED HAVE BEEN DELETED. I GUARANTEE.
```

How can this program be useful? Every application or system programmer, whether working with CICS or not, will have to delete some records from VSAM files, especially in the test environment and while problem solving. So, rather than write his or her own program for it, this program can be used.

To make this facility really general-purpose and highly useful, consider this scheme. You can define in your CICS test system a file that is not really used; it is there only for special needs. Let us suppose you have given it the DDname of SPCLFILE. It is defined in the FCT (File Control Table) as a file with variable-length records, so it can be used with files that have fixed-length records as well as with files that have variable-length records. Anytime you want to delete some records from any VSAM KSDS file, whether it is allocated to CICS or not, you can just allocate this file to your CICS test system under DDname SPCLFILE, using the CEMT transaction. Now use BNU1 to delete the records, and then close the file on CICS using the CEMT transaction. This will also deallocate the VSAM file from the CICS test system. But before using the BNU1 transaction, make sure your VSAM file was successfully allocated under SPCLFILE and that it is open. If this file is open on some other CICS system, (e.g., a production CICS system), the open on the CICS test system might not succeed. If the file is not open, BNU1 cannot delete records from it. In fact, if a file is not defined to CICS, or is closed, or in the event of some other kind of error, BNU1 will issue the following error message:

```
AN ERROR OF SOME KIND HAS OCCURRED. CONTACT BARRY FOR HELP.
```

In this case, you must run BNU1 under CEDF (CICS Execution Debugging Facility) in order to find the exact cause of the problem.

Explanation of Program BNUTL01

Let us suppose that the user typed "BNU1/H D" on the screen and pressed the Enter key. CICS checks the PCT and finds that transaction BNU1 is associated with program BNUTL01. So, it creates a new task and assigns to it a fresh copy of the working storage section of this program. This area has

```
BNU1/D/DDNAME    /T/NN/F/KEY-VALUE-GENERIC-OR-FULL
***** PLEASE JUST OVERTYPE ON FIRST LINE AND PRESS ENTER
   T= KEY TYPE (G= GENERIC, F = FULL)
   NN= KEY LENGTH; MUST BE ONE OF 01,02,03.....20
   F= FORMAT OF DATA (C= CHARACTER, H = HEX)
   KEY VALUE: IN CHAR MAX 20 BYTES; IN HEX MAX 40 BYTES
```

Figure 2.9. The help screen displayed when user enters BNU1/H D

```
BNU1/C/FROM-DD /TO-DD        /
***** PLEASE JUST OVERTYPE ON FIRST LINE AND PRESS ENTER.
      FROM-DD = DDNAME OF INPUT VSAM KSDS
      TO-DD   = DDNAME OF OUTPUT VSAM KSDS
*****************************************************************
NOTE: ALL RECORDS OF INPUT FILE WILL GET COPIED TO OUTPUT
FILE. RECORDS WITH DUPLICATE KEYS WILL BE IGNORED, BUT
THEIR COUNT WILL BE REPORTED. IF OUTPUT FILE IS OF FIXED
LENGTH, ENSURE INPUT FILE HAS ALL RECORDS OF SAME LENGTH
AS OUTPUT FILE.
```

Figure 2.10. The help screen displayed when user enters BNU1/H C

```
RECORDS FROM INPUT VSAM HAVE BEEN ADDED TO OUTPUT VSAM
TOTAL RECORDS READ FROM INPUT  VSAM FILE: 00012
TOTAL RECORDS WRITTEN TO OUTPUT VSAM FILE: 00008
TOTAL RECORDS THAT WERE NOT COPIED (DUPLICATE KEYS) : 00004
```

Figure 2.11. Screen displayed by program BNUTLO1 when copying is successful.

data initialized to the initial values shown by the VALUE clauses in the working storage section of Figure 2.8. CICS then gives control to program BNUTL01.

So execution starts from line number 164 in Figure 2.8. On line 168, we receive into variable WS-DATA-IN whatever was typed on the screen. So, if the user typed "BNU1/H D" (quotation marks are not entered) after the receive command, the content of WS-DATA-IN will be "BNU1/H D". Next, on line 170, we test if the user wants help with delete, i.e., if he entered "BNU1/H D". If so, on line 171, WS-MSG-HELP-D is moved into WS-DATA-IN and control flows to line 299, where the content of WS-DATA-IN is sent out to the terminal and the task is ended. At this time the screen appears as shown in Figure 2.9.

Now suppose that the user enters data to request deletion of some records. When he presses the Enter key, a new task is created with a fresh copy of the working storage section of the program and control flows to line 164 in Figure 2.8. Again, on line 168, whatever was received from the screen is moved into WS-DATA-IN. On line 176, the WANTS-DELETE condition will be true, and control will flow to line 237. You can easily read the program and figure out that on lines 238 through 261 it is validating the data entered on the screen. If any error is detected, control flows to line 299. If all data is found valid, then, on line 267, a test is made whether the generic key was entered. If so, a DELETE command on lines 268 through 273 is issued, otherwise the DELETE command on lines 275 through 279 is issued. If no error occurred while executing the DELETE command, control will come to line 280. At this point, the same screen that was received from the user is redisplayed after changing the last line to contain the "success" message.

However, if the "Record(s) Not Found" condition occurred on the DELETE command, control will flow to the line with the label NOT-FOUND, and if any other error occurred, control will flow to the line with the label SOME-ERROR. This is due to the fact that on line 166 we executed the HANDLE CONDITION command to set up these actions.

2.7 A PROGRAM TO COPY ALL RECORDS FROM ONE KEY-SEQUENCED VSAM DATASET TO ANOTHER

The program shown in Figure 2.8 will also copy all records from a source VSAM KSDS into a target VSAM KSDS. Both files should have the same kind of records (i.e., fixed-length or variable-length records) with the same key length, key position, and record layout. If a record being copied already exists on the target file, it will not get copied and a count of all such records will be reported by the program.

Procedure to Use This Program

Let us illustrate the procedure for using this program through an example.

Example 1: Suppose you want to copy all records from file VPPY001A into file VPPY001B. The first thing you must do is enter the following on a blank screen and the press the Enter key:

BNU1/H C

where H stands for Help, and C stands for Copy. So, you are asking for help using the copy function of transaction BNU1. The system will display a screen as shown in Figure 2.10. On this screen, the first line is formatted for you. There are four fields on this line, each of fixed length. The slash character is used to separate these fields. You only need to enter the relevant information on the first line. The other lines on the screen are there merely to guide you. So, change the first line so it looks like this, and then press the Enter key;

BNU1/C/VPPY001A/VPPY001B

The first field is BNU1, which is the transaction ID associated with the program in Figure 2.8. The next field is C to indicate Copy. The third field of eight characters indicates the DDname of the source KSDS file from which records are to be read. The fourth field of eight characters indicates the DDname of the target file into which records are to be written. (If the DDname of a file is less than eight characters long, the third and/or fourth field will have one or more spaces at the end.)

The program will perform the copy, and if there was no error, it will display a screen similar to the one shown in Figure 2.11. If the source or target file is not defined to CICS, or is defined but not open, the user will receive the same screen he sent but with the following message on the last line:

AN ERROR OF SOME KIND HAS OCCURRED. CONTACT BARRY FOR HELP.

And if the source file has no records, you will get the following message on the last line:

STARTBR HAD A PROBLEM LOCATING FIRST RECORD ON FILE.

In what way can this program be useful? Suppose that file SGTLIB1 is defined to your CICS test region but it is opened for update. It can be a file with fixed-length or variable-length records. Many users are updating this file through CICS. To fix some problem you must add some records to this file. You can do this through a batch job using a program such as IDCAMS. But the problem is that because this file is defined with share options of (2, 3), you can't update it in batch until it is closed on the CICS test region. You can't close it on CICS because many CICS users are updating it. So, what do you do? Wait until CICS comes down? Probably, if you are not in a hurry. But there is a better way, now that you have this program.

Suppose you have defined in your CICS test system a file that is not really used; it is there only for special needs. Let us suppose you have given it the DDname of SPCLFILE. It is defined in the FCT as a variable-length file. So, you can do this:

1. Define through IDCAMS DEFINE command a file with any name that has the same characteristics as file SGTLIB1.
2. Load this file with the record(s) you want to copy to SGTLIB1.
3. Sign on to CICS test region and close file SPCLFILE, using the CEMT transaction if it is open.
4. Now allocate the file defined in step 1 under DDname SPCLFILE.
5. Open SPCLFILE. Make sure SPCLFILE is open and the file defined in Step 1 is allocated to it.

Now, using the copy feature of BNU1 transaction described above, copy all records from SPCLFILE to SGTLIB1. Your mission has been accomplished.

While using BNU1 to copy records, if an error situation occurs, e.g., a DDname specified is not defined to CICS, or is defined but not open, BNU1 will issue the following error message:

AN ERROR OF SOME KIND HAS OCCURRED. CONTACT BARRY FOR HELP.

In this case, you must run BNU1 under CEDF (CICS Execution Debugging Facility) in order to find the exact cause of the problem.

Explanation of Program BNUTL01

Let us suppose that the user typed "BNU1/H C" on the screen and pressed the Enter key. CICS checks the PCT and finds that transaction BNU1 is associated with program BNUTL01. So, it creates a new task and assigns to it a fresh copy of the working storage section of this program. This area has data initialized to the initial values shown by the VALUE clauses in the working storage section of Figure 2.8. CICS then gives control to program BNUTL01.

So execution starts from line number 164 in Figure 2.8. On line 168, we receive into variable WS-DATA-IN whatever was typed on the screen. If the user typed "BNU1/H C" (quotation marks are not typed) after the receive command, the content of WS-DATA-IN will be "BNU1/H C". Next, on line 173, we test if the user wants help with the copy, i.e., if he entered "BNU1/H C". If so, on line 174, WS-MSG-HELP-C is moved into WS-DATA-IN, and control flows to line 299, where the content of WS-DATA-IN is sent out to the terminal and the task is ended. At this time the screen appears as shown in Figure 2.10.

Now suppose that the user enters data to request copying of all records from a source file to a target file. When he presses the Enter key, a new task is created with a fresh copy of the working storage section of the program, and control flows to line 164 in Figure 2.8. Again, on line 168, whatever was received from the screen is moved into WS-DATA-IN. On line 179, the WANTS-COPY condition will be true and control will flow to line 185. You can easily read the program and figure out that on line numbers 186 through 189 it is validating the data entered on the screen. If any error is detected, control flows to line 299. If all data is found valid, the copy operation is performed on lines 191 through 225 by successively reading each record from the source file and writing it to the target file. When the end of the file is reached on the source file, control flows to the line with label THATSALL (line 233). This is because on line 200 we set up things so that if ENDFILE condition occurs, control would flow to the line with label THATSALL. Eventually, while executing READ-NEXT command on line 205, the ENDFILE condition will occur that will send control to line 233. At this point, the screen shown in Figure 2.11 will be sent to the terminal and the task will be terminated.

2.8 A PROGRAM TO WRITE A SPECIFIED RECORD ON ANY VSAM KEY-SEQUENCED DATASET

Figure 2.12 shows a program that can be easily changed to enter one or more records into any VSAM KSDS defined to CICS. Let us examine what this program does before we discuss changing it. Suppose file BNFILE2 is defined to CICS. It has record key in positions 1 through 16. It can have fixed-length records, 400 bytes long, in which case this file should be defined in the CICS FCT as a fixed-length file. Or it can have variable-length records with maximum record length being 400 or more, in which case this file should be defined in the CICS FCT as a variable-length file. Suppose you want to add a record into it with the 16 bytes key being "NIRMAL/BARRY + + + +" and the data portion containing $ in all 384 positions. This program will do this job.

Procedure For Installing Program BNADDREC

Step 1. Enter this program in member BNADDREC of a source PDS.

Step 2. Make suitable changes to it to add a record in a file already defined in your CICS system. Or, if you want to use this program without any change, do the following. Ask your system programmer to define file BNFILE2 in the test CICS system as a fixed-length file that has all options in the SERVREQ parameter. Then you should define a VSAM KSDS using IDCAMS that has fixed-length records of 400 bytes with the key in positions 1 through 16. Next you should load in this VSAM file a record of 400 bytes with the key of all 9's. Then you can use this program without any change.

```
 ***********************************************************************
1      IDENTIFICATION DIVISION.
2      PROGRAM-ID.    BNADDREC.
3      AUTHOR.        BARRY NIRMAL.
4  * *****************************************************************
5  * THIS PROGRAM WILL ADD ONE RECORD ON ANY FILE DEFINED TO CICS
6  * WHICH HAS FIXED OR VARIABLE LENGTH RECORDS.
7  * *****************************************************************
8  * THIS PGM CAN BE EASILY CHANGED TO ADD MULTIPLE RECORDS.
9  * *****************************************************************
10     ENVIRONMENT DIVISION.
11     DATA DIVISION.
12     WORKING-STORAGE SECTION.
13     01  IX                        PIC S9(04) COMP.
14     01  WS-FILE-RECORD.
15         05  WS-FILE-KEY      PIC X(16) VALUE 'NIRMAL/BARRY++++'.
16         05  WS-FILE-DATA     PIC X(384) VALUE ALL '$'.
17  ***********
18  * CONSTANTS AND VARIABLES FOR CICS CALLS
19  ***********
20     01  CICS-LENGTHS.
 ***********************************************************************
```

62

```
21              05  LEN-RECORD              PIC S9(04) COMP SYNC.
22          01  WS-MSG-OK.
23              05  FILLER  PIC X(80) VALUE
24                  'BARRY, RECORD YOU SPECIFIED HAS BEEN ADDED TO THE FILE'.
25
26          PROCEDURE DIVISION.
27          1000-MAINLINE.
28              MOVE +400 TO LEN-RECORD.
29              EXEC CICS WRITE
30                  FROM (WS-FILE-RECORD)
31                  DATASET ('BNFILE2')
32                  RIDFLD(WS-FILE-KEY)
33                  LENGTH (LEN-RECORD)
34              END-EXEC.
35              EXEC CICS SEND FROM(WS-MSG-OK) LENGTH(80) ERASE END-EXEC.
36              EXEC CICS RETURN END-EXEC.
37              GOBACK.
****************************************************************************
```

Figure 2.12. Source code of program BNADDREC

Step 3. Compile and link this program using the JCL given in Section B.1 in Appendix B. This job will create load module BNADDREC in your load library. This load library must be included under DDname DFHRPL in the CICS start-up procedure or job.

Step 4. Define the following in CICS tables:

Definition of Program BNADDREC in the PPT

```
PROGRAM    BNADDREC
GROUP      CICSBOOK
LANGUAGE   COBOL
```

Other parameters for BNADDREC in the PPT should be the same as those for the sample program BNPROG1 given in Section 1.6.

Definition of Transaction BNVA in the PCT

```
TRANSACTION  BNVA
GROUP        CICSBOOK
PROGRAM      BNADDREC
```

Other parameters for BNVA in the PCT should be the same as those for the sample transaction BNC1 given in Section 1.6.

Procedure for Using This Program

On a blank screen, type BNVA and press the Enter key. If there was no error, you will receive the following message on the first line:

```
BARRY, RECORD YOU SPECIFIED HAS BEEN ADDED TO THE FILE
```

If there was any error, the task would abend and you would get the abend message on the last line of the screen. This can happen if, for example, the file being used on line 31 in Figure 2.12 is not defined to CICS, or is defined but not open, or if a length error condition arose. In this case you must execute this transaction under CEDF to find out what went wrong.

In what way can this program be useful? Application and system programmers often have to add one or more records to a VSAM file during their development work or while problem solving. This program can be easily modified for this use. In fact, to make this program really general-purpose and highly useful, you can do the following. Define in the FCT of your CICS test system a file named SPCLFILE as a variable-length file. It is not really used by any application; it is there for special needs. Now suppose you want to add a record of 1400 bytes in your payroll master file. You can then do the following:

Close SPCLFILE on CICS. Allocate your payroll master under SPCLFILE using CEMT transaction.

Open SPCLFILE using CEMT, and make sure it gets open.

Change program in Figure 2.12 so that on line 28, 1400 gets moved to LEN-RECORD. Change line 31 to use file SPCLFILE. Change the definitions under WS-FILE-RECORD on line 14 to reflect your payroll master file layout.

Compile and link this program as BNADDREC.

Execute transaction BNVA to execute your new program. Your record should get added and you should receive a confirmation message. If any abend occurs, find out the cause of the problem, fix the error, and rerun transaction BNVA.

Explanation of Program BNADDREC

This program is straightforward. When you type BNVA and press the Enter key, control flows to line 28 in Figure 2.12 which is the first line of the procedure division. Here we are moving 400 to LEN-RECORD because the length of record being added is 400. LEN-RECORD must be defined in working storage as S9(4) COMP, i.e., two bytes binary, because this is a CICS requirement. You can't define it as S9(4) or S9(4) COMP-3. Next, we issue the WRITE command of CICS to write out 400 bytes from WS-FILE-RECORD as a record into file BNFILE2. On line 35, we are writing 80 bytes from WS-MSG-OK onto the screen after first erasing it. On line 36, we transfer control to CICS, which signals the end of this transaction.

2.9 A FACILITY TO VIEW RECORDS ON ANY VSAM KEY-SEQUENCED DATASET

Figure 2.13 shows program BNVSVIEW that can be used to view records on any VSAM KSDS, whether allocated to CICS or not. The VSAM KSDS can have fixed- or variable-length records. The VSAM key can be in any position in the record; it need not be in the beginning. The procedures for installing and using this program follow:

Procedure For Installing Program BNVSVIEW

Step 1. Enter this program in member BNVSVIEW of a source PDS. Enter the map shown in Figure 2.14 in member BNVIEWM of the same source PDS.

Step 2. Assemble and link map BNVIEWM using the JCL given in Section B.4 in Appendix B. This job will create member BNVIEWM in your copybook library and load module BNVIEWM in your load library. This load library must be included under DDname DFHRPL in the CICS start-up procedure or job.

```
**********************************************************************
*  IDENTIFICATION DIVISION.
*  PROGRAM-ID.  BNVSVIEW.
*  ENVIRONMENT DIVISION.
*  DATA DIVISION.
*  WORKING-STORAGE SECTION.
*  01 KEY-IN.
*     05 CHAR-IN      OCCURS 50 TIMES  PIC X.
*  01 KEY-OUT.
*     05 CHAR-OUT     OCCURS 50 TIMES  PIC X.
*  01 GUIDE.
*     05 FILLER    PIC X(40) VALUE
*     '....+....1....+....2....+....3....+....4'.
*     05 FILLER    PIC X(35) VALUE
*     '....+....5....+....6....+....7....+'.
*  01 IX1           PIC S9(8) COMP.
*  01 IX2           PIC S9(8) COMP.
**********************************************************************
*  # THE KEY CAN BE ANYWHERE IN THE RECORD. IT NEED NOT BE IN THE
*  # BEGINNING. THE LARGEST RECORD ON FILE CAN HAVE ANY LENGTH. BUT
*  # ONLY THE FIRST 3750 BYTES OF EACH RECORD WILL BE DISPLAYED.
**********************************************************************
*  01 RECORDS-ALL.
*     05 RECORD-ONE  OCCURS 15 TIMES.
*        10 REC-SEGMENT OCCURS 50 TIMES
*           PIC X(75).
*  01 COMMUNICATION-AREA.
*     05 FIRST-KEY            PIC X(50).
*     05 LAST-KEY             PIC X(50).
*     05 RECORD-PART-X.
```

Line numbers:
```
 1  IDENTIFICATION DIVISION.
 2  PROGRAM-ID.  BNVSVIEW.
 3  ENVIRONMENT DIVISION.
 4  DATA DIVISION.
 5  WORKING-STORAGE SECTION.
 6  01 KEY-IN.
 7     05 CHAR-IN      OCCURS 50 TIMES  PIC X.
 8  01 KEY-OUT.
 9     05 CHAR-OUT     OCCURS 50 TIMES  PIC X.
10  01 GUIDE.
11     05 FILLER    PIC X(40) VALUE
12     '....+....1....+....2....+....3....+....4'.
13     05 FILLER    PIC X(35) VALUE
14     '....+....5....+....6....+....7....+'.
15  01 IX1           PIC S9(8) COMP.
16  01 IX2           PIC S9(8) COMP.
17  # THE KEY CAN BE ANYWHERE IN THE RECORD. IT NEED NOT BE IN THE
18  # BEGINNING. THE LARGEST RECORD ON FILE CAN HAVE ANY LENGTH. BUT
19  # ONLY THE FIRST 3750 BYTES OF EACH RECORD WILL BE DISPLAYED.
20
21  01 RECORDS-ALL.
22     05 RECORD-ONE  OCCURS 15 TIMES.
23        10 REC-SEGMENT OCCURS 50 TIMES
24           PIC X(75).
25
26  01 COMMUNICATION-AREA.
27     05 FIRST-KEY            PIC X(50).
28     05 LAST-KEY             PIC X(50).
29     05 RECORD-PART-X.
```

```
30              10 RECORD-PART              PIC 9(2).
31       01  REC-LENGTH-X.
32           05  REC-LENGTH              PIC 9(4).
33       01  WORK-FIELD              PIC 9(4).
34       01  KEY-LENGTH-X.
35           05  KEY-LENGTH              PIC 9(2).
36       01  REC-LENGTH-CICS          PIC S9(4) COMP.
37       01  KEY-LENGTH-CICS          PIC S9(4) COMP.
38       01  WS-OFFSET                PIC 9(4).
39       01  WS-KEY                   PIC X(50).
40   COPY BNVIEWW.
41   LINKAGE SECTION.
42       01  DFHCOMMAREA              PIC X(102).
43   PROCEDURE DIVISION.
44       EXEC CICS HANDLE CONDITION
45                 LENGERR(LENGTH-ERROR)
46                 ERROR(SERIOUS-ERROR)
47                 NOTOPEN(NOT-OPEN)
48       END-EXEC.
49       IF EIBCALEN NOT = ZERO
50          MOVE DFHCOMMAREA TO COMMUNICATION-AREA
51          PERFORM PROCESS-SCREEN
52       ELSE
53          PERFORM SEND-FIRST-SCREEN.
54
55   FROM-SCREEN-TO-WS.
56       MOVE RECLENI TO REC-LENGTH-X.
```

Figure 2.13. Source code of program BNVSVIEW

67

```
57      IF REC-LENGTH NOT NUMERIC
58          MOVE 'RECORD LENGTH FIELD IS NOT NUMERIC' TO MSGO
59          PERFORM SEND-MAP-END-PGM.
60      IF REC-LENGTH = 0
61          MOVE 'RECORD LENGTH ON SCREEN IS ZERO. INVALID' TO MSGO
62          PERFORM SEND-MAP-END-PGM.
63      MOVE KEYLENI TO KEY-LENGTH-X.
64      IF KEY-LENGTH NOT NUMERIC
65          MOVE 'KEY LENGTH FIELD IS NOT NUMERIC' TO MSGO
66          PERFORM SEND-MAP-END-PGM.
67      IF KEY-LENGTH = 0 OR KEY-LENGTH GREATER THAN 50
68          MOVE 'KEY LENGTH ZERO OR GREATER THAN 50' TO MSGO
69          PERFORM SEND-MAP-END-PGM.
70      MOVE SEGMENTI TO RECORD-PART-X.
71      IF RECORD-PART NOT NUMERIC
72          MOVE 'RECORD SEGMENT ON MAP IS NOT NUMERIC' TO MSGO
73          PERFORM SEND-MAP-END-PGM.
74      IF RECORD-PART = 0 OR RECORD-PART GREATER THAN 50
75          MOVE 'RECORD SEGMENT IS ZERO OR GREATER THAN 50' TO MSGO
76          PERFORM SEND-MAP-END-PGM.
77      MOVE KEY-LENGTH TO KEY-LENGTH-CICS.
78  PROCESS-SCREEN.
79      MOVE SPACES TO RECORDS-ALL.
80      EXEC CICS HANDLE AID CLEAR(END-PROGRAM)
81                         PF8(BROWSE-FORWARD)
82                         PF10(BROWSE-LEFT)
83                         PF11(BROWSE-RIGHT)
84                         ENTER(ENTER-KEY)
85                         ANYKEY(ANY-OTHER-KEY)
86      END-EXEC.
```

```
 87        EXEC CICS RECEIVE MAP('BNVIEWM') INTO(BNVIEWMI) END-EXEC.
 88        MOVE 'ERROR CONDITON 1. CHECK PROGRAM SOURCE' TO MSGO.
 89        PERFORM SEND-MAP-END-PGM.
 90
 91   END-PROGRAM.
 92        EXEC CICS RETURN END-EXEC.
 93        GOBACK.
 94
 95   ANY-OTHER-KEY.
 96        MOVE 'INVALID KEY PRESSED. PLEASE PRESS A KEY SHOWN BELOW'
 97             TO MSGO.
 98        PERFORM SEND-MAP-END-PGM.
 99
100   BROWSE-FORWARD.
101        MOVE SPACES TO MSGO.
102        PERFORM FROM-SCREEN-TO-WS.
103        MOVE LAST-KEY TO FIRST-KEY.
104        PERFORM READ-STORE-RECORDS.
105        PERFORM FROM-WS-TO-SCREEN.
106        PERFORM SEND-MAP-END-PGM.
107   BROWSE-LEFT.
108        MOVE SPACES TO MSGO.
109        PERFORM FROM-SCREEN-TO-WS
110        IF RECORD-PART = 1
111             MOVE 'THIS IS ALREADY THE LEFT-MOST PORTION OF RECORD'
112                  TO MSGO
113        ELSE
114             SUBTRACT 1 FROM RECORD-PART.
```

Figure 2.13. continued.

69

```
115        PERFORM READ-STORE-RECORDS.
116        PERFORM FROM-WS-TO-SCREEN.
117        PERFORM SEND-MAP-END-PGM.
118    BROWSE-RIGHT.
119        MOVE SPACES TO MSGO.
120        PERFORM FROM-SCREEN-TO-WS
121        IF RECORD-PART = 50
122        MOVE 'THIS IS ALREADY THE RIGHT-MOST PORTION OF THE RECORD'
123            TO MSGO
124    ELSE
125        ADD 1 TO RECORD-PART.
126        PERFORM READ-STORE-RECORDS.
127        PERFORM FROM-WS-TO-SCREEN.
128        PERFORM SEND-MAP-END-PGM.
129    ENTER-KEY.
130        MOVE SPACES TO MSGO.
131        PERFORM FROM-SCREEN-TO-WS
132        EXAMINE RECKEYI  REPLACING ALL SPACE BY LOW-VALUE.
133        EXAMINE RECKEYI  REPLACING ALL '.'    BY LOW-VALUE.
134        MOVE RECKEYI TO FIRST-KEY.
135        PERFORM READ-STORE-RECORDS.
136        PERFORM FROM-WS-TO-SCREEN.
137        PERFORM SEND-MAP-END-PGM.
138    READ-STORE-RECORDS.
139        MOVE FIRST-KEY TO WS-KEY.
140        EXEC CICS HANDLE CONDITION NOTFND(RECORD-NOTFND)
141            END-EXEC.
142        EXEC CICS STARTBR DATASET(FILEI)
143            RIDFLD(WS-KEY)
144            KEYLENGTH(KEY-LENGTH-CICS)
```

```
145                 END-EXEC.
146     EXEC CICS HANDLE CONDITION ENDFILE(END-OF-FILE)
147                 END-EXEC.
148     COMPUTE WS-OFFSET = (RECORD-PART - 1) * 75.
149     MOVE WS-OFFSET TO OFFSETO.
150     MOVE SPACES TO RECLENFO, RECLENLO.
151     IF REC-LENGTH GREATER THAN 3750
152         MOVE 3750 TO REC-LENGTH
153         MOVE 'RECORD LENGTH USED ON CICS READNEXT COMMAND IS 3750'
154             TO MSGO
155     EXEC CICS IGNORE CONDITION LENGERR END-EXEC.
156     PERFORM READ-NEXT-RECORD
157         VARYING IX1 FROM 1 BY 1 UNTIL IX1 GREATER THAN 15.
158     MOVE WS-KEY TO LAST-KEY.
159     MOVE REC-LENGTH-CICS TO WORK-FIELD
160     MOVE WORK-FIELD        TO RECLENLO.
161
162 READ-NEXT-RECORD.
163     MOVE REC-LENGTH   TO REC-LENGTH-CICS.
164     EXEC CICS READNEXT DATASET(FILEI)
165                 INTO(RECORD-ONE (IX1))
166                 LENGTH(REC-LENGTH-CICS)
167                 RIDFLD(WS-KEY)
168                 KEYLENGTH(KEY-LENGTH-CICS)
169                 END-EXEC.
170     IF IX1 = 1
171         MOVE WS-KEY TO FIRST-KEY
```

Figure 2.13. continued.

```
            MOVE REC-LENGTH-CICS TO WORK-FIELD
            MOVE WORK-FIELD         TO RECLENFO.

        END-OF-FILE.
            IF RECORD-ONE (1) = SPACES
               MOVE HIGH-VALUE TO FIRST-KEY.
               MOVE HIGH-VALUE TO LAST-KEY.
            PERFORM FROM-WS-TO-SCREEN.
            MOVE 'END OF FILE REACHED' TO MSGO.
            PERFORM SEND-MAP-END-PGM.

        RECORD-NOTFND.
            MOVE 'RECORD WITH FULL OR PARTIAL KEY SPECIFIED NOT FOUND'
               TO MSGO.
            PERFORM FROM-WS-TO-SCREEN.
            PERFORM SEND-MAP-END-PGM.

        FROM-WS-TO-SCREEN.
            PERFORM MAKE-PRINTABLE-1 VARYING IX1 FROM 1 BY 1 UNTIL
               IX1 GREATER THAN 15.
            IF RECORD-ONE (1) NOT = SPACES
               MOVE FIRST-KEY TO RECKEYO
            ELSE
               MOVE SPACES TO RECKEYO.
            EXEC CICS LINK PROGRAM('BNTRNSL') COMMAREA(RECKEYO)
               LENGTH(50)     END-EXEC.
        ** MOVE SPACES TO END OF RECKEYO, THAT DON'T BELONG TO ACTUAL KEY
            MOVE RECKEYO TO KEY-IN.
            MOVE SPACES TO KEY-OUT.
            PERFORM MOVE-CHAR VARYING IX1 FROM 1 BY 1 UNTIL IX1 GREATER
```

172
173
174
175
176
177
178
179
180
181
182
183
184
185
186
187
188
189
190
191
192
193
194
195
196
197
198
199
200
201

```
202                 THAN KEY-LENGTH-CICS
203            MOVE KEY-OUT    TO RECKEYO.
204            MOVE RECORD-PART TO SEGMENTO.

205            MOVE REC-SEGMENT (1,  RECORD-PART)  TO LINE010.
206            MOVE REC-SEGMENT (2,  RECORD-PART)  TO LINE020.
207            MOVE REC-SEGMENT (3,  RECORD-PART)  TO LINE030.
208            MOVE REC-SEGMENT (4,  RECORD-PART)  TO LINE040.
209            MOVE REC-SEGMENT (5,  RECORD-PART)  TO LINE050.
210            MOVE REC-SEGMENT (6,  RECORD-PART)  TO LINE060.
211            MOVE REC-SEGMENT (7,  RECORD-PART)  TO LINE070.
212            MOVE REC-SEGMENT (8,  RECORD-PART)  TO LINE080.
213            MOVE REC-SEGMENT (9,  RECORD-PART)  TO LINE090.
214            MOVE REC-SEGMENT (10, RECORD-PART)  TO LINE100.
215            MOVE REC-SEGMENT (11, RECORD-PART)  TO LINE110.
216            MOVE REC-SEGMENT (12, RECORD-PART)  TO LINE120.
217            MOVE REC-SEGMENT (13, RECORD-PART)  TO LINE130.
218            MOVE REC-SEGMENT (14, RECORD-PART)  TO LINE140.
219            MOVE REC-SEGMENT (15, RECORD-PART)  TO LINE150.
220
221        MOVE-CHAR.
222            MOVE CHAR-IN (IX1) TO CHAR-OUT (IX1).
223
224        MAKE-PRINTABLE-1.
225            PERFORM MAKE-PRINTABLE-2 VARYING IX2 FROM 1 BY 1 UNTIL
226                IX2 GREATER THAN 50.
227
228        MAKE-PRINTABLE-2.
```

Figure 2.13. continued.

73

```
229        EXEC CICS LINK PROGRAM('BNTRNSL')
230            COMMAREA (REC-SEGMENT (IX1 IX2))
231            LENGTH(75) END-EXEC.
232
233    NOT-OPEN.
234        MOVE 'FILE NOT OPEN ON CICS. CHECK THIS USING CEMT' TO MSGO.
235        PERFORM SEND-MAP-END-PGM.
236
237    LENGTH-ERROR.
238        MOVE 'LENGTH ERROR CONDITION RAISED. USE CEDF TO DEBUG'
239            TO MSGO.
240        PERFORM SEND-MAP-END-PGM.
241
242    SERIOUS-ERROR.
243        MOVE 'ERROR. FILE NOT DEFINED OR WRONG KEY LENGTH. USE CEDF'
244            TO MSGO.
245        PERFORM SEND-MAP-END-PGM.
246
247    SEND-MAP-END-PGM.
248        EXEC CICS SEND MAP ('BNVIEWM')
249            DATAONLY
250            FROM(BNVIEWMO)
251            END-EXEC.
```

```
252        EXEC CICS RETURN TRANSID('BNVR')
253                     COMMAREA(COMMUNICATION-AREA)
254                     LENGTH(102)
255                     END-EXEC.
256
257   SEND-FIRST-SCREEN.
258        MOVE 'FOR VAR LENGTH FILES, ENTER MAX REC LENGTH ON SCREEN'
259             TO MSGO.
260        MOVE '01' TO SEGMENTO.
261        MOVE '0000' TO OFFSETO.
262        MOVE GUIDE TO RULERO.
263        EXEC CICS SEND MAP('BNVIEWM')
264             ERASE
265             END-EXEC.
266        EXEC CICS RETURN TRANSID('BNVR')
267                     COMMAREA(COMMUNICATION-AREA)
268                     LENGTH(102)
269                     END-EXEC.
```
****

Figure 2.13.   continued.

75

Step 3. Compile and link program BNVSVIEW using the JCL given in Section B.1 in Appendix B. This job will create load module BNVSVIEW in your load library. This load library must be included under DDname DFHRPL in the CICS start-up procedure or job.

Step 4. Make sure CICS subprogram BNTRNSL has been installed, as described in Section C.4 in Appendix C. This is because program BNVSVIEW issues a CICS LINK to BNTRNSL.

Step 5. Define the following in CICS tables:

Definition of Program BNVSVIEW in the PPT

```
PROGRAM    BNVSVIEW
GROUP      CICSBOOK
LANGUAGE   COBOL
```

Other parameters for BNVSVIEW in the PPT should be the same as those for the sample program BNPROG1 given in Section 1.6.

Definition of Mapset BNVIEWM in the PPT

```
MAPSET  BNVIEWM
GROUP   CICSBOOK
RSL     00
STATUS  ENABLED
```

Definition of Transaction BNVR in the PCT

```
TRANSACTION  BNVR
GROUP        CICSBOOK
PROGRAM      BNVSVIEW
```

Other parameters for BNVR in the PCT should be the same as those for the sample transaction BNC1 given in Section 1.6.

Procedure for Using This Program

On a blank screen, type BNVR and press the Enter key. You will receive a screen as shown in Figure 2.15. Now let us suppose you want to view records on file PAYMAST which is defined in the FCT as a file having fixed-length records. The record length is 1300, and the key length is 13. So you should enter the following and then press the Enter key:

```
FILE: PAYMAST
KEY LENGTH: 13
RECORD LENGTH: 1300
```

```
********************************************************************************
 1   PASSION   DFHMSD  TYPE=MAP,MODE=INOUT,CTRL=FREEKB,LANG=COBOL,TIOAPFX=YES
 2   BNVIEWM   DFHMDI  SIZE=(24,80),LINE=1,COLUMN=1
 3   MSG       DFHMDF  POS=(01,01),LENGTH=79,ATTRB=(BRT,ASKIP)               *
 4             DFHMDF  POS=(02,01),LENGTH=43,ATTRB=(ASKIP),                  *
 5                     INITIAL='FACILITY TO VIEW RECORDS ON ANY VSAM KSDS'
 6             DFHMDF  POS=(02,45),LENGTH=18,ATTRB=(BRT,ASKIP),              *
 7                     INITIAL='BY BARRY K. NIRMAL'
 8   FILE      DFHMDF  POS=(03,01),LENGTH=05,ATTRB=(ASKIP),INITIAL='FILE:'   *
 9             DFHMDF  POS=(03,07),LENGTH=08,ATTRB=(UNPROT,IC,FSET,BRT),     *
10                     INITIAL='                '
11   KEYLEN    DFHMDF  POS=(03,16),LENGTH=11,ATTRB=(ASKIP),                  *
12                     INITIAL='KEY LENGTH:'
13             DFHMDF  POS=(03,28),LENGTH=02,ATTRB=(UNPROT,FSET,BRT),        *
14                     INITIAL='00'
15   RECLEN    DFHMDF  POS=(03,31),LENGTH=14,ATTRB=(ASKIP),                  *
16                     INITIAL='RECORD LENGTH:'
17             DFHMDF  POS=(03,46),LENGTH=04,ATTRB=(BRT,UNPROT,FSET),        *
18                     INITIAL='0000'
19   SEGMENT   DFHMDF  POS=(03,51),LENGTH=11,ATTRB=(ASKIP),                  *
20                     INITIAL='REC SEGMENT'
21             DFHMDF  POS=(03,63),LENGTH=02,ATTRB=(BRT,UNPROT,FSET)
22             DFHMDF  POS=(03,66),LENGTH=01,ATTRB=(ASKIP)
23             DFHMDF  POS=(04,01),LENGTH=23,ATTRB=(ASKIP),                  *
24                     INITIAL='KEY VALUE(FULL/PARTIAL)'
25   RECKEY    DFHMDF  POS=(04,25),LENGTH=50,ATTRB=(BRT,UNPROT,FSET)
26             DFHMDF  POS=(04,76),LENGTH=01,ATTRB=(ASKIP)
```

Figure 2.14.   Source code of mapset BNVIEWM

```
               *      *    *     *      *

27          DFHMDF POS=(05,01),LENGTH=20,ATTRB=(ASKIP),
28                 INITIAL='OFFSET WITHIN RECORD'
29 OFFSET   DFHMDF POS=(05,22),LENGTH=04,ATTRB=(ASKIP,BRT)
30          DFHMDF POS=(05,27),LENGTH=38,ATTRB=(ASKIP),
31                 INITIAL='ACTUAL POSITION WITHIN RECORD =OFFSET+'
32          DFHMDF POS=(05,66),LENGTH=14,ATTRB=(ASKIP),
33                 INITIAL='RULER POSITION'
34          DFHMDF POS=(06,01),LENGTH=22,ATTRB=(ASKIP),
35                 INITIAL='LENGTH OF FIRST RECORD'
36 RECLENF  DFHMDF POS=(06,24),LENGTH=04,ATTRB=(BRT,ASKIP)
37          DFHMDF POS=(06,29),LENGTH=22,ATTRB=(ASKIP),
38                 INITIAL='LENGTH OF LAST RECORD'
39 RECLENL  DFHMDF POS=(06,52),LENGTH=04,ATTRB=(BRT,ASKIP)
40 RULER    DFHMDF POS=(07,01),LENGTH=75,ATTRB=(ASKIP)
41 LINE01   DFHMDF POS=(08,01),LENGTH=75,ATTRB=(BRT,ASKIP)
42 LINE02   DFHMDF POS=(09,01),LENGTH=75,ATTRB=(BRT,ASKIP)
43 LINE03   DFHMDF POS=(10,01),LENGTH=75,ATTRB=(BRT,ASKIP)
44 LINE04   DFHMDF POS=(11,01),LENGTH=75,ATTRB=(BRT,ASKIP)
45 LINE05   DFHMDF POS=(12,01),LENGTH=75,ATTRB=(BRT,ASKIP)
46 LINE06   DFHMDF POS=(13,01),LENGTH=75,ATTRB=(BRT,ASKIP)
47 LINE07   DFHMDF POS=(14,01),LENGTH=75,ATTRB=(BRT,ASKIP)
48 LINE08   DFHMDF POS=(15,01),LENGTH=75,ATTRB=(BRT,ASKIP)
```

```
49 LINE09  DFHMDF POS=(16,01),LENGTH=75,ATTRB=(BRT,ASKIP)
50 LINE10  DFHMDF POS=(17,01),LENGTH=75,ATTRB=(BRT,ASKIP)
51 LINE11  DFHMDF POS=(18,01),LENGTH=75,ATTRB=(BRT,ASKIP)
52 LINE12  DFHMDF POS=(19,01),LENGTH=75,ATTRB=(BRT,ASKIP)
53 LINE13  DFHMDF POS=(20,01),LENGTH=75,ATTRB=(BRT,ASKIP)
54 LINE14  DFHMDF POS=(21,01),LENGTH=75,ATTRB=(BRT,ASKIP)
55 LINE15  DFHMDF POS=(22,01),LENGTH=75,ATTRB=(BRT,ASKIP)
56         DFHMDF POS=(23,01),LENGTH=29,ATTRB=(ASKIP),              *
57                INITIAL='ENTER=INQUIRE SPECIFIC RECORD'
58         DFHMDF POS=(23,31),LENGTH=28,ATTRB=(ASKIP),              *
59                INITIAL='PF8=FWD PF10=LEFT PF11=RIGHT'
60         DFHMDF POS=(24,01),LENGTH=32,ATTRB=(ASKIP),              *
61                INITIAL='MAX RECORD LENGTH DISPLAYED=3750'
62         DFHMDF POS=(24,34),LENGTH=25,ATTRB=(ASKIP),              *
63                INITIAL='MAX KEY LENGTH ALLOWED=50'
64         DFHMSD TYPE=FINAL
65         END
```

****

Figure 2.14. continued.

FOR VAR LENGTH FILES, ENTER MAX REC LENGTH ON SCREEN

FACILITY TO VIEW RECORDS ON ANY VSAM KSDS   BY BARRY K. NIRMAL

FILE: _____   KEY LENGTH: 00 RECORD LENGTH: 0000 REC SEGMENT 01

KEY VALUE(FULL/PARTIAL)

OFFSET WITHIN RECORD 0000 ACTUAL POSITION WITHIN RECORD =OFFSET+ RULER POSITION

LENGTH OF FIRST RECORD   LENGTH OF LAST RECORD

....+....1....+....2....+....3....+....4....+....5....+....6....+....7....+

```
ENTER=INQUIRE SPECIFIC RECORD  PF8=FWD PF10=LEFT  PF11=RIGHT

MAX RECORD LENGTH DISPLAYED=3750 MAX KEY LENGTH ALLOWED=50
```

Figure 2.15. Initial screen displayed by program BNVSVIEW

(Leave the REC SEGMENT field as 01 if you want to see positions 1 through 75 of the first 15 records. But, for example, if you want to see positions 76 through 150 of the first 15 records, enter 02 in the REC SEGMENT field.) You will receive a screen similar to the one shown in Figure 2.15 but with data on lines 8 through 22 on the screen. Line 7 will have the ruler. The KEY-VALUE field will have the key of the first record displayed. On line number 6, the lengths of the first and the last record displayed will also be shown. (Note: These are not the lengths of the first and last records on the file.)

How large can the records on file be?   This program allows us to view the first 3750 bytes of each record. If a file has records larger than 3750 bytes, this program will work fine, but it will display only the first 3750 bytes of each record. If a file has records with lengths less than 3750, there is no problem either. Positions following the record length will display as blank on the screen. Each record of 3750 bytes is conceptually divided into 50 segments of 75 bytes each. To illustrate this concept, suppose that the REC SEGMENT field on the screen has 3 in it. So, you are viewing the third segment of each record. In this case you are viewing positions 151 through 225 on each record. In this case you will find that line 5 on the screen has this:

```
OFFSET WITHIN RECORD 0150
```

And the remainder of line 5 always has this informative message:

```
ACTUAL POSITION WITHIN RECORD = OFFSET + RULER POSITION
```

There is also a ruler marking positions 1 through 75 of the data displayed on screen. So, in this example, a character corresponding to ruler position 12 is actually at position 162 (150 + 12) within the record.

When you receive a screen with data from the file, you can do the following:

If you want to view the next segment of the same set of records, press PF11.

If you want to view the previous segment of the same set of records, press PF10.

If you want to see the next 15 records from the file, press PF8.

If you want to see the same set of records as shown on the screen, but the Nth segment of the records, change SEGMENT field to $N - 1$ and press PF11 (Browse Right), or change SEGMENT to $N + 1$ and press PF10 (Browse Left).

Suppose you are viewing records 41 through 55 and you want to view the first 15 records of the file. To do this, take the cursor to the KEY VALUE field and blank it out (or press EOF key), and then press the Enter key. It should be noted that when you press PF10, PF11, or PF8, any value you enter in the KEY VALUE field is ignored. This is to say that for PF10 and PF11, the same set of records is displayed, and for PF8, the next set of 15 records is displayed, regardless of what you entered in the KEY-VALUE field.

No matter which one of these keys you press—Enter, PF8, PF10, or PF11—any data entered in the following fields are always captured and used in the program:

```
FILE ID
KEY LENGTH
RECORD LENGTH
REC SEGMENT
```

So, KEY VALUE is the only field that gets captured and used only when you press the Enter key.

What are the valid keys that can be pressed? Pressing the Clear key terminates the program and gives you a blank screen, where you can enter this or any other transaction. The functions of Enter, PF8, PF10, and PF11 have been described above. Pressing any other key simply results in INVALID KEY PRESSED message being displayed; no other change occurs to the program or screen displayed.

What if file record has nonprintable characters such as binary zero (Hex '00')? All data displayed on the KEY-VALUE field as well as the 15 data lines are converted to printable characters by linking to program BNTRNSL. (See lines 196 and 229 in program BNVSVIEW.) Characters such as binary zero (Hex '00') and high value (Hex 'FF') are converted to dots. If the program did not do this conversion and sent data containing nonprintable characters, the user would get a PROG 403 or PROG 470 message at the bottom of the screen and would have to press the RESET key to delete these messages. (If he was using an IBM PS/2 connected to the mainframe, he would not be able to get out of PROG 403 by pressing the Reset key.)

In this connection, it should be noted that whatever data is received in the KEY VALUE field, it is first scanned, and any dots and spaces are changed to low values (Hex '00') before being used on start browse command. (See lines 132 and 133 in Figure 2.13.) This explains the following phenomenon: Suppose that a file has its first record with key having low-value (Hex '00') in the first position. So if you blank out the KEY VALUE field and press Enter, the program would display the first record whose key has Hex '00' in position 1 and the following 14 records from the file.

How to use this program to read records with partial key. Suppose there is a file with key length of 6. The key is always numeric. You want to start browsing this file from the first record that has 9 in the first position of the key. To do this on the initial screen displayed when you issue transaction BNVR, or on any other screen, take the cursor to the KEY-VALUE field, enter 9 in first position, and blank out the rest of the field. Make sure the KEY LENGTH field has the full key length. Now press Enter. The first record displayed will be the one with 9 in the first key position. If there is no such record, you will get a message to this effect on the top of the screen, and nothing will be displayed from file.

What should you enter in the key and record length fields? Issue the TSO LISTCAT command for the full VSAM cluster name, and find out the record length and key length. Use the key length displayed by LISTCAT in the KEY LENGTH field. If LISTCAT shows that the file has fixed-length records (i.e., average and maximum record lengths are the same), then enter that value in the RECORD LENGTH field. But if the file has variable length records (i.e., average and maximum record length shown by LISTCAT are not the same), then use 9999 as RECORD LENGTH. In this case, the program will use 3750 as record length, because this is the maximum that the program can display. But in this case, the DDname under which this variable length file is allocated to CICS must be defined in CICS FCT as a variable-length file. See "How to use this program to view records on any VSAM KSDS" below.

In what way can this program be useful? Application and system programmers often have to view records on VSAM files either during their development work or while problem solving. This program can be used for this purpose. If a file is already allocated to CICS and is open, you can just issue transaction BNVR and use it as described above.

How to use this program to view records on any VSAM KSDS. Even if a VSAM KSDS is not allocated to CICS, you can still browse it using this program. To do this, you can do the following. Define in the FCT of your CICS test system a file named SPCLFILE as a variable-length file. It is not really used by any application; it is there for special needs. Now suppose you want to view records on your payroll master file. You can then do the following:

> Close and disable SPCLFILE on CICS and then allocate your payroll master file under SPCLFILE using the CEMT transaction.
>
> Open and enable SPCLFILE using CEMT and make sure it gets open.
>
> Execute transaction BNVR. When the map shown in Figure 2.15 appears, enter the following data and then press the Enter key:

```
FILE = SPCLFILE
KEY LENGTH = 08 (assuming that the key length of your payroll
                    master file is 8)
RECORD LENGTH = 9999 (because SPCLFILE is a variable length
    file)
```

The program will display the first 15 records from the file. Now you can press PF8 to browse forward, PF10 to browse to the left, PF11 to browse to the right, and so on as described above.

Once you are finished viewing records, use the CEMT transaction to close file SPCLFILE. Now your payroll master file has been detached from CICS test system. You can now use SPCLFILE to view records on some other file or for some other purpose.

Explanation of Program BNVSVIEW

When you type BNVR and press the Enter key, control flows to line 44 in Figure 2.13, i.e., to the first line of the procedure division. Here we set up some traps: We tell CICS which labels to branch to in the event of various conditions arising upon execution of any CICS command. So, we have set up things so that when the LENGERR condition occurs, control would automatically go to label LENGTH-ERROR. On line 49, we are testing if the length of communication area passed to this program is zero. This would be true when you just typed BNVR on a blank screen and pressed Enter. In this case, line 53 would get executed. So, control would flow to label SEND-FIRST-SCREEN (line 257). Here on line 263, we send the entire map BNVIEWM after erasing the screen. After that, on line 266 we return to CICS and pass out the 102-byte-long communication area from the field COMMUNICATION-AREA.

What does the EXEC CICS RETURN command of line 266 do? It tells CICS that the next time the user presses any key on his terminal, including Clear, PA1, etc., transaction BNVR should automatically get started, and the program associated with BNVR should automatically receive the communication area we are passing out.

At this time you have on your terminal the map shown in Figure 2.15. On this map the following are the only fields that are unprotected, i.e., the cursor can go to these fields, and you can enter some data in them:

```
FILE
KEY LENGTH
RECORD LENGTH
REC SEGMENT
KEY VALUE
```

Suppose that you modified only the following fields and then pressed the Enter key:

```
FILE: PAYRMAST
KEY LENGTH: 08
RECORD LENGTH: 1200
```

Since all unprotected fields on the map have FSET attribute, whatever data are there in those fields on the screen will get transmitted to the program. So, when you press Enter, control flows to line 44 in Figure 2.13. On line 49, EIBCALEN, the length of communication area will be found to be 102, so lines 50 and 51 would get executed. So, we go to line 79. On line 80, we are setting up some traps so that when the EXEC RECEIVE MAP command is subsequently executed and it is found that the user pressed the Clear key, control would flow to label END-PROGRAM, and if he pressed the Enter key, control would flow to label ENTER-KEY, and so on. Then, on line 87, we receive the data entered on the map in field BNVIEWMI. As soon as the RECEIVE is done, CICS checks the traps set up earlier. It would find that the Enter key was pressed, and since the trap for Enter key was set up to branch to label ENTER-KEY, this branch would take place. So, control would flow to line 129. Here on line 131, we perform routine FROM-SCREEN-TO-WS. In this routine we capture all data transmitted from the map and store them in various fields in the working storage. So, the various fields in working storage are as follows:

```
RECKEYI = LOW-VALUES (because the user did not enter anything in
                      this field)
RECLENI = 1200
KEYLENI = 08
FILEI = PAYRMAST
RECORD-PART = 01
KEY-LENGTH-CICS = 08
```

Next on line 135, we perform READ-STORE-RECORDS. So, on line 139, low values get moved into WS-KEY. On line 142 we issue the STARTBR command to position the pointer at that record in file PAYRMAST, whose key is greater than or equal to low values. So, the pointer would get positioned at the very first record in the file. Next on line 156, we perform READ-NEXT-RECORD 15 times. So, the first time, on line 164 when the READNEXT command is issued, it will read the first record from the file and store it into RECORD-ONE (1). The next time routine READ-NEXT-RECORD is performed, it would read the next record from the file into RECORD-ONE (2), and so on up to the fifteenth record. Then when routine READ-STORE-RECORDS has been performed, control would flow to line 136 where routine FROM-WS-TO-SCREEN would get performed. In this routine, we move data into those fields in working storage that correspond to map fields. After this routine has been performed, control would flow to line 137 where we perform SEND-MAP-END-PGM. So, control flows to line 248, where only data fields are sent for map BNVIEWM (because of DATAONLY on SEND MAP command.) This means only those fields that have labels in the map of Figure 2.14, and that have nonbinary zero values in the program, will be sent. Next on line 252, we return to CICS and pass out the 102-byte area at COMMUNICATION-AREA. So, we are telling CICS that the next time any key is pressed on that terminal, transaction BNVR should be started, and the program should receive 102 byte communication area that we have just passed out.

Next time, suppose that you pressed the PF8 key. You can follow through this program as we did above. You will find that in this case, control would flow to label BROWSE-FORWARD, due to the trap set up on line 81. In this routine, on lines 104 through 106, we would perform the same three routines that were performed in ENTER-KEY, but the records read from file this time would be records 16 through 30.

This way you can study this program. The description of this program given above under the heading "PROCEDURE FOR USING THIS PROGRAM" will also help you in obtaining a thorough and detailed understanding of this program.

2.10 FACILITY TO SUBMIT BATCH JOBS FROM CICS OR GENER/OL APPLICATION PROGRAMS

Figures 2.16 through 2.22 give the various components of a facility to submit batch jobs from a CICS application program. The calling program can be written in any language such as CICS COBOL, GENER/OL, or CSP. This facility works in the following way. A JCL deck consisting of n lines (where n is from 1 to 9999) is first stored in a VSAM file under an eight-character JCL ID. The VSAM file has 92-bytes-long records. Its key is in the first 12 positions; the first 8 bytes represent the JCL ID, and the next 4 bytes contain the record sequence number. So, if you stored your JCL of 10 lines under JCL ID of MATERIAL, they would be stored on the VSAM file as records with keys MATERIAL0001, MATERIAL0002, and so on up to MATERIAL0010. Having stored your JCL on the VSAM file, you can submit it from a CICS program simply by linking to program JSCICSUB and passing it a communication area of 1697 bytes, one of whose fields contains the JCL ID to be submitted.

Loading of a JCL deck is done by executing a batch program. There is also another program that can be used to read a specific JCL deck from the VSAM file and store it in a sequential dataset, which can be a member of a PDS. When you link to JSCICSUB, you can also request that one or more lines in the JCL deck on the VSAM file be modified prior to job submission. This modification is done only to the JCL cards submitted, not to the records on the VSAM file. This makes this facility a powerful tool for building on-line applications, which use batch jobs to perform processing or produce reports that can be automatically routed to a remote printer located in the user's offices.

Usefulness of This Facility in Applications Design

A common question is "Why is there a need to submit a batch job from CICS? I thought CICS was an on-line system and had nothing to do with batch jobs." The people who feel this way are either those with little experience in data processing or those who have not dirtied their hands with programming work for a long time and have lost touch with the needs of the people on the shop floor. The main benefit of this facility is that it allows you to put your

```
++++++++++++++++++++++++++++++++++++++++++++++++++++++++++++++++++++++++++++++++
      1       ID DIVISION.
      2       PROGRAM-ID.  JSLOAD.
      3       REMARKS.
      4           THIS PROGRAM IS USED TO LOAD ANY JCL DECK TO JCL VSAM KSDS
      5           FILE WHICH IS ALLOCATED TO CICS. CICS PROGRAM BNSUBJOB READS
      6           THIS VSAM KSDS AND SUBMITS ONE JOB FROM IT TO MVS.
      7       ENVIRONMENT DIVISION.
      8       INPUT-OUTPUT SECTION.
      9       FILE-CONTROL.
     10           SELECT SEQFILE ASSIGN TO SEQFILE.
     11           SELECT VSAMFILE ASSIGN TO VSAMFILE
     12               ORGANIZATION IS INDEXED
     13               ACCESS MODE IS DYNAMIC
     14               RECORD KEY IS JCL-KEY
     15               FILE STATUS IS STAT.
     16       DATA DIVISION.
     17       FILE SECTION.
     18       FD  SEQFILE
     19           LABEL RECORDS OMITTED
     20           BLOCK CONTAINS 0 RECORDS.
     21       01  IN-JCL-REC      PIC X(80).
     22       FD  VSAMFILE
     23           LABEL RECORDS OMITTED.
     24       01  OUTPUT-JCL.
     25           03  JCL-KEY             PIC X(12).
     26           03  FILLER REDEFINES JCL-KEY.
     27               05  JCL-SUB-KEY.
     28                   08  JCL-ID      PIC X(8).
     29               05  JCL-SEQ         PIC 9(4).
++++++++++++++++++++++++++++++++++++++++++++++++++++++++++++++++++++++++++++++++
```

88

```
30              03  OUT-JCL-REC                PIC X(80).
31      WORKING-STORAGE SECTION.
32      77  DASHES                      PIC X(120) VALUE ALL '='.
33      77  CTR-JCL-LOADED              PIC 999 VALUE 0.
34      77  CTR-DELETED                 PIC 999 VALUE 0.
35      77  STAT                        PIC XX  VALUE SPACES.
36      77  IN-JCL-ID                   PIC X(8).
37      77  INPUT-SW                    PIC 9 VALUE 0.
38          88 END-OF-INPUT             VALUE 1.
39      77  VSAM-SW                     PIC 9 VALUE 0.
40          88 END-OF-VSAM              VALUE 1.
41      ***************************************************************
42      PROCEDURE DIVISION.
43      ***************************************************************
44          OPEN INPUT SEQFILE
45               I-O  VSAMFILE.
46          IF STAT NOT = '00'
47              DISPLAY DASHES
48              DISPLAY 'ERROR OCCURED DURING OPENING VSAM FILE'
49              DISPLAY 'VSAM STATUS CODE ............' STAT
50              DISPLAY 'PROGRAM HAS BEEN TERMINATED '
51              DISPLAY DASHES
52              CLOSE SEQFILE VSAMFILE
53              STOP RUN.
54          ACCEPT IN-JCL-ID.
55          DISPLAY DASHES.
56          DISPLAY 'NOTE: JCL KEY STARTS WITH ' IN-JCL-ID.
```

Figure 2.16. Source code of program JSLOAD

```
       MOVE IN-JCL-ID TO JCL-ID.
       START VSAMFILE KEY = JCL-SUB-KEY.
       IF STAT = '00'
       READ VSAMFILE NEXT
       IF IN-JCL-ID = JCL-ID
           PERFORM DELETE-JCL-CARDS THRU DELETE-EXIT
               UNTIL (JCL-ID NOT = IN-JCL-ID)
                   OR END-OF-VSAM.

       DISPLAY DASHES.
       DISPLAY 'NUMBER OF RECORDS DELETED FOR JCL ID: ' IN-JCL-ID
           ' ======> ' CTR-DELETED.

       DISPLAY DASHES.
       DISPLAY 'THE RECORDS LOADED TO VSAM FILE ARE AS FOLLOWS: '
       DISPLAY DASHES.
       PERFORM WRITE-NEW-JCL THRU WRITE-EXIT UNTIL END-OF-INPUT.
       DISPLAY DASHES.
       DISPLAY 'NUMBER OF RECORDS WRITTEN TO VSAM FILE FOR JCL ID: '
           IN-JCL-ID ' ======> ' CTR-JCL-LOADED
       DISPLAY DASHES.
       CLOSE SEQFILE
             VSAMFILE.

       GOBACK.

   DELETE-JCL-CARDS.
       DELETE VSAMFILE RECORD.
       IF STAT NOT = '00'
           DISPLAY DASHES
           DISPLAY 'ERROR OCCURED DURING DELETING A RECORD FROM FILE'
           DISPLAY 'VSAM STATUS CODE ::::::::::::: ' STAT
           DISPLAY 'PROGRAM IS TERMINATED'
```

57
58
59
60
61
62
63
64
65
66
67
68
69
70
71
72
73
74
75
76
77
78
79
80
81
82
33
84
85
86

```
 87          DISPLAY DASHES
 88          CLOSE SEQFILE VSAMFILE
 89          STOP RUN.
 90          ADD 1 TO CTR-DELETED.
 91          READ VSAMFILE NEXT AT END MOVE 1 TO VSAM-SW.
 92      DELETE-EXIT. EXIT.
 93
 94      WRITE-NEW-JCL.
 95          READ SEQFILE AT END
 96              MOVE 1 TO INPUT-SW
 97              GO TO WRITE-EXIT.
 98          IF CTR-JCL-LOADED > 9999
 99              DISPLAY DASHES
100              DISPLAY 'JCL CARDS IN INPUT FILE ARE MORE THAN 9999'
101              DISPLAY 'JCL RECORDS HAVE NOT BEEN LOADED'
102              DISPLAY 'PROGRAM HAS BEEN TERMINATED'
103              START VSAMFILE KEY = JCL-SUB-KEY
104              READ VSAMFILE NEXT
105              IF JCL-ID = IN-JCL-ID
106                  PERFORM DELETE-JCL-CARDS UNTIL (JCL-ID NOT = IN-JCL-ID)
107              CLOSE SEQFILE VSAMFILE
108              STOP RUN.
109          ADD 1 TO CTR-JCL-LOADED.
110          MOVE IN-JCL-ID TO JCL-ID
111          MOVE CTR-JCL-LOADED TO JCL-SEQ.
112          MOVE IN-JCL-REC TO OUT-JCL-REC.
113          WRITE OUTPUT-JCL.
114          IF STAT NOT = '00'
```

Figure 2.16. continued.

```
115          DISPLAY DASHES
116          DISPLAY 'ERROR OCCURED DURING WRITING A RECORD TO VSAM '
117                  'FILE'
118          DISPLAY 'VSAM STATUS CODE ................ ' STAT
119          DISPLAY 'PROGRAM IS TERMINATED'
120          DISPLAY DASHES
121          CLOSE SEQFILE VSAMFILE
122          STOP RUN.
123      DISPLAY OUTPUT-JCL.
124   WRITE-EXIT. EXIT.
*************************************************************
```

Figure 2.16. continued.

```
***************************************************************
 1   //JOBNAME   JOB CARD GOES HERE
 2   //*=========================================================
 3   //* LOAD A JCL FROM A 80-BYTE RECORD FILE TO VSAM JCL MASTER FILE
 4   //*=========================================================
 5   //STEP01    EXEC  PGM=IDCAMS
 6   //SYSPRINT  DD    SYSOUT=*
 7   //FILE01    DD    DISP=SHR,DSN=VSAM.KSDS.NAME
 8   //SYSIN     DD    *
 9        VERIFY FILE(FILE01)
10        VERIFY FILE(FILE01)
11   //*=========================================================
12   //STEP02    EXEC  PGM=JSLOAD
13   //STEPLIB   DD    DISP=SHR,DSN=NAME.OF.LOAD.LIBRARY
14   //SYSUDUMP  DD    SYSOUT=*
15   //SYSDBOUT  DD    SYSOUT=*
16   //SYSOUT    DD    SYSOUT=*
17   //SEQFILE   DD    DISP=SHR,DSN=SEQ.FILE.NAME
18   //*SEQFILE  DD    DUMMY,DCB=(RECFM=FB,LRECL=80,BLKSIZE=9040)
19   //VSAMFILE  DD    DISP=SHR,DSN=VSAM.KSDS.NAME
20   //*=========================================================
21   //* JCL ID (PART OF VSAM KEY) MUST BE ENTERED IN COLUMNS 1 THRU
22   //* 8 OF THE RECORDS UNDER SYSIN.
23   //*=========================================================
24   //SYSIN     DD    *
25   PAYROLL1
***************************************************************
```

Figure 2.17. JCL to load a JCL onto VSAM
JCL master file

```
***************************************************************
1  *=============================================================*
2  * HISTORY OF CHANGES TO THIS PROGRAM
3  *=============================================================*
4  * DATE    |PGMR |DESCRIPTION
5  *=============================================================*
6  *YY/MM/DD|BARRY|NEW PROGRAM
7  *=============================================================*
8         COPY REGDEF
9  JSCICSUB DFHEIENT CODEREG=(9,10),DATAREG=11,EIBREG=12
10        EXEC CICS IGNORE CONDITION LENGERR
11        EXEC CICS HANDLE CONDITION ERROR(ERRFILE)
12        MVC   RECOUT(3),=X'000000C'
13        CLC   EIBCALEN(2),=H'1697'
14        BNE   SORRYO
15 OKSIR  EQU   *
16        L     R4,DFHEICAP
17        CLC   C(8,R4),=CL8'00000000'
18        BE    DEFFILE
19        CLC   O(8,R4),BLANKS
20        BE    DEFFILE
21        CLC   O(8,R4),NULLS
22        BE    DEFFILE
23        CLC   C(8,R4),=CL8'_____'
24        BNE   ALRIGHT2
25 DEFFILE EQU  *
26        MVC   O(8,R4),=CL8'VSAMJCL1'
27 ALRIGHT2 EQU *
28  *=============================================================*
29  * INSERT VALIDATION FOR FILES OTHER THAN VSAMJCL1 AFTER THIS LINE. FOR
```

```
30  * EXAMPLE IF YOU WANT TO ALLOW FILE JCLFILE, THEN UNCOMMENT THE
31  * FOLLOWING TWO LINES:
32  *        CLC  0(8,R4),=CL8'JCLFILE'
33  *        BE   FILEOK
34  *==================================================================
35           CLC  0(8,R4),=CL8'VSAMJCL1'
36           BE   FILEOK
37           MVC  ERRMSG(80),ERRMSG2
38           B    SORRY
39  FILEOK   EQU  *
40           MVC  DATASET,0(4)
41           MVC  WSJCLID,8(4)
42           MVC  WSRECSEQ,=C'0001'
43           LA   R1,21(4)          POINT R1 TO FIRST 'NEW LINE' FIELD.
44           LA   R2,20             20=NUMBER OF TIMES LOOP IS TO BE EXECUTED
45  LOOP1    EQU  *
46           BAL  R14,SCAN1
47           LA   R1,84(R1)         POINT R1 TO NEXT 'NEW LINE' FIELD.
48           BCT  R2,LOOP1
49           LR   R1,R4             POINT R1 TO COMM AREA.
50           LA   R1,20(R1)         POINT R1 TO FIRST SEQUENCE NUMBER
51           LA   R2,20             20=NUMBER OF TIMES LOOP2 IS TO BE EXECUTED
52  LOOP2    EQU  *
53           OI   0(R1),X'F0'       CHANGE C OR D IN FIRST NIBBLE TO F.
54           LA   R1,84(R1)         POINT R1 TO NEXT SEQUENCE NUMBER.
55           BCT  R2,LOOP2
56  NEXTWRK1 EQU  *
57           EXEC CICS HANDLE CONDITION NOTFND(STBRERR)
```

Figure 2.18.   Source code of program JSCICSUB

```
58          EXEC CICS STARTBR DATASET(DATASET) RIDFLD(WSKEY)          X
59               KEYLENGTH(12) EQUAL
60          EXEC CICS HANDLE CONDITION NOTFND(EOF) ENDFILE(ECF)
61          EXEC CICS ENQ RESOURCE(RESNAME) LENGTH(5)
62 READREC  EQU  *
63          EXEC CICS READNEXT DATASET(DATASET) INTO(FILEREC)         X
64               RIDFLD(WSKEY) KEYLENGTH(12) LENGTH(LENREC)
65          CLC  FRJCLID,8(4)   IS THE JCL ID OF RECORD DESIRED ONE?
66          BNE  EOF            NO, TREAT IT LIKE  END OF FILE
67          LR   R1,R4          POINT R1 TO COMM AREA
68          LA   R1,17(R1)      POINT R1 TO FIRST SEQUENCE NUMBER
69          LA   R2,20          WE WANT TO CHECK 20 SEQUENCE NUMBERS
70 LOOP3    EQU  *
71          CLC  0(4,R1),=C'0000'
72          BE   NOCHNG
73          CLC  0(4,R1),FRRECSEQ
74          BNE  NOCHNG
75          MVC  FRDATA,4(R1)
76          B    WRITEREC
77 NOCHNG   EQU  *
78          LA   R1,84(R1)
79          BCT  R2,LOOP3
80 WRITEREC EQU  *
81          EXEC CICS WRITEQ TD QUEUE('INT1') FROM(FRDATA) LENGTH(80)
82          AP   RECOUT,=P'1'   INCREMENT RECOUT
83          B    READREC
84 EOF      EQU  *
85          EXEC CICS ENDBR DATASET(DATASET)
86          MVI  16(4),C'P'     SET RETURN CODE TO P= PASSED
87 GETOUT   EQU  *
```

```
88          CP    RECOUT,=P'0'
89          BE    NONEED
90          MVC   FRDATA,BLANKS
91          MVC   FRDATA(5),=C'/*EOF'
92          EXEC CICS WRITEQ TD QUEUE('INT1') FROM(FRDATA) LENGTH(80)
93 NONEED   EQU   *
94          EXEC CICS DEQ RESOURCE(RESNAME) LENGTH(5)
95 ALRIGHT1 EQU   *
96          EXEC CICS RETURN
97 STBRERR  EQU   *
98          MVC   ERRMSG(130),ERRMSG4
99          MVC   ERRMSG+35(12),WSKEY
100         MVI   16(R4),C'F'   INSERT RETURN CODE IN COMM AREA
101         EXEC CICS SEND FROM(ERRMSG) LENGTH(130) ERASE
102         EXEC CICS RECEIVE INTO(WSDATAIN) LENGTH(LEN160)
103         EXEC CICS RETURN
104 ERRFILE  MVC   ERRMSG(80),ERRMSG3
105          B    SORRY
106 *==========================================================*
107 SCAN1    EQU   *
108 *** SCAN 80 BYTES FROM WHERE R1 IS POINTING AND REPLACE HEX '00' WITH
109 *** BLANK.
110          ST    R1,SAVER1     SAVE R1
111          ST    R2,SAVER2     SAVE R2
112          SR    R2,R2
113          LA    R2,80         WE WANT TO SACN 80 BYTES
114 LOOP     CLI   0(R1),X'00'
115          BNE   ADVANCE1
```

Figure 2.18. continued.

```
116 ADVANCE1 MVI   0(R1),X'40'        POINT R1 TO NEXT BYTE
117          LA    R1,1(R1)
118          BCT   R2,LOOP            LOOP BACK IF NECESSARY
119          L     R1,SAVER1          RESTORE R1
120          L     R2,SAVER2          RESTROE R2
121          BR    14
122 *=========================================================*
123 SORRY0   EQU   *
124          MVC   ERRMSG(80),ERRMSG1
125          B     SORRY
126 *=========================================================*
127 SORRY    EQU   *
128          MVI   12(R4),C'F'
129          EXEC CICS SEND FROM(ERRMSG) LENGTH(80) ERASE
130          EXEC CICS RECEIVE INTO(WSDATAIN) LENGTH(LEN160)
131          EXEC CICS RETURN
132 *=========================================================*
133 BLANKS   DC    80X'40'
134 NULLS    DC    80X'00'
135 RESNAME  DC    CL5'DFH99'
136 ERRMSG1  DS    OCL80
137          DC    CL50'LENGTH OF COMM AREA PASSED TO JSCICSUB IS NOT 1697'
138          DC    CL30'. CORRECT THIS ERROR AND RETRY'
139 ERRMSG2  DS    OCL80
140          DC    CL50'UNSUPPORTED FILE PASSED THRU COMM AREA. CALL BARRY'
141          DC    CL30'. NIRMAL IMMEDIATELY FOR HELP. '
142 ERRMSG3  DS    OCL80
143          DC    CL50'AN ERROR OF SOME KIND HAS OCCURRED IN FILE PROCESS'
```

```
144          DC       CL30'. PHONE BARRY NIRMAL PLEASE.   '
145 ERRMSG4  DS       0CL130
146          DC       CL35'NO RECORD FOUND ON FILE WITH KEY = '
147          DC       CL12'XXXXXXXXXXXX'
148          DC       CL33' *** JOB COULD NOT BE SUBMITTED. '
149          DC       CL50'LOAD THIS JCL TO VSAM JCL FILE BEFORE SUBMITTING. '
150 *=========================================================================*
151 LENREC   DC       H'92'
152 LEN160   DC       H'160'
153 LEN80    DC       H'80'
154          DFHEISTG
155 SAVER1   DS       F
156 SAVER2   DS       F
157 DATASET  DS       CL8        DDNAME OF THE VSAM FILE THAT HAS JCL DECK
158 ERRMSG   DS       CL160
159 WSDATAIN DS       CL160
160 RECOUT   DS       PL3        NUMBER OF LINES WRITTEN TO INTERNL READER
161 FILEREC  DS       0CL92      RECORD FROM FILE GETS READ HERE
162 FRKEY    DS       0CL12
163 FRJCLID  DS       CL8
164 FRRECSEQ DS       CL4
165 FRDATA   DS       CL80
166 WSKEY    DS       0CL12      KEY USED IN STARTBR AND READNEXT COMMANDS
167 WSJCLID  DS       CL8
168 WSRECSEQ DS       CL4
169          END
```

****

Figure 2.18. continued.

```
     ***********************************************************************
   1  IDENTIFICATION DIVISION.
   2  PROGRAM-ID. JSTSTPGM.
   3  ENVIRONMENT DIVISION.
   4 *---------------------------------------------------------------------*
   5 *   VER.   DATE PROGRAMMER      DESCRIPTION/MODIFICATIONS             *
   6 *   ---   ---- ----------       -----------------------              *
   7 *   0000 YY/MM/DD BARRY    NEW PROGRAM                               *
   8 ***********************************************************************
   9 * THIS PGM IS A DRIVER TO TEST ROUTINE JSCICSUB. IT SUBMITS
  10 * FROM THE VSAM JCL FILE, JCL DECK WITH ID = PAYROLL1. LINE
  11 * NUMBER 9 IN THE JCL IS CHANGED TO THE FOLLOWING PRIOR TO JOB
  12 * SUBMISSION:
  13 * //SYSPRINT  DD SYSOUT=X
  14 ***********************************************************************
  15  DATA DIVISION.
  16  WORKING-STORAGE SECTION.
  17 *=====================================================================*
  18 *  WORK AREA FOR LINKING TO JSCICSUB FROM A CICS COMMAND LEVEL        *
  19 *  OR A CICS COOBOL/XE PROGRAM.                                       *
  20 *=====================================================================*
  21  01  COMM-AREA.
  22      05  JSCIC-FILE-ID           PIC X(8)  VALUE SPACES.
  23      05  JSCIC-JCL-ID            PIC X(8)  VALUE SPACES.
  24      05  JSCIC-RET-CODE          PIC X(1).
  25      05  JSCIC-JCL-SEQ1          PIC 9999  VALUE ZERO.
  26      05  JSCIC-NEW-LINE1         PIC X(80).
  27      05  JSCIC-JCL-SEQ2          PIC 9999  VALUE ZERO.
  28      05  JSCIC-NEW-LINE2         PIC X(80).
  29      05  JSCIC-JCL-SEQ3          PIC 9999  VALUE ZERO.
```

100

```
30   05   JSCIC-NEW-LINE3                  PIC  X(80).
31   05   JSCIC-JCL-SEQ4                   PIC  9999 VALUE ZERO.
32   05   JSCIC-NEW-LINE4                  PIC  X(80).
33   05   JSCIC-JCL-SEQ5                   PIC  9999 VALUE ZERO.
34   05   JSCIC-NEW-LINE5                  PIC  X(80).
35   05   JSCIC-JCL-SEQ6                   PIC  9999 VALUE ZERO.
36   05   JSCIC-NEW-LINE6                  PIC  X(80).
37   05   JSCIC-JCL-SEQ7                   PIC  9999 VALUE ZERO.
38   05   JSCIC-NEW-LINE7                  PIC  X(80).
39   05   JSCIC-JCL-SEQ8                   PIC  9999 VALUE ZERO.
40   05   JSCIC-NEW-LINE8                  PIC  X(80).
41   05   JSCIC-JCL-SEQ9                   PIC  9999 VALUE ZERO.
42   05   JSCIC-NEW-LINE9                  PIC  X(80).
43   05   JSCIC-JCL-SEQ10                  PIC  9999 VALUE ZERO.
44   05   JSCIC-NEW-LINE10                 PIC  X(80).
45   05   JSCIC-JCL-SEQ11                  PIC  9999 VALUE ZERO.
46   05   JSCIC-NEW-LINE11                 PIC  X(80).
47   05   JSCIC-JCL-SEQ12                  PIC  9999 VALUE ZERO.
48   05   JSCIC-NEW-LINE12                 PIC  X(80).
49   05   JSCIC-JCL-SEQ13                  PIC  9999 VALUE ZERO.
50   05   JSCIC-NEW-LINE13                 PIC  X(80).
51   05   JSCIC-JCL-SEQ14                  PIC  9999 VALUE ZERO.
52   05   JSCIC-NEW-LINE14                 PIC  X(80).
53   05   JSCIC-JCL-SEQ15                  PIC  9999 VALUE ZERO.
54   05   JSCIC-NEW-LINE15                 PIC  X(80).
55   05   JSCIC-JCL-SEQ16                  PIC  9999 VALUE ZERO.
56   05   JSCIC-NEW-LINE16                 PIC  X(80).
57   05   JSCIC-JCL-SEQ17                  PIC  9999 VALUE ZERO.
```

Figure 2.19. Source code of program JSTSTPGM

```
58    05  JSCIC-NEW-LINE17               PIC X(80).
59    05  JSCIC-JCL-SEQ18                PIC 9999 VALUE ZERO.
60    05  JSCIC-NEW-LINE18               PIC X(80).
61    05  JSCIC-JCL-SEQ19                PIC 9999 VALUE ZERO.
62    05  JSCIC-NEW-LINE19               PIC X(80).
63    05  JSCIC-JCL-SEQ20                PIC 9999 VALUE ZERO.
64    05  JSCIC-NEW-LINE20               PIC X(80).
65  01  IX1                             PIC S9(04) COMP SYNC.
66  01  WS-DATA-IN                      PIC X(160).
67  01  LENGTH-160                      PIC S9(04) COMP SYNC VALUE +160.
68  01  WS-OUT-MSG-1.
69    05  FILLER              PIC X(80) VALUE
70    'AN ERROR OF SOME KIND HAS OCCURRED IN PROGRAM JSTSTPGM. '.
71    05  FILLER              PIC X(80) VALUE
72    'CONTACT BARRY NIRMAL IMMEDIATELY FOR PROBLEM RESOLUTION. '.
73  01  WS-OUT-MSG-2.
74    05  FILLER              PIC X(40) VALUE
75    'PROGRAM JSTSTPGM HAS ENDED SUCCESSFULLY.'.
76    05  FILLER              PIC X(40) VALUE
77    ' JOB HAS BEEN SUBMITTED AS SPECIFIED. '.
78
79  LINKAGE SECTION.
80  PROCEDURE DIVISION.
81  *==================================================================
82    EXEC CICS IGNORE CONDITION LENGERR END-EXEC.
83    EXEC CICS HANDLE CONDITION ERROR (ERROR-RTN)
84    END-EXEC.
85    MOVE 'PAYROLLI' TO JSCIC-JCL-ID.
```

```
86          MOVE 9               TO JSCIC-JCL-SEQ1.
87          MOVE '//SYSPRINT DD SYSOUT=X' TO JSCIC-NEW-LINE1.
88    ****  MOVE 3               TO JSCIC-JCL-SEQ2.
89    ****  MOVE '//* LINE THREE IN JCL DECK' TO JSCIC-NEW-LINE2.
90          EXEC CICS LINK PROGRAM('JSCICSUB') COMMAREA(COMM-AREA)
91             LENGTH(1697)
92          END-EXEC.
93          IF JSCIC-RET-CODE NOT = 'P'
94             PERFORM ERROR-RTN.
95          EXEC CICS SEND FROM (WS-OUT-MSG-2)
96             LENGTH(80)
97             ERASE
98          END-EXEC.
99          EXEC CICS RETURN END-EXEC.
100         GOBACK.
101   ERROR-RTN.
102         EXEC CICS SEND FROM (WS-OUT-MSG-1)
103            LENGTH(160)
104            ERASE
105         END-EXEC.
106         EXEC CICS RECEIVE INTO(WS-DATA-IN)
107            LENGTH(LENGTH-160)
108         END-EXEC.
109         EXEC CICS RETURN END-EXEC.
```

****

Figure 2.19. continued.

103

```
********************************************************************************
   1    //JOBNAME  JOB CARD GOES HERE
   2    //*========================================================================
   3    //* THIS JCL CAN BE USED TO DEFINE ANY VSAM KEY-SEQUENCED DATA SET.
   4    //*========================================================================
   5    //STEP01   EXEC PGM=IDCAMS
   6    //SYSPRINT DD SYSOUT=*
   7    //SYSIN    DD *
   8    DELETE VSAMT.ZZBKN.VSAMJCL.NEW.CLUSTER
   9    DEF CLUSTER ( NAME(VSAMT.ZZBKN.VSAMJCL.NEW.CLUSTER) -
  10                  INDEXED -
  11                  SHAREOPTIONS(2 3) -
  12                  FSPC (10 10) -
  13                  KEYS(12 0) -
  14                  RECSZ(92 92) -
  15                  TRACKS(5 5) -
  16                  VOLUME (CICTIO) -
  17                  ) -
  18         DATA   ( NAME(VSAMT.ZZBKN.VSAMJCL.NEW.DATA) -
  19                  CISZ (4096) -
  20                  ) -
```

104

```
21        INDEX    (    NAME(VSAMT.Z28KN.VSAMJCL.NEW.INDEX)  -
22                      CISZ (2048)  -
23                      )
24   //*===========================================================
25   //* THIS STEP WILL ADD INTO THE VSAM FILE A RECORD OF 92 BYTES LENGTH
26   //* WHOSE KEY CONSISTS OF ALL 9'S. MAKE SURE SEQUENTIAL DATA SET UNDER
27   //* DDNAME INPUT HAS RECORD LENGTH OF 92 AND IT HAS ONLY ONE RECORD
28   //* WHICH HAS 9'S IN KEY POSITIONS. OTHER POSITIONS IN THE RECORD CAN
29   //* BE ANYTHING.THIS IS BECAUSE THIS RECORD IS ACTUALLY A DUMMY RECORD.
30   //* AFTER THIS RECORD HAS BEEN ADDED, YOU MAY DELETE THIS RECORD FROM
31   //* THE VSAM FILE, OR YOU MAY LEAVE IT AND IGNORE IT WHEN IT IS READ.
32   //*===========================================================
33   //STEP02    EXEC PGM=IDCAMS
34   //INPUT     DD   DISP=SHR,DSN=Z28KN.TEMPFILE
35   //OUTPUT    DD   DISP=SHR,DSN=VSAMT.Z28KN.VSAMJCL.NEW.CLUSTER
36   //SYSPRINT  DD   SYSOUT=*
37   //SYSIN     DD   *
38      REPRO  INFILE(INPUT)  OUTFILE(OUTPUT)
     ***************************************************************
```

Figure 2.20. JCL to define VSAM JCL master file and load it with one record

```
**************************************************************************
    1   ID DIVISION.
    2   PROGRAM-ID.  JSCOPY.
    3   REMARKS.
    4       THIS PROGRAM IS USED TO READ ANY JCL DECK FROM JCL VSAM FILE
    5       AND WRITE IT TO A SEQUENTIAL FILE THAT HAS RECORD LENGTH=92.
    6       THE VSAM FILE HAS 12 BYTE KEY IN THE FORMAT XXXXXXXXSSSS
    7       WHERE XXXXXXXX=JCL CODE; SSSS= RECORD SEQUENCE NUMBER. THE
    8       JCL ID CAN HAVE ANY VALUE, WHILE SEQUENCE NUMBER MUST BE
    9       A NUMBER FROM 0001 THRU 9999.
   10   ENVIRONMENT DIVISION.
   11   INPUT-OUTPUT SECTION.
   12   FILE-CONTROL.
   13       SELECT VSAMFILE ASSIGN TO VSAMFILE
   14              ORGANIZATION IS INDEXED
   15              ACCESS MODE IS DYNAMIC
   16              RECORD KEY IS VSAM-KEY
   17              FILE STATUS IS STAT.
   18       SELECT SEQFILE ASSIGN TO SEQFILE.
   19   DATA DIVISION.
   20   FILE SECTION.
   21   FD  SEQFILE
   22       LABEL RECORDS STANDARD
   23       BLOCK CONTAINS 0 RECORDS.
   24   01  SEQFILE-REC       PIC X(80).
   25
   26   FD  VSAMFILE
   27       LABEL RECORDS STANDARD.
   28   01  VSAMFILE-REC.
   29       05 VSAM-KEY          PIC X(12).
```

106

```
30        05  FILLER REDEFINES VSAM-KEY.
31            10 JCL-SUB-KEY.
32                15 JCL-ID       PIC X(8).
33                    PIC 9(4).
34            10 JCL-SEQ          PIC 9(4).
35        05 VSAM-REC             PIC X(80).
36    WORKING-STORAGE SECTION.
37    77  DASHES             PIC X(120) VALUE ALL '='.
38    77  CTR-RECORDS-COPIED  PIC 999 VALUE 0.
39    77  STAT               PIC XX VALUE SPACES.
40    77  IN-JCL-ID          PIC X(8).
41    77  VSAM-SW            PIC 9 VALUE 0.
42        88 END-OF-VSAM          VALUE 1.
43    ***************************************************************
44    PROCEDURE DIVISION.
45    ***************************************************************
46        OPEN INPUT VSAMFILE
47             OUTPUT SEQFILE.
48        IF STAT NOT = '00'
49            DISPLAY DASHES
50            DISPLAY 'ERROR OCCURED DURING OPENING VSAM FILE'
51            DISPLAY 'VSAM STATUS CODE ........... ' STAT
52            DISPLAY 'PROGRAM PROCESSING IS TERMINATED'
53            DISPLAY DASHES
54            CLOSE VSAMFILE SEQFILE
55            STOP RUN.

56        ACCEPT IN-JCL-ID.
57        DISPLAY DASHES
```

Figure 2.21. Source code of program JSCOPY

```cobol
58         DISPLAY 'NOTE: JCL KEY STARTS WITH '  IN-JCL-ID.
59         DISPLAY DASHES
60         MOVE IN-JCL-ID TO JCL-ID.
61         START VSAMFILE KEY = JCL-SUB-KEY.
62         IF STAT = ZERO
63            READ  VSAMFILE NEXT
64            PERFORM READ-JCL-CARDS
65               UNTIL (JCL-ID NOT = IN-JCL-ID)  OR END-OF-VSAM.
66         DISPLAY DASHES.
67         DISPLAY 'TOTAL LINES COPIED FOR JCL CODE: ' IN-JCL-ID
68            ' =====>' CTR-RECORDS-COPIED.
69         DISPLAY DASHES.
70         CLOSE SEQFILE
71               VSAMFILE.
72
73         GOBACK.
74     READ-JCL-CARDS.
75         WRITE SEQFILE-REC FROM VSAM-REC.
76         ADD 1 TO CTR-RECORDS-COPIED.
77         READ  VSAMFILE NEXT AT END MOVE 1 TO VSAM-SW.
```

****

Figure 2.21. continued.

108

```
***********************************************************************
1    //JOBNAME   JOB CARD GOES HERE
2    //*================================================================
3    //* COPY A JCL DECK FROM THE VSAM KSDS TO A SEQUENTIAL FILE WHICH HAS
4    //* RECORD LENGTH OF 80. THE SEQUENTIAL FILE CAN BE A MEMBER OF A JCL
5    //* LIBRARY (PDS).
6    //*================================================================
7    //STEP01    EXEC  PGM=IDCAMS
8    //SYSPRINT  DD    SYSOUT=*
9    //FILE01    DD    DISP=SHR,DSN=VSAM.KSDS.NAME
10   //SYSIN     DD    *
11      VERIFY FILE(FILE01)
12      VERIFY FILE(FILE01)
13   //*================================================================
14   //STEP02    EXEC  PGM=JSCOPY
15   //STEPLIB   DD    DISP=SHR,DSN=NAME.OF.LOAD.LIBRARY
16   //SYSUDUMP  DD    SYSOUT=*
17   //SYSDBOUT  DD    SYSOUT=*
18   //SYSPRINT  DD    SYSOUT=*
19   //SYSOUT    DD    SYSOUT=*
20   //SEQFILE   DD    DISP=SHR,DSN=SEQ.FILE.NAME
21   //VSAMFILE  DD    DISP=SHR,DSN=VSAM.KSDS.NAME
22   //*================================================================
23   //* ENTER THE JCL ID (PART OF VSAM KEY) IN FIRST 8 POSITIONS OF THE
24   //* SINGLE RECORD UNDER DDNAME SYSIN.
25   //*================================================================
26   //SYSIN     DD    *
27   PAYROLL1
***********************************************************************
```

Figure 2.22. JCL to copy a JCL from VSAM JCL master file onto a Sequential file

109

knowledge of writing "batch" report-generation programs in Easytrieve or SAS, or other kinds of programs in COBOL, FORTRAN, etc., to good use in building on-line systems. For example, suppose you have a batch COBOL program that reads the material master file and generates a report of all items that have not been used for many months. The JCL to execute this program consists of the following seven lines:

```
//JOBNAME JOB CARD GOES HERE
//STEP01 EXEC PGM=MMSREP1
//STEPLIB DD DISP=SHR,DSN=MMS.LOADLIB
//MMSMAST DD DISP=SHR,DSN=MMS.MASTER.VSAM.CLUSTER
//REPORT DD SYSOUT=Z,DEST=R00
//SYSIN DD *
 PERIOD IN MONTHS FOR WHICH REPORT IS DESIRED: XX
```

Now suppose that your user would like to have an on-line facility as a part of the material management system so that he or she can enter on the screen the period in months and the remote printer ID where he wants his report printed and press the Enter key. The system will generate this report and automatically route it to the remote printer specified by the user.

Instead of developing an on-line CICS program that reads the MMS master file and prints the report on a printer defined to CICS, you may like to use your batch program MMSREP1 that has been debugged, tried, and tested. You can do this by using this facility to submit batch jobs from a CICS application program, the detailed description of whose components is given later in this section. You store the batch job shown above in the VSAM file that is defined to CICS. Then you capture the period and remote printer ID entered by the user in a work area. You then link to program JSCICSUB, specifying in the communication area passed to it the ID of the JCL deck you want submitted. You must also indicate that before submission, line number 7 is to be modified by the new line that contains the period entered by the user, and that line number 5 is to be modified by the new line that specifies the remote printer ID where the printout is to be routed. Program JSCICSUB will then submit the job and return control to the calling program. The calling program will display a number of message lines informing the user that the report will be printed out in a few minutes, along with the phone number of the systems analyst in case of problems.

The main advantages of this facility are as follows:

1. It allows you to utilize your knowledge of writing batch programs, especially those for report generation, in building on-line systems. This does not mean that submitting batch jobs through CICS is always the best solution and that it must be used in all circumstances. Sometimes it may be more desirable to present a report on the user's CRT rather than print it on a printer. It may also be more practical to write a

program in CICS COBOL, or preferably in a 4GL language such as CSP or GENER/OL, which reads the file allocated to CICS and generates the report in real-time on a printer defined to CICS.

2. It allows all programmers in the EDP department to store their JCL for job submission on a common VSAM file, rather than each application using its own single or multiple VSAM files. Thus, it is necessary to define a single VSAM file in CICS FCT for job submission. This will reduce VSAM storage requirements in CICS and contribute to smoother operation of your CICS system. It will also make it easy for the Quality Assurance personnel to control the VSAM JCL file that contains production JCL.

Procedure for Installing This Facility

Step 1. Enter the program shown in Figure 2.16 in member JSLOAD of a source PDS. Enter the program shown in Figure 2.18 in member JSCICSUB in a source PDS, and enter the program shown in Figure 2.21 in member JSCOPY in the source PDS.

Step 2. Compile and link program JSLOAD into a load library using a JCL that is used to compile and link batch COBOL program.

Step 3. Compile and link program JSCOPY into a load library using a JCL that is used to compile and link batch COBOL program.

Step 4. Decide the DDname you want to use for the VSAM JCL file in CICS FCT. Choose VSAMJCL1 if it is not already being used in the FCT or use some other name. Ask your CICS system programmer to define it in the CICS FCT as a VSAM file with fixed-length records, which has only READ and BROWSE options in the SERVREQ parameter. Use the definition of file BASCLUST given in Section 1.6 as a guide. When the calling program leaves FILE ID in the communication area blank, JSCICSUB will use this file by default.

Step 5. If you decided not to use VSAMJCL1 but some other name, you must make suitable changes to program JSCICSUB. Suppose you decided to use DDname CICSSUB instead of VSAMJCL1, then on lines 26 and 35, change CL8 'VSAMJCL1' to CL8 'CICSSUB'.

Step 6. When the calling program leaves FILE ID in the communication area blank, JSCICSUB uses file VSAMJCL1 by default. (See lines 26 and 35 in Figure 2.18.) You may like to use this or its replacement as a default, but additionally, for example, you may desire that the calling program can also specify VSAMJCL2 in FILE ID in the communication area to indicate that this JCL should be read from file VSAMJCL2. To support this additional file, you have to add the following lines after line 34 in Figure 2.18:

```
CLC   0(8,R4),=CL8'VSAMJCL2'
BE    FILEOK
```

(See the explanation on lines 29 through 33 in Figure 2.18.)

Step 7. Next you should define a VSAM KSDS using IDCAMS which has fixed-length records of 92 bytes with the key in positions 1 through 12. Next you should load into this VSAM file a record of 92 bytes with the key of all 9's. Use the sample JCL shown in Figure 2.20 for this purpose.

Step 8. Assemble and link program JSCICSUB using the JCL given in Section B.2 in Appendix B. This job will create load module JSCICSUB in your load library. This load library must be included under DDname DFHRPL in the CICS start-up procedure or job.

Step 9. Define the following in CICS tables, in addition to defining the VSAM JCL file in the FCT as described above:

Definition of Program JSCICSUB in the PPT

```
PROGRAM    JSCICSUB
GROUP      CICSBOOK
LANGUAGE   ASSEMBLER
```

Other parameters for JSCICSUB in the PPT should be the same as those for the sample program BNPROG1 given in Section 1.6.

Definitions for extra-partition queue INT1 in the DCT

```
DFHDCT TYPE=EXTRA,                            X
       DESTID=INT1,                           X
       DSCNAME=IEINTRDR,
(Other TYPE=EXTRA entries go here)
DFHDCT TYPE=SDSCI,                            X
       BLKSIZE=80,                            X
       BUFNO=1,                               X
       DSCNAME=IEINTRDR,                      X
       RECSIZE=80,                            X
       RECFORM=FIXUNB,                        X
       TYPFLE=OUTPUT
```

In the start-up procedure or job for CICS, the following must be present:

```
//IEINTRDR DD SYSOUT=(Q,INTRDR)
```

Procedure for Loading a JCL Deck onto the VSAM JCL File

Enter the JCL shown in Figure 2.17 into a JCL library. Modify this JCL as follows:

1. Replace line 1 with a valid JOB card, which may consist of one or more lines.
2. On lines 7 and 19, replace VSAM.KSDS.NAME with the full name of your VSAM KSDS that will be loaded with your JCL.
3. On line 13, replace NAME.OF.LOAD.LIBRARY with the full name of the PDS that contains load module JSLOAD.
4. On line 17, replace SEQ.FILE.NAME with the name of the sequential file that has logical record length of 80 and that contains the JCL that is to be loaded. This sequential file can be a member of a PDS. For example:

```
//SEQFILE DD DISP = SHR,DSN = P1BKN.SEQ.FILE
OR
//SEQFILE DD DISP = SHR,DSN = P1BKN.JCL.PDS (REPJCL1)
```

5. On line 25, change PAYROLL1 to the eight-character JCL ID under which you want to store your JCL on the VSAM file.
6. Submit this job. Ensure that both job steps ended in condition code of zero. If not, find the cause of the problem, resolve it, and resubmit the job.

Salient Features of Program JSLOAD

1. If a JCL with a certain JCL ID already exists on the VSAM file, and you submit the job shown in Figure 2.17 to load another JCL under the same JCL ID, the old JCL deck for that JCL ID will be deleted from the VSAM file, and the new JCL deck will get loaded. This is because of the way program JSLOAD is designed. When you run it to load a JCL deck under a certain JCL ID, it first deletes all records for that JCL ID from the VSAM file and displays a line informing you of the number of lines that were deleted. Next it loads all records from the sequential file into the VSAM file and fully displays each record that is written to the VSAM file.
2. If a JCL deck with a certain JCL ID exists on the VSAM file, you can delete it from the VSAM file by running the job shown in Figure 2.17 which executes program JSLOAD with the following changes:

Comment out line 17 and uncomment line 18. This will allocate DDname SEQFILE as a dummy file.

Enter the JCL ID which you want to delete on line 25.

3. Sometimes it can happen that you have replaced a JCL deck on the VSAM file with a new deck. When you view the records for this JCL deck on the CICS system through an on-line facility, you find that the records for the old JCL deck are being displayed. To solve this problem related to VSAM pointers, all you have to do is close the VSAM JCL file on CICS and then reopen it.

Procedure for Submitting a Batch Job from a CICS COBOL Program

The best way of understanding how to submit a batch job from a CICS COBOL program is to take an example. Figure 2.19 gives a sample CICS COBOL program that submits from the VSAM JCL file JCL deck with ID of PAYROLL1. It also specifies that line number 9 in the JCL on the VSAM file be changed to the following prior to job submission:

```
//SYSPRINT DD SYSOUT=X
```

How does this program work? Let's see how this program works and how you can link to JSCICSUB from any other COBOL program. In the working-storage on line 21 is an area called COMM-AREA that has 43 fields totalling 1697 bytes in length. In your own program, you must use the same layout as shown under COMM-AREA in this figure. Of course, the group level name COMM-AREA and the names of fields under it can be changed, but nothing else, including the picture clauses and initial values, should be changed. On line 90, a LINK is issued to JSCICSUB passing out 1697 bytes from COMM-AREA. But before issuing the LINK, various fields in COMM-AREA must be set properly. Here is how:

The first field of 8 bytes in the communication area has spaces, so JSCIC-SUB will use the default DDname. If you wanted JSCICSUB to use another file and if it was supported by JSCICSUB, you would move that file's DDname into JSCIC-FILE-ID.

The next field of 8 bytes in the communication area must contain the JCL ID of the JCL deck that you want to have submitted. In this example, on line 85, we are moving PAYROLL1 into this field.

The next field of one byte can contain anything before issuing the LINK. But when control comes back from JSCICSUB, this field will contain P if job was submitted successfully, or it will contain F. The calling program must check this field, and if it is not P, proper error messages should be displayed on the screen. The program in Figure 2.19 does this checking, and if the return code is not P, it performs routine ERROR-RTN where an error message is displayed. So if JCL with ID of PAYROLL1 did not exist on the VSAM file, program JSCICSUB would display a message to this effect, and when control came back to program JSTSTPGM, it would also display two lines of error message. It should be noted that if any kind of error occurs in job submission, JSCICSUB displays an error message so that the user would be informed.

Since this program wants to modify line 9 in the JCL, on line 86 it moves 9 into JSCIC-JCL-SEQ1, and on line 87 it moves into JSCIC-NEW-LINE1, the new line that will replace line 9 from the VSAM file. Now suppose this program also wanted to change line 3 in the JCL to a comment. To do this, you would have to uncomment lines 88 and 89 in Figure 2.19.

Suppose you want to modify the program in Figure 2.19 so that no lines are modified prior to job submission. To achieve this, you simply have to delete or comment out lines 86 and 87.

The calling program can specify that none or up to 20 lines in the JCL on VSAM file be changed prior to job submission. Program JSCICSUB checks fields JSCIC-JCL-SEQ1, JSCIC-JCL-SEQ2, and so on, up to JSCIC-JCL-SEQ20. If a sequence number field has a zero in it, it indicates that the caller does not want a change, and the next sequence number field is examined. The content of sequence number 1, sequence number 2, and so on, need not be in ascending sequence. They can be in any sequence.

Procedure for Submitting a Batch Job from a GENER/OL Program

Suppose you have stored JCL for a job under JCL ID of ACCTNG1 on the VSAM JCL file, and you wish to submit this job from your GENER/OL program. Then you must do the following:

Step 1. Create a work area named JCLWORK. Its total length must be 1697 bytes, and its layout must match exactly with that of COMM-AREA shown in Figure 2.19, including the length, type, and initial values of fields. Suppose your work area with prefix of JW looks like this:

FIELD NAME	START AT	LENGTH	TYPE	COMMENTS
COMMAREA	1	1697	C	WHOLE AREA
FILEID	1	8	C	V = ' '
JCLID	9	8	C	V = ' '

FIELD NAME	START AT	LENGTH	TYPE	COMMENTS
RETCODE	17	1	C	
JCLSEQ1	18	4	N	V = 0
NEWLINE1	22	80	C	
JCLSEQ2	102	4	N	V = 0
NEWLINE2	106	80	C	
– – – – – –				
– – – –				
JCLSEQ20	1614	4	N	V = 0
NEWLINE20	1618	80	C	

***Step* 2.** In the beginning of your program, you must declare the work area, as follows:

```
JCLWORK          WORK                 PREFIX=JW         AREANAME
```

In the program, following code is all that is required to submit your job:

```
          MOVE          'ACCTNG1' TO JWJCLID
          LINK          (JSCICSUB),JWCOMMAREA
          JWRETCODE EQ  'P'                              YES  SUCCESS
          PRINT         'JOB WAS NOT SUBMITTED'
          ENDJOB
SUCCESS   SKIP
          PRINT         'JOB WAS SUCCESSFULLY SUBMITTED'
```

As shown here, after control comes back from JSCICSUB, you must check the return code. If it has "P," then the job was submitted; otherwise there was some error in job submission. Now suppose you want to modify the fifth line from the JCL deck before submitting this job. Then before linking to JSCIC-SUB, you should move 5 to JWJCLSEQ1 and move the new JCL line to JWNEWLINE1. You can modify none or up to 20 lines before submitting the job. No change is made to the content of the VSAM file. The change is made only to the record(s) read from the VSAM file before job submission.

Explanation of Program JSCICSUB

When a calling program issues a CICS LINK to program JSCICSUB, control flows to line 9 in Figure 2.18. Here the DFHEIENT macro sets up entry logic using registers 9 and 10 for addressing code, register 11 to address data, and register 12 to address the EIB. Next on lines 10 and 11, we set up the trap so that if LENGERR condition arose, it would be ignored, and if any other condition arose that is not trapped, control would flow to the line with label ERRFILE. On line 13, we are checking if the length of the communication area passed by the caller is 1697. If not, control flows to label SORRYO where the content of ERRMSG1 is displayed, and when the user presses any key, EXEC CICS RETURN gets executed which would cause control to flow to the caller.

Now let us suppose that the length of the communication area passed is 1697. So, on line 16, R4 is loaded with the address of the incoming communication area. Next we are checking if the file ID in the communication area is zero, blank, or low values. If so, we go to line 26 where VSAMJCL1 is moved to the file ID field in the communication area. Next in LOOP1 on line 46, we branch to routine SCAN1 where the NEW LINE 1 field of 80 bytes is scanned and all low values are replaced with blanks. This is repeated for NEW LINE 2, NEW LINE 3, and so on, up to NEW LINE 20. In LOOP2 on line 52 we scan SEQUENCE NUMBER 1, SEQUENCE NUMBER 2, and so on, up to SEQUENCE NUMBER 20 in the communication area and replace any C or D found in the first nibble of the last byte with F. So, for example, if a sequence number field has HEX 'F0F1F0C1', it would be changed to HEX 'F0F1F0F1'.

On line 58 we issue the STARTBR command to position the pointer at the beginning of the record with key equal to JCLID supplied in the communication area followed by 0001. If no such record is found, control flows to label STBRERR, where an appropriate error message is displayed, and the program ends. If the STARTBR command was successful, on line 61 we issue the ENQ command to cause single threading. Next on line 63 we read the next record from file. This is followed by comparison of JCL ID of the record read with the JCL ID supplied by the caller. If there is no match, control flows to label EOF. If there is a match, we check in LOOP3 to see if the sequence number of the record read matches with any of the 20 sequence numbers supplied by the caller. If so, the record's data area is replaced with the NEW LINE field supplied by the caller. Next, we come to label WRITEREC, where the data portion of the record read is written to queue 'INT1'. Control then flows to label READREC, where the next read from the file is read and the above process repeated, until the JCL ID of the record read does not match that supplied by the caller or end of file condition occurs. In either case, control flows to label EOF, where the ENDBR command is issued to terminate the browse operation. Next on line 88 we check that at least one record was written to queue 'INT1'. If so, we enter into INT1 a line that has /*EOF in the beginning followed by 75 blanks. This causes all lines previously written to the queue INT1 to be submitted to MVS as a batch job. (The line with /*EOF itself is not written as part of the job. It is merely a trigger to cause job submission.) Next, on line 94 we issue the DEQ command to terminate single-threading. This is followed by the RETURN command on line 96, which sends control back to the calling program.

Procedure for Copying a JCL Deck from VSAM JCL File to a Sequential File

Sometimes you may want to copy a JCL deck from the VSAM file into a sequential file so that you can modify the JCL and again reload it onto the VSAM file. Changing a JCL deck and testing it through TSO/ISPF is easy if it is in a sequential dataset, or in a member of a PDS. The following is the required procedure: First, enter the JCL shown in Figure 2.22 into a JCL library; then modify it as follows:

1. Replace line 1 with a valid JOB card, which may consist of one or more lines.
2. On lines 9 and 21, replace VSAM.KSDS.NAME with the full name of your VSAM KSDS that contains the JCL deck.
3. On line 15, replace NAME.OF.LOAD.LIBRARY with the full name of the PDS that contains load module JSCOPY.
4. On line 20, replace SEQ.FILE.NAME with the name of the sequential file that has logical record length of 80. The JCL deck will be written into this file. This sequential file can be a member of a PDS. For example:

```
//SEQFILE DD DISP=SHR,DSN=P1BKN.SEQ.FILE
//SEQFILE DD  DISP=SHR,DSN=P1BKN.JCL.PDS(REPJCL1)
```

5. On line 27, change PAYROLL1 to the eight-character JCL ID of the JCL deck that you want to copy from the VSAM file.
6. Submit this job. Ensure that both steps ended in the condition code of zero. If not, find the cause of the problem, resolve the problem, and resubmit the job.

2.11 A FACILITY FOR OPENING/ CLOSING OF CICS FILES AND ENABLING/ DISABLING OF TRANSACTIONS THROUGH A BATCH JOB

Figures 2.23 through 2.25 give the various components of a facility to issue CEMT transaction through a batch job. In fact, this facility can be used to issue any MVS or JES command if the job name is given special attribute in the authorization table. Let us discuss the various issues involved.

Why Do You Need This Facility?

Suppose you have a master file that is allocated and open on a CICS production region. In a production batch job, this file is deleted, redefined, and loaded with records. Since this file is open on CICS, your production job step

```
***************************************************************
*  ===========================================================
*  * PROGRAM ID:    MVSCMD1
*  * AUTHOR:        BARRY KUMAR NIRMAL
*  *===========================================================
*  * THIS IS THE MAIN PROGRAM THAT IS EXECUTED IN THE JCL. THIS
*  * PROGRAM WILL PASS THE COMMAND SPECIFIED AS PARAMETER ON THE
*  * EXEC CARD TO MVS. ANY MVS OR JES COMMAND CAN BE ISSUED THRU
*  * THIS PROGRAM, SUBJECT TO THE USER BEING AUTHORIZED TO ISSUE
*  * IT. AUTHORIZATION CHECKING IS DONE BY PROGRAM MVSCMD2.
*  ===========================================================
MVSCMD1  CSECT
         PRINT ESYSPARM.GEN
         COPY  REGDEF
         USING MVSCMD1,R15
         B     BEGIN
         DC    C'MVSCMD1  ASSEMBLED AT ESYSTIME ON ESYSDATE'
         DROP  R15
         USING MVSCMD1,R11
BEGIN    STM   R14,R12,12(R13)        SAVE R14,R15...R12
         LR    R11,R15                SAVE R15 INTO R11
         LR    R10,R13                SAVE R13 INTO R10
         LA    R13,SAVEAREA           POINT R13 TO MY SAVE AREA
         ST    R13,8(R10)             SAVE MY R13 INTO HIS SAVE AREA
         ST    R10,SAVEAREA+4         SAVE HIS R13 INTO MY SAVE AREA
REALWORK EQU   *
         L     R1,0(R1)
         LH    R4,0(R1)               LOAD R4 WITH LENGTH OF PARM
```

Figure 2.23. Source code of program MVSCMD1

119

```
28  LTR    R4,R4                        PARM LENGTH = ZERO?
29  BE     MISPARM                      YES, BRANCH TO MISPARM
30  CH     R4,=H'80'                    PARM LENGTH GREATER THAN 80?
31  BH     BADPARM                      YES, BRANCH TO BADPARM
32 *** PREPARE TO LINK TO AUTHORIZATION CHECKING PROGRAM.
33  ST     R1,PARMADDR                  SAVE R1
34  LA     R1,PARMADDR
35  LINK   EP=MYSCMD2
36  LTR    R15,R15                      R15 CONTAINS ZERO?
37  BNZ    GETOUT                       NO, USER IS NOT AUTHORIZED
38 *** USER HAS PASSED AUTHORIZATION CHECKING. NOW SERVICE THE REQUEST.
39  L      R1,PARMADDR                  RESTORE R1
40  LA     R5,2(R1)                     POINT R5 TO ACTUAL COMMAND IN PARM
41  LR     R3,R4                        LOAD R3 WITH LENGTH OF PARAMETER
42  AH     R3,=H'6'                     INCREMENT R3 BY 6
43  STH    R3,SVC34LEN                  STORE R3 INTO SVC34LEN
44 ****************************         R4 CONTAINS LENGTH OF PARAMETER PASS
45  SH     R4,=H'1'                     SUBTRACT 1 FROM R4
46  STC    R4,MOVTXT+1                  STORE R4 INTO LENGTH BYTE OF MVC
47 MOVTXT  MVC  SVC34TXT,0(R5)          MOVE PARAMETER TO SVC34TXT
48  MODESET KEY=ZERO,MODE=SUP           SWITCH TO SUPERVISOR STATE
49  SR     R0,R0                        CLEAR R0
50  LA     R1,SVC34LEN                  R1 POINTS TO SVC34LEN FOR SVC 3
51  SVC    34                           ISSUE SVC 34 TO ISSUE COMMAND
52  MODESET KEY=NZERO,MODE=PROB         SWITCH TO PROBLEM STATE
53  SR     R15,R15                      CLEAR R15
54  B      GETOUT
```

```
55 MISPARM  EQU  *
56          LA   R15,4                LOAD 4 INTO R15 (CC = 4)
57          B    GETOUT               BRANCH TO OPERATING SYSTEM.
58 BADPARM  EQU  *
59          LA   R15,8                LOAD 8 INTO R15 (CC = 8)
60          B    GETOUT               BRANCH TO OPERATING SYSTEM
61 GETOUT   EQU  *
62 ************** DON'T WAIT IF THE COMMAND WAS NOT ISSUED.
63          LTR  R15,R15
64          BNZ  NONEED
65          STIMER WAIT,BINTVL=TIMEWAIT
66 NONEED   L    R13,SAVEAREA+4       RESTORE CALLER'S R13
67          L    R14,12(R13)          RESTORE R14
68          LM   R0,R12,20(R13)       RESTORE R0,R1...R12
69          BR   R14                  BRANCH TO OPERATING SYSTEM.
70 *******************************************************
71 PARMADDR DC   F'-1'
72 TIMEWAIT DC   F'3000'   WAIT TIME IN .01 SECONDS, I.E. 30 SECONDS
73 TEMP     DC   C'**BARRY**'
74 SVC34LEN DC   F'0'
75 SVC34TXT DC   82C' '
76 SAVEAREA DC   18F'-1'
77          LTORG
78          END
*******************************************************
```

Figure 2.23.   continued.

121

```
#######################################################################
#=====================================================================#
1  # THIS IS THE AUTHORIZATION CHECKING PROGRAM. IT IS LINKED TO BY THE
2  # MAIN PROGRAM MVSCMD1.
3  # PROGRAM NAME= MVSCMD2
4  # AUTHOR: BARRY KUMAR NIRMAL
5  #=====================================================================#
6
7  MVSCMD2  CSECT
8           COPY  REGDEF
9           USING MVSCMD2,R15
10          B     BEGIN
11 REFER    DC    C'MVSCMD2 ASSEMBLED AT &SYSTIME ON &SYSDATE'
12          DROP  R15
13          USING MVSCMD2,R11
14 BEGIN    STM   R14,R12,12(R13)
15          LR    R11,R15           SAVE R15 INTO R11
16          LR    R10,R13           SAVE HIS R13 INTO R10
17          LA    R13,SAVEAREA      POINT R13 TO MY SAVE AREA
18          ST    R13,8(R10)        SAVE MY R13 INTO HIS SAVE AREA
19          ST    R10,SAVEAREA+4    SAVE HIS R13 INTO MY SAVE AREA
20 REALWRK  EQU   *
21          L     R1,0(R1)          LOAD R1 WIH ADDRESS OF PARAMETER
22          ST    R1,PARMADDR       SAVE R1 AT PARMADDR
23          EXTRACT TIOTADDR,'S',FIELDS=(TIOT)
24          L     R4,TIOTADDR
25          MVC   JOBNAME,0(R4)     SAVE JOB NAME IN JOBNAME FIELD.
26 PROCEED  L     R1,PARMADDR       POINT R1 TO PARAMETER
27          LA    R5,JOBNAM00
28 ## AFTER THIS POINT R1 MUST NOT BE CHANGED. R5 WILL BE MOVED ONE
29 ## SLOT AT A TIME IN THE AUTHORIZATION TABLE.
```

```
30   NEXTUSER   EQU   *
31              CLC   =C'ZZZZZZZ',0(R5)
32              BE    NOPASS11
33              LA    R4,JOBNAME
34              LA    R2,8
35   * R5 POINTS TO THE PARTICULAR 8-BYTE SLOT IN THE AUTHORIZATION TABLE
36   * R4 POINTS TO THE JOB NAME FIELD.
37              BAL   R14,COMPARE
38              LTR   15,15
39              BZ    NEXTBKN1
40   * ADVANCE TO BEGINNING OF NEXT JOB NAME IN THE AUTH TABLE.
41   LOOP1      LA    R5,8(R5)
42              CLC   =C'ZZZZZZZ',0(R5)
43              BE    NOPASS11
44              CLC   =C'*******',0(R5)
45              BNE   LOOP1
46              LA    R5,8(R5)
47              B     NEXTUSER
48   NEXTBKN1   EQU   *
49   *rrrrrrrrrrrrrrrrrrrrrrrrrrrrrrrrrrrrrrrrrrrrrrrrrrr
50   * JOB NAME MATCHED. NOW CHECK THE TYPE OF THIS USER.
51   *rrrrrrrrrrrrrrrrrrrrrrrrrrrrrrrrrrrrrrrrrrrrrrrrrrr
52              CLC   =CL8'MVSGUY',8(R5)
53              BE    GOBACK
54              CLC   =CL8'CICSGUY',8(R5)
55              BE    CICSGUY
56   *rrrrrrrrrrrrrrrrrrrrrrrrrrrrrrrrrrrrrrrrrrrrrrrrrrr
57   * THIS IS ORDINARY CICS USER. CHECK CICS ID IN TABLE.
```

Figure 2.24.   Source code of program MVSCMD2

```
58  *
59  NEXTSIR1 EQU  *
60           LA   R5,16(R5)
61           LA   R4,4(R1)    POINT R4 TO CICS ID IN PARM
62           LA   R2,8
63           BAL  R14,COMPARE
64           LTR  15,15
65           BZ   NEXTSIR2
66  * CICS ID NOT MATCHED. ADVANCE UNTIL NEXT SET.
67  LOOP2    LA   R5,8(R5)
68           CLC  =C'ZZZZZZZ',0(R5)
69           BE   NOPASS12
70           CLC  =C'########',0(R5)
71           BNE  LOOP2
72           LA   R5,8(R5)
73           B    NEXTUSER
74  NEXTSIR2 EQU  *
75  *
76  * CICS ID MATCHED. NOW CHECK THE RESOURCE TYPE (FILE, TRAN. ETC)
77  *
78           CLC  =C'DA',20(R1)
79           BE   TSTFILE
80           CLC  =C'TRAN',20(R1)
81           BE   TSTTRAN
82  ** RESOURCE TYPE IS INVALID. GET OUT OF HERE
83           B    NOPASS13
84  TSTFILE  EQU  *
85           LA   R5,8(R5)
86           CLC  =C'ZZZZZZZ',0(R5)
87           BE   NOPASS12
```

```
88          CLC   =C'********',0(R5)
89          BE    TSTNXT1
90          CLC   =C'*********',0(R5)
91          BE    NEXTJOB1
92          LA    R4,23(R1)    POINT R4 TO DDNAME IN PARAMETER
93          LA    R2,8
94          BAL   R14,COMPARE
95          LTR   15,15
96          BZ    GOBACK
97          B     TSTFILE
98   TSTNXT1  EQU   *
99   * ADVANCE R5 TO NEXT JOB NAME FIELD. THEN START OVER.
100         LA    R5,8(R5)
101         B     NEXTUSER
102  *rrrrrrrrrrrrrrrrrrrrrrrrrrrrrrrrrrrrrrrrrrrrrrrrrrr
103  NEXTJOB1 EQU   *
104  * ADVANCE R5 TO NEXT JOB NAME FIELD. THEN START OVER.
105         LA    R5,8(R5)
106         CLC   =C'********',0(R5)
107         BE    TSTNXT1
108         B     NEXTJOB1
109  *rrrrrrrrrrrrrrrrrrrrrrrrrrrrrrrrrrrrrrrrrrrrrrrrrrr
110  TSTTRAN  EQU   *
111         LA    R5,8(R5)
112         CLC   =C'ZZZZZZZ',0(R5)
113         BE    NOPASS12
114         CLC   =C'*********',0(R5)
115         BE    TSTNXT2
```

Figure 2.24. continued.

125

```
116          CLC     =C'++++++++',0(R5)
117          BE      ENDFILE
118          B       TSTTRAN
119 ENDFILE  EQU     *
120          LA      R5,8(R5)
121          CLC     =C'ZZZZZZZZ',0(R5)
122          BE      NOPASS12
123          CLC     =C'########',0(R5)
124          BE      TSTNXT2
125          LA      R4,25(R1)      POINT R4 TO TRANSACTION ID IN PARAMETER
126          LA      R2,4
127          BAL     R14,COMPARE
128          LTR     15,15
129          BZ      GOBACK
130          B       ENDFILE
131 TSTNXT2  EQU     *
132 * ADVANCE R5 TO NEXT JOB NAME FIELD. THEN START OVER.
133          LA      R5,8(R5)
134          B       NEXTUSER
135 *rrrrrrrrrrrrrrrrrrrrrrrrrrrrrrrrrrrrrrrrrrrrrrrrrrrrrrrrrrrrrrrrrrrr
136 * THIS IS THE ROUTINE TO COMPARE TWO FIELDS OF EQUAL LENGTH. LENGTH
137 * IS CONTAINED IN R2 AND CAN HAVE ANY VALUE. LENGTH IS 8 FOR FILES AND
138 * 4 FOR TRANSACTIONS.
139 * R5 POINTS TO AREA IN AUTH. TABLE AND R4 POINTS TO USER'S DATA.
140 * NOTE: EITHER OR BOTH FIELDS BEING COMPARED MAY CONTAIN ASTERISK.
141 *rrrrrrrrrrrrrrrrrrrrrrrrrrrrrrrrrrrrrrrrrrrrrrrrrrrrrrrrrrrrrrrrrrrr
142 COMPARE  EQU     *
143          ST      R4,SAVER4
144          ST      R5,SAVER5
145 LOOPA    EQU     *
```

```
146             CLI    0(R5),C'*'
147             BE     PASSHIM
148             CLC    0(1,R4),0(R5)
149             BNE    DONTPASS
150             LA     R4,1(R4)
151             LA     R5,1(R5)
152             BCT    R2,LOOPA
153   PASSHIM   SR     R15,R15
154             B      EXIT1
155   DONTPASS  LA     R15,8
156   EXIT1     L      R4,SAVER4
157             L      R5,SAVER5
158             BR     R14
159   *========================================*
160   NOPASS11  MVC    RETCODE(4),=F'11'
161             B      GOBACK
162   NOPASS12  MVC    RETCODE(4),=F'12'
163             B      GOBACK
164   NOPASS13  MVC    RETCODE(4),=F'13'
165             B      GOBACK
166   CICSGUY   EQU    *
167             CLC    =C'CEMT',13(R1)
168             BE     GOBACK
169             MVC    RETCODE(4),=F'21'
170             B      GOBACK
171   GOBACK    EQU    *
172             L      R13,SAVEAREA+4      RESTORE R13
173             L      R15,RETCODE         LOAD RET CODE IN R15
```

Figure 2.24. continued.

```
174              L     R14,12(R13)      RESTORE R14
175              LM    R0,R12,20(R13)   RESTORE R0, THRU R12
176              BR    R14              BRANCH TO CALLER
177      #===============================================#
178      RETCODE  DC    F'0'
179      SAVER4   DS    F
180      SAVER5   DS    F
181      PARMADDR DS    F
182      TIOTADDR DS    F
183      SAVEAREA DS    18F'-1'
184      JOBNAME  DS    CL8' '
185               DC    C'###BARRY NIRMAL###'
186               LTORG
187               COPY MVSAUTH
188               END
#****************************************************************
```

Figure 2.24.   continued.

```
*================================================================*
* THIS IS THE AUTHORIZATION TABLE FOR THE PROGRAM TO ISSUE MVS OR JES
* COMMAND IN BATCH. IF YOU CHANGE THIS TABLE, YOU MUST ASSEMBLE PROGRAM
* MVSCMD2.
*================================================================*
* THE LAST ENTRY IN THIS TABLE MUST BE 'ZZZZZZZZ'. THIS IS IMPORTANT.
*================================================================*
* ADD NEW ENTRIES AT THE END OF THIS TABLE, AND DO NOT FORGET TO PUT
* A RECORD OF CHANGE YOU MADE IN THE HISTORY AREA BELOW:
*================================================================*
* DATE     |PGMR |DESCRIPTION OF CHANGE
*--------|-----|-----
*YY/MM/DD|BARRY|INITIAL SETUP
*================================================================*
* TYPE FIELD IS 8 BYTES LONG, AND FOLLOWS THE JOB NAME FIELD.
* IF TYPE FIELD = MVSGUY
*   USER IS AUTHORIZED TO ISSUE ANY MVS OR JES COMMAND.
* IF TYPE FIELD = CICSGUY
*   USER IS AUTHORIZED TO ISSUE ANY MODIFY COMMAND FOR ANY CICS REGION
*   FOR EXECUTING ANY CEMT TRANSACTION.
* IF TYPE FIELD = CICSUSER
*   USER IS AUTHORIZED TO ISSUE ONLY MODIFY COMMANDS WITH CEMT IN ORDER
*   TO DISPLAY AND CHANGE STATUS OF FILES AND TRANSACTIONS ONLY. THE
*   FILES AND TRANSACTIONS TO WHICH THE USER IS AUTHORIZED MUST BE
*   GIVEN IN THE TABLE BELOW.
*================================================================*
* THE FIRST LINE MUST HAVE LABEL OF JOBNAM00. OTHER LINES MAY NOT HAVE
```

Figure 2.25. Source code of copybook MVSAUTH

```
28  *  LABELS. EACH JOB NAME ENTRY IS TERMINATED WITH A LINE CONTAINING
29  *  CL8'********'. A LINE WITH CL8'++++++++' IS OPTIONAL AND IS ONLY
30  *  NEEDED IF YOU HAVE FILES AND TRANSACTIONS OR NO FILES BUT ONE OR MORE
31  *  TRANSACTIONS. IN THIS CASE, ALL FILES NAMES MUST BE FOLLOWED WITH A
32  *  LINE WITH CL8'++++++++' AND THIS IS FOLLOWED BY TRANSACTIONS.
33  *  ENTRIES BELOW ARE CODED CORRECTLY.
34  *===================================================================#
35  JOBNAM00  DC    CL8'Z3ATT# '
36            DC    CL8'MVSGUY '
37            DC    CL8'********'
38  *------------------
39  JOBNAM01  DC    CL8'Z3JRA# '
40            DC    CL8'CICSGUY '
41            DC    CL8'********'
42  *------------------
43  JOBNAM02  DC    CL8'Z2BKN# '
44            DC    CL8'CICSUSER'
45  CICSID2   DC    CL8'# '
46  FILES02   DC    CL8'++++++++'
47  TRAN02    DC    CL8'GOL1 '
48            DC    CL8'********'
```

```
49  #-----------------------------
50  JOBNAM03  DC    CL8'Z28BKN#'
51            DC    CL8'CICSUSER'
52  CICSID03  DC    CL8'CICSTST1'
53  FILES03   DC    CL8'SGTLIB1'
54            DC    CL8'++++++++'
55  TRAN03    DC    CL8'GOL2'
56            DC    CL8'########'
57  #-----------------------------
58  JOBNAM04  DC    CL8'Z38BKN#'
59            DC    CL8'CICSUSER'
60  CICSID04  DC    CL8'CICSPRD1'
61  FILES04   DC    CL8'SGT#'
62            DC    CL8'########'
63  #-----------------------------
64  ENDAUTH   DC    CL8'ZZZZZZZZ'
    #############################
```

Figure 2.25. continued.

131

that deletes this file using IDCAMS DELETE command will fail, and you will get a message saying that the file is allocated to some other job or user. So, you have two alternatives:

Alternative 1

Manually close the file on CICS using CEMT or some other transaction.

Run the batch job that deletes, redefines, and loads it.

Manually open the file on CICS using CEMT or some other transaction.

Alternative 2

Include the following step in the beginning of the job, so as to close it on CICS:

```
//STEP01 EXEC PGM=MVSCMD1,
//         PARM='F cicsname,CEMT S DA(ddname) CLOSE'
//STEPLIB  DD DISP=SHR,DSN=LOAD.LIB.NAME
//SYSABEND DD SYSOUT=X
//SYSUDUMP DD SYSOUT=X
```

(where cicsname must be replaced with the name of the CICS region and ddname with the ddname of the file or files to be closed or opened).

Include the following step at the end of the job, so as to open it on CICS:

```
//STEP99 EXEC PGM=MVSCMD1,
//         PARM='F cicsname,CEMT S DA(ddname) OPEN'
//STEPLIB  DD DISP=SHR,DSN=LOAD.LIB.NAME
//SYSABEND DD SYSOUT=X
//SYSUDUMP DD SYSOUT=X
```

Save the job.

Now any time you need to run this job, you can just submit it without having to manually close and open files on CICS.

The benefit of the second alternative is that your job needs to be modified only once by inserting steps to execute program MVSCMD1. After this one-time change, it can simply be submitted, whereas with the first alternative you have to manually close and open the file every time this job is to be run. The use of program MVSCMD1 eliminates manual intervention and frees you to do more important things than close and open files.

Similarly, sometimes a need may arise where you want to disable a transaction while a batch job is running and enable it when it has finished. The batch job may be processing the data in your files, and you may not want your users to enter any data on the on-line system until the job has finished. Rather than disable and enable the transaction manually using the CEMT transaction, you can just run program MVSCMD1 with the following parameter to disable your transaction:

```
//  PARM='F cicsname,CEMT S TRAN(tran) DISABLE'
```

(where tran is to be replaced with the actual transaction ID to be disabled, and cicsname is to be replaced with the name of the CICS region.) At the end of the job, you can execute MVSCMD1 with the following parameter to enable your transaction:

```
//  PARM='F cicsname,CEMT S TRAN(tran) ENABLE'
```

Procedure for Installing This Facility

Step 1. Enter the contents of Figure 2.25 in member MVSAUTH of a source dataset used to contain macros and copybooks.

Step 2. Enter the program shown in Figure 2.23 in member MVSCMD1 of a source PDS, and enter the program shown in Figure 2.24 in member MVSCMD2 of the same source PDS.

Step 3. Now change the content of MVSAUTH created in Step 1 to suit your requirements. You must understand the rules for creating entries in this table. Comments in Figure 2.25 should be read and understood. Let us illustrate the rules by studying the table in this figure. In this figure, there are five job name entries, labelled JOBNAM00, JOBNAM01, and so on up to JOBNAM04.

The first entry specifies that any job with a name beginning with Z3ATT has the attribute of MVSGUY. So, such a job can issue any MVS or JES command. Let us take some examples:

Example 1: If the job name is Z3ATT001, for example, it can execute program MVSCMD1 with the following parameter to display all active tasks in the MVS system:

```
PARM='D A,L'
```

Example 2: If the job name is Z3ATT111, it can execute program MVSCMD1 with the following parameter to cancel the current session of TSO user EBVISYS:

```
PARM='C U=EBVISYS'
```

Example 3: A job with name Z3ATTX can execute MVSCMD1 with the following parameter to display all the JES initiators in the system:

```
PARM='$DI'
```

The second job entry on lines 39 through 41 specifies that any job whose name starts with Z3JRA has the attribute of CICSGUY. Such a job can issue any Modify command for any CICS region in order to execute any CEMT transaction. Let us take some examples:

Example 4: A job with name Z3JRAA can execute program MVSCMD1 with the following parameter to put out of service all terminals in CICSPRD1 with IDs that begin with CA*:

```
PARM = 'F CICSPRD1,CEMT S TERM(CA*) OUT'
```

Example 5: A job with name Z3JRA001 can execute program MVSCMD1 with the following parameter to open and enable all files in CICSTST1:

```
PARM = 'F CICSTST1,CEMT S DA(*) OPEN ENABLED'
```

The job name entry on lines 43 through 48 specifies that any job with a name starting with Z2BKN has the attribute of CICSUSER. A job with CICSUSER attribute can only issue CEMT transaction for inquiring or modifying status of files or transactions only. And the name of the CICS region, as well as the IDs of files and transactions to which such a job is authorized, is specified in the table. For example, line 45 specifies that this job can issue transactions for any CICS region. Line 46 indicates the end of files for this entry. So this job is not allowed to inquire or modify status of any files, unless some other entry in the table authorizes it. Line 47 specifies that this job can issue CEMT transaction against transaction GOL1 only.

Example 6: Job with name Z2BKN111 is authorized to execute MVSCMD1 with the following parameter:

```
PARM = 'F CICSTST1,CEMT S TRAN(GOL1) DISABLE'
```

But such a job is not allowed the following, because for CICSTST1 files SGT* are not included either on JOBNAM02 or JOBNAM03.

```
PARM = 'F CICSTST1,CEMT S DA(SGT*) CLOSED'
```

The entry on lines 50 through 56 specifies that a job with name starting with Z2BKN has the attribute of CICSUSER. Such a job can issue CEMT transactions for CICSTST1 only, and is authorized for the single file SGTLIB1 and for the single transaction GOL2.

Example 7: Job named Z2BKNX can issue the following:

```
PARM = 'F CICSTST1,CEMT S DA(SGTLIB1 ) OPEN'
```

(Note the space after SGTLIB1. It is mandatory here because the DDname is not generic, i.e., has no asterisk in it.)

But this job is not authorized to issue the following, because this CICS job name and file combination is not in the table:

```
PARM='F CICSPRD1,CEMT S DA(SGTLIB1 ) OPEN'
```

Example 8: Job named Z3BKNX can issue any of the following:

```
PARM='F CICSPRD1,CEMT S DA(SGT*) OPEN ENABLED'
PARM='F CICSPRD1,CEMT S DA(SGTL*) CLOSED'
PARM='F CICSPRD1,CEMT S DA(SGTLIB1) OPEN'
PARM='F CICSPRD1,CEMT I DA(SGTLIBAA)'
```

This is permitted by the job name entry on lines 58 through 62. But such a job has no access to any transaction on any CICS region. Also such a job has no access to any file on any CICS region other than CICSPRD1.

Step 4. Assemble and link program MVSCMD2 using the JCL given in Section B.3 in Appendix B. This job will require that the name of the macro library in which you stored copybooks REGDEF and MVSAUTH be allocated under DDname SYSLIB in the assembly step. (See lines 8 and 187 in Figure 2.24.) This job will create load module MVSCMD2 in a load library. The name of this load library is used under DDname STEPLIB in the job step that executes program MVSCMD1.

Step 5. Assemble and link program MVSCMD1 using the JCL given in Section B.3 in Appendix B. This job will require that the name of the macro library in which you stored REGDEF be allocated under DDname SYSLIB in the assembly step. (See line 13 in Figure 2.23.)

This program must be linked with authorization code (AC) of 1. So, insert the following lines after line 25 in the JCL given in Figure B.5:

```
//  DD *
    SETCODE AC(1)
```

This job will create load module MVSCMD1 in a load library. The name of this load library is used under DDname STEPLIB in the job step that executes program MVSCMD1.

Step 6. Ask your MVS systems programmer to place the load library which contains MVSCMD1 and MVSCMD2 in the APF (Authorized Program Facility) list in SYS1.PARMLIB, or use a load library that is already in the APF list to store these programs. This is because MVSCMD1 issues the MODESET macro to place itself in the supervisor state. See *Important Note* at the end of this section regarding using authorization SVC available at your installation.

Step 7. If you are going to use this program to issue CEMT transaction on a CICS region, make sure that terminal CJCL is defined in the TCT of that CICS system as follows:

```
TERMINAL                        : CJCL
GROUP                           : CICSBOOK
AUTINSTMODEL                    : NO
AUTINSTNAME                     :
TERMINAL IDENTIFIERS
  TYPETERM                      : CONSL000            Note 1
  NETNAME                       : CJCL
  CONSOLE                       : 00                  Note 2
  REMOTESYSTEM                  :
  REMOTENAME                    :
  MODENAME                      :
ASSOCIATED PRINTERS
  PRINTER                       :
  PRINTERCOPY                   : NO
  ALTPRINTER                    :
  ALTPRINTCOPY                  : NO
PIPELINE PROPERTIES
  POOL                          :
  TASKLIMIT                     : NO
OPERATOR DEFAULTS
  OPERID                        :
  OPERPRIORITY                  : 000
  OPERRSL                       : 0
  OPERSECURITY                  : 1,4                 Note 3.
  USERID                        :
TERMINAL USAGE
  TRANSACTION                   :
  TERMPRIORITY                  : 000
  INSERVICE                     : YES
SESSION SECURITY
  SECURITYNAME                  :
  ATTACHSEC                     : LOCAL
  BINDPASSWORD                  :
```

(This definition is from a CICS system without external security installed and has been tested to work in both test and production environments.)

Note 1. TYPETERM value here is CONSL000. This is and should be the same as the value for TYPETERM used in the definition of terminal CN01, which is the first MVS console. CN01 is usually defined in the TCT with CONSOLE parameter being 01. Such an entry is required if you wish to use the MVS console as the master terminal for CICS, which can issue CEMT transaction through the MODIFY command. For example,

```
MODIFY CICSTST1,CEMT INQUIRE TASK
            OR
F CICSTST1,CEMT I TAS
```

Note 2. In the definition of CJCL above, we are using 00 as the value for CONSOLE. For an example of the DFHTCT TYPE = TERMINAL macro instruction needed to support CICS command using JCL, see the sample TCT, DFHTCT5$ in CICS.SAMPLIB that was created from the IBM tape at the time of CICS installation.

Note 3. 4 is assumed to be the security level of the CEMT transaction. If your CEMT has a different security level, change the value in OPERSECURITY accordingly.

Step 8. Execute this program as shown above under "WHY DO YOU NEED THIS FACILITY?" and make sure that the job step ends in condition code of zero, which means that the command was issued. If the command was successfully issued, it will appear in the MVS system log (SYSLOG), and the response of the system to the command will follow in the SYSLOG.

Salient Features of This Facility

If program MVSCMD1 ends in condition code of zero, this means that the command was successfully issued. If the requested command was not issued, condition code will indicate the cause of the error, as follows:

```
Condition
Code         Cause of Error

 4 ———→      PARM missing on EXEC card
 8 ———→      Length of parameter passed to program MVSCMD1 is
             greater than 80.
11 ———→      Job name not present in the table in MVSAUTH or end of
             table was encountered while searching.
12 ———→      Job not authorized to issue this command.
13 ———→      Job with CICSUSER attribute is specifying in command
             resource type other than DA and TRAN.
21 ———→      Job with CICUSER attribute is not issuing CEMT.
```

Program MVSCMD2, which validates the command entered as the parameter, handles different types of jobs differently.

Jobs with CICSGUY attribute must use an eight character name for the CICS region in the command. They can only issue a CEMT command, but any kind of CEMT command can be issued.

Jobs with MVSGUY attribute are not subject to any restrictions. They can issue any MVS or JES command.

Jobs with the attribute of CICSUSER, being the weakest of the three types of users, are subject to the following restrictions:

1. The name of the CICS region on the PARM must be eight characters long, e.g., CICSTST1, CICSPRD2, etc.
2. The format of the parameter for a job with CICSUSER attribute must follow one of the following valid formats:

```
PARM='F cicsname,CEMT I DA(ffffffff)'
PARM='F cicsname,CEMT S DA(ffffffff) options'
PARM='F cicsname,CEMT I TRAN(tttt)'
PARM='F cicsname,CEMT S TRAN(tttt) options'
```

where ffffffff may be from one to eight characters long, if it is generic, i.e., has an asterisk at the end. It must be eight characters long if it is not generic in the table, i.e., has no asterisk in it. If the file name in the table and on the command is not generic, and is less than eight characters long, insert one or more spaces at the end. Similarly, tttt may be from one to four characters long if it is generic. It must be four characters long if it is not generic in the table and on the command. So if the transaction ID is not generic and is less than four characters long, you must insert one or more spaces at the end.
3. Note that for a job with CICSUSER attribute, program MVSCMD2 does not check for the presence of CEMT in the command, even though this would be desirable.
4. Please note that in the command, you must use DA and not DATASET and use TRAN and not TRANS or TRANSACTIONS. Options that follow 'S DA' or 'S TRAN' can be anything and are not validated.
5. The program checks all entries in the table before declaring that the job is not authorized to issue the specified command. However, when a job is found to be authorized, the search stops and control is transferred to calling program MVSCMD1. For the same job name, there can be multiple entries in the authorization table and all are searched for deciding whether the command should be allowed.
6. If the user type in the table is anything other than MVSGUY and CICSGUY, the job is treated as if its attribute was CICSUSER.

Explanation of Programs for This Facility

Program MVSCMD1 is the one that gets executed in the job. Execution starts from line 15 in Figure 2.23, which is the first executable instruction. On lines 26 through 31, it is checking if the length of parameter passed is zero or greater than 80. If so, control flows to label MISPARM and BADPARM respectively. On line 35, a LINK is issued to pass control to program MVSCMD2, which is a separate load module. Program MVSCMD2 carries out authorization checking. If it finds that the job name is authorized, it returns zero in Register 15, or it returns a non-zero value in Register 15. On line 36, a test is made if

Register 15 contains zero, If not, branch to label GETOUT is taken. If the user passed the authorization checking, line 39 would be executed. The instructions that follow, among other things, move the actual parameter into field SVC34TXT. Then the MODESET macro is issued on line 48 to place the task in the supervisor state. This is required for issuing SVC 34 on line 51. SVC 34 is a restricted SVC, and the task must be in supervisor state to issue it.

Issuing of SVC 34 causes the MVS or JES command in SVC34TXT to be passed to the system. Next, on line 52, the MODESET macro is issued to put the task back in problem state. Then branch is taken to label GETOUT, where we test the content of Register 15. If it is zero, it means that the command was issued, in which case the STIMER macro is issued on line 65 to delay the task by 30 seconds. (This is done to allow the command issued to get executed. This is because, in a job, one step might execute this program to issue a CEMT transaction to close some files. The next step might execute DELETE commands against those files. So, you want to ensure that the close command was successful before you attempt to delete the files.) This is followed by return to the operating system on lines 66 through 69.

Important Note: If you have an authorization SVC at your installation, you may issue it in MVSCMD1 prior to issuing the first MODESET macro. This will make the task authorized to issue the MODESET macro. Then after the second MODESET macro, you may again issue that SVC to make the task unauthorized. If you do so, you can assemble and link MVSCMD1 as any ordinary program, without AC = 1, and the load library need not be in the APF list. The point is that if you know how to use the authorization SVC available at your installation, you are not dependent on your friendly or unfriendly MVS system programmer.

Another point is that suppose you are not using the authorization SVC to make your program authorized. In this case, even if you linked MVSCMD1 with AC = 1, if the load library in which it resides is not APF authorized, when you execute the program, it will abend with system completion code 047. If you look up the Messages and Codes manual, this abend code says that an unauthorized program requested a restricted SVC. This is part of the security feature of MVS.

2.12 A FACILITY FOR ISSUING ANY CEMT TRANSACTION THROUGH A BATCH JOB

The facility discussed in Section 2.11 can also be used to issue, through a batch job, any CEMT transaction for any CICS region. You are urged to read and understand Section 2.11. If a job name is present in the authorization table and its user type is CICSGUY, this job can issue any CEMT transaction for any CICS region without restriction. However, the name of the CICS on the PARM must be eight characters long, and only CEMT transactions are allowed. So the following parameter is invalid for a job name with CICSGUY attribute, because the name of CICS region is less than eight characters long:

```
PARM='F CICSPR1,CEMT S JOURN(10) CLOSED'
```

But the following is valid:

```
PARM='F CICSPRD1,CEMT S JOURN(10) CLOSED'
```

2.13 A FACILITY FOR ISSUING ANY MVS OR JES COMMAND THROUGH A BATCH JOB

The facility discussed in Section 2.11 can also be used to issue any MVS or JES command through a batch job. So, if you are an MVS system programmer, and even if you know nothing about CICS, you can easily use the facility described in Section 2.11. You are urged to read and understand Section 2.11. If a job name is present in the authorization table and its user type is MVSGUY, this job can issue any MVS or JES command without any restriction. So, a job with MVSGUY attribute can execute program MVSCMD1 with the following parameter to cancel the current session of TSO user Z3BKN:

```
PARM='C U=Z3BKN'
```

This command will be issued and result in the cancellation of TSO user Z3BKN if this user is currently logged on to TSO.

2.14 A FACILITY TO PRINT A REPORT OF ANY SIZE ON A PRINTER DEFINED TO CICS.

If you are a COBOL programmer or, for that matter, any kind of programmer in the IBM environment, you know how reports are usually generated and printed. The record length of the report file is usually 133 characters long, with the first character of each record being the carriage control character. The record format of the report file is usually FBA. The carriage control character follows the ANSI standard, which is as follows:

Code   Action before Printing Record

```
blank  Space 1 line
0      Space 2 lines
-      Space 3 lines
+      Suppress Space, i.e., overprint on the same line
1      Skip to line 1 on new page
```

Such a report file can be sent for printing on remote printer destination Rxx by issuing the following TSO command:

```
PRINTOFF 'full.name.of.data.set' DEST(Rxx) CLASS(c)
```

where the items in lower-case characters must be replaced with proper values.

Now suppose that you want to generate a report from within a CICS application program for printing on a printer defined to CICS. In this section we give you a facility that you can use with ease and which resembles the method of generating reports from TSO described above. Let us first discuss how to install it.

Procedure for Installing This Facility

Step 1. Suppose you want to print reports on a printer whose CICS terminal ID is D917. So, in the DCT (Destination Control Table) of CICS, your system programmer must define the following entry:

```
DFHDCT TYPE=INTRA,                                            X
       TRANSID=BNPT,                                          X
       DESTFAC=TERMINAL,                                      X
       REUSE=YES,                                             X
       RSL=PUBLIC,                                            X
       TRIGLEV=1,                                             X
       DESTID=D917
```

Note: The value of TRANSID here is BNPT, because that is what we will define in the PCT. But you can choose some other ID for it. The character X at the end of each line must be in column 72. The word DFHDCT starts in column 10 and TYPE starts in column 17. DESTID is equated to D917 because this is the terminal ID of our printer in this example. Change D917 to the CICS terminal ID of the printer you want to use. Each printer that you want to use for printing through this facility must have an entry for itself in the DCT.

Step 2. Define program BNREPORT in the PPT as follows:

```
PROGRAM    BNREPORT
GROUP      CICSBOOK
LANGUAGE   COBOL
```

Other parameters for BNREPORT in the PPT should be the same as those for the sample program BNPROG1 given in Section 1.6.

Step 3. Define transaction BNPT in the PCT as follows:

```
TRANSACTION    BNPT
GROUP          CICSBOOK
PROGRAM        BNREPORT
```

Other parameters for BNPT in the PCT should be the same as those for the sample transaction BNC1 given in Section 1.6, but ensure that BNPT has security level of 1, so that anyone can execute it without any restriction.

Step 4. Enter the program shown in Figure 2.26 in a source PDS as member BNREPORT. Then compile and link it using the JCL given in Section B.1 in Appendix B. This job will create member BNREPORT in a load library which must be allocated under DDname DFHRPL in a CICS startup procedure or job.

Procedure for Using This Facility in a Cobol Program

In an application program, the procedure to follow to print a report of one or more lines on any printer defined to CICS is as follows:

Step 1. In the working storage section, define a work area of 133 bytes, whose first position will have the carriage control character. Let us suppose this area is defined as follows:

```
01  WS-PRINT-RECORD.
    05 WS-CC-CHAR       PIC X.
    05 WS-PRINT-DATA    PIC X(132).
```

Step 2. Move the proper carriage control character in the first byte of WS-PRINT-RECORD. The valid ANSI carriage control codes and their meanings were given above. (The program in Figure 2.26 does not support the plus character as carriage control. It is treated as if it were space. This is the only carriage control character that is not supported. You are urged to do some research, talk to some knowledgeable people, and change the program in Figure 2.26 to support this carriage control character.)

Step 3. Move the data to be printed in WS-PRINT-DATA.

Step 4. Execute the following CICS command to write out this line to transient data queue qqqq, where qqqq should be replaced with the terminal ID of the printer where the report is to be printed:

```
EXEC CICS WRITEQ TD QUEUE('qqqq') FROM(WS-PRINT-AREA)
LENGTH(133) END-EXEC.
```

Step 5. Repeat steps 2 through 4 for all other lines of the report. See the program in Figure 2.27 for an example of a program that generates a report of four lines using this facility.

Generating a Sample Report on Printer ID D917

Figure 2.27 shows a sample program written in CICS Command Level COBOL that generates a report consisting of the following four lines:

```
SAMPLE REPORT
-------------
ABC ELECTRONICS COMPANY
HEAD OFFICE
```

The printer skips to the top of a new page before printing this report. This report is printed on the printer with terminal ID D917.

You can copy the program in Figure 2.27 into a dataset, change D917 to the terminal ID of a printer at your installation, compile and link the program, and execute it. (Suppose you compiled and linked this program as load module TSTPGM, and transaction ID TST1 is defined in the PCT and is associated with program TSTPGM. You can type TST1 on a blank screen and press Enter to execute the program of Figure 2.27.)

You will find that this report of four lines will print on your printer. If it does not print, or prints incorrectly, check that this facility was correctly installed as described above and that you are correctly following the instructions for using this facility.

Procedure for Using This Facility in a GENER/OL, CSP or Other Programs

You must understand how this facility is used in a CICS Command Level COBOL program. This understanding will enable you to use this facility with ease in a program written in any other language.

Explanation of How This Facility Works

Let us explain this facility through the example of the program in Figure 2.27. The program writes four report lines, each 133 characters long, to the transient data queue D917, which is defined in the DCT as an intrapartition queue. What this means is that these four records get stored in the intrapartition transient data file, which is a VSAM file allocated to CICS under DDname DFHINTRA. As shown above, under installation instructions, the DCT entry for queue D917 specifies DESTFAC as TERMINAL, TRANSID as BNPT, and TRIGLEV (Trigger Level) as 1. This means that when there are one or more records stored under queue D917, then CICS is to start transaction BNPT on terminal D917. (If the Trigger Level was changed to, say, 10, then this would mean that transaction BNPT would be started only after at least 10 records were written under queue named D917.) So, after the application program has finished writing all the records to queue D917, transaction BNPT is started by CICS and is associated with terminal ID D917. CICS searches the PCT and finds that transaction BNPT is associated with program BNREPORT. So control flows to the first statement in the procedure division of Figure 2.26.

Program BNREPORT, being in COBOL and of small size, is easy to understand. You should go through this program and understand what it does.

```
****************************************************************
****************************************************************
* THIS PROGRAM IS USED TO PRINT TO A 3270 PRINTER DEFINED TO CICS.
* IT CONVERTS ASA CONTROL CHARACTERS TO THEIR NEW REPRESENTATION
* SO THAT THEY CAN BE PRINTED ON 3270 PRINTERS DEFINED TO CICS.
****************************************************************
  IDENTIFICATION DIVISION.
  PROGRAM-ID.    BNREPORT.
  AUTHOR.        BARRY K. NIRMAL.
  DATE-COMPILED.
  ENVIRONMENT DIVISION.
  INPUT-OUTPUT SECTION.
  FILE-CONTROL.
  DATA DIVISION.
  FILE SECTION.
  WORKING-STORAGE SECTION.
  01  CONTROL-FIELDS.
      05  HEX-12                  PIC 9(4)    COMP VALUE 12.
      05  FF-FIELD.
          10  FILLER              PIC X       VALUE SPACES.
          10  FF-COMMAND          PIC X       VALUE SPACES.
      05  HEX-13                  PIC 9(4)    COMP VALUE 13.
      05  CR-FIELD.
          10  FILLER              PIC X       VALUE SPACES.
          10  CR-COMMAND          PIC X       VALUE SPACES.
      05  HEX-21                  PIC 9(4)    COMP VALUE 21.
      05  NL-FIELD.
          10  FILLER              PIC X       VALUE SPACES.
          10  NL-COMMAND          PIC X       VALUE SPACES.
```

1
2
3
4
5
6
7
8
9
10
11
12
13
14
15
16
17
18
19
20
21
22
23
24
25
26
27
28
29

144

```
30     01   PROGRAM-INDICATORS.
31          02   EOF-SW                    PIC 9          VALUE 0.
32               88   EOF                                 VALUE 1.
33
34     01   PROGRAM-CONSTANTS.
35          02   LENGTH-OF-BUFFER          PIC S9(4) COMP.
36          02   LENGTH-OF-PRINT-RECORD    PIC S9(4) COMP.
37          02   CONTROL-CHAR              PIC X          VALUE 'H'.
38
39     01   PROGRAM-VARIABLES.
40          02   NL-COUNT                  PIC 9          VALUE ZEROS.
41          02   SET-CHAR                  PIC X          VALUE SPACES.
42
43     01   PRINT-RECORD.
44          02   PRINT-ASA                 PIC X.
45               88   ASA-CHARACTER                       VALUE '1', '0', '-'.
46               88   FORM-FEED                           VALUE '1'.
47               88   SINGLE-SPACE                        VALUE ' '.
48               88   DOUBLE-SPACE                        VALUE '0'.
49               88   TRIPLE-SPACE                        VALUE '-'.
50          02   PRINT-CHAR                PIC X          OCCURS 132 TIMES
51               INDEXED BY PRINT-INDEX.
52
53     #   PRINTER-DEFINITON
54     #   FOR CICS 1.6.1 USE 4000
55     #   FOR CICS 1.7.0 USE 1920
56     01   BUFFER-AREA.
57          02   BUFFER-CHAR              PIC X          OCCURS 1920 TIMES
```

Figure 2.26. Source code of program BNREPORT

145

```
                 INDEXED BY BUFFER-INDEX.

         PROCEDURE DIVISION.
             MOVE HEX-12 TO FF-FIELD.
             MOVE HEX-13 TO CR-FIELD.
             MOVE HEX-21 TO NL-FIELD.
             EXEC CICS
                 HANDLE CONDITION QZERO(QUEUE-EMPTY)
             END-EXEC.
             MOVE LOW-VALUES TO BUFFER-AREA.
             SET BUFFER-INDEX TO 1.
             MOVE 0 TO LENGTH-OF-BUFFER.
             PERFORM PRINT-QUEUE-RECORD
                 UNTIL EOF.
             EXEC CICS ISSUE DISCONNECT SESSION(EIBTRMID)
             END-EXEC.
             EXEC CICS RETURN END-EXEC.
             GOBACK.
         PRINT-QUEUE-RECORD.
             PERFORM READ-QUEUE-RECORD THRU READ-QUEUE-EXIT.
             IF EOF
                 PERFORM SEND-BUFFER-DATA
             ELSE
                 PERFORM FORMAT-BUFFER-DATA.

         READ-QUEUE-RECORD.
             MOVE 133 TO LENGTH-OF-PRINT-RECORD.
             EXEC CICS
                 READQ TD QUEUE(EIBTRMID)
                     INTO(PRINT-RECORD)
                     LENGTH(LENGTH-OF-PRINT-RECORD)
```

58
59
60
61
62
63
64
65
66
67
68
69
70
71
72
73
74
75
76
77
78
79
80
81
82
83
84
85
86
87
88

```
 89          END-EXEC.
 90      SET PRINT-INDEX TO 1.
 91      GO TO READ-QUEUE-EXIT.
 92
 93  QUEUE-EMPTY.
 94      MOVE 1 TO EOF-SW.
 95
 96  READ-QUEUE-EXIT.  EXIT.
 97
 98  FORMAT-BUFFER-DATA.
 99  ***** PRINTER-DEFINITION ***********************
100  * FOR CICS 1.6.1 USE 3996
101  * FOR CICS 1.7.0 USE 1916
102  ***********************************************
103  **** IF BUFFER-INDEX > 3996 - LENGTH-OF-PRINT-RECORD
104      IF BUFFER-INDEX > 1916 - LENGTH-OF-PRINT-RECORD
105          PERFORM SEND-BUFFER-DATA
106          MOVE LOW-VALUES TO BUFFER-AREA
107          SET BUFFER-INDEX TO 1.
108      PERFORM FORMAT-CONTROL-CHARACTERS THRU FORMAT-CONTROL-EXIT.
109      PERFORM MOVE-PRINT-CHARACTER
110          VARYING PRINT-INDEX FROM 1 BY 1
111          UNTIL PRINT-INDEX = 132.
112
113  FORMAT-CONTROL-CHARACTERS.
114      IF NOT (FORM-FEED OR
115              SINGLE-SPACE OR
116              DOUBLE-SPACE OR
```

Figure 2.26. continued.

```
117              TRIPLE-SPACE)
118         MOVE • • TO PRINT-ASA.
119
120    IF FORM-FEED
121       MOVE CR-COMMAND TO SET-CHAR
122       PERFORM SET-BUFFER-CHARACTER
123       MOVE FF-COMMAND TO SET-CHAR
124       PERFORM SET-BUFFER-CHARACTER
125       MOVE CR-COMMAND TO SET-CHAR
126       PERFORM SET-BUFFER-CHARACTER
127    ELSE
128    IF SINGLE-SPACE
129       MOVE 1 TO NL-COUNT
130    ELSE
131    IF DOUBLE-SPACE
132       MOVE 2 TO NL-COUNT
133    ELSE
134    IF TRIPLE-SPACE
135       MOVE 3 TO NL-COUNT.
136
137    IF NOT FORM-FEED
138       IF BUFFER-INDEX = 1
139          SUBTRACT 1 FROM NL-COUNT.
140
141    IF NOT FORM-FEED
142       MOVE NL-COMMAND TO SET-CHAR
143       IF NL-COUNT NOT = ZEROS
144          PERFORM SET-BUFFER-CHARACTER
145             NL-COUNT TIMES.
```

```
146     FORMAT-CONTROL-EXIT. EXIT.
147
148     SET-BUFFER-CHARACTER.
149         ADD 1 TO LENGTH-OF-BUFFER.
150         MOVE SET-CHAR TO BUFFER-CHAR (BUFFER-INDEX).
151         SET BUFFER-INDEX UP BY 1.
152
153
154     MOVE-PRINT-CHARACTER.
155         MOVE PRINT-CHAR (PRINT-INDEX) TO SET-CHAR.
156         PERFORM SET-BUFFER-CHARACTER.
157
158     SEND-BUFFER-DATA.
159         MOVE CR-COMMAND TO SET-CHAR.
160         PERFORM SET-BUFFER-CHARACTER.
161
162     ***** PRINTER-DEFINITION
163     * FOR CICS 1.6.1 USE 4000
164     * FOR CICS 1.7.0 USE 1920
165         EXEC CICS
166             SEND FROM(BUFFER-AREA)
167                  LENGTH(LENGTH-OF-BUFFER)
168                  CTLCHAR(CONTROL-CHAR)
169                  ERASE
170         END-EXEC.
171         MOVE 0 TO LENGTH-OF-BUFFER.
**************************************************************
```

Figure 2.26. continued.

```
*******************************************************
     1      IDENTIFICATION DIVISION.
     2      PROGRAM-ID. BNREPRT.
     3  *=================================================
     4  * THIS PROGRAM WILL WRITE A REPORT CONSISTING OF THREE LINES.
     5  * THE PRINTER WILL SKIP TO NEW PAGE BEFORE PRINTING THIS REPORT,
     6  * WHICH WILL BE PRINTED ON PRINTER WITH CICS TERMINAL ID D917.
     7  * NOTE: THIS IS ACTUALLY ONLY A SAMPLE PROGRAM THAT SHOWS HOW A
     8  * REPORT OF ANY SIZE CAN BE PRINTED ON ANY PRINTER DEFINED TO
     9  * CICS.
    10  *=================================================
    11      ENVIRONMENT DIVISION.
    12      DATA DIVISION.
    13      WORKING-STORAGE SECTION.
    14      01  WS-REC-AREA-1    PIC X(133) VALUE '1 SAMPLE REPORT'.
    15      01  WS-REC-AREA-2    PIC X(133) VALUE ' --------'.
    16      01  WS-REC-AREA-3    PIC X(133) VALUE
    17          ' ABC ELECTRONICS COMPANY'.
    18      01  WS-REC-AREA-4    PIC X(133) VALUE '   HEAD OFFICE'.
    19
    20      01  WS-OUT-MSG-1.
    21          05 FILLER            PIC X(80) VALUE
    22          'AN ERROR OF SOME KIND HAS OCCURRED IN PROGRAM BNREPRT. '.
    23          05 FILLER            PIC X(80) VALUE
    24          'USE CEDF TO DEBUG. NOW PRESS CLEAR KEY TO CONTINUE. '.
    25
    26      01  WS-OUT-MSG-3.
    27          05 FILLER            PIC X(80) VALUE
    28          'MISSION SUCCESSFUL. '.
    29
    30      PROCEDURE DIVISION.
    31          EXEC CICS IGNORE CONDITION LENGERR END-EXEC.
    32          EXEC CICS HANDLE CONDITION
    33              ERROR(ERROR-COND)
```

```
34              END-EXEC.
35          PERFORM MAIN-RTN.
36          GOBACK.
37
38      MAIN-RTN.
39          PERFORM WRITE-TD-QUEUE.
40          EXEC CICS SEND FROM (WS-OUT-MSG-3)
41              ERASE
42              LENGTH(80)
43          END-EXEC.
44          EXEC CICS RETURN END-EXEC.
45 ***************************************************************
46      WRITE-TD-QUEUE.
47          EXEC CICS WRITEQ TD QUEUE('D917') FROM(WS-REC-AREA-1)
48              LENGTH(133) END-EXEC.
49          EXEC CICS WRITEQ TD QUEUE('D917') FROM(WS-REC-AREA-2)
50              LENGTH(133) END-EXEC.
51          EXEC CICS WRITEQ TD QUEUE('D917') FROM(WS-REC-AREA-3)
52              LENGTH(133) END-EXEC.
53          EXEC CICS WRITEQ TD QUEUE('D917') FROM(WS-REC-AREA-4)
54              LENGTH(133) END-EXEC.
55 ***************************************************************
56      ERROR-COND.
57          EXEC CICS SEND FROM (WS-OUT-MSG-1)
58              ERASE
59              LENGTH(160)
60          END-EXEC.
61          EXEC CICS RETURN END-EXEC.
62 ***************************************************************
```

Figure 2.27. Source code of program BNREPRT

151

Basically, the processing is as follows. Each record of 133 bytes is read from transient data queue, and it is accumulated in BUFFER-AREA, which is defined in working storage on line 56 as an area of 1920 bytes. In the example of Figure 2.27, all four records would be stored in BUFFER-AREA. When the READQ command on line 86 is executed to read the fifth record from the queue, the QZERO condition would occur. Due to the HANDLE CONDITION COMMAND on line 65, control would flow to line 94, where EOF-SW would be set to 1. Next, control would flow to line 78, where, due to EOF-SW being 1, routine SEND-BUFFER-DATA would get executed. In this routine, the content of BUFFER-AREA would be sent to the terminal on which this transaction is executing, which, in this example, is terminal ID D917. After that, control would flow to line 72, where the DISCONNECT SESSION command would be executed, which would disconnect the printer from CICS. Next, the RETURN command on line 74 would send control to CICS, which would terminate this task. The end result would be that the four-line report would have been printed on printer D917, and, from the transient data queue D917, all records would have been removed. This is because when a record is read from the intrapartition transient data queue, it gets deleted automatically.

2.15 A FACILITY TO INQUIRE/MODIFY STATUS OF CICS RESOURCES WITHOUT USING THE CEMT TRANSACTION

Figures 2.28 through 2.33 give the various components of a facility to inquire or modify the status of files, transactions, programs, and journals in a running CICS system. These will be referred to as resources. IBM-supplied transaction CEMT can be used to perform the functions performed by the facility and more. So, the question arises:

Why Do We Need This facility?

The main reason why a CICS shop would need this facility is so the CEMT transaction can be controlled. The CEMT transaction is a very powerful tool, designed solely for the use of system programmers and, in some cases, by the operators, who start and stop CICS or monitor the status (in service, out of service, etc.) of terminals. Through the CEMT transaction, one can change the status of all kinds of CICS resources, including transactions, programs, files, and journals, without any restriction. For example, one can place all terminals out of service, thereby preventing everyone from using the system. So, if one is allowed to use the CEMT transaction, he or she has access to all resources, assuming that external security is not present on the system. Using CEMT, one can also dynamically change system parameters, such as maximum number of tasks, maximum number of active tasks, and so on. Incorrect changes to system parameters can adversely affect the performance of the CICS system and, in some cases, can even result in system crash. It is obvious that such a powerful tool cannot be made available to all the programmers and analysts.

```
***********************************************************************
 1    UNUSED1    DFHMSD  TYPE=&SYSPARM,MODE=INOUT,CTRL=(FREEKB),         *
 2                       LANG=ASM,TIOAPFX=YES,EXTATT=MAPONLY,COLOR=GREEN
 3    BEMTMS1    DFHMDI  SIZE=(24,80)
 4    APPLID1    DFHMDF  POS=(01,1),LENGTH=8,ATTRB=(ASKIP,BRT)
 5               DFHMDF  POS=(01,15),LENGTH=39,ATTRB=(ASKIP,BRT),        X
 6                       INITIAL='NIRMAL''S FACILITY TO INQUIRE/SET STATUS'
 7               DFHMDF  POS=(01,55),LENGTH=19,ATTRB=(ASKIP,BRT),        X
 8                       INITIAL='OF CICS RESOURCES'
 9               DFHMDF  POS=(05,10),LENGTH=31,ATTRB=(ASKIP,BRT),        X
10                       INITIAL='ENTER YOUR USER ID HERE =====>>'
11    USERID     DFHMDF  POS=(05,48),LENGTH=08,ATTRB=(IC,UNPROT,FSET),  X
12                       INITIAL='
13               DFHMDF  POS=(05,57),LENGTH=01
14               DFHMDF  POS=(06,25),LENGTH=3,ATTRB=(ASKIP),            X
15                       INITIAL='AND'
16               DFHMDF  POS=(07,10),LENGTH=31,ATTRB=(ASKIP,BRT),       X
17                       INITIAL='    YOUR PASSWORD HERE ===>>'
18    PASSWD     DFHMDF  POS=(07,48),LENGTH=08,ATTRB=(UNPROT,FSET,DRK)  X
19               DFHMDF  POS=(07,57),LENGTH=01
20               DFHMDF  POS=(11,01),LENGTH=17,                         X
21                       INITIAL='SYSTEM MESSAGE:  '
22    SYSMSG1    DFHMDF  POS=(11,19),LENGTH=58,ATTRB=(ASKIP,BRT)
23               DFHMDF  POS=(13,01),LENGTH=41,                         X
24                       INITIAL='PRESS <ENTER> TO RECEIVE THE MAIN SCREEN.'
25               DFHMDF  POS=(13,43),LENGTH=21,                         X
26                       INITIAL='PRESS <CLEAR> TO EXIT'
27               DFHMSD  TYPE=FINAL
28               END
***********************************************************************
```

Figure 2.28. Source code of map BEMTMS1

153

```
***********************************************************************
1  UNUSED2  DFHMSD TYPE=&SYSPARM,MODE=INOUT,CTRL=(FREEKB),               *
2           LANG=ASM,TIOAPFX=YES,EXTATT=MAPONLY,COLOR=GREEN
3  BEMTMS2  DFHMDI SIZE=(24,80)
4  APPLID2  DFHMDF POS=(01,1),LENGTH=8,ATTRB=(ASKIP,BRT)                 X
5           DFHMDF POS=(01,15),LENGTH=39,ATTRB=(ASKIP,BRT),
6            INITIAL='NIRMAL''S FACILITY TO INQUIRE/SET STATUS'          X
7           DFHMDF POS=(01,55),LENGTH=19,ATTRB=(ASKIP,BRT),              X
8            INITIAL='OF CICS RESOURCES'
9           DFHMDF POS=(03,01),LENGTH=08,INITIAL='USER ID:'
10 USER     DFHMDF POS=(03,10),LENGTH=08,ATTRB=(ASKIP,BRT)               X
11          DFHMDF POS=(05,01),LENGTH=20,
12           INITIAL='YOUR WISH (I,S,R)==>'
13 WISH     DFHMDF POS=(05,23),LENGTH=08,ATTRB=(IC,UNPROT,FSET)          X
14          DFHMDF POS=(05,32),LENGTH=01
15          DFHMDF POS=(06,01),LENGTH=20,
16           INITIAL='RESOURCE-TYPE  =====>'
17 RESTYPE  DFHMDF POS=(06,23),LENGTH=08,ATTRB=(UNPROT,FSET)             X
18          DFHMDF POS=(06,32),LENGTH=01
19          DFHMDF POS=(07,01),LENGTH=20,                               X
20           INITIAL='RESOURCE-NAME   ====>'
21 RESNAME  DFHMDF POS=(07,23),LENGTH=08,ATTRB=(UNPROT,FSET)            X
22          DFHMDF POS=(07,32),LENGTH=01
23          DFHMDF POS=(08,01),LENGTH=20,                               X
24           INITIAL='DESIRED STATUS  ====>'
25 STATUS   DFHMDF POS=(08,23),LENGTH=08,ATTRB=(UNPROT,FSET)            X
26          DFHMDF POS=(08,32),LENGTH=01
27          DFHMDF POS=(10,01),LENGTH=17,                               X
28           INITIAL='SYSTEM ANSWER 1:'
29 SYSANS1  DFHMDF POS=(10,19),LENGTH=58,ATTRB=(ASKIP,BRT)
```

```
30          DFHMDF  POS=(11,01),LENGTH=17,                              X
31                  INITIAL='SYSTEM ANSWER 2: '
32  SYSANS2  DFHMDF  POS=(11,19),LENGTH=58,ATTRB=(ASKIP,BRT)             X
33          DFHMDF  POS=(13,01),LENGTH=46,                              X
34                  INITIAL='PRESS <ENTER> TO PERFORM WORK.  <CLEAR> TO QUIT'
35          DFHMDF  POS=(14,01),LENGTH=40,ATTRB=(ASKIP,BRT),            X
36                  INITIAL='--------------------------------------'
37          DFHMDF  POS=(14,42),LENGTH=38,ATTRB=(ASKIP,BRT),            X
38                  INITIAL='--------------------------------------'
39          DFHMDF  POS=(15,01),LENGTH=05,COLOR=GREEN,                  X
40                  INITIAL='WISH:'
41          DFHMDF  POS=(15,12),LENGTH=02,ATTRB=(ASKIP,BRT),            X
42                  INITIAL='I='
43          DFHMDF  POS=(15,15),LENGTH=07,COLOR=GREEN,                  X
44                  INITIAL='INQUIRE'
45          DFHMDF  POS=(15,25),LENGTH=02,ATTRB=(ASKIP,BRT),            X
46                  INITIAL='S='
47          DFHMDF  POS=(15,28),LENGTH=03,COLOR=GREEN,                  X
48                  INITIAL='SET'
49          DFHMDF  POS=(15,33),LENGTH=02,ATTRB=(ASKIP,BRT),            X
50                  INITIAL='R='
51          DFHMDF  POS=(15,36),LENGTH=24,COLOR=GREEN,                  X
52                  INITIAL='REFRESH A PROGRAM OR MAP'
53          DFHMDF  POS=(16,01),LENGTH=14,COLOR=GREEN,                  X
54                  INITIAL='RESOURCE TYPE:'
55          DFHMDF  POS=(16,16),LENGTH=03,ATTRB=(ASKIP,BRT),            X
56                  INITIAL='DA='
```

Figure 2.29. Source code of map BEMTMS2

155

```
57   DFHMDF POS=(16,20),LENGTH=04,COLOR=GREEN,              X
58          INITIAL='FILE'
59   DFHMDF POS=(16,25),LENGTH=05,ATTRB=(ASKIP,BRT),        X
60          INITIAL='TRAN='
61   DFHMDF POS=(16,31),LENGTH=11,COLOR=GREEN,              X
62          INITIAL='TRANSACTION'
63   DFHMDF POS=(16,43),LENGTH=05,ATTRB=(ASKIP,BRT),        X
64          INITIAL='PROG='
65   DFHMDF POS=(16,49),LENGTH=14,COLOR=GREEN,              X
66          INITIAL='PROGRAM OR MAP'
67   DFHMDF POS=(16,64),LENGTH=06,ATTRB=(ASKIP,BRT),        X
68          INITIAL='JOURN='
69   DFHMDF POS=(16,71),LENGTH=08,COLOR=GREEN,              X
70          INITIAL='JOURNAL'
71   DFHMDF POS=(17,01),LENGTH=07,COLOR=GREEN,              X
72          INITIAL='STATUS:'
73   DFHMDF POS=(17,09),LENGTH=03,ATTRB=(ASKIP,BRT),        X
74          INITIAL='OP='
75   DFHMDF POS=(17,13),LENGTH=04,COLOR=GREEN,              X
76          INITIAL='OPEN'
77   DFHMDF POS=(17,18),LENGTH=03,ATTRB=(ASKIP,BRT),        X
78          INITIAL='CL='
79   DFHMDF POS=(17,22),LENGTH=05,COLOR=GREEN,              X
80          INITIAL='CLOSE'
81   DFHMDF POS=(17,28),LENGTH=05,ATTRB=(ASKIP,BRT),        X
82          INITIAL='ENAB='
83   DFHMDF POS=(17,34),LENGTH=06,COLOR=GREEN,              X
84          INITIAL='ENABLE'
```

```
85       DFHMDF POS=(17,41),LENGTH=06,ATTRB=(ASKIP,BRT),          X
86              INITIAL='DISAB='
87       DFHMDF POS=(17,48),LENGTH=07,COLOR=GREEN,                X
88              INITIAL='DISABLE'
89       DFHMDF POS=(18,01),LENGTH=41,                            X
90              INITIAL='INQUIRY IS PERMITTED EVEN IF RESOURCE(S) '
91       DFHMDF POS=(18,43),LENGTH=37,                            X
92              INITIAL='REQUESTED ARE NOT INCLUDED IN TABLE. '
93       DFHMDF POS=(19,01),LENGTH=41,ATTRB=(ASKIP,BRT),          X
94              INITIAL='FOR INQUIRING FILES, RESOURCE NAME CAN BE'
95       DFHMDF POS=(19,43),LENGTH=37,ATTRB=(ASKIP,BRT),          X
96              INITIAL='FULL OR GENERIC, E.G. BK* IS GENERIC.'
97       DFHMDF POS=(20,01),LENGTH=39,                            X
98              INITIAL='SUPPOSE WISH=S, RESOURCE NAME=AB*  .THIS'
99       DFHMDF POS=(20,41),LENGTH=36,                            X
100             INITIAL='WILL AFFECT ALL RESOURCES WHOSE NAME'
101      DFHMDF POS=(21,01),LENGTH=42,                            X
102             INITIAL='STARTS WITH AB. THIS IS TRUE FOR FILES AND'
103      DFHMDF POS=(21,44),LENGTH=36,                            X
104             INITIAL='TRANSACTIONS ONLY AS OF THIS RELEASE'
105      DFHMDF POS=(22,01),LENGTH=42,ATTRB=(ASKIP,BRT),          X
106             INITIAL='JOURNALS CAN ONLY BE CLOSED, THEN OPENED. '
107      DFHMSD TYPE=FINAL
108      END
*******************************************************************
```

Figure 2.29. continued.

157

```
*********************************************************  *
 1  UNUSED3   DFHMSD TYPE=&SYSPARM,MODE=INOUT,CTRL=(FREEKB),
 2                   LANG=ASM,TIOAPFX=YES,EXTATT=MAPONLY
 3  BEMTMS3   DFHMDI SIZE=(24,80)
 4  DD01      DFHMDF POS=(01,01),LENGTH=08,ATTRB=(ASKIP,BRT,FSET)
 5  DSN01     DFHMDF POS=(01,10),LENGTH=44,ATTRB=(ASKIP)
 6  OSTAT01   DFHMDF POS=(01,55),LENGTH=12,ATTRB=(ASKIP,BRT)
 7  ESTAT01   DFHMDF POS=(01,68),LENGTH=12,ATTRB=(ASKIP)
 8  DD02      DFHMDF POS=(02,01),LENGTH=08,ATTRB=(ASKIP,BRT)
 9  DSN02     DFHMDF POS=(02,10),LENGTH=44,ATTRB=(ASKIP)
10  OSTAT02   DFHMDF POS=(02,55),LENGTH=12,ATTRB=(ASKIP,BRT)
11  ESTAT02   DFHMDF POS=(02,68),LENGTH=12,ATTRB=(ASKIP)
12  DD03      DFHMDF POS=(03,01),LENGTH=08,ATTRB=(ASKIP,BRT)
13  DSN03     DFHMDF POS=(03,10),LENGTH=44,ATTRB=(ASKIP)
14  OSTAT03   DFHMDF POS=(03,55),LENGTH=12,ATTRB=(ASKIP,BRT)
15  ESTAT03   DFHMDF POS=(03,68),LENGTH=12,ATTRB=(ASKIP)
16  DD04      DFHMDF POS=(04,01),LENGTH=08,ATTRB=(ASKIP,BRT)
17  DSN04     DFHMDF POS=(04,10),LENGTH=44,ATTRB=(ASKIP)
18  OSTAT04   DFHMDF POS=(04,55),LENGTH=12,ATTRB=(ASKIP,BRT)
19  ESTAT04   DFHMDF POS=(04,68),LENGTH=12,ATTRB=(ASKIP)
20  DD05      DFHMDF POS=(05,01),LENGTH=08,ATTRB=(ASKIP,BRT)
21  DSN05     DFHMDF POS=(05,10),LENGTH=44,ATTRB=(ASKIP)
22  OSTAT05   DFHMDF POS=(05,55),LENGTH=12,ATTRB=(ASKIP,BRT)
23  ESTAT05   DFHMDF POS=(05,68),LENGTH=12,ATTRB=(ASKIP)
24  DD06      DFHMDF POS=(06,01),LENGTH=08,ATTRB=(ASKIP,BRT)
25  DSN06     DFHMDF POS=(06,10),LENGTH=44,ATTRB=(ASKIP)
26  OSTAT06   DFHMDF POS=(06,55),LENGTH=12,ATTRB=(ASKIP,BRT)
27  ESTAT06   DFHMDF POS=(06,68),LENGTH=12,ATTRB=(ASKIP)
28  DD07      DFHMDF POS=(07,01),LENGTH=08,ATTRB=(ASKIP,BRT)
29  DSN07     DFHMDF POS=(07,10),LENGTH=44,ATTRB=(ASKIP)
```

```
30  OSTAT07   DFHMDF POS=(07,55),LENGTH=12,ATTRB=(ASKIP,BRT)
31  ESTAT07   DFHMDF POS=(07,68),LENGTH=12,ATTRB=(ASKIP)
32  DD08      DFHMDF POS=(08,01),LENGTH=08,ATTRB=(ASKIP,BRT)
33  DSN08     DFHMDF POS=(08,10),LENGTH=44,ATTRB=(ASKIP)
34  OSTAT08   DFHMDF POS=(08,55),LENGTH=12,ATTRB=(ASKIP,BRT)
35  ESTAT08   DFHMDF POS=(08,68),LENGTH=12,ATTRB=(ASKIP)
36  DD09      DFHMDF POS=(09,01),LENGTH=08,ATTRB=(ASKIP,BRT)
37  DSN09     DFHMDF POS=(09,10),LENGTH=44,ATTRB=(ASKIP)
38  OSTAT09   DFHMDF POS=(09,55),LENGTH=12,ATTRB=(ASKIP,BRT)
39  ESTAT09   DFHMDF POS=(09,68),LENGTH=12,ATTRB=(ASKIP)
40  DD10      DFHMDF POS=(10,01),LENGTH=08,ATTRB=(ASKIP,BRT)
41  DSN10     DFHMDF POS=(10,10),LENGTH=44,ATTRB=(ASKIP)
42  OSTAT10   DFHMDF POS=(10,55),LENGTH=12,ATTRB=(ASKIP,BRT)
43  ESTAT10   DFHMDF POS=(10,68),LENGTH=12,ATTRB=(ASKIP)
44  DD11      DFHMDF POS=(11,01),LENGTH=08,ATTRB=(ASKIP,BRT)
45  DSN11     DFHMDF POS=(11,10),LENGTH=44,ATTRB=(ASKIP)
46  OSTAT11   DFHMDF POS=(11,55),LENGTH=12,ATTRB=(ASKIP,BRT)
47  ESTAT11   DFHMDF POS=(11,68),LENGTH=12,ATTRB=(ASKIP)
48  DD12      DFHMDF POS=(12,01),LENGTH=08,ATTRB=(ASKIP,BRT)
49  DSN12     DFHMDF POS=(12,10),LENGTH=44,ATTRB=(ASKIP)
50  OSTAT12   DFHMDF POS=(12,55),LENGTH=12,ATTRB=(ASKIP,BRT)
51  ESTAT12   DFHMDF POS=(12,68),LENGTH=12,ATTRB=(ASKIP)
52  DD13      DFHMDF POS=(13,01),LENGTH=08,ATTRB=(ASKIP,BRT)
53  DSN13     DFHMDF POS=(13,10),LENGTH=44,ATTRB=(ASKIP)
54  OSTAT13   DFHMDF POS=(13,55),LENGTH=12,ATTRB=(ASKIP,BRT)
55  ESTAT13   DFHMDF POS=(13,68),LENGTH=12,ATTRB=(ASKIP)
56  DD14      DFHMDF POS=(14,01),LENGTH=08,ATTRB=(ASKIP,BRT)
57  DSN14     DFHMDF POS=(14,10),LENGTH=44,ATTRB=(ASKIP)
```

Figure 2.30. Source code of map BEMTMS3

```
58  OSTAT14   DFHMDF POS=(14,55),LENGTH=12,ATTRB=(ASKIP,BRT)
59  ESTAT14   DFHMDF POS=(14,68),LENGTH=12,ATTRB=(ASKIP)
60  DD15      DFHMDF POS=(15,01),LENGTH=08,ATTRB=(ASKIP,BRT)
61  DSN15     DFHMDF POS=(15,10),LENGTH=44,ATTRB=(ASKIP)
62  OSTAT15   DFHMDF POS=(15,55),LENGTH=12,ATTRB=(ASKIP,BRT)
63  ESTAT15   DFHMDF POS=(15,68),LENGTH=12,ATTRB=(ASKIP)
64  DD16      DFHMDF POS=(16,01),LENGTH=08,ATTRB=(ASKIP,BRT)
65  DSN16     DFHMDF POS=(16,10),LENGTH=44,ATTRB=(ASKIP)
66  OSTAT16   DFHMDF POS=(16,55),LENGTH=12,ATTRB=(ASKIP,BRT)
67  ESTAT16   DFHMDF POS=(16,68),LENGTH=12,ATTRB=(ASKIP)
68  DD17      DFHMDF POS=(17,01),LENGTH=08,ATTRB=(ASKIP,BRT)
69  DSN17     DFHMDF POS=(17,10),LENGTH=44,ATTRB=(ASKIP)
70  OSTAT17   DFHMDF POS=(17,55),LENGTH=12,ATTRB=(ASKIP,BRT)
71  ESTAT17   DFHMDF POS=(17,68),LENGTH=12,ATTRB=(ASKIP)
72  DD18      DFHMDF POS=(18,01),LENGTH=08,ATTRB=(ASKIP,BRT)
73  DSN18     DFHMDF POS=(18,10),LENGTH=44,ATTRB=(ASKIP)
74  OSTAT18   DFHMDF POS=(18,55),LENGTH=12,ATTRB=(ASKIP,BRT)
75  ESTAT18   DFHMDF POS=(18,68),LENGTH=12,ATTRB=(ASKIP)
76  DD19      DFHMDF POS=(19,01),LENGTH=08,ATTRB=(ASKIP,BRT)
77  DSN19     DFHMDF POS=(19,10),LENGTH=44,ATTRB=(ASKIP)
78  OSTAT19   DFHMDF POS=(19,55),LENGTH=12,ATTRB=(ASKIP,BRT)
79  ESTAT19   DFHMDF POS=(19,68),LENGTH=12,ATTRB=(ASKIP)
80  DD20      DFHMDF POS=(20,01),LENGTH=08,ATTRB=(ASKIP,BRT)
81  DSN20     DFHMDF POS=(20,10),LENGTH=44,ATTRB=(ASKIP)
82  OSTAT20   DFHMDF POS=(20,55),LENGTH=12,ATTRB=(ASKIP,BRT)
83  ESTAT20   DFHMDF POS=(20,68),LENGTH=12,ATTRB=(ASKIP)
84  DD21      DFHMDF POS=(21,01),LENGTH=08,ATTRB=(ASKIP,BRT)
85  DSN21     DFHMDF POS=(21,10),LENGTH=44,ATTRB=(ASKIP)
86  OSTAT21   DFHMDF POS=(21,55),LENGTH=12,ATTRB=(ASKIP,BRT)
```

```
87  ESTAT21   DFHMDF  POS=(21,68),LENGTH=12,ATTRB=(ASKIP)
88  DD22      DFHMDF  POS=(22,01),LENGTH=08,ATTRB=(ASKIP,BRT)
89  DSN22     DFHMDF  POS=(22,10),LENGTH=44,ATTRB=(ASKIP)
90  OSTAT22   DFHMDF  POS=(22,55),LENGTH=12,ATTRB=(ASKIP,BRT)
91  ESTAT22   DFHMDF  POS=(22,68),LENGTH=12,ATTRB=(ASKIP)
92  DD23      DFHMDF  POS=(23,01),LENGTH=08,ATTRB=(ASKIP,BRT)
93  DSN23     DFHMDF  POS=(23,10),LENGTH=44,ATTRB=(ASKIP)
94  OSTAT23   DFHMDF  POS=(23,55),LENGTH=12,ATTRB=(ASKIP,BRT)
95  ESTAT23   DFHMDF  POS=(23,68),LENGTH=12,ATTRB=(ASKIP)
96            DFHMDF  POS=(24,01),LENGTH=06,ATTRB=(ASKIP,BRT),
97                    INITIAL='ENTER='
98            DFHMDF  POS=(24,08),LENGTH=17,ATTRB=(ASKIP),
99                    INITIAL='NEXT PAGE OF DATA'
100           DFHMDF  POS=(24,26),LENGTH=04,ATTRB=(ASKIP,BRT),      X
101                   INITIAL='PF3='
102           DFHMDF  POS=(24,31),LENGTH=23,ATTRB=(ASKIP),
103                   INITIAL='EXIT TO MAIN SCREEN'
104           DFHMDF  POS=(24,55),LENGTH=06,ATTRB=(ASKIP,BRT),      X
105                   INITIAL='CLEAR='
106           DFHMDF  POS=(24,62),LENGTH=09,ATTRB=(ASKIP),
107                   INITIAL='EXIT'
108  FMORE    DFHMDF  POS=(24,72),LENGTH=07,ATTRB=(ASKIP,BRT),      X
109                   INITIAL='...MORE'
110           DFHMSD  TYPE=FINAL
111           END
```

****

Figure 2.30. continued.

161

```
********************************************************************************
 1         COPY  REGDEF
 2         COPY  DFHAID
 3  BEMTPG1 DFHEIENT CODEREG=(9,10),DATAREG=11,EIBREG=12
 4         EXEC  CICS IGNORE CONDITION MAPFAIL LENGERR                         X
 5         EXEC  CICS HANDLE CONDITION ERROR(ERRCOND)                          X
 6               DSIDERR(DSIDERR)                                              X
 7               TRANSIDERR(TRANERR)                                           X
 8               PGMIDERR(PGMIDERR)                                            X
 9               END(ENDBROWS)
10         LH    R4,EIBCALEN     LOAD R4 WITH COMMAREA LENGTH
11         LTR   R4,R4           IS COMM AREA LENGTH = ZERO?
12         BZ    INITIAL         YES, BRANCH
13         CH    R4,=H'40'       IS COMMAREA OF 40 BYTES?
14         BE    AGAIN02         YES, BRANCH
15         CH    R4,=H'8'        IS COMMAREA OF 8 BYTES?
16         BE    AGAIN01         YES, BRANCH
17         MVC   OUTMSG,ERRMSG99
18         B     ABENDRTN
                 *
19  AGAIN01 EQU  *
20         CLI   EIBAID,DFHENTER      WAS ENTER KEY PRESSED?
21         BE    ENTER01
22         CLI   EIBAID,DFHCLEAR      WAS CLEAR KEY PRESSED?
23         BE    CLEARKEY
24         MVC   SYSMSG10,ERRMSG3
25         B     GOBACK1
                 *
26  ENTER01 EQU  *
27         EXEC  CICS RECEIVE MAP('BEMTMS1') INTO(BEMTMS1I)
28         MVC   CUSER,USERIDI        SAVE USER ID IN COMM AREA
29         MVC   CPWD,PASSWDI
```

```
30          MVI   CTYPE,C'U'
31          MVI   CFLAG,C'F'
32          EXEC  CICS LINK PROGRAM('BEMTPG2') COMMAREA(COMM01)        X
33                LENGTH(40)
34          CLI   CFLAG,C'P'
35          BNE   REJECT
36  PASSED  EQU   *
37          MVC   USER0,CUSER        MOVE USER ID TO MAP
38          MVC   APPLID20,APPLID
39          EXEC  CICS SEND MAP('BEMTMS2') ERASE
40          EXEC  CICS RETURN TRANSID('BEMT') COMMAREA(COMM01)         X
41                LENGTH(40)
42  REJECT  EQU   *
43          MVC   SYSMSG10,ERRMSG6
44          B     GOBACK1
45  AGAIN02 EQU   *
46          L     R4,DFHEICAP        POINT R4 IN    COMMAREA
47          MVC   COMM01(40),0(R4)   STORE COMMAREA INTO WORKING STORAGE
48          CLI   EIBAID,DFHENTER    WAS ENTER KEY PRESSED?
49          BE    ENTERKEY           YES, BRANCH
50          CLI   EIBAID,DFHCLEAR    WAS CLEAR KEY PRESSED?
51          BE    CLEARKEY           YES, BRANCH
52          MVC   SYSANS20,ERRMSG3
53          MVC   WISHL,=H'-1'
54          B     GOBACK
55  *=========================================================*
56  ENTERKEY EQU   *
57          EXEC  CICS RECEIVE MAP('BEMTMS2') INTO(BEMTMS2I)
```

Figure 2.31. Source code of program BEMTPG1

```
58  MVC       OUTMSG,BLANKS            MOVE BLANKS TO FIELD ON MAP
59  MVC       SYSANS1O,BLANKS          MOVE BLANKS TO FIELD ON MAP
60  MVC       SYSANS2O,BLANKS          MOVE BLANKS TO FIELD ON MAP
61  CLI       WISHI,C'S'               IS WISH = S
62  BE        DECIDE01                 YES, BRANCH
63  MVC       STATUSO,BLANKS           MOVE BLANKS TO STATUS FIELD ON MAP
64  CLI       WISHI,C'R'               IS WISH = R
65  BE        DECIDE01                 YES, BRANCH
66  CLI       WISHI,C'I'               IS WISH = I
67  BE        DECIDE01                 YES, BRANCH
68  MVC       SYSANS2O,ERRMSG4
69  MVC       WISHL,=H'-1'
70  B         GOBACK
71  DECIDE01  EQU       *
72  MVC       CWISH,WISHI              SAVE WISH IN COMMAREA
73  MVC       CENTRY,RESNAMEI          SAVE RESOURCE NAME IN COMMAREA
74  MVC       CEMTOBJ,RESNAMEI         MOVE RESOURCE NAME TO CEMT AREA
75  MVI       CEMTPAR,C')'
76  MVC       CEMTACT,STATUSI          MOVE DESIRED STATUS TO CEMT AREA
77  LA        R1,CEMTCMD               POINT R1 TO CEMTCMD
78  ST        R1,PARMCMD
79  LA        R1,CEMTCLN
80  ST        R1,PARMCLN
81  LA        R1,CEMTIND
82  ST        R1,PARMIND
83  LA        R1,CEMTOUT
84  ST        R1,PARMOUT
85  LA        R1,CEMTOLN
86  ST        R1,PARMOLN
87  CLC       RESTYPEI(2),=CL2'DA'     RESOURCE TYPE ON SCREEN = DA
```

```
88           BE    FILERTN                    YES,  BRANCH
89           CLC   RESTYPEI(4),=CL4'TRAN'
90           BE    TRANRTN
91           CLC   RESTYPEI(4),=CL4'PROG'
92           BE    PROGRTN
93           CLC   RESTYPEI(5),=CL5'JOURN'
94           BE    JOURNRTN
95           MVC   SYSANS20,ERRMSG5
96           MVC   RESTYPEL,=H'-1'
97           B     GOBACK
98  JOURNRTN EQU   *
99           MVI   CTYPE,C'J'
100          MVI   CFLAG,C'F'
101          EXEC  CICS LINK PROGRAM('BEMTPG2') COMMAREA(COMM01)
102                LENGTH(40)
103          CLI   CFLAG,C'P'
104          BNE   JREJECT
105          CLI   WISHI,C'S'
106          BE    SETJOURN
107  SORRYJ  EQU   *
108          MVC   SYSANS20,ERRMSG19
109          MVC   WISHL,=H'-1'
110          B     GOBACK
111  SETJOURN EQU  *
112  ****  USER WANTS TO SET JOURNAL TO WHICH HE IS AUTHORIZED.
113          CLC   STATUSI(2),=CL2'CL'
114          BNE   SORRYJ
115          MVC   CEMTCMD,=CL9'SET JOUR('
```

Figure 2.31. continued.

165

```
116 JCLOSE   EQU  *
117          EXEC CICS LINK PROGRAM('DFHEMTA') COMMAREA(CEMTPARM)
118 ASKAGAIN EQU  *
119          MVC  TOLEN(2),=H'8'
120          EXEC CICS CONVERSE FROM(FROMDATA) FROMLENGTH(FROMLEN)        X
121          INTO(TODATA) TOLENGTH(TOLEN) ERASE
122          CLI  EIBAID,DFHENTER
123          BNE  ASKAGAIN
124          CLC  TODATA(8),=CL8'LOVEHATE'
125          BNE  ASKAGAIN
126 JOPEN    EQU  *
127          MVC  CEMTACT,=CL8'OUTPUT'
128          EXEC CICS LINK PROGRAM('DFHEMTA') COMMAREA(CEMTPARM)
129          MVC  CEMTACT,=CL8'SWITCH'
130          EXEC CICS LINK PROGRAM('DFHEMTA') COMMAREA(CEMTPARM)
131          MVC  SYSANS20,ERRMSG21
132          MVC  STATUS0,BLANKS
133          B    PASSED
134 FILERTN  EQU  *
135          MVI  CTYPE,C'F'
136          MVI  CFLAG,C'F'
137          EXEC CICS LINK PROGRAM('BEMTPG2') COMMAREA(COMM01)           X
138          LENGTH(40)
139          CLI  CFLAG,C'P'
140          BNE  FREJECT
141          CLI  WISHI,C'I'
142          BE   INQFILE
143 SETFILE  EQU  *
144          MVC  SYSANS20,ERRMSG7
145          CLI  CASTFND,C'N'
```

```
146            BE       SETFILE1
147   SETFILEG EQU      *
148   ****     USER WANTS TO SET FILES GENERICALLY
149            MVC      CEMTCMD,=CL9'SET DATA('
150            EXEC     CICS LINK PROGRAM('DFHEMTA') COMMAREA(CEMTPARM)
151            MVC      WISHL,=H'-1'
152            B        GOBACK
153   SETFILE1 EQU      *
154            CLC      STATUSI(2),=CL2'OP'
155            BE       FILEOPEN
156            CLC      STATUSI(2),=CL2'CL'
157            BE       FILECLOS
158            CLC      STATUSI(4),=CL4'ENAB'
159            BE       FILEENA
160            CLC      STATUSI(5),=CL5'DISAB'
161            BE       FILEDIS
162            MVC      SYSANS20,ERRMSG8
163            MVC      STATUSL,=H'-1'
164            B        GOBACK
165   FILEOPEN EXEC     CICS SET DATASET(RESNAMEI) OPEN
166            B        RETURN01
167   FILECLOS EXEC     CICS SET DATASET(RESNAMEI) CLOSED
168            B        RETURN01
169   FILEENA  EXEC     CICS SET DATASET(RESNAMEI) ENABLED
170            B        RETURN01
171   FILEDIS  EXEC     CICS SET DATASET(RESNAMEI) DISABLED
172            B        RETURN01
173   RETURN01 EQU      *
```

Figure 2.31. continued.

```
       MVC   WISHL,=H'-1'
       B     GOBACK
*----------------------------------------------------------------------
* YOU CAN USE R4 IN LOGIC BELOW. NO PROBLEM. IT DOES NOT POINT TO
* FIELD COMM01. IT POINTS TO COMM AREA AS INPUT TO THIS PROGRAM.
*----------------------------------------------------------------------
INQFILE  EQU   *
         CLI   CASTFND,C'N'
         BE    INQFILE1
*----------------------------------------------------------------------
INQFGEN  EQU   *
         ZAP   KOUNT,=P'0'
         MVI   SWENDBR,C'N'     RESET END BROWSE SWITCH
         EXEC CICS INQUIRE DATASET START
**** USER INQUIRING ABOUT FILES GENERICALLY
LOOP50   EQU   *
         SR    R3,R3
         LA    R3,23            23 LINES OF DATA ON SCREEN
         LA    R5,DD010
         LA    R6,DSN010
         LA    R7,OSTAT010
         LA    R8,ESTAT010
INQFNEXT EQU   *
         EXEC CICS INQUIRE DATASET(DD00) NEXT OBJECTNAME(DSN00)          X
               OPENSTATUS(FOPST) ENABLESTATUS(FENST)
         LA    R15,TESTAST
         BALR  14,15
         LTR   15,15
         BNZ   INQFNEXT
         AP    KOUNT,=P'1'
```

174
175
176
177
178
179
180
181
182
183
184
185
186
187
188
189
190
191
192
193
194
195
196
197
198
199
200
201
202
203

```
204        MVC    0(8,R5),DD00
205        MVC    0(44,R6),DSN00
206        CLC    FOPST,DFHVALUE(OPEN)
207        BE     OPEN1
208        CLC    FOPST,DFHVALUE(CLOSED)
209        BE     CLOSED1
210        CLC    FOPST,DFHVALUE(OPENING)
211        BE     OPENING1
212        CLC    FOPST,DFHVALUE(CLOSING)
213        BE     CLOSING1
214        CLC    FOPST,DFHVALUE(CLOSEREQUEST)
215        BE     CLOSERQ1
216        B      EXAM2
217 OPEN1    MVC    0(12,R7),=CL12'OPEN'
218        B      EXAM2
219 CLOSED1  MVC    0(12,R7),=CL12'CLOSED'
220        B      EXAM2
221 OPENING1 MVC    0(12,R7),=CL12'OPENING'
222        B      EXAM2
223 CLOSING1 MVC    0(12,R7),=CL12'CLOSING'
224        B      EXAM2
225 CLOSERQ1 MVC    0(12,R7),=CL12'CLOSEREQUEST'
226        B      EXAM2
227 EXAM2    EQU    *
228        CLC    FENST,DFHVALUE(ENABLED)
229        BE     ENAB1
230        CLC    FENST,DFHVALUE(DISABLED)
231        BE     DISAB1
```

Figure 2.31. continued.

169

```
232          CLC   FENST,DFHVALUE(UNENABLED)
233          BE    UNENAB1
234          CLC   FENST,DFHVALUE(DISABLING)
235          BE    DISABLN1
236          B     FINITO1
237 ENAB1    MVC   0(12,R8),=CL12'ENABLED'
238          B     FINITO1
239 DISAB1   MVC   0(12,R8),=CL12'DISABLED'
240          B     FINITO1
241 UNENAB1  MVC   0(12,R8),=CL12'UNENABLED'
242          B     FINITO1
243 DISABLN1 MVC   0(12,R8),=CL12'DISABLING'
244          B     FINITO1
245 FINITO1  EQU   *
246          LA    R5,88(R5)
247          LA    R6,88(R6)
248          LA    R7,88(R7)
249          LA    R8,88(R8)
250          BCT   R3,INQFNEXT
251 SENDMAP1 EQU   *
252          C     R3,=F'23'
253          BE    DONESIR
254          EXEC  CICS SEND MAP('BEMTMS3') ERASE WAIT
255          EXEC  CICS RECEIVE MAP('BEMTMS3') INTO(BEMTMS3I)
256          CLI   EIBAID,DFHCLEAR
257          BE    CLEARKEY
258          CLI   SWENDBR,C'Y'
259          BE    DONESIR
260          CLI   EIBAID,DFHPF3
261          BE    DONESIR
```

```
262          CLI   EIBAID,DFHENTER
263          BE    LOOP50
264 * NOW GET READY TO SEND ANOTHER PAGE OF MAP BEMTMS3
265          B     LOOP50
266 *---------------------------------------------------------------
267 DONESIR  EQU   *
268          CP    KOUNT,=P'0'
269          BE    NAFILE
270          MVC   OKOUNT,=X'402020202020'
271          ED    OKOUNT,KOUNT
272          MVC   SYSANS10(5),OKOUNT+1
273          MVC   SYSANS10+6(15),=C'FILES DISPLAYED'
274          B     PASSED
275 NAFILE   MVC   SYSANS10(18),=C'NO FILE TO DISPLAY'
276          B     PASSED
277 *---------------------------------------------------------------
278 INQFILE1 EQU   *
279          EXEC CICS INQUIRE DATASET(RESNAMEI) OBJECTNAME(FILENAME)    X
280               OPENSTATUS(FOPST) ENABLESTATUS(FENST)
281          MVC   SYSANS10(14),=CL14'FILE NAME = '
282          MVC   SYSANS10+14(44),FILENAME
283          MVC   OUTMSG,BLANKS
284          CLC   FOPST,DFHVALUE(OPEN)
285          BE    OPEN
286          CLC   FOPST,DFHVALUE(CLOSED)
287          BE    CLOSED
288          CLC   FOPST,DFHVALUE(OPENING)
289          BE    OPENING
```

Figure 2.31. continued.

171

```
290            CLC   FOPST,DFHVALUE(CLOSING)
291            BE    CLOSING
292            CLC   FOPST,DFHVALUE(CLOSEREQUEST)
293            BE    CLOSEREQ
294            B     EXAMINE2
295   OPEN     MVC   MSG1,=CL12'OPEN'
296            B     EXAMINE2
297   CLOSED   MVC   MSG1,=CL12'CLOSED'
298            B     EXAMINE2
299   OPENING  MVC   MSG1,=CL12'OPENING'
300            B     EXAMINE2
301   CLOSING  MVC   MSG1,=CL12'CLOSING'
302            B     EXAMINE2
303   CLOSEREQ MVC   MSG1,=CL12'CLOSEREQUEST'
304            B     EXAMINE2
305   EXAMINE2 EQU   *
306            CLC   FENST,DFHVALUE(ENABLED)
307            BE    ENABLED
308            CLC   FENST,DFHVALUE(DISABLED)
309            BE    DISABLED
310            CLC   FENST,DFHVALUE(UNENABLED)
311            BE    UNENABLE
312            CLC   FENST,DFHVALUE(DISABLING)
313            BE    DISABLNG
314            B     FINITO
315   ENABLED  MVC   MSG2,=CL12'ENABLED'
316            B     FINITO
317   DISABLED MVC   MSG2,=CL12'DISABLED'
318            B     FINITO
319   UNENABLE MVC   MSG2,=CL12'UNENABLED'
```

```
320          B     FINITO
321 DISABLNG MVC   MSG2,=CL12'DISABLING'
322          B     FINITO
323 *===========================================*
324 JREJECT  EQU   *
325          MVC   SYSANS20,ERRMSG20
326          MVC   RESNAMEL,=H'-1'
327          B     GOBACK
328 *===========================================*
329 FREJECT  EQU   *
330          MVC   SYSANS20,ERRMSG10
331          MVC   RESNAMEL,=H'-1'
332          B     GOBACK
333 *===========================================*
334 TREJECT  EQU   *
335          MVC   SYSANS20,ERRMSG11
336          MVC   RESNAMEL,=H'-1'
337          B     GOBACK
338 *===========================================*
339 PREJECT  EQU   *
340          MVC   SYSANS20,ERRMSG14
341          MVC   RESNAMEL,=H'-1'
342          B     GOBACK
343 *===========================================*
344 FINITO   EQU   *
345          MVC   SYSANS20,OUTMSG
346          MVC   WISHL,=H'-1'
347          B     GOBACK
```

Figure 2.31. continued.

```
348  *=================================================================*
349  ENDBROWS EQU   *
350           MVI   SWENDBR,C'Y'
351           CLI   CTYPE,C'F'
352           BE    ENDFILE
353           B     INITIAL
354  *=================================================================*
355  ENDFILE  EQU   *
356           MVC   FMOREO,=CL7'NO MORE'
357           B     SENDMAP1
358  *=================================================================*
359  PROGRTN  EQU   *
360           MVI   CTYPE,C'P'
361           MVI   CFLAG,C'F'
362           EXEC CICS LINK PROGRAM('BEMTPG2') COMMAREA(COMM01)       X
363                 LENGTH(40)
364           CLI   CFLAG,C'P'
365           BNE   PREJECT
366           CLI   WISHI,C'I'
367           BE    INQPROG
368           CLI   WISHI,C'R'
369           BE    PROGNEW
370  SETPROG  EQU   *
371           MVC   SYSANS20,ERRMSG7
372           CLC   STATUSI(4),=CL4'ENAB'
373           BE    PROGENA
374           CLC   STATUSI(5),=CL5'DISAB'
375           BE    PROGDIS
376           MVC   SYSANS20,ERRMSG16
377           MVC   STATUSL,=H'-1'
```

```
378          B      GOBACK
379 PROGENA  EQU    *
380          MVC    PENST,DFHVALUE(ENABLED)
381          B      PISSUE
382 PROGDIS  EQU    *
383          MVC    PENST,DFHVALUE(DISABLED)
384 PISSUE   EQU    *
385          EXEC   CICS SET PROGRAM(RESNAMEI) STATUS(PENST)
386 RETURN02 EQU    *
387          MVC    WISHL,=H'-1'
388          B      GOBACK
389 PROGNEW  EQU    *
390          EXEC   CICS SET PROGRAM(RESNAMEI) NEWCOPY
391          MVC    SYSANS20,ERRMSG17
392          B      RETURN02
393 *----------------------------------------------------------------------
394 INQPROG  EQU    *
395 INQPGEN  EQU    *
396          EXEC   CICS INQUIRE PROGRAM(RESNAMEI)                          X
397                 LANGUAGE(PLANG) PROGTYPE(PTYPE) STATUS(PENST)
398          CLC    PLANG,DFHVALUE(COBOL)
399          BE     PCOBOL
400          CLC    PLANG,DFHVALUE(PL1)
401          BE     PPL1
402          CLC    PLANG,DFHVALUE(ASSEMBLER)
403          BE     PASSEM
404          B      NEXTAA
405 PCOBOL   MVC    MSG1,=CL12'COBOL'
```

Figure 2.31. continued.

```
406           B     NEXTAA
407  PPL1     MVC   MSG1,=CL12'PL/1'
408           B     NEXTAA
409  PASSEM   MVC   MSG1,=CL12'ASSEMBLER'
410  NEXTAA   EQU   *
411           CLC   PTYPE,DFHVALUE(PROGRAM)
412           BE    PPROG
413           CLC   PTYPE,DFHVALUE(MAP)
414           BE    PMAP
415           CLC   PTYPE,DFHVALUE(PARTITIONSET)
416           BE    PPART
417           B     NEXTBB
418  PPROG    MVC   MSG2,=CL12'PROGRAM'
419           B     NEXTBB
420  PMAP     MVC   MSG2,=CL12'MAP'
421           B     NEXTBB
422  PPART    MVC   MSG2,=CL12'PARTITIONSET'
423  NEXTBB   CLC   PENST,DFHVALUE(ENABLED)
424           BE    PENAB
425           CLC   PENST,DFHVALUE(DISABLED)
426           BE    PDISAB
427           B     FINITO
428  PENAB    MVC   MSG3,=CL12'ENABLED'
429           B     FINITO
430  PDISAB   MVC   MSG3,=CL12'DISABLED'
431           B     FINITO
432  *===============================================*
433  TRANRTN  EQU   *
434           MVI   CTYPE,C'T'
435           MVC   TRAN,RESNAMEI
```

```
436         MVI    CFLAG,C'F'      INITIALIZE FLAG TO F FOR FAILED.
437         EXEC   CICS LINK PROGRAM('BEMTPG2') COMMAREA(COMM01)            X
438                LENGTH(40)
439         CLI    CFLAG,C'P'      IS USER AUTHORIZED?
440         BNE    TREJECT         NO, BRANCH
441         CLI    WISHI,C'I'      IS USER INQUIRING?
442         BE     INQTRAN         YES, BRANCH
443  SETTRAN EQU   *
444         MVC    SYSANS20,ERRMSG7
445         CLI    CASTFND,C'N'
446         BE     SETTRAN1
447  SETTRANG EQU  *
448  **** USER WANTS TO SET TRANS GENERICALLY
449         MVC    CEMTCMD,=CL9'SET TRAN('
450         EXEC   CICS LINK PROGRAM('DFHEMTA') COMMAREA(CEMTPARM)
451         MVC    WISHL,=H'-1'
452         B      GOBACK
453  SETTRAN1 EQU  *
454         CLC    STATUSI(4),=CL4'ENAB'
455         BE     TRANENA
456         CLC    STATUSI(5),=CL5'DISAB'
457         BE     TRANDIS
458         MVC    SYSANS20,ERRMSG13
459         MVC    STATUSL,=H'-1'
460         B      GOBACK
461  TRANENA EQU   *
462         MVC    TENST,DFHVALUE(ENABLED)
463         B      TISSUE
```

Figure 2.31. continued.

```
464  TRANDIS  EQU   *
465           MVC   TENST,DFHVALUE(DISABLED)
466  TISSUE   EQU   *
467           EXEC  CICS SET TRANSACTION(TRAN) STATUS(TENST)
468           MVC   WISHL,=H'-1'
469           B     GOBACK
470  *rrrrrrrrrrrrrrrrrrrrrrrrrrrrrrrrrrrrrrrrrrrrrrrrrrrrrrrrrrrrr
471  INQTRAN  EQU   *
472  INQTGEN  EQU   *
473           EXEC  CICS INQUIRE TRANSACTION(TRAN) PROGRAM(PROGRAM)   X
474                 STATUS(TENST)
475           MVC   SYSANS10(14),=CL14'PROGRAM NAME= '
476           MVC   SYSANS10+14(8),PROGRAM
477           CLC   TENST,DFHVALUE(ENABLED)
478           BE    TENA
479           CLC   TENST,DFHVALUE(DISABLED)
480           BE    TDIS
481           B     FINITO
482  TENA     MVC   MSG2,=CL12'ENABLED'
483           B     FINITO
484  TDIS     MVC   MSG2,=CL12'DISABLED'
485           B     FINITO
486  *===========================================================*
487  INITIAL  EQU   *
488           EXEC  CICS ASSIGN APPLID(APPLID)
489           MVC   APPLID10,APPLID
490           EXEC  CICS SEND MAP('BEMTMS1') ERASE
491           EXEC  CICS RETURN TRANSID('BEMT') COMMAREA(COMM01)      X
492                 LENGTH(8)
493  *===========================================================*
```

```
494   ERRCOND   EQU    *   CICS HANDLE CONDITION ERROR(RETURN)
495             EXEC   CLC    RESTYPEI(2),=CL2'DA'
496             BNE    OTHERE
497             CLC    STATUSI(2),=CL2'OP'
498             BNE    OTHERE
499             MVC    SYSANS2O,ERRMSG1A
500             B      RETURN1
501   OTHERE    EQU    *
502             MVC    SYSANS2O,ERRMSG1
503   RETURN1   MVC    WISHL,=H'-1'
504             B      GOBACK
505   RETURN    EXEC   CICS RETURN
506 *===============================================*
507   DSIDERR   EQU    *
508             MVC    SYSANS2O,ERRMSG2
509             MVC    RESNAMEL,=H'-1'
510             B      GOBACK
511 *===============================================*
512   TRANERR   EQU    *
513             MVC    SYSANS2O,ERRMSG12
514             MVC    RESNAMEL,=H'-1'
515             B      GOBACK
516 *===============================================*
517   PGMIDERR  EQU    *
518             MVC    SYSANS2O,ERRMSG15
519             MVC    RESNAMEL,=H'-1'
520             B      GOBACK
```

Figure 2.31. continued.

179

```
*=================================================================*
ABENDRTN EQU  *
         EXEC CICS SEND FROM(OUTMSG) LENGTH(58) ERASE
         EXEC CICS RETURN
*=================================================================*
CLEARKEY EQU  *
         MVI   OUTMSG,C' '
         EXEC CICS SEND FROM(OUTMSG) LENGTH(1) ERASE
         EXEC CICS RETURN
*=================================================================*
GOBACK1  EQU  *
         EXEC CICS SEND MAP('BEMTMS1') DATAONLY
         EXEC CICS RETURN TRANSID('BEMT') COMMAREA(COMM01)         X
               LENGTH(8)
*=================================================================*
GOBACK   EQU  *
         EXEC CICS SEND MAP('BEMTMS2') DATAONLY CURSOR
         EXEC CICS RETURN TRANSID('BEMT') COMMAREA(COMM01)         X
               LENGTH(40)
*=================================================================*
TESTAST  EQU  *
*=================================================================*
* TEST IF THE DDNAME AT DD00 MATCHES WHAT THE USER SPECIFIED IN
* RESOURCE NAME FIELD. FOR EXAMPLE IF USER SPECIFIED PACIV* AND THE
* VALUE AT DD00 IS PACIV810, THEN THERE IS A MATCH.
* R14 IS THE RETURN REGISTER
* AT ENTRY, R15 HAS ADDRESS OF THIS ROUTINE.
* UPON RETURN, R15 = 0 MEANS PASSED, ELSE FAILED.
* USES REG 2,4,15 ONLY
*=================================================================*
```

522
523
524
525
526
527
528
529
530
531
532
533
534
535
536
537
538
539
540
541
542
543
544
545
546
547
548
549
550
551

```
552            L      R15,=F'8'
553            LA     R2,RESNAMEI
554            LA     R4,DD00
555   LOOP00   EQU    *
556            CLI    0(R2),C'*'
557            BE     SUKCESS
558            CLC    0(1,R2),0(R4)
559            BNE    FAILED
560            LA     R2,1(R2)
561            LA     R4,1(R4)
562            BCT    R15,LOOP00
563   SUKCESS  EQU    *
564            SR     15,15
565            BR     14
566   FAILED   EQU    *
567            BR     14
568   *===============================================================*
569   BLANKS   DC     80C' '
570   ERRMSG1  DS     0CL58
571            DC     CL45'REQUEST FAILED. CONTACT BARRY NIRMAL FOR ASSI'
572            DC     CL13'STANCE.                                       '
573   ERRMSG1A DS     0CL58
574            DC     CL45'FILE OPEN FAILED. CHECK IF DATA SET EXISTS. I'
575            DC     CL13'SSUE LISTCAT.                                 '
576   ERRMSG2  DS     0CL58
577            DC     CL45'SPECIFIED DDNAME NOT DEFINED TO CICS. CHECK  '
578            DC     CL13'IT PLEASE.                                    '
579   ERRMSG3  DS     0CL58
```

Figure 2.31. continued.

```
580          DC    CL45'ON THIS SCREEN, ONLY <ENTER> AND <CLEAR> KEYS'
581          DC    CL13' ARE ALLOWED.'
582 ERRMSG4  DS    0CL58
583          DC    CL45'INVALID WISH. VALID WISH CODES ARE I=INQ, S=S'
584          DC    CL13'ET, R=REFRESH'
585 ERRMSG5  DS    0CL58
586          DC    CL45'INVALID RESOURCE TYPE. ENTER DA,TRAN,PROG, OR'
587          DC    CL13' JOURN.'
588 ERRMSG6  DS    0CL58
589          DC    CL45'USER ID AND/OR PASSWORD YOU ENTERED NOT MATCH'
590          DC    CL13'ED. TRY AGAIN'
591 ERRMSG7  DS    0CL58
592          DC    CL45'REQUESTED ACTION PERFORMED. CONFIRM IT BY ISS'
593          DC    CL13'UING INQUIRE.'
594 ERRMSG8  DS    0CL58
595          DC    CL45'VALID STATUS VALUES FOR FILES ARE OP, CL, ENA'
596          DC    CL13'B, DISAB.'
597 ERRMSG9  DS    0CL58
598          DC    CL45'FREE ERROR MESSAGE SLOT.'
599          DC    CL13' '
600 ERRMSG10 DS    0CL58
601          DC    CL45'YOU ARE NOT AUTHORIZED FOR THIS FILE. SORRY.'
602          DC    CL13' '
603 ERRMSG11 DS    0CL58
604          DC    CL45'YOU ARE NOT AUTHORIZED FOR THIS TRANSACTION.'
605          DC    CL13'SORRY.'
606 ERRMSG12 DS    0CL58
607          DC    CL45'THE SPECIFIED TRANSACTION NOT DEFINED TO CICS'
608          DC    CL13'. CHECK IT.'
609 ERRMSG13 DS    0CL58
```

```
610          DC    CL45'VALID STATUS VALUES FOR TRANSACTIONS: ENAB,    '
611          DC    CL13'DISAB.       '
612 ERRMSG14 DS    0CL58
613          DC    CL45'YOU ARE NOT AUTHORIZED FOR THIS PROGRAM. SORR'
614          DC    CL13'Y.           '
615 ERRMSG15 DS    0CL58
616          DC    CL45'REQUESTED PROGRAM NOT DEFINED TO CICS. CHECK '
617          DC    CL13'IT PLEASE.   '
618 ERRMSG16 DS    0CL58
619          DC    CL45'VALID STATUS VALUES FOR PROGRAMS ARE: ENAB OR'
620          DC    CL13'DISAB.       '
621 ERRMSG17 DS    0CL58
622          DC    CL45'SPECIFIED PROGRAM HAS BEEN REFRESHED. THANK  '
623          DC    CL13'GOD.         '
624 ERRMSG18 DS    0CL58
625          DC    CL45'NO RESOURCES SELECTED. HAVE A GOOD DAY AND A '
626          DC    CL13'GOOD NIGHT.  '
627 ERRMSG19 DS    0CL58
628          DC    CL45'YOU CAN ONLY CLOSE JOURNAL TO WHICH YOU ARE A'
629          DC    CL13'UTHORIZED.   '
630 ERRMSG20 DS    0CL58
631          DC    CL45'YOU MAY NOT ACCESS THIS JOURNAL. HAVE A GOOD '
632          DC    CL13'DAY.........'
633 ERRMSG21 DS    0CL58
634          DC    CL45'JOURNAL SPECIFIED HAS BEEN OPENED. HAVE A WON'
635          DC    CL13'DERFUL DAY.  '
636 ERRMSG98 DS    0CL58
637          DC    CL45'ERROR MESSAGE 98 IN BEMTPG1. CONTACT BARRY K.'
```

Figure 2.31. continued.

183

```
638          DC    CL13' NIRMAL.'
639 ERRMSG99  DS    0CL58
640          DC    CL45'CATASTROPHIC ERROR DETECTED IN BEMTPG1.  CONTA'
641          DC    CL13'CT B. NIRMAL '
642 *=================================================================*
643 APPLID    DS    CL8
644 FROMLEN   DC    H'1280'
645 FROMDATA  DC    CL80'????????'
646          DC    CL80'JOURNAL YOU SPECIFIED HAS BEEN CLOSED. NOW YOU CAN'
647          DC    CL80'RUN YOUR BATCH JOBS. WHEN BOTH THE JOURNAL DATA '
648          DC    CL80'SETS HAVE BEEN FORMATTED, AND YOU WANT ME TO OPEN '
649          DC    CL80'THIS JOURNAL FOR YOU, TYPE MAGIC WORD ON TOP LEFT '
650          DC    CL80'CORNER OF THE SCREEN AND PRESS ENTER KEY. I WILL '
651          DC    CL80'THEN OPEN THE JOURNAL FOR YOU. WAIT TILL I INFORM '
652          DC    CL80'YOU THAT YOUR JOURNAL HAS BEEN OPENED SUCCESSFULLY'
653          DC    CL80' '
654          DC    CL80' $$$ WARNING $$$  WARNING $$$$$ WARNING $$$$$ ----'
655          DC    CL80' '
656          DC    CL80'DO NOT TYPE MAGIC WORD UNTIL YOUR JOURNAL HAS BEEN'
657          DC    CL80'FORMATTED, ELSE SERIOUS SYSTEM PROBLEM WILL OCCUR'
658          DC    CL80' '
659          DC    CL80'CONTACT MR. NIRMAL, DESIGNER OF THIS PGM FOR HELP'
660          DC    CL80' '
661 CEMTCLN   DC    H'26'
662 CEMTIND   DC    X'00'
663 CEMTOLN   DC    H'80'
664 *=================================================================*
665          DFHEISTG
666          COPY  BEMTMS1
667          COPY  BEMTMS2
```

184

```
668            COPY BEMTMS3
669 *=================================*
670 CEMTOUT    DS   CL80
671            DS   0D
672 CEMTPARM   EQU  *
673 PARMCMD    DS   F
674 PARMCLN    DS   F
675 PARMIND    DS   F
676 PARMOUT    DS   F
677 PARMOLN    DS   F
678 *=================================*
679 CEMTCMD    DS   CL9        'SET DATA('
680 CEMTOBJ    DS   CL8
681 CEMTPAR    DS   CL1        RIGHT PARA
682 CEMTACT    DS   CL8
683 *=================================*
684 KOUNT      DS   PL3        99 99 9C
685 OKOUNT     DS   CL6        ZZZZZZ
686 DD00       DS   CL8
687 DSN00      DS   CL44
688 OUTMSG     DS   0CL58
689 MSG1       DS   CL12
690            DS   C
691 MSG2       DS   CL12
692            DS   C
693 MSG3       DS   CL12
694            DS   C
695 MSG4       DS   CL12
```

Figure 2.31. continued.

185

```
696              DS    C
697              DS    CL6
698     *-------------------------------------------------*
699     FOPST    DS    F
700     FENST    DS    F
701     TENST    DS    F
702     PLANG    DS    F
703     PTYPE    DS    F
704     PENST    DS    F
705     TRAN     DS    CL4
706     PROGRAM  DS    CL8
707     FILENAME DS    CL44
708     SWENDBR  DS    C
709     *-------------------------------------------------*
710     COMM01   DS    0CL40    COMMUNICATION AREA PASSED TO BEMTPG2
711     CUSER    DS    CL8      USER ID ENTERED BY THE USER
712     CPWD     DS    CL8      PASSWORD ENTERED BY TH USER
713     CTYPE    DS    C        TYPE OF ENTRY TO VALIDATE: F=FILE,P=PROG,T=TRAN
714     CENTRY   DS    CL8      RESOURCE NAME AS ENTERED BY THE USER ON SCREEN
715     CFLAG    DS    C        FLAG SET BY BEMTPG2: P= PASSED, F = FAILED
716     CFILLER1 DS    C        FOR FUTURE USE
717     CASTFND  DS    C        FLAG SET BY BEMTPG2: ASTERISK IN RESOURCE NAME
718     *                       ENTERED BY USER: Y = FOUND, N = NOT FOUND
719     CWISH    DS    C        WISH OF USER: I=INQUIRE, S = SET, R = REFRESH
720     CFILLER  DS    CL11     FOR FUTURE USE
721     *-------------------------------------------------*
722     TOLEN    DS    H
723     TODATA   DS    CL8
724              END
*****************************************************************
```

Figure 2.31. continued.

```
**********************************************************************
    1   *============================================================*
    2   * DATE    |USER  | DESCRIPTION OF CHANGE                      *
    3   *---------|------|-------------------------------------------*
    4   *YY/MM/DD|NIRMAL|NEW PROGRAM                                  *
    5   *--------|------|--------                                      *
    6   *        |      |                                             *
    7   *============================================================*
    8           COPY  REGDEF
    9   BEMTPG2 DFHEIENT CODEREG=(10,11),DATAREG=12,EIBREG=3
   10           L     R4,DFHEICAP
   11           CLI   16(R4),C'U'    CALLER ASKING TO VERIFY USER ID AND PWD?
   12           BE    USERRTN        YES, BRANCH
   13           CLI   16(R4),C'F'    CALLER ASKING TO VERIFY FILE ID?
   14           BE    FILERTN        YES, BRANCH.
   15           CLI   16(R4),C'T'    CALLER ASKING TO VERIFY TRANSACTION ID?
   16           BE    TRANRTN        YES, BRANCH
   17           CLI   16(R4),C'P'    CALLER ASKING TO VERIFY PROGRAM ID?
   18           BE    PROGRTN        YES, BRANCH
   19           CLI   16(R4),C'J'    CALLER ASKING TO VERIFY JOURNAL ID?
   20           BE    JOURNRTN       YES, BRANCH.
   21   *============================================================*
   22   GOBACK  EQU   *
   23           EXEC CICS RETURN
   24   *============================================================*
   25   JOURNRTN EQU  *
   26           LA    R5,JOURN01
   27           B     NODE01
```

Figure 2.32. Source code of program BEMTPG2

```
28  FILERTN  EQU  *
29           LA   R5,FILE01
30           B    NODE01
31  TRANRTN  EQU  *
32           LA   R5,TRAN01
33           B    NODE01
34  PROGRTN  EQU  *
35           LA   R5,PROG01
36           B    NODE01
37  NODE01   EQU  *
38  *=====================================================*
39  * DECIDE IF INPUT ENTRY (8 BYTES) HAS AN ASTERISK ANYWHERE IN IT.
40  *=====================================================*
41           MVI  27(R4),C'N'      BE PESSIMISTIC. IT HELPS.
42           L    R8,=F'8'
43           LA   R9,17(R4)        POINT R9 TO RESOURCE NAME ENTERED BY USER
44  LOOPAA   EQU  *
45           CLI  0(R9),C'*'
46           BE   ASTFND
47           LA   R9,1(R9)
48           BCT  R8,LOOPAA
49           B    NEXTWORK
50  ASTFND   MVI  27(R4),C'Y'
51  *=====================================================*
52  NEXTWORK EQU  *
53           CLI  28(R4),C'I'      ONLY INQUIRING?
54           BNE  NORM02           NO, BRANCH
55           MVI  25(R4),C'P'      PASS HIM; HE IS ONLY INQUIRING.
56           B    GOBACK
57  NORM02   EQU  *
```

```
58            CLC   0(8,R5),=CL8'ZZZZZZZZ'    END OF TABLE?
59            BE    GOBACK
60            CLC   0(8,R5),0(R4)        MATCH FOUND?
61            BE    FLOOP99              YES, BRANCH.
62  FLOOP2    EQU   *
63  *=============================================================*
64  * ADVANCE R5 UNTIL IT POINTS TO A NEW USER ID SLOT
65  *=============================================================*
66            LA    R5,8(R5)            ADVANCE R5 TO NEW SLOT IN TABLE
67            CLC   0(8,R5),=CL8'$$$$$$$$'
68            BNE   FLOOP2
69            LA    R5,8(R5)        ADVANCE R5 TO NEW SLOT
70            B     NORM02
71  FLOOP99   EQU   *
72  *=============================================================*
73  * R5 POINTS TO THE CORRECT        SLOT IN FILE, TRAN, PROG OR
74  * JOURNAL AREA IN THE AUTHORIZATION TABLE.
75  *=============================================================*
76            LA    R5,8(R5)        ADVANCE R5 TO NEXT SLOT IN TABLE.
77            CLC   0(8,R5),=CL8'$$$$$$$$'
78            BE    GOBACK
79            CLI   0(R5),C'*'
80            BE    PASSED
81            LR    R6,R5
82            LA    R7,17(R4)        POINT R7 TO RESOURCE NAME ENTERED BY USER
83            L     R8,=F'8'
84  LOOP00    EQU   *
85            CLI   0(R6),C'*'
```

Figure 2.32. continued.

189

```
86          BE    PASSED
87          CLC   0(1,R7),0(R6)
88          BE    NEXTCHAR
89          B     FLOOP99
90  PASSED  MVI   25(R4),C'P'
91          B     GOBACK
92  *==================================================*
93  NEXTCHAR EQU  *
94          LA    R7,1(R7)
95          LA    R6,1(R6)
96          BCT   R8,LOOP00
97          B     PASSED
98  *==================================================*
99  USERRTN EQU   *
100         LA    R5,USER01
101 LOOP1   EQU   *
102         CLC   0(8,R5),=CL8'ZZZZZZZZ'
```

```
103             BE    GOBACK
104             CLC   0(8,R4),0(R5)
105             BE    TESTPWD
106   ADVANCE1  EQU   *
107             LA    R5,16(R5)
108             B     LOOP1
109   TESTPWD   EQU   *
110             CLC   8(8,R5),8(R4)
111             BNE   ADVANCE1
112             MVI   25(R4),C'P'
113             B     GOBACK
114   *========================================================*
115             COPY  BEMTAUTH
116             DFHEISTG
117             END
******************************************************************
```

Figure 2.32. continued.

```
***********************************************************
********************************************
*  AUTHORIZATION TABLE USED BY PROGRAM BEMTPG2.
********************************************

 1
 2
 3
 4   USER01    DC    CL8'Z2BKN  '
 5             DC    CL8'Z2BKN  '
 6   USER02    DC    CL8'Z3BKN  '
 7             DC    CL8'Z3BKN  '
 8   USEREND   DC    CL8'ZZZZZZZZ'
 9   FILE01    DC    CL8'Z2BKN  '
10             DC    CL8'*      '
11             DC    CL8'$$$$$$$$'
12   FILE02    DC    CL8'Z3BKN  '
13             DC    CL8'T*     '
14             DC    CL8'$$$$$$$$'
15   FILEEND   DC    CL8'ZZZZZZZZ'
16   TRAN01.   DC    CL8'Z2BKN  '
```

```
17          DC    CL8'*        '
18          DC    CL8'$$$$$$$$'
19   TRAN02 DC    CL8'Z3BKN   '
20          DC    CL8'C*      '
21          DC    CL8'$$$$$$$$'
22   TRANEND DC   CL8'ZZZZZZZZ'
23   PROG01 DC    CL8'Z2BKN   '
24          DC    CL8'*       '
25          DC    CL8'$$$$$$$$'
26          DC    CL8'Z3BKN   '
27          DC    CL8'C*      '
28          DC    CL8'$$$$$$$$'
29   PROGEND DC   CL8'ZZZZZZZZ'
30   JOURN01 DC   CL8'Z2BKN   '
31          DC    CL8'*       '
32          DC    CL8'$$$$$$$$'
33   JOURNEND DC  CL8'ZZZZZZZZ'
```

****

Figure 2.33. Source code of copybook BEMTAUTH

However, the applications programmers and analysts need a facility with which they can refresh their programs, open/close their application files, or enable/disable their transactions. Such a facility is presented in this section. This facility is designed so that a particular user can be granted access to only a limited number of resources, such as transactions, files, programs, and journals that belong to his or her application. This restriction is beneficial to everyone and helps to stabilize the CICS system as a whole.

In some shops, the system programming group denies the CEMT transaction to the applications staff, particularly in the production regions. So, when a systems analyst needs to close or open one or more files belonging to his or her application, he has to either telephone or visit his friendly system programmer, who performs this function for him. This is definitely not in the interest of the applications staff, who would like to have a facility wherein they could do these things themselves, without being dependent on someone else. Such a facility is described in this section.

Procedure for Installing This Facility

Step 1. Enter the content of Figure 2.28 in member BEMTMS1 of a source PDS. Enter the content of Figure 2.29 in member BEMTMS2, the content of Figure 2.30 in member BEMTMS3, the content of Figure 2.31 in member BEMTPG1, and the content of Figure 2.32 in member BEMTPG2 of the same source library.

Step 2. Enter the copybook shown in Figure 2.33 in member BEMTAUTH of a PDS used to contain macros and copybooks.

Step 3. Assemble and link the map shown in Figure 2.28 using the JCL given in Section B.4 in Appendix B. This job will create load module BEMTMS1 in a load library that must be allocated under DDname DFHRPL in the CICS start-up procedure or JCL. This job will also create copybook member BEMTMS1 in a copybook library. This copybook member will be required when assembling program BEMTPG1.

Step 4. Assemble and link the map shown in Figure 2.29 using the JCL given in Section B.4 in Appendix B. This job will create load module BEMTMS2 in a load library that must be allocated under DDname DFHRPL in the CICS start-up procedure or JCL. This job will also create copybook member BEMTMS2 in a copybook library. This copybook member will be required when assembling program BEMTPG1.

Step 5. Assemble and link the map shown in Figure 2.30 using the JCL given in Section B.4 in Appendix B. This job will create load module BEMTMS3 in a load library that must be allocated under DDname DFHRPL in the CICS start-up procedure or JCL. This job will also create copybook member BEMTMS3 in a copybook library. This copybook member will be required when assembling program BEMTPG1.

Step 6. Now change the content of BEMTAUTH, created in Step 2, to suit your requirements. See "Rules for Setting Up Authorization Table in BEM-TAUTH" in this section which will help you in this. But to start with, you may just use the entries shown in Figure 2.33, because they are used here to illustrate the concepts. After you become familiar with this facility, you may then change the authorization table to suit your requirements. Remember, every time you make a change to the authorization table in BEMTAUTH, you must assemble and link program BEMTPG2, which is the authorization checking program.

Step 7. Assemble and link program BEMTPG2 using the JCL given in Section B.2 in Appendix B. This job will require that the name of the macro library in which you stored copybooks REGDEF and BEMTAUTH be allocated under DDname SYSLIB in the assembly step. (See lines 8 and 115 in Figure 2.32.) This job will create load module BEMTPG2 in a load library. This load library must be allocated under DDname DFHRPL in the CICS start-up procedure or JCL.

Step 8. Assemble and link program BEMTPG1 using the JCL given in Section B.2 in Appendix B. This job will require that the name of the macro library in which you stored copybooks REGDEF, BEMTMS1, BEMTMS2, and BEMTMS3 be allocated under DDname SYSLIB in the assembly step. (See lines 1, 666, 667, and 668 in Figure 2.31.) This job will create load module BEMTPG1 in a load library. This load library must be allocated under DDname DFHRPL in the CICS start-up procedure or JCL.

Step 9. Ask the CICS system programmer to define the following entries in CICS tables:

Definition of Mapset BEMTMS1 in the PPT

```
MAPSET  BEMTMS1
GROUP   CICSBOOK
RSL     00
STATUS  ENABLED
```

Definition of Mapset BEMTMS2 in the PPT

```
MAPSET  BEMTMS2
GROUP   CICSBOOK
RSL     00
STATUS  ENABLED
```

Definition of Mapset BEMTMS3 in the PPT

```
MAPSET  BEMTMS3
GROUP   CICSBOOK
```

```
RSL      00
STATUS   ENABLED
```

Definition of Program BEMTPG1 in the PPT

```
PROGRAM   BEMTPG1
GROUP     CICSBOOK
LANGUAGE  ASSEMBLER
```

Definition of Program BEMTPG2 in the PPT

```
PROGRAM   BEMTPG2
GROUP     CICSBOOK
LANGUAGE  ASSEMBLER
```

Other parameters for BEMTPG1 and BEMTPG2 in the PPT should be the same as those for the sample program BNPROG1, given in Section 1.6.

Definition of Transaction BEMT in the PCT

```
TRANSACTION  BEMT
GROUP        CICSBOOK
PROGRAM      BEMTPG1
```

Other parameters for BEMT in the PCT should be the same as those for the sample transaction BNC1, given in Section 1.6.

Step 10. Execute transaction BEMT, as shown below, under "HOW TO USE THIS FACILITY", and make sure it works. If there is an error, execute the transaction under CEDF, find and correct the cause of the problem, and test this facility again.

Rules for Setting Up the Authorization Table in BEMTAUTH

You must understand the rules for creating entries in this table. Let us illustrate the rules by studying the content of Figure 2.33.

Line Explanation

```
4  User ID of the first user is Z2BKN.
5  Password of this user is Z2BKN.
6  User ID of the second user is Z3BKN
7  Password of the second user.
8  Signals the end of the User ID table.
```

9 Start of file entries for user Z2BKN. The user ID specified here need not be that of the first user in the user ID table.

10 Specifies that user Z2BKN is allowed to access any file.

11 Signals the end of file entries for this user.

12 Start of file entries for user Z3BKN.

13 Specifies that this user is allowed to access all files whose DDname starts with character T.

14 Signals the end of file entries for this user.

15 Signals the end of file entries for all users.

16 Start of transaction entries for user Z2BKN. The user ID specified on this line need not be that of the first user in the User ID table.

17 Specifies that this user has access to all transactions.

18 Signals the end of transaction entries for this user.

19 Start of transaction entries for user Z3BKN.

20 Specifies that this user can access all transaction IDs that start with character C.

21 Signals the end of transaction entries for user Z3BKN.

22 Signals the end of transaction entries for all users.

23 Start of program entries for user Z32BKN. This user ID here need not be that of the first in the user ID and password table.

24 Specifies that this user can access all programs.

25 Signals the end of program entries for this user.

26 Start of program entries for user Z3BKN

27 Specifies that this user is authorized to access programs whose ID starts with character C.

28 Signals the end of program entries for this user.

29 Signals the end of program entries for all users.

30 Start of journal entries for user Z2BKN.

31 Specifies that this user can access all journals.

32 Signals the end of journal entries for this user.

33 Signals the end of journal entries for all users.

Some Remarks about This Table.

1. The line with label USER01 signals the start of the user ID and password table. This table is ended with a line that has CL8'ZZZZZZZZ'. The line with label FILE01 signals the start of file entries for all users. These entries are similarly ended with a line that has CL8'ZZZZZZZZ'. The line with label TRAN01 signals the start of transaction entries for all users. These entries are again ended with a line that has CL8'ZZZZZZZZ'. The line with label PROG01 signals the start of program entries for all users. These entries are ended with a line that has CL8'ZZZZZZZZ'. The line with label JOURN01 signals the start of journal entries for all users. These entries are ended with a line

that has CL8'ZZZZZZZZ'. These are the only labels required. Other lines may or may not have labels, but having them helps by making the tables readable, as shown by Figure 2.33.

2. If a user has no authorization for a particular resource, that user need not be present in the table for that resource. For example, in the sample authorization table of Figure 2.33, user Z3BKN has no access to journals. So, this user's entries are missing from the journal table.

3. Suppose you wanted to prevent user Z3BKN from accessing any files. To achieve this, you could simply delete line 13 from Figure 2.33. Another way to achieve the same result would be to delete lines 12, 13, and 14. In either case, you would have to reassemble and link program BEMTPG2 so that the new authorization copybook gets included in the load module of BEMTPG2.

4. The user ID specified in resource tables need not be in the same sequence as that in the user ID and password table.

5. Because a user can have access to none, one, or more than one resource, the resource entries for each user must be ended with a line that has CL8'$$$$$$$$'.

6. This facility provides unrestricted access to resources for inquire only. But a user must be present in the table in order to perform sign-on and obtain the screen shown in Figure 2.35. So what you can do is define a user ID that can be used by everyone in the EDP department for inquiry purpose only. This user should not be present in the individual resource tables. The reason is that the author feels that the EDP programmers and analysts should be allowed to inquire against resources without restriction. This ability helps in quick problem solving and does no harm, because one can only inquire; one can't inadvertently change status of resources.

7. The same user ID should not be present more than once in the user ID and password table and in the resource tables. If duplication is present, the first entry from the top will be the one used in authorization checking, and the duplicates will be ignored.

How to Use This Facility

On a blank screen, type BEMT and press the Enter key. A screen resembling the one shown in Figure 2.34 will appear. On this screen, enter your user ID and password and press the Enter key. If the user ID and password you entered are present in the authorization table that is included in the load module of authorization checking program BEMTPG2, you will receive a screen resembling the one shown in Figure 2.35. If either the user ID or password you entered is not present in the table, the program will redisplay the same map along with a message to this effect. Note also that, on the Figures 2.34 and 2.35 screens, only Enter and Clear keys are valid. The Clear key on all

```
C170TST1      NIRMAL'S FACILITY TO INQUIRE/SET STATUS OF CICS RESOURCES


        ENTER YOUR  USER ID HERE  ====>>      _____
                       AND
                YOUR PASSWORD HERE  ===>>



SYSTEM MESSAGE:

PRESS <ENTER> TO RECEIVE THE MAIN SCREEN.  PRESS <CLEAR> TO EXIT
```

Figure 2.34. First screen displayed when user enters BEMT on a blank screen

```
C170TST1        NIRMAL'S FACILITY TO INQUIRE/SET STATUS OF CICS RESOURCES

USER ID: Z2BKN

YOUR WISH (I,S,R)==>      I
RESOURCE TYPE  =====>     DA
RESOURCE NAME  ====>      SGTLIB1
DESIRED STATUS =====>

SYSTEM ANSWER 1:   FILE NAME =      CICS.GENEROL.TST1.SGTLIB1.KSDS
SYSTEM ANSWER 2:   OPEN             ENABLED

PRESS <ENTER> TO PERFORM WORK.  <CLEAR> TO QUIT
-----------------------------------------------------------------------
WISH:      I= INQUIRE     S= SET   R= REFRESH A PROGRAM OR MAP
RESOURCE TYPE: DA= FILE TRAN=TRANSACTION PROG= PROGRAM OR MAP JOURN= JOURNAL
STATUS: OP= OPEN CL= CLOSE ENAB= ENABLE DISAB= DISABLE
INQUIRY IS PERMITTED EVEN IF RESOURCE(S)  REQUESTED ARE NOT INCLUDED IN TABLE.
FOR INQUIRING FILES, RESOURCE NAME CAN BE FULL OR GENERIC. E,G, BK* IS GENERIC.
SUPPOSE WISH=S, RESOURCE NAME=AB* .  THIS WILL AFFECT ALL RESOURCES WHOSE NAME
STARTS WITH AB. THIS IS TRUE FOR FILES AND TRANSACTIONS ONLY AS OF THIS RELEASE.
JOURNALS CAN ONLY BE CLOSED, THEN OPENED.
```

Figure 2.35. Main screen displayed when user enters correct user ID and password on the screen shown in Figure 2.34.

```
SGTLIB1   CICS.GENEROL.TST1.SGTLIB1.CLUSTER     OPEN     ENABLED
SGTLIBU   CICS.GENEROL.SGTLIBU.CLUSTER          OPEN     ENABLED




ENTER= NEXT PAGE OF DATA PF3= EXIT TO MAIN SCREEN     CLEAR= EXIT     NO MORE
```

Figure 2.36. A sample of the screen displayed when user enteres generic file name on the main screen

three screens terminates this transaction and gives you a blank screen where you can enter any CICS transaction.

Now, suppose you receive the second screen as shown in Figure 2.35. This is the main screen of this facility. Here you can enter I, INQ, S, or SET in the WISH field. "I" stands for Inquire, and "S" stands for Set or Change. In the RESOURCE TYPE field, you specify whether you want to work on a program, a transaction, and so on. The valid values allowed in all the fields are given at the bottom of the screen. In the RESOURCE NAME field, you can either specify the full or generic name of the resource. A full name is one that does not contain an asterisk, whereas a generic name contains an asterisk at the end of the name. In the DESIRED STATUS field, you enter the type of action you want performed, provided your WISH is to Set. The valid values that can be entered in this field depend on the type of resource. That is, programs, transactions, and files can be enabled or disabled, but a program or transaction cannot be opened or closed. Files can be opened or closed.

A journal can only be closed on this screen, as indicated on the last line of Figure 2.35. After you close a journal, the program will display a screen on which you will have to enter the so-called magic word in the top left corner of the screen in order to open that journal. The magic word is hard-coded in program BEMTPG1 and it is LOVEHATE. You can change this magic word and reassemble BEMTPG1 if you are concerned about security exposure.

When would you need to close a journal? The facility for closing a journal is desired when a journal is open on CICS and you want to process the data on that journal, reformat it, and then reopen it on CICS. You should first disable the main transaction for your application so that the users cannot use the system. Then you can close the journal on the screen of Figure 2.35 by entering S in the WISH field, JOURN in the RESOURCE TYPE field, journal ID (e.g., 20) in the RESOURCE NAME field, and CLOSE in the DESIRED STATUS field. The program will inform you that the journal has been closed. You can then process the data on that journal and then reformat the journal. Only then do you enter the magic word on the screen and press the Enter key. The program will then open the journal for you and display the main screen of Figure 2.35. The reason why the journals are handled this way is that CICS requires that *when a task closes a journal, the same task must open it*. If a task closes a journal and then ends without opening it, another task will not be able to open it.

Let us further explain how to use this facility through some examples of man-machine dialog:

Example 1: Suppose a user wants to inquire the status of all files whose DDname starts with string VPPA. He or she then enters the following data and presses the Enter key:

```
YOUR WISH: I
RESOURCE TYPE: DA
RESOURCE NAME: VPPA*
```

The system will display a screen similar to that of Figure 2.36, containing one line for each file whose DDname has VPPA in the first four positions. On each line, the first field is the DDname, the second field is the full data set name, the third field indicates whether the file is open or closed, and the last field indicates whether the file is enabled, unenabled, or disabled. If the bottom right-hand corner of the screen shows NO MORE, this means there are no more files to display, and the Enter key will take the user to the main screen of Figure 2.25. However, if the bottom right-hand corner of the screen has . . . MORE, this means that there are more files, and pressing the Enter key will display the next set of files. On the screen of Figure 2.36, the user may decide that he does not want to view any more files. If so, he can press PF3 to go back to the main screen.

Example 2: A user wants to close all files whose DDname starts with string PAY. He or she can enter the following data and press the Enter key:

```
YOUR WISH: S
RESOURCE TYPE: DA
RESOURCE NAME: PAY*
DESIRED STATUS: CL
```

The system will send a confirmation message indicating that the requested action was taken. The user can verify this simply by changing the S in the WISH field to I and pressing the Enter key. The program will then display a screen similar to Figure 2.36, showing the status of all files whose DDname is or starts with string PAY. All files should display as CLOSED.

Example 3: Suppose a user has forgotten the DDnames under which his application's files are allocated to CICS. He or she can display all the files defined to CICS by entering the following and pressing the Enter key:

```
YOUR WISH: I
RESOURCE TYPE: DA
RESOURCE NAME: *
```

The program will display a screen like that in Figure 2.36. On this screen, the user presses the Enter key to display the next page of the screen, and PF3 to return to the main screen. Since the files displayed are in ascending sequence of DDnames, the user can easily find out the information he is looking for.

Example 4: A user wants to inquire as to the status of program BNCOBOL1. He or she can enter the following data and press the Enter key:

```
YOUR WISH: I
RESOURCE TYPE: PROG
RESOURCE NAME: BNCOBOL1
```

If this program is not defined to CICS, a message to this effect will be displayed, otherwise the following information about this program will be displayed:

> Program's language
>
> Whether it is a program or map
>
> Whether it is enabled or disabled

Example 5: A user has compiled and linked a new version of program BNROUTE and wants to refresh it on CICS. Without this refreshing, CICS would continue to use the previous version of this program. The user can enter the following and press the Enter key:

```
YOUR WISH: R
RESOURCE TYPE: PROG
RESOURCE NAME: BNROUTE
```

The program will send a confirmation message and thank God for having made this possible. (Remember, even if you want to refresh a mapset, you must enter PROG in the RESOURCE TYPE field, because a mapset is also considered an assembler language program.)

Example 6: Suppose a user wants to disable transaction GOL1. He or she can do so by entering the following and pressing the Enter key:

```
YOUR WISH: S
RESOURCE TYPE: TRAN
RESOURCE NAME: GOL1
```

The system will send a confirmation message indicating that the desired action was taken. The user can verify this by simply changing the WISH field from S to I and pressing the Enter key.

Example 7: A user wants to know the program associated with transaction GOL2 as well as other information about this transaction. He or she can enter the following and press the Enter key:

```
YOUR WISH: I
RESOURCE TYPE: TRAN
RESOURCE NAME: GOL2
```

If this transaction is not defined to CICS, the program would send a message to this effect, otherwise the response will indicate the program ID associated with this transaction, and whether GOL2 is enabled or disabled.

Example 8: A user wants to inquire about mapset BNMAPS1. He or she can do so by entering the following and pressing the Enter key:

```
YOUR WISH: I
RESOURCE TYPE: PROG
RESOURCE NAME: BNMAPS1
```

The program will display the status of BNMAPS1, indicating whether it is enabled or disabled and also indicating whether it is a program or a map. (Note: Even if you are inquiring about or changing the status of a map, you must enter PROG in the RESOURCE TYPE field. This is because a map is considered an assembler program. Note that the explanation at the bottom of Figure 2.35 indicates that the RESOURCE TYPE must be PROG for both programs and maps.)

Explanation of How This Facility Works

When you type BEMT on a blank screen and press the Enter key, CICS searches the PCT and finds that BEMT is associated with program BEMTPG1. So, it gives control to this program, shown in Figure 2.31. Execution starts with the first executable statement. On line 5 thru 9, we are setting up traps for future possible use. On line 11, we are checking if the length of the communication area passed to this program is zero. This would be the case if you entered BEMT on a blank screen. So control would flow to line 487, which has the label INITIAL. On line 488, we store in field APPLID, the VTAM application ID of the CICS region. On line 490, we send the first map BEMTMS1, after erasing what might already be on the screen. Next, we execute the RETURN command and specify BEMT in the TRANSID option and pass out 8 bytes at COMM01 using the COMMAREA option. So, control is passed to CICS, and the task is terminated. But CICS has been told that the next time the user presses any key on that terminal, transaction BEMT is to be started and the program is to receive the 8 bytes communication area being passed out.

Now suppose that program BEMTPG2 has been assembled with the authorization table shown in Figure 2.33. Suppose further that the user enters Z2BKN as user ID and Z2BKN as the password on the sign-on screen and presses the Enter key. The control then flows to the first executable statement in program BEMTPG1. The test being made on line 15 would be true, because the length of communication area passed is 8. So, control flows to line 19 with the label AGAIN01. And since the Enter key was pressed, control would flow to line 26 with the label ENTER01. On line 27, we receive the map and store the data entered into fields in working storage. Next, we store the user ID and password entered in the fields under COMM01, and, on line 32, we LINK to program BEMTPG2, passing it 40 bytes at COMM01 as communication area.

BEMTPG2 is the authorization checking program. It always receives a 40-byte area as communication area, whose layout is at COMM01 in BEMTPG1.

In this case, field CTYPE, at line 713 in Figure 2.31, contains U, meaning that the request is to check if the user ID and password stored in CUSER and CPWD, respectively, are in the authorization table. Program BEMTPG2 would carry out the validation, and if they were in the table, it would place P in field CFLAG (line 715 in Figure 2.31), and if they were not in the table, it would leave CFLAG unchanged. In this example, since user ID and password entered are in the table, BEMTPG2 would move P in CFLAG, and control would come back to line 34 in Figure 2.31. On line 39, the main map BEMTMS2 would be displayed after erasing what might already be on the screen. On line 40, the RETURN command is issued to terminate the task and specify BEMT under TRANSID and pass out 40 bytes at COMM01 as communication area.

So, the user is now presented with the map of Figure 2.35. Let us suppose that the user enters I in the WISH field, TRAN in the RESOURCE TYPE field, and GOL1 in the RESOURCE NAME field, and then presses the Enter key. CICS then starts transaction BEMT and passes the 40-byte area, passed before, to the program. So, control flows to the first executable instruction in Figure 2.31. Again, on lines 5 through 9, traps would be set up. And on line 13, we check if the length of the communication area passed is 40. Since this is true, control would flow to line 45 with the label AGAIN02. On line 47, we store 40 bytes of the incoming communication area into storage area at COMM01. Next, we check if the Enter key was pressed. Since this is the case, control flows to line 56 with label ENTERKEY. On line 57, we receive the data entered on map and store them in working storage. On line 66, the comparison being made would be true, and control would flow to line 71. On lines 72 through 86, we store data in various fields. On line 89, we are checking if the resource type entered on the screen is TRAN. In this example, this would be the case, and control would flow to line 433 with the label TRANRTN. On line 434, we move T to CTYPE, which will indicate to BEMTPG2 that the resource whose authorization checking is being requested is transaction. Then, on line 437, we LINK to BEMTPG2, passing it to the 40-byte communication area at COMM01.

BEMTPG2 will find that the WISH in the communication area is inquire. So, it will pass it, because inquiry is unrestricted. (See lines 53 through 56 in Figure 2.32.) So, BEMTPG2 would move P in field CFLAG in the communication area at COMM01. Control would then flow to line 439 in Figure 2.31. On line 441, a test is made if the wish of the user is to inquire. In this example, this would be true; so, control would flow to line 471 with label INQTRAN. On line 473, the INQUIRE TRANSACTION command is issued. If the transaction ID being inquired is not defined to CICS, control would flow to label TRANERR. This is due to the trap set up on line 7. Let us suppose that this transaction is defined to CICS. So, CICS stores in field PROGRAM the program ID associated with the transaction being inquired. It stores in field TENST the Enabled/Disabled status of the transaction. On lines 475 through 484, we move proper values in fields that will appear on the map. Then we branch to label FINITO on line 344. On line 346, the cursor is positioned at the WISH field. Next, we branch to label GOBACK, on line 537. On line 538, the main map is displayed again with the DATAONLY option. This is followed by the RETURN command on line 539, which terminates the task. The user is now viewing the map that responds to his inquiry in the SYSTEM ANSWER 1 and SYSTEM ANSWER 2 fields.

At this point, the user can enter any other data in the various keyable (unprotected) fields on the screen and press the Enter key to process data entered, or he can press the Clear key to terminate the transaction and receive a blank screen where any valid CICS transaction can be entered.

We have described in sufficient detail what happens when the user enters one set of values in the fields on the main map shown in Figure 2.35. If you want to understand the flow of control through the programs for some other combination of data, you can easily do so. The information given above, about using this facility and the way the authorization checking is carried out, will also help you obtain a good understanding of these two programs. Only good comprehension will enable you to modify these programs to suit your unique needs, or to write similar programs to meet your needs. The CICS commands INQUIRE TRANSACTION, INQUIRE PROGRAM, INQUIRE DATA SET, SET PROGRAM, SET TRANSACTION, and SET DATA SET, are described in the following IBM publication: *CICS/VS Customization Guide* (manual number: SC33-0239). Other CICS commands are described in the following publication: *CICS/VS Application Programmer's Reference Manual (Command Level)* (Manual Number: SC33-0241).

Program BEMTPG1, in some situations, executes a CEMT transaction by linking to program DFHEMTA (see lines 117, 128, 130, 150, and 450 in Figure 2.31). This works the same way as if you entered that CEMT transaction on the terminal, but the command is not entered on the terminal and the result of execution is not displayed. The procedure for executing the CEMT transaction in a program is described in the following IBM publications: *CICS-Supplied Transactions* (manual number: SC33-0240) and *CICS/VS Customization Guide* (manual number: SC33-0239).

3

Commonly Asked Questions Regarding Application Programming Answered

In this chapter, we answer some questions that are commonly asked by the application programmer. But the concepts discussed here are of great interest to the system programmer as well. This is because a system programmer must have good knowledge of application programming in order to be most effective in his or her job. The author was asked most of the questions in this chapter by programmers, both application and system, as well as by data processing managers, application systems managers, and others, during the course of his work as a consulting CICS specialist at corporations in Canada and Saudi Arabia.

3.1 USER ENTERS ON BLANK SCREEN A TRANSACTION ID FOLLOWED BY PARAMETERS. HOW CAN I ACCESS THE PARAMETERS IN A COMMAND LEVEL PROGRAM?

Let us first consider a COBOL program. Suppose your program is designed so the user can enter the transaction ID (4 characters) followed by a parameter of up to 20 characters. For example, the user can enter transaction ID PAY1, followed by a slash, followed by employee number, (8 characters) of the employee whose record is to be inquired, as follows:

PAY/109014500

So, you have to do the following:

1. Define in the working storage the following:

```
01  CICS-LEN-24    PIC S9(4) COMP SYNC VALUE +24.
```

```
01  WS-DATA-IN.
     05 TRANS-ID-IN  PIC X(4).
     05 PARM-IN    PIC X(20).
```

2. In the Procedure Division, you can do this:

```
PROCEDURE DIVISION.
     EXEC CICS IGNORE CONDITION LENGERR END-EXEC.
     EXEC CICS RECEIVE INTO(WS-DATA-IN) LENGTH (CICS-LEN-
     24)
     END-EXEC.
```

After the RECEIVE command has executed, the first 24 characters of whatever the user entered on the screen is available in WS-DATA-IN. (If the user entered less than 24 characters, the content of WS-DATA-IN would be what the user entered followed by one or more bytes, which, in this example, would be binary zeros, because they are not changed by the execution of the RECEIVE command.) The first 4 characters of WS-DATA-IN must be transaction ID for this program, otherwise control would not have come here. You can now examine the content of PARM-IN and take appropriate action.

The reason why we have the IGNORE CONDITION command is that the user may only enter the transaction ID, or he or she may enter the transaction ID followed by more than 20 characters. So, if the IGNORE CONDITION LENGERR command is omitted, and more than 24 characters are entered on the screen, a LENGERR condition would occur, and if you did not provide for it through a HANDLE CONDITION command, your program would abend.

In an assembler program, the technique is similar. For a sample program in command level that captures the parameter entered by the user, see program BNUTLO1 in Figure 2.8 in Chapter 2 for COBOL, and see program BNUTLO2 in Figure 5.13 in Chapter 5 for Assembler.

3.2 EXPLAIN HOW THE INTERNAL SECURITY OF CICS WORKS. HOW CAN I PROTECT A TRANSACTION SO THAT ONLY SPECIFIC USERS CAN USE IT?

Suppose your transaction ID is PAY2 and you want only certain users to be able to access this transaction. This is the procedure:

Step 1. Assign a security key in the range 2 through 64. Suppose you assign the key of 30. This transaction's definition in the PCT (on the DFHCSD file) must have TRANSEC = 30. (Remember, if a transaction has TRANSEC = 1, any user can access it without having to first perform sign-on using the CSSN transaction.)

Step 2. Now decide on a name, ID, and password to be defined in the sign-on table that can access this transaction. Let's say the name is PAY1ABC; the

ID, PAY (should be three characters); and password, XYZ1. Define an entry in the CICS sign-on table (DFHSNT) that has the following parameters among other required ones:

```
EXTSEC=NO,
OPNAME=PAY1ABC,
OPIDENT=PAY,
PASSWRD=XYZ1,
SCTYKEY=(1,30),
```

EXTSEC=NO specifies that external security is absent on this CICS. OPI-DENT is a three-character string that is the ID of this user. SCTYKEY has two keys here, 1 and 30. The security key of 1 is given to everyone by default, whether it is specified in the SNT or not. By including 30 under SCTYKEY of this user, we have allowed him to access all transactions that have a security key of 30 in their definitions.

Step 3. Assemble and link the sign-on table as load module DFHSNT. This table will be picked up on the next start-up of CICS. Make sure the correct definition of PAY1 with TRANSEC = 30 will also be picked up at the next start-up of CICS.

Step 4. Give the user name and password to the users who are authorized to access PAY1 and wait for the next start-up of CICS.

Now, suppose a user has not performed sign-on using CSSN or has performed sign-on using a user name and password that does not have 30 in the SCTYKEY parameter in the SNT. When such a user tries to access PAY1 by entering PAY1 on a blank screen, he will be greeted with the message SE-CURITY VIOLATION HAS BEEN DETECTED at the bottom of the screen. This message will also be logged to the CICS log, so the system programmer will know the ID and the terminal where an attempt was made to access PAY1. This log can initiate an investigation into why that user was trying to access a secured transaction.

Users who know the name of PAY1ABC and password of XYZ1 can access this transaction. They must first sign-on to CICS using CSSN. CSSN will ask them for the user name and password. They must enter PAY1ABC in the user name field and XYZ1 in the password field and press the Enter key. They should then get a SIGN-ON COMPLETE message at the bottom of the screen. Now they can clear the screen and enter PAY1. They should receive the first screen displayed by the program associated with transaction PAY1.

This is how the internal security of CICS works. Remember, a transaction has only one key assigned to it, while an entry in the sign-on table can have multiple security keys assigned to it under SCTYKEY parameter. A user who has performed sign-on using a user name and password combination can access all transactions whose security key matches with one of the keys specified under SCTKEY parameters in that user's entry in the SNT.

3.3 AFTER RELINKING A NEW VERSION OF A PROGRAM, HOW CAN I TELL CICS TO USE THE NEW VERSION?

After CICS start-up, if you have linked a new version of a program, you must issue either of the following commands for CICS to pick up the new version from the load library:

```
CSMT NEW,PGRMID=progname
CEMT S PROG(progname) NEW
```

where progname is to be replaced with the program name defined in the PPT or on the DFHCSD file. When you use the CEMT command, you will receive a screen displaying the size of the new load module. On this screen, press PF3 to get out and then press the Clear key.

Now suppose you want to refresh all programs whose name starts with string BKN. There are two ways of doing this:

Method 1: issue the following command:

```
CEMT S PROG(BKN*) NEW
```

When the CEMT screen appears, press PF3 to quit and then press the Clear key.

Method 2: Issue the following to inquire about all programs that start with BKN:

```
CEMT I PROG(BKN*)
```

This will display a screen with this command minus CEMT appearing on the top line. There will be one line for each program whose ID starts with BKN. If you want to refresh all programs, change the top line to the following and then press the Enter key:

```
S PROG(BKN*) NEW
```

But you may like to refresh only some of the programs displayed. So, with the tab key, take the cursor to the end of the program line that you want to refresh and add NEW to the end of the line. Do this with each program you want refreshed. Then press the Enter key. You will receive the confirmation message NEWCOPY at the end of each line indicating programs that were refreshed.

3.4 HOW CAN I ENSURE THAT MY PAYROLL MASTER FILE CAN ONLY BE READ AND NEVER UPDATED BY A CICS PROGRAM?

Your payroll master file must be defined in the FCT (File Control Table) of the CICS region. In the FCT entry for every file, there is one parameter called

SERVREQ, which stands for service request. If you want an application program to be allowed only to read and browse this file, ask your CICS system programmer to make sure that this parameter for your payroll master file is as follows:

```
SERVREQ=(READ,BROWSE),
```

If you want a VSAM file to be available for all kinds of operations by application programs, make sure all options are present under SERVREQ for this file, as follows:

```
SERVREQ=(READ,BROWSE,UPDATE,ADD,DELETE),
```

A path for an alternate index cluster should have only READ, BROWSE under SERVREQ. This means the alternate index file is only for reading or browsing and not updating records on the base cluster.

3.5 CAN I CHANGE THE DEFINITION OF A TRANSACTION—FOR EXAMPLE, PROGRAM NAME AND SECURITY KEY DYNAMICALLY—WHILE CICS IS UP?

Yes. Use the restricted CEDA transaction to copy the definition of the transaction to a temporary group called TEMPNIRM. Then change the definition of the transaction in TEMPNIRM. Make sure TEMPNIRM has only one entry, i.e., your transaction, and no other entry. Now issue the following to activate the new definition of your transaction on the running system:

```
CEDA INSTALL G(TEMPNIRM)
```

Make sure the install was successful. It might not be if some task in the system is using your transaction. If so, wait until that task finishes and then try installing again. Now, the new definition of your transaction should be active. If you want to make the change permanent, you should alter the definition of this transaction in its proper group, which is included in the list for the CICS.

This facility is useful in situations like these. Suppose transaction ABC1 is associated with program PROG1, but for some reason you want to associate it with program PROG2 temporarily. Or suppose that a transaction has a security key which is not part of your user ID, but you have access to CEDA transaction and want to execute that transaction. You can use the procedure given above to change the security key of the transaction to a value that your user ID has. After installing TEMPNIRM containing the new definition, you would be able to use the transaction.

Note that using transaction CEDA and following a procedure similar to the one described above enables you to change the definition of any program, transaction, or terminal in a running CICS system.

3.6 EXPLAIN HOW I CAN SHARE A VSAM FILE AMONG DIFFERENT REGIONS, E.G., CICSPRD1, CICSPRD2, AND A BATCH REGION.

Suppose you have a VSAM file that has been defined using the DEFINE command of Access Methods Services with share options of (2.3). (Defining all VSAM files with share options of 2,3 is strongly recommended.) You want to perform all kinds of operations—read, browse, update, delete, etc.—through CICS application programs. So, this file's FCT entry must have the following:

```
SERVREQ=(READ,BROWSE,UPDATE,ADD,DELETE)
```

Once this file is opened on CICS, it cannot be opened on another region, batch, or CICS for update. So if you want to read this file on another CICS, makes sure its FCT entry on that CICS has the following:

```
SERVREQ=(READ,BROWSE)
```

This will allow it to be opened on another CICS region, but only for read and browse. This file can also be opened by a batch program for read and browse. For example, you can use the PRINT command of IDCAMS to print records on this file in a batch job.

Similarly, if you want a file to be updated only through batch jobs, you have to make sure that in all CICS systems where this file is defined, its FCT entry has only READ and BROWSE under the SERVREQ parameter. Then this file can be opened on multiple CICS regions for read and browse only, and at the same time, it can be opened by a batch program for read or update.

3.7 MY BILLING TRANSACTIONS FILE IS OPEN ON CICSPRD1. WHAT MUST I DO TO DELETE, REDEFINE, AND LOAD IT?

Before you can delete a VSAM file, either through TSO or a batch job, you must make sure that it is not allocated to any other user in the system. If your billing transactions file is open on CICSPRD1, you should close it on CICSPRD1. To close the file using an on-line facility, you can use the IBM-supplied CEMT transaction or the BEMT transaction presented in Section 2.15 in Chapter 2. You can also close it through a batch job using the program presented in Section 2.11 in Chapter 2. These tools will close the file, and CICS will automatically deallocate or free your file from CICSPRD1. If this file is open on any other CICS regions, you must close it on those regions as well. (If you are running a CICS release earlier than 1.7, you may have to close the file on CICS and then deallocate it using the ADYN transaction.)

Confirm that your file is indeed freed up from CICSPRD1 and any other region by using a TSO command called WHOHAS. (This command may be called something else at your installation.) For example, from option 6 of TSO/ISPF, issue this command:

```
WHOHAS 'full.name.of.your.file'
```

If the response is that this file is not allocated to any user, you can proceed to delete it using the IDCAMS DELETE command, redefine it using the IDCAMS DEFINE command, and reload it using the IDCAMS REPRO command. The command WHOHAS can be used with any kind of file.

3.8 MY CUSTOMER MASTER FILE IS OPEN ON CICSTST1 FOR UPDATE. WHAT MUST I DO TO UPDATE IT USING A BATCH PROGRAM?

Assuming that your master file has been correctly defined with share options (2,3), you will not be able to open this file for update (e.g., OPEN I/O in a COBOL program) in a batch program. So, you must do one of two things before you can run your batch program:

Option 1. Close it on CICSTST1, or

Option 2. Using CEMT, close and disable it on CICSTST1. Then change its service requests dynamically to READ, BROWSE only. Then open and enable it and ensure that its service requests are READ and BROWSE only, nothing else.

As regards Option 1, you can close it using IBM-supplied transaction CEMT or the BEMT transaction presented in Section 2.15 in Chapter 2. You can also close it through a batch job using the program presented in Section 2.11 in Chapter 2. These tools will close the file and CICS will automatically deallocate or free your file from CICSTST1.

As for Option 2, you must use transaction CEMT, which will enable you to carry out all activities on the same screen, one after another, after you have issued CEMT I DA(ddname). Read the chapter on CEMT in *CICS-Supplied Transactions* manual for more information.

3.9 IN MY CICS COBOL PROGRAM, CAN I INVOKE AN ASSEMBLER ROUTINE THAT IS ALSO CALLED BY BATCH PROGRAMS? HOW SHOULD SUBROUTINES BE DESIGNED TO BE INVOKED THROUGH CALL OR EXEC CICS LINK?

The answer to the first question is: Yes, you can. Let us explain this using program BNDATETI given in Figure 2.1. This is a simple command level COBOL program that calls date conversion routine BNDATE. On line 110 in this figure we have:

```
CALL 'BNDATE' USING IN-TYPE OUT-TYPE CD-CURR-DATE-G.
```

where IN-TYPE and OUT-TYPE are defined in the working storage section and CD-CURR-DATE-G is defined in the linkage section. BNDATE is an assembler routine that can be invoked via the CALL statement of COBOL from a batch COBOL or a CICS command level COBOL program. This routine can also be invoked via the CALL macro from a batch assembler or a CICS command level assembler program.

In all cases, the load module of the called routine is linked with the calling program by the linkage-editor, provided the calling COBOL program was compiled using NODYNAM option. So the load module for the calling program, which in this example is BNDATETI, includes the load module of the called subroutine, which is BNDATE. Because of this, the size of the calling program increases. Imagine a CICS system that has 100 programs in virtual storage, each of which calls the date conversion routine. So, you have a situation where the date conversion routine of perhaps 1000 bytes is present in 100 load modules. Would it not be better if the date conversion routine was a separate module that would be invoked via the LINK command of CICS? Undoubtedly it would be, because this way you would save around 90K of storage, having only one copy of the date conversion routine in virtual storage instead of 100 copies.

Also, imagine a program that calls 10 different subroutines. Because the load module of the calling program includes all the called routines, its size may become enormous, and it may contribute to a virtual storage shortage in the CICS region.

To alleviate this virtual storage shortage, you should design a routine as a separate CICS subprogram that can be invoked by means of EXEC CICS LINK command. Such a routine is not linked with the calling program. When there is shortage of virtual storage, CICS, using a process called program compression, gets rid of programs that are in storage but are not being used.

3.10 HOW CAN I INVOKE A COBOL SUBPROGRAM DESIGNED TO BE CALLED BY A BATCH COBOL PROGRAM IN MY CICS COMMAND LEVEL COBOL PROGRAM?

Suppose you have a COBOL subprogram that receives two fields. The length of the first field can be from 1 to 1024 bytes; the second field indicates the length of the first field. This program works on the first field and modifies its content in some way. **This program only modifies the first n bytes of the first field where n is the value of the second field.** This program will appear as follows:

```
IDENTIFICATION DIVISION.
PROGRAM-ID. MODPGM1.
- - - -
WORKING-STORAGE SECTION.
- - - -
```

```
LINKAGE SECTION.
01 FIRST-FIELD   PIC X(1024).
01 SECOND-FIELD  PIC 9(4).
PROCEDURE DIVISION USING FIRST-FIELD SECOND-FIELD.
- - - -
```

Suppose this subprogram is compiled and linked into a load library as member MODPGM1. In a batch or a CICS command-level program, it can be called by means of the following statement:

```
CALL 'MODPGM1' USING AREA-TO-BE-MODIFIED AREA-LENGTH.
```

where AREA-TO-BE-MODIFIED and AREA-LENGTH would normally be defined in the working storage section, but they could also be in linkage section. When the calling program is compiled and linked, the linkage editor will include the load module of MODPGM1 into the output load module for the calling program, assuming that NODYNAM option was used while compiling the calling program.

So, the way you call a COBOL subprogram is the same, whether the calling program is for execution in batch or under CICS command level.

A few words of caution: We pointed out that program MODPGM1 only modifies n bytes of the first field where n is specified in the second field passed to it. But suppose that program MODPGM1 has a flaw (bug) in it. It has a field called WS-F1 in the working storage with PIC X(1024). In the linkage section, it has FIRST-FIELD defined with PIC X(1024). Suppose, in the procedure division, it does this:

```
MOVE FIRST-FIELD TO WS-F1.
```

Then it modifies first n bytes of WS-F1 where n is the value in SECOND-FIELD. After that, rather than moving only n bytes from WS-F1 to FIRST-FIELD, it errs by executing this:

```
MOVE WS-F1 TO FIRST-FIELD.
```

This moves 1024 bytes into FIRST-FIELD. Now suppose that in the GENER/OL work area or in a calling COBOL program, we have defined the first parameter (PARM1) as having a length of 70 bytes rather than 1024 bytes. When MODPGM1 is called, it will first move 1024 bytes from the calling program's first parameter area (PARM1) into WS-F1, which is in its own working storage section. It will change first 70 bytes of WS-F1 and then it will move 1024 bytes into the calling program's first parameter area (PARM1). This will cause 70 bytes to be moved into PARM1 and 954 (1024–70) bytes to be moved beyond. This means some other area that does not belong to the calling program's task might get overlaid, causing storage violation in CICS. This could even cause the whole CICS to crash down, if a critical control block of CICS, such as the CSA, was overlaid.

3.11 HOW CAN I INVOKE A COBOL SUBPROGRAM DESIGNED TO BE CALLED BY A BATCH COBOL PROGRAM IN MY GENER/OL PROGRAM?

Consider the COBOL subprogram MODPGM1 discussed in Section 3.10. This subprogram can easily be called in a GENER/OL program, provided you first perform the following two steps:

   a. Compile and link MODPGM1 in the same way you compile and link batch COBOL programs. The load library where it resides must be allocated to CICS under DDname DFHRPL.

   b. In CICS PPT, specify the language of MODPGM1 as assembler and not COBOL, even though the program really is written in COBOL.

Now let us talk about using it. Suppose in a work area with prefix W1 you have the following two fields:

```
Field            Starts at        Length       Type        Comments

FIELD            1                1024         C
LENGTH           1040             4            N
```

The starting positions of the fields can be anything. In the program, if you want the first 10 bytes of W1FIELD to be modified, you would need to do this:

```
MOVE  10 to W1LENGTH
CALL  (MODPGM1), W1FIELD, W1LENGTH
```

3.12 HOW CAN I ENSURE THAT CICS WILL BACKOUT THE EFFECT OF AN INCOMPLETE TRANSACTION IN THE EVENT IT IS TERMINATED ABNORMALLY?

To illustrate the concepts of recovery and backout, let us use an example that you can simulate on your own CICS test system. Suppose you have transaction BNC3 that is associated with program BNCOBOL3, which is shown in Figure 3.1. This is a command-level program. BNC3 has INDOUBT = BACKOUT in its definition on the DFHCSD file. (In fact, at the author's installation, all transactions have INDOUBT = BACKOUT.) In program BNCOBOL3, we add a record to file SPCLFILE. This is followed by the CONVERSE command, which results in a message being sent to the terminal, and the task gets suspended. The user must enter something on the terminal and press the Enter key, at which time control will come back to the program, the task will be activated, and the ABEND command that follows the CONVERSE command will get executed, causing the task to abend with abend code BARY.

After the task has ended, will the file contain the record that was added using the WRITE command? Well, it depends. If file SPCLFILE is defined in the file control table with LOG = YES, and a value other than NO for JID, then this record will be removed by CICS when the task abends, and if it has LOG = NO, then the record added will not be removed by CICS. Why does CICS remove the record? It is related to the concepts of **recovery, backout, logical units of work (LUWs), in-flight tasks**, and **syncpoint**.

The reason why CICS removes the record is that file SPCLFILE is defined as recoverable in the FCT (LOG = YES), and the task had abended. If a task is abnormally terminated, all changes made by the task to recoverable resources, including files, are backed out. The process of restoring the resources associated with a task is called **backout**. A task that has not yet completed is said to be **in-flight**.

The backout can occur in two circumstances. If an individual task fails, the backout is performed by the dynamic transaction backout (DTB) program, which is part of CICS. If the whole CICS abnormally terminates while a task is in-flight, the backout is performed as part of the **emergency restart** process.

You can simulate the emergency restart process as follows. Define SPCLFILE in your test system's file control table as a file with RECFORM = (VARIABLE, BLOCKED), LOG = YES, and JID = SYSTEM. Define this file with key length of 13, average record length of 80, and maximum record length of 200. Enter the code given in Figure 3.1 in a data set and compile it. Execute the transaction associated with this program. When the program executes the CONVERSE command, it will send a message to the terminal and wait for the user to enter something on the terminal. At this point, the task should appear suspended, when you display all the tasks in the system using the CEMT I TASK command. Now cancel the CICS region using the cancel command on MVS console. Then restart CICS and make sure START = AUTO option of SIT is effective. This will cause the system to start in emergency mode. After the system has come up, list the contents of file SPCLFILE. You will find that the record added by the task during the previous life of CICS is not there. This confirms that this record was removed during the emergency restart process.

If a program is long-running and updates many files, you may not want *all* changes made by it to be backed out in the event of abnormal termination of the program. You can achieve this by using the SYNCPOINT command to split the program into logically separate sections, termed **logical units of work (LUWs)**. The end of an LUW is called a synchronization point (**sync point**).

In addition to those points marked by SYNCPOINT commands, sync points also occur at the end of a task and at each DL/I termination or checkpoint (CHKP) call. For the purposes of backout, each of these sync points is treated as if it marked the end of a task. If a program or CICS fails after a sync point,

```
IDENTIFICATION DIVISION.
PROGRAM-ID. BNCOBOL3.
AUTHOR.    BARRY K. NIRMAL.
ENVIRONMENT DIVISION.
DATA DIVISION.
WORKING-STORAGE SECTION.
01  RECORD-LENGTH          PIC S9(4) COMP SYNC.
01  TO-LENGTH              PIC S9(4) COMP SYNC.
01  WS-FILE-RECORD.
    05 FILE-KEY            PIC X(13) VALUE '1234567890123'.
    05 FILE-DATA           PIC X(10) VALUE 'ABCDEFGHIJ'.
01  WS-MSG-IN              PIC X(80).
01  WS-MSG-OUT             PIC X(80) VALUE
    'ENTER ANYTHING ON SCREEN AND PRESS ENTER KEY'.
PROCEDURE DIVISION.
    EXEC CICS IGNORE CONDITION LENGERR END-EXEC.
```

```
MOVE +23 TO RECORD-LENGTH.
EXEC CICS WRITE FROM(WS-FILE-RECORD)
    DATASET('SPCLFILE')
    LENGTH(RECORD-LENGTH)
    RIDFLD(FILE-KEY)
    END-EXEC.
EXEC CICS CONVERSE FROM(WS-MSG-OUT)
    FROMLENGTH(80)
    INTO(WS-MSG-IN)
    ERASE
    MAXLENGTH(80)
    TOLENGTH(TO-LENGTH)
    END-EXEC.
EXEC CICS ABEND ABCODE('BARY') END-EXEC.
GOBACK.
```

Figure 3.1. Complete listing of a sample program to test that changes to recoverable files are backed out if task ends abnormally.

but before the task has completed, only changes made since the sync point are backed out.

To simulate a sync point, insert the following command before the CONVERSE command in the code given above:

```
EXEC CICS SYNCPOINT END-EXEC
```

Now, when the task abends due to the ABEND command, or when you cancel the CICS region when the task gets suspended at CONVERSE command, the record added to the file is not removed. This is because of the SYNCPOINT command, which marked the end of LUW.

3.13 I HAVE HEARD THAT CERTAIN VSAM FILES CAN BE DECLARED "RECOVERABLE." EXPLAIN WHAT THIS MEANS AND HOW IT CAN IMPROVE MY APPLICATION

There are two aspects to the problem of recoverability. One is related to keeping all files that are updated by a task in synchronization, and the other is related to our ability to repair a file without losing updates made to the file on-line if it suddenly gets corrupted or damaged.

Keeping All Files Updated by a Task in Synchronization

If a task updates multiple files and then ends abnormally, you may want all changes made to those files to be backed out so the files are in synchronization. This is because the task may have updated one file but not the other, and if the changes made to the first file are not backed out, the two files will not be in synchronization. For example, consider a banking application where an on-line program transfers money from one type of account to another. Assume that these two types of accounts are based on two different files. The program is designed to subtract the transfer amount from the first account and then to add the same amount to the other account. Now suppose that after the program has updated the first account file, but before it updates the second file, it abends.

So you have a situation where the customer's first account has been debited but the second account has not been credited. This means the two files are not in synchronization. If this situation is not remedied, it means certain loss of reputation for the bank.

How do we ensure that the files are kept in synchronization? We do this by defining them as recoverable in the file control table. This is done by having LOG=YES and a value other than NO for JID. When a file is marked recoverable in the FCT, any changes made to it by a task from the last sync point are backed out in the event of abnormal termination of the task. This was explained in the previous section.

Ensuring That Files Can Be Repaired without Losing On-Line Updates

Suppose you have a file that is updated by CICS transactions. This file could be a master file or a file to collect transactions data entered by the users. You have this file's backup that was taken before CICS was started. After 10 hours of update through CICS, the file is damaged. Now what do you do? You can delete the file, redefine it, and restore it from the backup taken earlier, but the updates made to it through CICS for 10 hours would be lost. The users would not agree to it unless you were working in a country where life is dull, where computer people are revered, and users never complain about anything these "saints" do. But, thanks to CICS, you don't have to be a saint to keep the user happy.

CICS provides a facility that enables you to recover files without losing any data. A file can be marked recoverable in the file control table by having LOG = YES and a value other than NO for JID. Suppose you have JID = 10, which means that journal 10 would be used to log changes. Now anytime a change is made to the file, whether by adding, deleting, or modifying records, a log of all such changes is kept by CICS in the journal dataset allocated under DDname DFHJ10A or DFHJ10B. When a file is damaged, you have to do the following:

Restore it from the last backup.

Run a program that will read the journal data set(s) and apply all changes made to it through CICS transactions after its last backup was taken. The program you run here can be one of many programs such as McKinney Systems Forward Recovery System (FRS).

Now your file is restored. You can open it on CICS and ask the users to use the transactions that access this file. The users may have lost some time in using the on-line system while you were repairing the file, but they have not lost any data.

3.14 CAN I HAVE MORE THAN ONE MAP IN A MAPSET?

Yes, you can, but this is not advisable. It is better to have a single map in each mapset. If a mapset has multiple maps, the mapset's load module contains code for all the maps. Suppose you have MAPSET1 that has four maps, MAP1, MAP2, MAP3, and MAP4. So, when you execute in your program:

```
EXEC CICS SEND MAP('MAP1') MAPSET('MAPSET1') END-EXEC
```

CICS brings into virtual storage the load module for MAPSET1, provided it is not already there. At this point, the user may decide to end the transaction and do something else. So, MAPSET1 is silently lying in virtual storage, occupying storage space until it is used again, probably a few hours later.

Now suppose you create one mapset for each of the four maps. So, you have MAPSET1, MAPSET2, MAPSET3, and MAPSET4, each containing a single map. Now, when you execute in your program:

```
EXEC CICS SEND MAP('MAP1') MAPSET('MAPSET1') END-EXEC
```

CICS brings into virtual storage the load module for MAPSET1, provided it is not already in storage. Even if this mapset is not used for a long time, there is not much loss, because its size now is small.

3.15 WHICH IS DEFINED IN CICS PPT—MAP OR MAPSET?

It is the mapset and not the map that is defined in the PPT or on the on-line resource definition file (DFHCSD). A mapset can have one or more maps within it. Only the mapset needs to be defined in the PPT; the maps contained within a mapset are not defined in the PPT.

3.16 WHEN I VIEW THE STATUS OF A FILE, I FIND IT IS CLOSED AND UNENABLED. EXPLAIN THE DIFFERENCE BETWEEN ENABLED, DISABLED, AND UNENABLED STATES OF A FILE.

If a VSAM file is closed and enabled, CICS will automatically open it upon first reference to this file in an application program, e.g., EXEC CICS READ in a command-level program. So, if a file is closed and enabled, and there is no reference to it during the whole day, it will remain closed and enabled at the end of the day.

Now, suppose a file is open and enabled, and you close it using IBM-supplied CEMT transaction or the BEMT transaction given in Chapter 2. CICS will change its status to closed and unenabled. This will prevent CICS from opening it either upon reference to the file in an application program or upon next warm start of CICS. The reasoning here is that since you closed it, probably for deleting the data set and redefining it, you know best when it should be opened. So, CICS will not interfere with your work. Once you are ready, you must open it using the CEMT transaction or the BEMT transaction presented in Chapter 2. When you open a file that has closed and unenabled status, CICS will automatically make it enabled.

Another point to remember is that if a file has the status of closed and unenabled at CICS termination time, its status will remain unchanged after CICS is restarted. The moral of the story is that if you closed a file using any tool, you must open it yourself. Otherwise, your application program will not be able to access it.

If a file is disabled, it cannot be accessed by an application program, whether it is open or not. Some attributes of a file, such as the dataset name allocated to the file or its service requests, can be changed using the CEMT transaction, but the file must first be closed and disabled before you make the change. In the file control table, a file should have FILSTAT = (CLOSED, EN-ABLED), so that upon cold start of CICS, it will be remain closed and enabled.

3.17 SHOULD ALL VSAM FILES DEFINED IN CICS FCT HAVE SHARE OPTIONS OF (2,3)?

Definitely. As a general rule, all VSAM files, whether for production or test environments, should be assigned share options of (2,3) while defining them using the DEFINE command of IDCAMS. This provides for proper data integrity. A dataset with share options (2,3) can be opened for update by only one system task. In other words, if it is open on CICSTST1 for update, it cannot be opened for update by any other task, but it can be opened for input only by any number of tasks, including a batch region, another CICS region, and so on. You may change the share options of a VSAM file to (3,3) so that it can be opened for update by more than one system task. This, however, might lead to data corruption or loss of data integrity. The IBM manual that describes the DEFINE command of IDCAMS says that the (3,3) share options could result in "VSAM program checks, lost or inaccessible records, uncorrectable dataset failures, and other unpredictable results. This option places heavy responsibility on each user sharing the dataset." (*MVS Extended Architecture Integrated Catalog Administration: Access Method Services Reference*, manual number GC26-4019.) This type of data corruption leading to problems in CICS system was observed by the author at one installation in Saudi Arabia, where he was working as the Chief CICS System Programmer.

How do you find the share options of your VSAM file? Issue the following command from any of the TSO/ISPF panels:

```
LISTC ENT('your.vsam.cluster.name') ALL
```

The system will display all information about this file from the catalog, one of which will be the share options. If it is not (2,3), you might have to back up the file using IDCAMS REPRO, redefine it using IDCAMS DEFINE with proper share options, and then reload it with the records on the backup file using IDCAMS REPRO. While defining, place the following parameter under DE-FINE CLUSTER, not DATA or INDEX:

```
SHR (2,3) -
```

3.18 IS IT WISE TO MINIMIZE THE NUMBER OF VSAM FILES DEFINED TO CICS?

Yes, it is better to have fewer VSAM files in CICS. Every VSAM file requires virtual storage for control blocks needed for opening it. A VSAM file that is open also requires storage for buffers during file I/O. (Note: All buffers in an MVS/XA DFP system go above the 16-meg line.) So, the fewer the number of VSAM files that are open on CICS, the better for CICS performance as a whole. Although, when a file is closed, the storage space (OSCOR) used by the file gets released. A file's opening and closing contributes to fragmentation of storage space (OSCOR). So, it is not a good idea to open and close VSAM files unnecessarily.

3.19 SUGGEST SOME TECHNIQUES TO MINIMIZE THE NUMBER OF VSAM FILES DEFINED TO CICS.

The general guideline is to consolidate logically related records on one VSAM file but not to over-consolidate. For example, suppose you need to store the following types of records on one or more VSAM key-sequenced datasets:

> Records with system broadcast messages to be displayed on the terminal when a user signs on to the application (maximum of 24 records).
>
> Payroll control record for the current month (only one record).
>
> Records containing the cutoff dates for payroll data entry for each month of a year (one record for each year).

One approach would be to have one VSAM file containing system broadcast messages, another having payroll control records, and a third having records with cutoff dates for all years. In fact, a novice designer might even consider having multiple VSAM files for the cutoff dates, one file for each year. Such an approach would cause little problem if the files were to be used in a batch system, apart from the fact that one would have the headache of managing so many files.

But, in a CICS system, the approach of having a VSAM file containing only one or two records is not a good idea. In this example, it is better to have just one VSAM file containing the three types of records described above. A sample design showing the content of record on such a file is shown in Figure 3.2. The first 10 bytes of each record is the key, and the remaining 79 bytes are for data.

```
CUTOFF1891/20212020212324243320212324
CUTOFF1992/2023242521201921233202120
CUTOFF1983/23242021202418202122321
PYRMSG0001    ****** WELCOME TO THE PAYROLL SYSTEM **********
PYRMSG0002 THE SYSTEM IS NOW AVAILABLE FOR ON-LINE DATA ENTRY.
PYRMSG0003
PYRMSG0004 CONTACT MR. RICHARD SCOTT, PROJECT LEADER OF PAYROLL
PYRMSG0005 RESYSTEMIZATION PROJECT AT EXTENSION 9876 IN CASE
PYRMSG0006 OF TECHNICAL PROBLEMS. FOR NON-TECHNICAL PROBLEMS
PYRMSG0007 CONTACT MR. WALTER SMITH AT EXTENSION 1234.
PAYROLLCNTP00001R0004A9876545
```

Figure 3.2. The content of a sample VSAM KSDS containing three types of records.

3.20 CAN THE SAME APPLICATION SYSTEM IN CICS TEST REGION BE USED BY PROGRAMMERS FOR TESTING AND BY USERS FOR TESTING AND TRAINING? IF SO, SUGGEST SOME TECHNIQUES FOR DOING SO.

Every application system, unless it is very big and very complex, can be developed in a CICS test region, and the same region can be used to train the users. There is no reason why you need one region to develop the application and another region to train your users. There are many advantages to this approach. You can use the same set of VSAM files for testing and training. There is no need to migrate software elements including programs and file contents from one CICS region to another. This will avoid problems caused by keeping many versions of the applications software in different regions.

The system programming group does not have to support numerous CICS regions. Having too many CICS regions on the same MVS machine is bad for the MVS system as a whole. Here is just one reason why. There is only one storage area in MVS called the common service area (CSA). This area is used by many tasks including IMS/VS and ACF/VTAM. If CSA is depleted during the course of the day, a re-IPL of the computer will most likely be required.

Two Techniques for Sharing Files by DP Professionals and Users:

You may ask, "How do I use the same set of VSAM files for my own testing as well as for user training?" The answer to this very important question is as follows. Sometimes, depending on the application, you and your users can share the same files. For example, if your VSAM record key is a purchase order number, you can reach an agreement with your users that all purchase order numbers starting with EDP will be entered by the programmers and analysts and all other purchase order numbers will be entered by the users. This way, if the users see purchase order numbers such as EDP001 and EDP002 on the screen or reports, they would know that these were not entered by them.

If this technique is not suitable for your application, the following procedure will always work. You can develop the system in a test CICS region. When you are satisfied with the system, you initialize the VSAM files allocated to CICS and train the users on how to use the system. After your users have started entering data, you can use the same system for your own testing by following the step-by-step method given below.

Step 1. Tell your users that when they try to sign-on to the application and receive the message

```
SYSTEM IN USE BY EDP PEOPLE. PLEASE WAIT.
```

they should wait until the following message appears on the sign-on screen:

```
SYSTEM NOW AVAILABLE TO USERS.
```

Or you can tell your users that you would telephone your user contact person and tell him or her that the system is now available for their use.

Step 2. Change your sign-on validation program, or preferably, the authorization table, if you have one, so that if the user ID entered is that of an EDP person, let the user through, or display the following message:

```
SYSTEM IN USE BY EDP PEOPLE. PLEASE WAIT.
```

Step 3. Close the VSAM files on CICS test system using the IBM-supplied CEMT transaction or the BEMT transaction presented in Chapter 2. The files will also get deallocated from CICS. But if you want to confirm that a file is not allocated by any user in the system, you can issue the following command from any TSO/ISPF panel:

```
TSO WHOHAS 'full.name.of.data.set'
```

At your installation, program WHOHAS may be known by a different name. Ask your MVS system programmer for the name of this command.

Step 4. Use the IDCAMS REPRO command to copy VSAM files to sequential files on tape. This is to save the training data of the users.

Step 5. Delete the VSAM files, redefine them, and load them with test data previously saved in backup files on tape.

Step 6. Open the VSAM files on the CICS test system, using the CEMT transaction or the BEMT transaction presented in Chapter 2. Make sure all files are now open on CICS.

Step 7. You can now carry out your own testing for as long as you want.

Once you are finished with your own testing, follow the procedure described below to make the system available to the users:

Step 1. Close the VSAM files on CICS test system. Use the TSO WHOHAS command given above to confirm that the VSAM files are not allocated to any user in the system.

Step 2. Use the IDCAMS REPRO command to copy the content of VSAM files that contain your test data onto sequential files on tape.

Step 3. Delete the VSAM files, redefine them, and load them with training data on backup files that were previously created.

Step 4. Open VSAM files on CICS, using the CEMT transaction or the BEMT transaction presented in Chapter 2. Make sure all files are now open on CICS.

Step 5. Change your sign-on validation program or, preferably, the authorization table, so the users can now sign on to the application successfully.

Step 6. Inform the user representative by telephone that the system is now available for their use. He or she will inform the other users.

3.21 WITH BASE CLUSTER AND AUXILIARY INDEX CLUSTER, WHICH IS DEFINED IN CICS FCT—AUXILIARY INDEX CLUSTER OR PATH?

When you have a VSAM key-sequenced dataset and you want to access its records, not through the primary key but through an alternate key, you have to define an alternate index cluster for it, using the DEFINE ALTERNATEIN-DEX command of IDCAMS. Next, you define a path entry that relates the alternate index cluster to the base cluster. You do this using the DEFINE PATH command of IDCAMS. Then you have to load the alternate index cluster using the BLDINDEX command of IDCAMS. The alternate index cluster has records whose key portion contains the alternate key value, and the data portion contains the primary keys of records that have this alternate key.

Whereas the base cluster and alternate index clusters are physical entities and are present on the DASD, the path entry is simply an entry in the MVS catalog; it is not present on the DASD.

It is the path name that is defined in CICS FCT (File Control Table). When CICS opens the path, it is the alternate index cluster that gets opened.

3.22 IF I AM GOING TO USE THE AUXILIARY INDEX CLUSTER BUT NOT THE BASE CLUSTER, DO I HAVE TO DEFINE THE BASE IN CICS FCT?

No. If you are going to use only the DDname of the path entry defined in the File Control Table (FCT), there is no need to define the base cluster in the FCT. Remember, when you read the records using the path entry defined in the FCT, you are actually reading records from the base cluster. But since you are not going to read records directly from the base cluster, using the primary key, there is no need to define the base cluster in the FCT.

3.23 A VSAM FILE THAT HAS BEEN DEFINED BUT NOT LOADED WITH ANY RECORDS IS SUPPOSED TO BE IN "LOAD MODE." CAN I OPEN SUCH A FILE ON CICS?

Suppose you have defined a VSAM data set using the IDCAMS DEFINE command and have not loaded it with one or more records using IDCAMS REPRO, or some other program. Such a file is considered an empty file that is ready for loading and can be opened by CICS without any problem. CICS opens the file with the access methods control block (ACB) settings that are appropriate to a dataset in VSAM LOAD mode. When the first record has been added, or a MASSINSERT request is complete, CICS closes the dataset and leaves it ready to be opened with the attributes specified in the file control table.

Suppose you have an empty file that is open on CICS. You can issue EXEC CICS READ command to read a record, and it will return NOT FOUND response. You can issue EXEC CICS WRITE to write a record and it will succeed.

If a dataset is defined with the REUSE option in the MVS catalog, it is considered a work file. This is not a common situation, so we will not discuss it here.

Problem Determination Techniques for the Application Programmer

In this chapter, we present some techniques and tools that will be useful to the application as well as system programmers in problem solving. The question-answer format is used to present these techniques and tools.

4.1 EVEN AFTER RELINKING A NEW VERSION OF A PROGRAM AND DOING NEWCOPY, CICS STILL EXECUTES THE OLD COPY OF THE PROGRAM. HOW DO I SOLVE THIS PROBLEM?

To solve this problem, you must understand how CICS fetches programs into virtual storage for execution. In the CICS start-up procedure or job, there is a DDname called DFHRPL to which more than one dataset is normally allocated. For example, suppose one CICS test system has the following:

```
//DFHRPL DISP=SHR,DSN=CICS.RELXXX.LOADLIB2
//       DISP=SHR,DSN=CICS.RELXXX.LOADLIB
//       DISP=SHR,DSN=CICS.RELXXX.TEST.TABLES
//       DISP=SHR,DSN=CICS.TEST.SYSPROG.LOAD
//       DISP=SHR,DSN=CICS.TEST.APPLPROG.LOAD
```

Now suppose you compile and link program P1 into CICS.TEST.APPLPROG.LOAD and refresh it on CICS. Suppose further that this program does not exist in any other library allocated to DDname DFHRPL. So, when you execute this program, CICS will fetch the load module of P1 from CICS.TEST.APPLPROG.LOAD into storage and give control to it.

Now suppose you have compiled and linked a new version of program P2 into CICS.TEST.APPLPROG.LOAD and have issued the CSMT or CEMT transaction (or the BEMT transaction described in Section 2.15) on CICS to refresh it. P2 also resides in CICS.TEST.SYSPROG.LOAD. So, when this program is executed, CICS will search all datasets allocated under DFHRPL. The first dataset to be searched will be CICS.RELXXX.LOADLIB2; the next to be searched will be CICS.RELXXX.LOADLIB, and so on, because this is the order in which they are allocated under DFHRPL. So, CICS, finding program P2 in CICS.TEST.SYSPROG.LOAD, will load it into storage and pass control to it. Even though you linked a new version of P2 into CICS.TEST.APPLPROG.LOAD, it would not be used.

If you have a problem like this, proceed as follows. Note the length of the program displayed by issuing CEMT INQ PROG(program) command. The length displayed is in decimal. Check that it is the same as the length of the program displayed on the linkage-editor map, where it is displayed in hexadecimal. If the two lengths are not the same, the problem is evident. Find out the names and concatenation order of load libraries allocated under DFHRPL. Next, scan the directory of each of these libraries and find out which libraries contain the program. The load module in the first library (from the beginning of the concatenation) is the one that CICS will load and use.

4.2   HOW DO I FIND OUT WHY A TRANSACTION IS ABENDING WITH A CICS OR USER ABEND CODE?

With command-level programs, the best tool for diagnosing the abend of any kind is the CEDF transaction supplied by IBM as part of CICS. CEDF stands for CICS Execution Diagnostic Facility. It is one of the best software diagnostic tools that IBM ever produced. This facility allows you to test command-level programs on-line without modifying them. You can also test command-level programs for which only load modules (and not source) are available, like vendor programs such as GENER/OL. In fact, the author has used CEDF to trace the execution flow of GENER/OL programs in order to gain an understanding of how GENER/OL works. This was necessary in the absence of source code or adequate documentation about the internals of this product.

CEDF intercepts program execution at various points, including points where CICS commands are present, and displays information about it at these points. CEDF displays screens both before and after the execution of CICS commands. This allows the user to change things before command execution. CEDF also displays any screens sent by the application program so you can converse with the program and simulate actual execution of the program.

CEDF intercepts the program execution and displays the current status by indentifying the cause of interception at the following points:

1. At transaction initiation, after the EIB (EXEC Interface Block) has been initialized, but before the application program is given control.
2. At the start of the execution of every EXEC CICS and EXEC DLI command, after the initial trace entry has been made, but before the command has executed.

3. After executing every command, except ABEND, XCTL, and RETURN. This is done after the requested command has been performed, but before the HANDLE CONDITION mechanism has been invoked, and before the response trace entry is made.

4. At each program's termination.

5. At normal task termination.

6. At abnormal task termination.

7. When an ABEND occurs.

At any of these points of interception, you can do the following to aid in problem determination or speed things up:

1. If the current command is being displayed before it is executed, you can change the values of any parameter by overtyping the value displayed on the screen. You can also suppress command execution, but you cannot delete an existing parameter or add a new parameter to a command.

2. You can modify the program's working storage and most fields of the EIB and the DIB.

3. You can display the contents of any temporary storage queue. Press PF5 to display the working storage, then PF2 to invoke CEBR. From CEBR, when you press PF3 to end it, CICS will restore the original EDF working storage screen.

4. You can terminate EDF mode (except at point 2) and continue running the application without EDF.

5. You can force an abend.

6. You can request that displays by CEDF be suppressed until a specific condition, including execution of a specific command, or a specific exceptional condition occurs. You can specify these conditions by pressing PF9 (STOP CONDITIONS) on the EDF screen. Even if you do not specify the conditions using the STOP CONDITIONS key, certain default conditions will take effect, and you can use the SUPPRESS DISPLAY key on the screen to suppress displays. This will speed up the testing process.

How do I run my application under EDF? On a blank screen, type CEDF and press the Enter key. The system will respond by saying that the EDF mode is on. Clear the screen and enter the transaction code of the transaction to be tested. After that, keep on pressing the Enter key to trace through as program execution proceeds. The explanation of keys at the bottom of the screen will also help. For example, pressing PF4 will suppress displays. This is helpful if the transaction is pseudo-conversational and the point to be examined is very far ahead of where you currently are.

For further information on the CEDF transaction, refer to the chapter entitled "Execution (Command Level) Diagnostic Facility" in *Application Programmer's Reference Manual (Command Level)*.

4.3 WHAT ARE THE OTHER USEFUL TOOLS FOR PROBLEM DETERMINATION?

CICS application programmers should be familiar with the following transactions that are available to aid in problem determination:

> CEBR to browse any temporary storage queue
> CECI to interpret and execute any CICS command

The CEBR Transaction

This transaction allows you to browse and delete data on temporary storage queues. You can also copy data in a transient data queue into a temporary storage queue so that it can be browsed. The transient data queue can be an intrapartition data queue or an extrapartition data queue that is open for input. You can also copy the contents of a temporary storage queue being browsed to a transient data queue, which, again, can be an intrapartition queue or an extrapartition queue that is open for output.

To display the full list of commands that can be entered on the command line, enter CEBR without queue name. Then press PF1 to display help.

Press the Enter key on the help screen to return to the main screen.

Example 1: Suppose there exists a temporary storage queue named UTIL$$$$. You can browse it by issuing the following from a blank CICS screen:

```
CEBR UTIL$$$$
```

The response will indicate how many records there are in the queue, as well as the length of each record. If you want to purge all records of this queue and delete it, enter PURGE on the command line and press the Enter key. Do not use PURGE to erase the contents of an internally generated queue, such as the one for storing BMS logical message.

On the main screen displayed by CEBR, press PF3 to end the transaction, and press PF1 to obtain the help screen. From the help screen, press the Enter key to return to the main screen. Functions performed by other keys are shown at the bottom of the main screen.

Example 2: Suppose the name of a temporary storage queue is X'C100004040123400', i.e., it has nonprintable characters. To view it, do the following:

Enter CEBR on a blank screen. The main CEBR screen will be displayed. On the command line, enter the following and press the Enter key:

```
QUEUE X'C100004040123400'
```

For further information on the CEBR transaction, refer to the chapter entitled "Temporary Storage Browse" in *Application Programmer's Reference Manual (Command Level)*.

The CECI (CECS) Transaction

The CECI transaction is used to enter any CICS command permitted under command-level programming interface (except DL/I) for syntax checking and then, optionally, for execution. The results of execution can be displayed. So this transaction is useful to both application and system programmers:

Application programmers can use it for quick generation of test data online, simply by entering CICS commands. They can also use it to find out the full syntax of a command in case the command level reference manual is not handy. They can also use it for other purposes, as shown by examples below.

System programmers can use it to repair a damaged record on file or to create or delete a temporary storage queue, and so on. In this way, CECI is a natural extension of the CEMT transaction.

The fact that CECI can be used to execute any command means that it can be used to read or even update records in any file, even a sensitive file like a payroll master file. For this reason, many installations have made this transaction available only on the test CICS system.

Example 1: Suppose you want to read a record with key = 090157 from VSAM file PAYMAST. You can simply enter the following on a blank screen:

```
CECI READ DATASET('PAYMAST') RIDFLD('090157')
```

This will display a screen with the message ABOUT TO EXECUTE COMMAND. If you want to execute it, press the Enter key. The result of execution will be displayed on the screen. Suppose you left out the RIDFLD parameter. You will receive a screen showing the full syntax of the READ command. You can correct the error and press the Enter key to resubmit the command.

A question mark (?) before the command always gives the syntax check screen and prevents command execution. This will suit you if you are concerned about inadvertent execution of powerful commands, such as those that write or update records in files. If transaction CECS is used, it always forces a question mark before the command. So, if you are concerned about security, you may restrict CECI but make CECS more widely available to application programmers.

Example 2: Suppose you have assembled and linked a new mapset. You can test it without having to write a command-level program. Simply enter the following on a blank screen:

```
CECI SEND MAP('mapname') MAPSET('mapsetname')
    ERASE
```

The map will be displayed. Now you can check that only the desired fields are unprotected, that stopper fields are placed at the end of each unprotected field, and so on.

For further information on the CECI and CECS transactions, refer to the chapter entitled "Command Level Interpreter" in *Application Programmer's Reference Manual (Command Level)*.

Useful Tools Especially for System Programmers

In this chapter we will present and explain a number of programs that will serve as useful tools for system programmers. Some of the programs can be useful to application programmers as well. There is no clear line of demarcation between application programmers and system programmers. In the author's opinion, in order to become a good system programmer, a person must have sound, if not extensive, background in application programming, which will give him a good appreciation for the work and needs of his colleagues in the application area.

Some of the programs presented in this chapter are in the Assembly language, which some system programmers do not know. But detailed instructions are given that will enable the reader to assemble and link these programs and use them. Once these Assembly language programs have been installed and put to use, responsibility for maintaining and supporting them can be assigned to a CICS system programmer who has expertise in the Assembly language.

5.1 A PROGRAM TO DISPLAY THE ACTUAL VTAM LOGICAL NODENAME OF A TERMINAL AND OTHER INFORMATION

Figure 5.1 lists the program WHOPGM, and Figure 5.2 lists the mapset WHOMSET. Program WHOPGM is associated with transaction WHO in the PCT. When you enter WHO on a blank screen, you receive a screen as shown in Figure 5.3. The top left corner of the screen contains the name of the started task or job used to bring up the CICS system. For example, Figure 5.3 is showing CICSTRN1 as the job name of this CICS. (This means that the operator used the MVS command "S CICSTRN1" to start this CICS as an MVS started task, or, if this is a job, the job name on the job card was CICSTRN1.)

```
***************************************************************
 1  *=============================================================*
 2  WHOPGM    TITLE 'WHOPGM - DISPLAY TERMINAL AND USER INFORMATION'
 3  *=============================================================*
 4  * TRANSACTION ID ASSOCIATED WITH THIS PROGRAM: WHO
 5  * THIS TRANSACTION IS INTENTIONALLY UNPROTECTED. ITS SEC. LEVEL IS 1.
 6  *=============================================================*
 7            COPY  REGDEF
 8  SNTBAR    EQU   7
 9  TCTTEAR   EQU   8
10            DFHSNT TYPE=DSECT
11            DFHTCTZE
12            DROP  TCTTEAR
13  DFHEISTG  DSECT
14            COPY  WHOMSET
15  HOWSTRT   DS    CL2
16  WHOPGM    DFHEIENT CODEREG=2,EIBREG=3,DATAREG=13
17            B     START
18            DC    CL16'WHOPGM '
19            DC    CL16'&SYSDATE'
20            DC    CL16'&SYSTIME'
21  START     EQU   *
22            EXEC  CICS ASSIGN STARTCODE(HOWSTRT)
23            CLC   HOWSTRT,=C'TD'
24            BNE   EXITPGM
25            EXEC  CICS HANDLE CONDITION INVREQ(EXITPGM)
26            MVC   DATEO,=X'402120202020'
27            ED    DATEO,EIBDATE+1
28            MVC   TIMEO,=X'402021204B20204B2020'
29            ED    TIMEO,EIBTIME
```

```
30            MVC    TERMIDO,EIBTRMID
31            EXTRACT TIOTADDR,'S',FIELDS=(TIOT)
32            L      R4,TIOTADDR
33            MVC    SYSNAMEO,0(R4)
34            EXEC   CICS ASSIGN OPID(OPIDO)                        X
35                   USERID(USERIDO)                                X
36                   NETNAME(TERMNETO)
37   CHKOPID  EQU    *
38            CLC    OPIDO(3),=XL3'000000'
39            BE     NULLOPID
40   GETSNT   EXEC   CICS HANDLE CONDITION NOTAUTH(BADPGM) PGMIDERR(BADPGM)
41            EXEC   CICS LOAD PROGRAM('DFHSNT') ENTRY(SNTBAR)
42            USING  DFHSNNT,SNTBAR
43   SNTLOOP  EQU    *
44            CLC    SNNTLNG(2),SNTFENCE
45            BE     NOTFND1
46            CLC    OPIDO(3),SNNTID
47            BE     GOODOPID
48            AH     SNTBAR,SNNTLNG
49            B      SNTLOOP
50   BADPGM   EQU    *
51            MVC    ERRMSGO(50),ERRMSG1
52            B      PUTMAP
53   NOTFND1  EQU    *
54            MVC    ERRMSGO(50),OPIDMSG
55            B      PUTMAP
56   NULLOPID EQU    *
57            MVC    ERRMSGO(50),CSSNMSG
```

Figure 5.1. Source code of program WHOPGM

241

```
58          B      PUTMAP
59 GOODOPID EQU    *
60          XR     R4,R4
61          IC     R4,SNNTNL
62          EX     R4,MOVENAME
63          B      NEXTWORK
64 MOVENAME MVC    OPNAMEO(0),SNNTN
65 NEXTWORK EQU    *
66          DROP   SNTBAR
67 PUTMAP   EXEC CICS SEND MAP('WHOMAP')   MAPSET('WHOMSET') ERASE FREEKB
68 EXITPGM  EXEC CICS RETURN
69 ** WORKING CONSTANTS AND LITERALS
70 TIOTADDR DC     F'0'
71 SNTFENCE DC     XL2'FFFF'
72 BLANKS   DC     40C' '
73 ERRMSG1  DC     CL50'ERROR CONDITION 1 OCCURRED IN WHOPGM.  CALL NIRMAL.'
74 OPIDMSG  DC     CL50'YOU HAVE DONE CSSN BUT OPER.  ID NOT FOUND IN SNT.'
75 CSSNMSG  DC     CL50'YOU HAVE NOT SIGNED ON USING CSSN TRANSACTION.'
76          LTORG
77          END
```

****

Figure 5.1. continued.

```
*****************************************************************
 1  WHOMSET   DFHMSD TYPE=&SYSPARM,MODE=OUT,CTRL=(FREEKB,FRSET),     *
 2                   LANG=ASM,TIOAPFX=YES,DATA=FIELD
 3  WHOMAP    DFHMDI SIZE=(24,80)
 4  SYSNAME   DFHMDF POS=(01,01),LENGTH=08,ATTRB=(ASKIP,BRT)
 5            DFHMDF POS=(01,19),LENGTH=42,ATTRB=(ASKIP),            *
 6                   INITIAL='*** CICS USER AND TERMINAL INFORMATION ***'
 7            DFHMDF POS=(05,01),LENGTH=30,ATTRB=(ASKIP),            *
 8                   INITIAL='CURRENT DATE (JULIAN)'
 9  DATE      DFHMDF POS=(05,32),LENGTH=06,ATTRB=(ASKIP,BRT)
10            DFHMDF POS=(06,01),LENGTH=30,ATTRB=(ASKIP),            *
11                   INITIAL='CURRENT TIME (HH.MM.SS)'
12  TIME      DFHMDF POS=(06,32),LENGTH=10,ATTRB=(ASKIP,BRT)
13            DFHMDF POS=(07,01),LENGTH=30,ATTRB=(ASKIP),            *
14                   INITIAL='SIGNON NAME:'
15  OPNAME    DFHMDF POS=(07,32),LENGTH=20,ATTRB=(ASKIP,BRT),        *
16                   INITIAL='????????????????????'
17            DFHMDF POS=(08,01),LENGTH=30,ATTRB=(ASKIP),            *
18                   INITIAL='USER ID:'
19  USERID    DFHMDF POS=(08,32),LENGTH=08,ATTRB=(ASKIP,BRT),        *
20                   INITIAL='????????'
21            DFHMDF POS=(09,01),LENGTH=30,ATTRB=(ASKIP),            *
22                   INITIAL='OPERATOR ID:'
23  OPID      DFHMDF POS=(09,32),LENGTH=03,ATTRB=(ASKIP,BRT),        *
24                   INITIAL='???'
25            DFHMDF POS=(10,01),LENGTH=30,ATTRB=(ASKIP),            *
26                   INITIAL='CICS TERMINAL ID:'
27  TERMID    DFHMDF POS=(10,32),LENGTH=04,ATTRB=(ASKIP,BRT),        *
```

Figure 5.2. Source code of mapset WHOMSET

```
28                 INITIAL='????'
29         DFHMDF POS=(11,01),LENGTH=30,ATTRB=(ASKIP),        X
30                 INITIAL='VTAM LOGICAL NODE (LU) NAME: '
31 TERMNET DFHMDF POS=(11,32),LENGTH=08,ATTRB=(ASKIP,BRT),   X
32                 INITIAL='????????'
33 ERRMSG  DFHMDF POS=(24,15),LENGTH=50,ATTRB=(ASKIP,BRT),   X
34                 INITIAL=' '                                X
35
36         DFHMSD TYPE=FINAL
37         END
*************************************************************************
```

Figure 5.2. continued.

```
CICSTRN1              *** CICS USER AND TERMINAL INFORMATION ***

CURRENT DATE (JULIAN)         91077
CURRENT TIME (HH.MM.SS)     10.10.31
SIGNON NAME:                R1RLM
USER ID:                    RLM1
OPERATOR ID:                RLM
CICS TERMINAL ID:           E901
VTAM LOGICAL NODE (LU) NAME:  L9E001
```

Figure 5.3. A sample screen displayed by the program shown in Figure 5.1.

This screen also contains other very useful information such as the VTAM logical nodename and CICS terminal ID of your terminal as well as User ID, Sign-On Name, and Operator ID of the user who is currently signed on to the terminal. If you have not signed on the CICS, you will receive question marks in Sign-On Name and Operator ID fields, and the following message will appear at the bottom of the screen:

```
YOU HAVE NOT SIGNED ON USING CSSN TRANSACTION
```

After reading the screen, you should press the Clear key to clear the screen and proceed with your work. There is no provision to refresh the screen displayed, because there is no need for it. The transaction ID associated with the program of Figure 5.1 should have a security level of 1 so that anyone can execute it without any restriction, i.e., without having to first execute the CSSN transaction.

Procedure for Installing This Facility

Step 1. Enter the map shown in Figure 5.2 in a source PDS (partitioned dataset) as member WHOMSET. Enter the program shown in Figure 5.1 in the same source PDS as member WHOPGM.

Step 2. Now assemble this map using the JCL given in Section B.4 in Appendix B. Let us suppose that the name of the load library where the load module for this map will be created is P1BKN.LOADLIB, and the name of the macro (copybook) library where the copybook for the map will be created is P1BKN.MACLIB. So after you have run the job given in Section B.4, it will create load module WHOMSET in P1BKN.LOADLIB, and copybook member WHOMSET in P1BKN.MACLIB. This load library must be included under DDname DFHRPL in the CICS start-up procedure or job.

Step 3. Now compile and link program WHOPGM using the JCL given in Section B.2 in Appendix B. During the assembly, copybook WHOMSET created in Step 2 will be included in the program. This job will create load module WHOPGM in your load library. This load library must be included under DDname DFHRPL in the CICS start-up procedure or job.

Step 4. Define the following resources in CICS tables:

Definition of Mapset in the PPT

```
MAPSET   WHOMSET
GROUP    CICSBOOK
RSL      00
STATUS   ENABLED
```

Definition of Program in the PPT

```
PROGRAM    WHOPGM
GROUP      CICSBOOK
LANGUAGE   ASSEMBLER
```

Other parameters for WHOPGM in the PPT should be the same as those for sample program BNPROG1, given in Section 1.6.

Definition of Transaction in the PCT

```
TRANSACTION  WHO
GROUP        CICSBOOK
PROGRAM      WHOPGM
TRANSEC      1
```

Other parameters for WHO in the PCT should be the same as those for sample transaction BNC1, given in Section 1.6.

In what way can this program be useful? Suppose your installation is running multiple CICS regions. Your user phones you and tells you that he cannot log on to CICSPRD1 with his terminal. You ask him for his terminal's VTAM logical node name. He reads the nodename written on the label glued to the terminal and tells you it is LU33A09. You investigate the problem and find that this logical node name is defined in the TCT of CICSPRD1 and is also defined in the application table and should be working. (Note: Applications should not include terminal IDs of CRT-type terminals in their tables, because a user should be able to use any CRT-type terminal to access the application.)

But his terminal is not working on CICSPRD1. So, you reason that probably the logical node name written on the label is not correct. You ask him to log on to one of the other CICS regions, enter WHO on a blank screen, and tell you the VTAM node name displayed by WHO. He does it and tells you that VTAM logical node name displayed by WHO is not what is written on the label, but it is LU33A01. Now you look at the tables for CICSPRD1 and find that this terminal is not defined in the TCT of CICSPRD1. No wonder the user is not able to log on to CICSPRD1 using this terminal.

This is the best instance of where the WHO transaction can be most helpful. Whenever an end user telephones the applications systems analyst, or an applications programmer or analyst telephones a system programmer, he or she should report the correct VTAM logical node name as reported by the WHO transaction. This will help them in solving the problem faster.

The following points should be noted.

1. When a terminal is accessing CICS directly rather than through a VTAM sessions manager software such as VTAM Switch, the logical

node name displayed by WHO will be the same, no matter which CICS region was accessed. But this may not be true for CICS terminal ID. A good system programmer tries to make the CICS terminal ID the same on all CICS regions. But it is possible that the same physical terminal has different terminal ID on different CICS regions, and still that terminal will be able to access the applications on different systems. This is because most applications are independent of the terminal used to access them.

2. Applications should be written so that they do not include the terminal IDs in their tables. (This is definitely true for CRT type terminals, because terminal ID's of printers may have to be included in application routing tables.) This way, any CRT type terminal defined to CICS can be used to access that application. CICS or applications sign-on ID and password should be used to control who has access to that application.

Explanation of Program WHOPGM

This program is straightforward. When you type WHO and press Enter, control goes to line 16 in Figure 5.1. Here we execute the entry logic. Next, on line 17, we branch to line 21. On line 22, we store in variable HOWSTRT, a code indicating how this task was initiated. If it was initiated through terminal input, the code would be TD. On line 23, we check if this task was initiated through terminal input. If not, control flows to label EXITPGM on line 68, where we terminate the task.

Supposing that the task was initiated by typing WHO on a blank screen, control would flow to line 25. On lines 26 through 30, we move the current date and time into map fields. On line 31, we use the EXTRACT macro of MVS to obtain the address of the TIOT and store it in variable TIOTADDR. On line 33, we store the job name of the CICS region in map field SYSNAMEO. On line 34, we store in map field OPIDO, the operator ID, in USERIDO, the user ID, and in TERMNETO, the VTAM logical node name of the terminal. On line 38, we check if the operator ID obtained using the ASSIGN command is binary zeros. If so, this means that the operator has not signed on to CICS using the CSSN transaction. In this case, we branch to label NULLOPID, where we move CSSNMSG into map field ERRMSGO, and then branch to line 67.

Suppose that the operator ID obtained with the ASSIGN command is not binary zeros. In this case, we would execute line 41, where we would load the sign-on table DFHSNT in storage and load its address into Register 7 (SNTBAR). We would then search the SNT, looking for an operator ID that matches the value in OPIDO. Supposing there is a match, on line 47 we would branch to label GOODOPID, where we would store the sign-on name in map field OPNAMEO, and then branch to label NEXTWORK. Next, we would execute the SEND MAP command on line 67, followed by return to CICS on line 66. At this time, the user is presented with a map resembling the one shown in Figure 5.3. The task that displayed this map has ended.

5.2 A PROGRAM TO DELETE ALL TEMPORARY STORAGE QUEUES ASSOCIATED WITH A TERMINAL

Figure 5.4 shows the listing of program BNTSQDEL. This program is associated with transaction BNPU in the PCT. If you want to delete all temporary storage queues that have your four-character CICS terminal ID, either in positions 1 through 4 or in positions 5 through 8 of the queue ID, you can enter BNPU on a blank screen. This program will perform the deletion and display the following message on the first line of the screen:

```
T.S QUEUE(S) FOR REQUESTED TERM HAVE BEEN DELETED
```

Now, suppose you want to delete all temporary storage queues for another terminal. In fact, you can delete all queues that have tttt either in positions 1 through 4 or in positions 5 through 8 of the queue ID. Where tttt may or may not represent the terminal ID of another terminal, you can enter the following on a blank screen:

```
BNPU/tttt
```

(Note: tttt must be replaced by any desired four-character string.) This program will perform the deletion and display the message shown above as confirmation. So, the data entered to execute this program can be either four characters long (e.g., BNPU) or nine characters long (e.g., BNPU/tttt). If you enter data of any other length (e.g., BNPU/), this program will reject your request and display the following message on the first line of the screen:

```
DATA ENTERED ON TERMINAL MUST BE 4 OR 9 BYTES LONG
```

In what way can this program be useful? Many applications store data in temporary storage queues whose IDs have the terminal ID of the terminal on which the task is running, either in the beginning or at the end of the queue ID. This is done to make the temporary storage queue IDs unique. Normally, when a transaction ends, it deletes such queues. But when a transaction ends abnormally, such queues may be left in storage. When a new transaction is initiated, they may cause problems. So, it may be necessary to delete such queues in order to clean things up and start afresh.

It is here that this program can be helpful. Rather than use a utility or a CICS monitor to find out the names of all such queues that have your terminal ID either in the beginning or at the end, and then delete them one by one using a utility such as the CEBR transaction, you can perform deletions of multiple queues with just one execution of this transaction.

```
****************************************************************************
 1   *
 2   * THIS PGM WILL DELETE MULTIPLE T.S. QUEUES, WITH QUEUE NAME IN THE
 3   * FORM 'TTTTXXXX' OR 'XXXXTTTT' WHERE TTTT= TERM. ID. SPECIFIED ON
 4   * THE TRANSACTION, AND XXXX CAN BE ANYTHING. THE TRANSACTION ID.
 5   * ASSOCIATED WITH THIS PROGRAM MUST HAVE TWA SIZE OF AT LEAST 54.
 6   *
 7           COPY   REGDEF
 8   TSMAPBAR EQU    R7
 9   TSUTEAR  EQU    R7
10   TSGIDBAR EQU    R7
11   TSUTBAR  EQU    R7
12   TCTTEAR  EQU    R10
13   TIOABAR  EQU    R11
14           COPY   DFHCSADS
15           DFHTCA CICSYST=YES
16   ***** TWA GOES HERE, BARRY, SIR.
17   TERMID   DS     CL4
18   MSGXX    DS     CL50
19           COPY   DFHTCTTE
20           COPY   DFHTSMDS
21           DROP   TSMAPBAR
22           COPY   DFHTIOA
23   BNTSQDEL CSECT
24           BALR   R8,0
25           USING  *,R8
26           L      TCTTEAR,TCAFCAAA        MAKE MY TCTTE ADDRESSABLE
27           L      TIOABAR,TCTTEDA         LOAD TIOABAR
28           CLC    TIOATDL,=H'4'           INCOMING DATA 4 BYTES LONG?
29           BE     YOURTERM
```

```
30        CLC    TIOATDL,=H'9'           INCOMING DATA 9 BYTES LONG?
31        BE     HISTERM
32 ****** REJECT THIS TRANSACTION BECAUSE INCOMING DATA IS NOT OF CORRECT
33 * LENGTH. IT MUST BE 4 OR 9 BYTES LONG.
34        MVC    MSGXX,MSG02
35        B      DISPMSG
36 YOURTERM MVC   TERMID,TCTTETI
37        B      PROCEED
38 HISTERM  MVC   TERMID,TIOADBA+5        MOVE TERM ID FROM INCOMING MESSAGE
39 PROCEED  EQU   *
40         L      R7,CSATSMTA
41         USING DFHTSUT,R7
42         CLC    TSUTCC,=F'0'            TEST FOR NO ENTRIES
43         BE     CHKNEXT
44         L      R4,TSUTAHI
45         USING DFHTSUTE,R4
46 LOOPHERE EQU   *
47         CLC    TERMID,TSUTEID
48         BE     TSPURGE
49         CLC    TERMID,TSUTEID+4
50         BNE    SKIPTHIS
51 TSPURGE  EQU   *
52         MVC    TCATSDI,TSUTEID
53         TM     TSUTETC,TSUTEGID        IS GROUP ID BIT ON
54         BZ     TSRLSE                  IF NOT BRANCH TO SINGLE RELEASE
55         DFHTS  TYPE=PURGE              PURGE GROUP
56         B      PROCEED
57 TSRLSE   EQU   *
```

Figure 5.4. Source code of program BNTSQDEL

251

```
58          DFHTS  TYPE=RELEASE
59          B      PROCEED
60 SKIPTHIS EQU    *
61          C      R4,TSUTALI        ANY MORE ON CHAIN ?
62          BNL    CHKNEXT
63          LA     R4,TSUTELN(R4)    CHECK NEXT ENTRY
64          B      LOOPHERE
65 CHKNEXT  EQU    *
66          L      R7,TSUTFC         LOAD R7
67          LTR    R7,R7             DOES R7 CONTAIN ZERO?
68          BE     EXITPRG           YES, TERMINATE PROGRAM.
69          CLC    TSUTCC,=F'0'      TEST FOR NO ENTRIES
70          BE     CHKNEXT
71          L      R4,TSUTAHI
72          B      LOOPHERE
73 EXITPRG  EQU    *
74          MVC    MSGXX,MSG01
75 DISPMSG  EQU    *
76          DFHSC  TYPE=GETMAIN,CLASS=TERMINAL,NUMBYTE=50,INITIMG=40
77          L      TIOABAR,TCASCSA
78          ST     TIOABAR,TCTTEDA
79          MVC    TIOATDL(2),=H'50'
80          MVC    TIOADBA(50),MSGXX
81          DFHTC  TYPE=(ERASE,WRITE)
82          DFHPC  TYPE=RETURN
83 MSG01    DC     CL50'T.S. QUEUE(S) FOR REQUESTED TERM HAVE BEEN DELETED'
84 MSG02    DC     CL50'DATA ENTERED ON TERMINAL MUST BE 4 OR 9 BYTES LONG'
85          LTORG
86          END
```

****

Figure 5.4. continued.

252

You can also use this program (after suitably modifying it, of course) so that whenever a transaction ends abnormally, this program is executed to clean up the temporary storage queues associated with the terminal. This can be easily achieved by using CICS exit facility described in the CICS *Customization Guide*.

Procedure for Installing This Facility

Step 1. Enter the program shown in Figure 5.4 in a source PDS as member BNTSQDEL.

Step 2. Now compile and link this program using the JCL given in Section B.3 in Appendix B. (Note: This program is a macro-level CICS program.) During the assembly, copybook REGDEF, shown in Section C.5 in Appendix C, will be required. This job will create load module BNTSQDEL in your load library. This load library must be included under DDname DFHRPL in the CICS start-up procedure or job.

Step 3. Define the following resources in CICS tables:

Definition of Program in the PPT

```
PROGRAM   BNTSQDEL
GROUP     CICSBOOK
LANGUAGE  ASSEMBLER
```

Other parameters for this program in the PPT should be the same as those for sample program BNPROG1 given in Section 1.6.

Definition of Transaction in the PCT

```
TRANSACTION BNPU
GROUP       CICSBOOK
PROGRAM     BNTSQDEL
TWASIZE     100
```

Other parameters for this transaction in the PCT should be the same as those for sample transaction BNC1 given in Section 1.6.

Explanation of program BNTSQDEL. Let us suppose the user enters BNPU on a blank screen. Control then flows to line 24 in Figure 5.4, because it is the first executable statement in the program. Here we load Register 8 with the starting address of the program, so that it serves as the base register. On line 28, we check if only 4 bytes were entered on the screen. In this example, this would be true, and control would flow to label YOURTERM on line 36. Here the terminal ID of the user's terminal would be moved into

TERMID, which is defined on line 17 in the TWA (Transaction Work Area). Control would then flow to line 39. The logic that follows on lines 40 through 72 is the core of the program. Here we scan the temporary storage unit table and check if there are queues that have the value stored in TERMID in positions 1 through 4 or in positions 5 through 8 of TSUTEID. This checking is done on lines 47 through 50.

If there is a match, control flows to label TSPURGE on line 51. After this, either the DFHTS macro on line 55 or the one on line 58 is executed, depending on the type of this queue. In either case, control would then flow to label PROCEED. After scanning all entries in the temporary storage unit table and deleting the queues that match our criteria, control would eventually flow to label EXITPRG on line 73. On lines 74 through 81, we obtain a storage area of 50 bytes, move the content of MSG01 into it, and send it to the terminal. This is followed by return to CICS on line 82. The user is now presented with a message confirming that the queues have been deleted, and the task that performed the deletion has ended completely and unconditionally.

5.3 FACILITY TO DISPLAY MESSAGES ON THE GOOD MORNING MESSAGE SCREEN TO ALL USERS LOGGING ON TO CICS

Here is a facility that allows you to display up to 24 lines of messages on the good morning message screen to all users logging on to CICS. This facility has been tested and found to be functioning like a charm under CICS Release 1.7 systems. It was developed by the author in his spare time and adopted at his employer's installation as the standard means of modifying the good morning message screen. Even though the JCL used to create the load module of DFHGMM shown in Figure 5.7 is an MVS JCL, you can easily set up JCL for the DOS or the DOS/VSE environment. The programs given in Figures 5.5 and 5.6 will work on MVS, DOS, and DOS/VSE.

The underlying concept behind this facility is as follows. Normally, in your system initialization table (SIT), you have GMTRAN = CSGM. This says that when a user logs on to CICS, transaction CSGM should be started. In the PCT, this transaction points to program DFHGMM, which normally resides in the LOADLIB dataset created at the time of CICS installation. Program DFHGMM, when invoked, displays a logo on which the word CICS appears slanted in big letters. Then the program ends completely and unconditionally. This means that the operator can clear the screen and enter any valid or invalid transaction code.

The basic concept of the facility the author developed is to create another version of program DFHGMM and store it in your own load library that is allocated under DDname DFHRPL in the CICS start-up procedure, but which appears ahead of the CICS LOADLIB dataset. This means that when CICS is searching the load libraries concatenated under DDname DFHRPL for program

DFHGMM, it would find it in your own load library and execute it. At any time, if you want to stop displaying your own messages, you can simply delete DFHGMM from your own load library and refresh the program using command: CEMT S PROGRAM(DFHGMM) NEW. CICS would then use this program from LOADLIB dataset, which displays the logo with the word CICS appearing in big letters.

In what way can this program be useful? Suppose CICSPRD4, your fourth production region, supports many applications such as payroll, billing, etc. Suppose you want to inform all the users of CICSPRD4 that the system will be down on a particular day for a specified duration. You can modify good morning messages and display them for the entire day for one or two days prior to the day when the system is scheduled to be down. However, when the system comes up after being down, you should remove those messages. You can do this simply by deleting member DFHGMM from your own load library and refreshing program DFHGMM through CEMT, thus letting DFHGMM be used from the CICS LOADLIB dataset. The point to remember is that when users see the same screen day after day, they tend to ignore it. This is due to human psychology. So, to make a message screen really effective, display it only for the duration needed, and display the default CICS logo at all other times.

Procedure for Installing This Facility

Step 1. Enter the batch COBOL program shown in Figure 5.5 in a source PDS as member MSGCONV.

Step 2. Now compile and link this program using a JCL that executes the COBOL compiler and the linkage editor, and store it in a load library used to contain batch programs.

Step 3. Enter the CICS assembler program shown in Figure 5.6 in a source PDS as member DFHGMM.

Step 4. Procedure for assembling and linking DFHGMM using the JCL given in Figure 5.7, is given later.

Step 5. Enter the JCL shown in Figure 5.7 in a PDS that contains JCLs. This JCL is using instream procedure CICSMSG. If you wish, you may store this procedure in a procedure library such as SYS2.PROCLIB.

Step 6. Modify the lines that have NOTE at the end in Figure 5.7 as follows:

Note 1: Change this line to contain a valid JOB statement that can consist of one or more lines.

```
      **************************************************************
       IDENTIFICATION DIVISION.
       PROGRAM-ID.  MSGCONV.
      * AUTHOR: BARRY K. NIRMAL.
      **************************************************************
      *      C O B O L   P R O G R A M   D E S C R I P T I O N    *
      *  TO BE COMPLETED IN THE FUTURE.                           *
      *-----------------------------------------------------------*
      *                   CHANGE CONTROL                          *
      *  VERSION#  DATE  PGMR  DESCRIPTION OF CHANGE              *
      *  -------  -----  ----  ----------------------            *
      *  000001   YY/MM  NIRMAL NEW PROGRAM                       *
      **************************************************************
       ENVIRONMENT DIVISION.
       CONFIGURATION SECTION.
       INPUT-OUTPUT SECTION.
       FILE-CONTROL.
           SELECT INFILE      ASSIGN INFILE.
           SELECT OUTFILE     ASSIGN OUTFILE.

       DATA DIVISION.
       FILE SECTION.
       FD  INFILE
           LABEL RECORDS ARE STANDARD
           BLOCK CONTAINS 0 RECORDS.
       01  INFILE-REC              PIC X(80).

       FD  OUTFILE
           LABEL RECORDS ARE STANDARD
           BLOCK CONTAINS 0 RECORDS.
```

256

```
30   01  OUTFILE-REC              PIC X(80).
31
32   WORKING-STORAGE SECTION.
33   *** IF DASHES IS 80 OR MORE BYTES LONG, IT WILL NOT FIT
34   *** ON ONE LINE WHEN DISPLAYED ON A 3270 DISPLAY DEVICE.
35   *=====================================================
36   77  DASHES                   PIC X(79)  VALUE ALL '='.
37   77  ALL-REC-READ             PIC 99999 VALUE ZERO.
38   77  VALID-REC-READ           PIC 99999 VALUE ZERO.
39   77  EOF-INFILE-SW            PIC 9(01) VALUE 0.
40       88  EOF-INFILE           VALUE 1.
41   01  INPUT-RECORD.
42       04  MSG-TEXT-1           PIC X(40).
43       04  MSG-TEXT-2           PIC X(32).
44       04  FILLER               PIC X(08).
45   01  INPUT-RECORD-X  REDEFINES INPUT-RECORD.
46       04  FIRST-CHAR           PIC X(01).
47       04  FILLER               PIC X(79).
48
49   01  OUTPUT-RECORD-1.
50       04  FILLER               PIC X(04) VALUE 'MSGL'.
51       04  OUT-SEQ              PIC 99 VALUE ZERO.
52       04  FILLER               PIC X(13) VALUE ' '     DC   CL40'.
53       04  FILLER               PIC X(01) VALUE ' '.
54       04  OUT-TEXT-1           PIC X(40).
55       04  FILLER               PIC X(01) VALUE ' '.
56
57   01  OUTPUT-RECORD-2.
```

Figure 5.5. Source code of program MSGCONV

```cobol
58          04  FILLER             PIC X(09)  VALUE SPACES.
59          04  FILLER             PIC X(10)  VALUE 'DC    CL32'.
60          04  FILLER             PIC X(01)  VALUE ' '.
61          04  OUT-TEXT-2         PIC X(32).
62          04  FILLER             PIC X(01)  VALUE ' '.
63      LINKAGE SECTION.
64      PROCEDURE DIVISION.
65          OPEN INPUT INFILE
66               OUTPUT OUTFILE.
67          PERFORM B100-PROCESS-ROUTINE
68              THRU B100-EXIT
69              UNTIL EOF-INFILE.
70          IF VALID-REC-READ LESS THAN 24
71          PERFORM FILL-UP-OUT-FILE THRU FILL-UP-EXIT UNTIL
72              OUT-SEQ = 24.
73          CLOSE INFILE OUTFILE.
74          IF VALID-REC-READ NOT = 24
75          DISPLAY DASHES
76          DISPLAY 'MSGCONV HAS DETECTED A SOFT ERROR DESCRIBED BELOW'
77          DISPLAY 'NUMBER OF VALID RECORDS READ FROM INPUT FILE = '
78              VALID-REC-READ
79          DISPLAY 'THIS VALUE WAS NOT 24'
80          DISPLAY 'PROGRAM MSGCONV HAS EITHER IGNORED EXTRA RECORDS'
81          DISPLAY 'OR IT HAS FILLED OU OUTPUT FILE WITH BLANK LINES'
82          DISPLAY 'DEPENDING ON HOW MANY VALID RECORD WERE READ'
83          DISPLAY DASHES.
84          STOP RUN.
```

```
86      B100-PROCESS-ROUTINE.
87          READ INFILE INTO INPUT-RECORD          AT END
88              MOVE 1 TO EOF-INFILE-SW
89              GO TO B100-EXIT.
90          ADD 1 TO ALL-REC-READ.
91          IF FIRST-CHAR = '$'
92              GO TO B100-EXIT.
93          ADD 1 TO VALID-REC-READ.
94          IF VALID-REC-READ > 24
95              GO TO B100-EXIT.
96          ADD 1 TO OUT-SEQ.
97          MOVE MSG-TEXT-1  TO OUT-TEXT-1.
98          MOVE MSG-TEXT-2  TO OUT-TEXT-2.
99          WRITE OUTFILE-REC FROM OUTPUT-RECORD-1.
100         WRITE OUTFILE-REC FROM OUTPUT-RECORD-2.
101     B100-EXIT.  EXIT.
102
103     FILL-UP-OUT-FILE.
104         ADD 1 TO OUT-SEQ.
105         MOVE SPACES      TO OUT-TEXT-1.
106         MOVE SPACES      TO OUT-TEXT-2.
107         WRITE OUTFILE-REC FROM OUTPUT-RECORD-1.
108         WRITE OUTFILE-REC FROM OUTPUT-RECORD-2.
109     FILL-UP-EXIT.  EXIT.
**********************************************************************
```

Figure 5.5. continued.

259

```
*******************************************************************************
               TITLE 'CICS GOOD MORNING MESSAGE DISPLAY PROGRAM BY NIRMAL'
     1    *=============================================================*
     2    * THIS PROGRAM IS USED FOR ALL CICS REGIONS. NO CHANGE IS NEEDED TO  *
     3    * IT BEFORE ASSEMBLING. IT IS A MACRO LEVEL CICS PROGRAM. IT MUST BE *
     4    * ASSEMBLED AND LINKED AS LOAD MODULE DFHGMM IN A LOAD LIBRARY THAT  *
     5    * IS ALLOCATED UNDER DDNAME DFHRPL IN THE CICS START-UP PROCEDURE.   *
     6    *=============================================================*
     7    *AUTHOR:      BARRY K. NIRMAL
     8    *=============================================================*
     9
    10    DFHGMM   CSECT
    11    *******   ESTABLISH STANDARD REGISTER EQUATES
    12    TCTPFBAR EQU   3
    13             COPY  REGDEF
    14    TSIOABAR EQU   7
    15    FWACBAR  EQU   9
    16    TCTTEAR  EQU   10
    17    TIOABAR  EQU   11
    18             PRINT NOGEN
    19             COPY  DFHCSADS
    20             DFHTCA CICSYST=YES                    GENERATE FULL TCA
    21             COPY  DFHTIOA
    22             COPY  DFHAID
    23             PRINT OFF
    24             DFHTCTZE CICSYST=YES                  GENERATE FULL TCTTE.
    25             COPY  DFHTCTFX                         TCT PREFIX.
    26             PRINT ON
    27             EJECT
    28    DFHGMM   CSECT
    29             USING *,R8                             SET BASE REGS
```

```
30          LR    R8,R14              LOAD BASE REG
31          L     TCTTEAR,TCAFCAAA    LOAD TCT ADDRESS
32 VALIDKEY EQU   *
33          MVC   TCASCNB,=AL2(1848)     SET MESSAGE LENGTH
34          DFHSC TYPE=GETMAIN,CLASS=TERMINAL,INITIMG=40
35          L     TIOABAR,TCASCSA
36          ST    TIOABAR,TCTTEDA
37          MVC   TIOATDL,=AL2(1848)
38          MVC   TIOADBA(5),=X'1140401DE8'
39          MVC   TIOADBA+5(72),MSGL01
40          MVC   TIOADBA+77(5),=X'11C1501DE8'
41          MVC   TIOADBA+82(72),MSGL02
42          MVC   TIOADBA+154(5),=X'11C2601DE8'
43          MVC   TIOADBA+159(72),MSGL03
44          MVC   TIOADBA+231(5),=X'11C3F01DE8'
45          MVC   TIOADBA+236(72),MSGL04
46          MVC   TIOADBA+308(5),=X'11C5401DE8'
47          MVC   TIOADBA+313(72),MSGL05
48          MVC   TIOADBA+385(5),=X'11C6501DE8'
49          MVC   TIOADBA+390(72),MSGL06
50          MVC   TIOADBA+462(5),=X'11C7601DE8'
51          MVC   TIOADBA+467(72),MSGL07
52          MVC   TIOADBA+539(5),=X'11C8F01DE8'
53          MVC   TIOADBA+544(72),MSGL08
54          MVC   TIOADBA+616(5),=X'114A401DE8'
55          MVC   TIOADBA+621(72),MSGL09
56          MVC   TIOADBA+693(5),=X'114B501DE8'
57          MVC   TIOADBA+698(72),MSGL10
```

Figure 5.6. Source code of program DFHGMM

```
58  MVC   TIOADBA+770(5),=X'114C601DE8'
59  MVC   TIOADBA+775(72),MSGL11
60  MVC   TIOADBA+847(5),=X'114DF01DE8'
61  MVC   TIOADBA+852(72),MSGL12
62  MVC   TIOADBA+924(5),=X'114F401DE8'
63  MVC   TIOADBA+929(72),MSGL13
64  MVC   TIOADBA+1001(5),=X'1150501DE8'
65  MVC   TIOADBA+1006(72),MSGL14
66  MVC   TIOADBA+1078(5),=X'11D1601DE8'
67  MVC   TIOADBA+1083(72),MSGL15
68  MVC   TIOADBA+1155(5),=X'11D2F01DE8'
69  MVC   TIOADBA+1160(72),MSGL16
70  MVC   TIOADBA+1232(5),=X'11D4401DE8'
71  MVC   TIOADBA+1237(72),MSGL17
72  MVC   TIOADBA+1309(5),=X'11D5501DE8'
73  MVC   TIOADBA+1314(72),MSGL18
74  MVC   TIOADBA+1386(5),=X'11D6601DE8'
75  MVC   TIOADBA+1391(72),MSGL19
```

```
76    MVC    TIOADBA+1463(5),=X'11D7F01DE8'
77    MVC    TIOADBA+1468(72),MSGL20
78    MVC    TIOADBA+1540(5),=X'11D9401DE8'
79    MVC    TIOADBA+1545(72),MSGL21
80    MVC    TIOADBA+1617(5),=X'115A501DE8'
81    MVC    TIOADBA+1622(72),MSGL22
82    MVC    TIOADBA+1694(5),=X'115B601DE8'
83    MVC    TIOADBA+1699(72),MSGL23
84    MVC    TIOADBA+1771(5),=X'115CF01DE8'
85    MVC    TIOADBA+1776(72),MSGL24
86    DFHTC  TYPE=(ERASE,WRITE)
87    DFHPC  TYPE=RETURN
88    COPY GMMBOOK
89    LTORG
90    END    DFHGMM
```

Figure 5.6. continued.

263

```
//* ================================================= NOTE 1
//*JOBNAME   JOB CARD     - - - - - - - - - - - - - -
//* =================================================
//CICSMSG   PROC SYSTEM=JUNK,WORK=SYSDA
//STEP01    EXEC PGM=MSGCONV
//STEPLIB   DD DISP=SHR,DSN=Z2BKN.MLOAD               NOTE 2
//INFILE    DD DISP=SHR,DSN=Z2BKN.HISLIB(MSG&SYSTEM)  NOTE 3
//OUTFILE   DD DISP=SHR,DSN=Z2BKN.MACLIB(GMMBOOK)     NOTE 4
//SYSOUT    DD SYSOUT=*
//SYSDBOUT  DD SYSOUT=*
//SYSUDUMP  DD SYSOUT=*
//* =================================================
//ASM       EXEC PGM=IEV90,PARM='DECK,NOOBJECT,LIST'
//SYSLIB    DD DISP=SHR,DSN=CICS.R170.MACLIB          NOTE 5
//          DD DISP=SHR,DSN=SYS1.MACLIB
//          DD DISP=SHR,DSN=Z2BKN.MACLIB
//SYSUT1    DD UNIT=&WORK,SPACE=(1700,(400,400))      NOTE 6
//SYSUT2    DD UNIT=&WORK,SPACE=(1700,(400,400))
```

```
19  //SYSUT3    DD   UNIT=&WORK,SPACE=(1700,(400,400))
20  //SYSPUNCH  DD   DSN=&&OBJSET,UNIT=&WORK,DISP=(,PASS),
21  //               SPACE=(400,(100,100,1)),DCB=(RECFM=FB,LRECL=80,BLKSIZE=3200)
22  //SYSPRINT  DD   SYSOUT=*
23  //SYSIN     DD   DISP=(OLD,PASS),DSN=Z2BKN.HISLIB(DFHGMM)      NOTE 7
24  //*===============================================================
25  //LKED      EXEC PGM=IEWL,COND=(0,LT,ASM),
26  //               PARM=(LIST,LET,XREF,MAP)
27  //SYSLIB    DD   DUMMY
28  //SYSLMOD   DD   DISP=SHR,DSN=CICSU.TEST.TRANLIB(DFHGMM)       NOTE 8
29  //SYSUT1    DD   UNIT=&WORK,DCB=BLKSIZE=1024,SPACE=(1024,(200,20))
30  //SYSPRINT  DD   SYSOUT=*
31  //SYSLIN    DD   DSN=&&OBJSET,DISP=(OLD,DELETE)
32  //          PEND
33  //JSTEP01   EXEC CICSMSG,SYSTEM=TST1                           NOTE 9
****************************************************************************
```

Figure 5.7. JCL to create load module DFHGMM

265

```
***********************************************************************
1
2
3
4
5
6                   WELCOME TO THIS CICS TEST SYSTEM
7                                    AT
8
9                    THE GREAT LAKES ELECTRONICS COMPANY
10
11   PLEASE BE ADVISED THAT THIS CICS SYSTEM WILL BE DOWN FROM 7 P.M. TILL
12   9 P.M. ON JANUARY 1, 1995 FOR PREVENTIVE MAINTENANCE.
13
14
15
16
17
18   AFTER READING THIS SCREEN, PRESS THE CLEAR KEY AND CONTINUE AS USUAL.
19
***********************************************************************
```

Figure 5.8. A Sample data Set containing brodcast messages

266

Note 2: Change Z2BKN.MLOAD to the name of the PDS that contains the load module of batch program MSGCONV.

Note 3: Change Z2BKN.HISLIB to the name of a PDS (Logical Record Length = 80, Record Format = Fixed Blocked) that will contain one member for each CICS region. For example, member MSGTST1 will contain messages for the first test system, member MSGPRD1 for the first production system, and so on.

Note 4 and Note 6: Change Z2BKN.MACLIB to the name of the macro library that will contain macro GMMBOOK, which will be created by MSGCONV.

Note 5: Change CICS.R170.MACLIB to the name of the CICS macro library that contains CICS macros.

Note 7: Change Z2BKN.HISLIB to the dataset that contains source program DFHGMM, which was copied from Figure 5.6 in Step 3 above.

Note 8: Change CICSU.TEST.TRANLIB to the name of the load library that will contain load module DFHGMM.

Note 9: Change TST1 to the four-character ID for the CICS system. For example, if you used PRD1, this job will read member MSGPRD1 of the PDS that is supposed to contain the message source. (See line with NOTE 3 in this same figure.)

Procedure for Using This Facility to Modify Good Morning Messages for Any CICS Region:

Step 1. Create member MSGxxxx in a source PDS that will contain a message source, where xxxx = TST1 for the first test region, PRD1 for the first production region, and so on. Use the content shown in Figure 5.8 as a guide. You can have any number of lines in this data set up to 24. Message text must be in positions 1 through 72 of each record. If the first character of any line is a $, it is considered a comment and is ignored. Otherwise, the first character is considered part of the message. Positions 73 through 80 of each record are ignored. If you have less than 24 non-comment lines, the program will add blank lines at the end. If you have more than 24 non-comment lines, all lines except the first 24 will be ignored.

Step 2. Edit the JCL copied from Figure 5.7 and modified as described in Step 6 of the installation procedure given above. Submit this JCL. Make sure that all the steps ended with a condition code of zero. Check that member GMMBOOK was created in your macro library and member DFHGMM was created in your load library.

Step 3. Program DFHGMM will be in effect at the next start-up of CICS. If you want to make it effective immediately, issue the following command on CICS:

```
CEMT S PROG(DFHGMM) NEW
```

How does this facility work? The underlying concept and the principle of this facility was presented above. Now let us see what happens when you submit this job shown in Figure 5.7. The first step executes program MSGCONV. This program reads the dataset containing the message text and creates a dataset containing the assembler copybook. This copybook contains the text of the message in coded form. In the second step, the assembler takes program DFHGMM shown in Figure 5.6 and assembles it. During assembly, copybook GMMBOOK created in the earlier step is included. In the third step, the linkage editor creates load module of DFHGMM in your own load library.

Program DFHGMM shown in Figure 5.6 is pretty straightforward. On line 34, it obtains a storage area of 1848 bytes and initializes it with blanks. On the lines that follow, message lines MSGL01, MSGL02, and so on up to MSGL24 are moved into the storage area obtained. These message lines are part of copybook GMMBOOK. On line 86, we send the content of 1848-byte area obtained earlier to the terminal after erasing whatever might already be there. On line 87, we return to CICS. The user is now presented with a screen containing 24 lines of message. He or she can read the screen, press the Clear key, and proceed with his or her work in the usual way.

5.4 A PROGRAM TO DISPLAY A SINGLE FIELD FROM THE TCTTE

Figure 5.9 shows the listing of program BNTERMID. This program is associated with transaction BNTE in the PCT. If you want to know the four-character CICS terminal ID of any terminal, enter BNTE on a blank screen. The response will be as follows:

```
SIR, YOUR TERM ID IS = xxxx
```

where xxxx will be replaced by the actual CICS terminal ID. After receiving the response, you can clear the screen and enter any valid or invalid CICS transaction.

How can this program be useful? This program is an example of a simple macro-level assembler program that displays a single field from one CICS control block, i.e., TCTTE (Terminal Control Table Terminal Entry). It can be easily modified to display any other field from the TCTTE. Being a simple program that does only one thing, it can be easily understood by beginning programmers. Even though it is recommended that all new programs be written using the command level of CICS, there are occasions when you have to understand macro-level programs, or when you have to write using macro level. In such situations, a good knowledge of macro-level programming makes you a hero.

Procedure for Installing This Facility

Step 1. Enter the program shown in Figure 5.9 in a source PDS as member BNTERMID.

Step 2. Now assemble and link this program using the JCL given in Section B.3 in Appendix B. During the assembly, copybook REGDEF shown in Section C.5 in Appendix C will be required. This job will create load module BNTER-MID in your library. This load library must be included under DDname DFHRPL in the CICS start-up procedure or job.

Step 3. Define the following resources in CICS tables:

Definition of Program in the PPT

```
PROGRAM     BNTERMID
GROUP       CICSBOOK
LANGUAGE    ASSEMBLER
```

Other parameters for this program in the PPT should be the same as those for sample program BNPROG1 given in Section 1.6.

Definition of Transaction in the PCT

```
TRANSACTION   BNTE
GROUP         CICSBOOK
PROGRAM       BNTERMID
```

Other parameters for this transaction in the PCT should be the same as those for sample transaction BNC1 given in Section 1.6.

Explanation of Program BNTERMID

Let us suppose the user enters BNTE on a blank screen. Control then flows to line 22 in the program of Figure 5.9, which is the first executable statement. At this point, the contents of Registers 15 and 0 through 11 are unknown, Register 12 contains the address of the TCA, Register 13 contains the address of the CSA, and Register 14 contains the address of the user-program. These conventions are given in Figure 6 (Register Usage Under CICS) on page 15 in *Applications Programmers Reference Manual Macro Level* (manual no. SC33-0079-4).

On line 23, we load Register 8 with the starting address of the program, so that it serves as the base register. On line 24, we load Register 10 (TCTTEAR) with the address of this terminal's TCTTE. On line 26, we issue the DFHSC macro to obtain a storage of 80 bytes and initialize it with blanks (INI-TIMG = 40). Then, on line 29, we move into this area the text of our message,

```
*****************************************************************************

 1              TITLE 'BNTERMID- DISPLAY TERM ID USING THIS TRANS'
 2    BNTERMID  CSECT
 3              COPY  REGDEF
 4    TCTPFBAR  EQU   3
 5    TSIOABAR  EQU   7
 6    FWACBAR   EQU   9
 7    TCTTEAR   EQU   10
 8    TIOABAR   EQU   11
 9              PRINT NOGEN
10              COPY  DFHCSADS
11              DFHTCA CICSYST=YES                      GENERATE FULL TCA
12    ********  TWA GOES HERE,  BARRY   ********
13              COPY  DFHTIOA
14              COPY  DFHAID
15              PRINT OFF
16              DFHTCTZE CICSYST=YES                    GENERATE FULL TCTTE
17              COPY  DFHTCTFX TCT PREFIX.
18              PRINT ON
19              EJECT
```

```
* * * * * * * * * * * * * * * * * * * * * * * * * * * *
20
21 BNTERMID CSECT
22          USING  *,R8                               SET BASE REGS
23          LR     R8,R14                             LOAD BASE REG
24          L      TCTTEAR,TCAFCAAA                   LOAD TCT ADDRESS
25          MVC    TCASCNB,=AL2(80)                   SET MESSAGE LENGTH
26          DFHSC  TYPE=GETMAIN,CLASS=TERMINAL,INITIMG=40
27          L      TIOABAR,TCASCSA                    GET STORAGE ADDRESS
28          MVC    TIOATDL,=AL2(80)                   SET WRITE LENGTH
29          MVC    TIOADBA(23),=C'SIR, YOUR TERM ID IS = '
30          MVC    TIOADBA+23(4),TCTTETI
31          ST     TIOABAR,TCTTEDA                    STORE MESSAGE ADDRESS FOR TC
32          DFHTC  TYPE=(ERASE,WRITE)
33          DFHPC  TYPE=RETURN
34          LTORG
35          END
```

* *

Figure 5.9. Source code of program BNTERMID

and on line 30, we move the terminal ID from the TCTTE. Then, on line 32, we send the content of the 80-byte area to the terminal after erasing whatever might already be on the screen. This is followed by return to CICS on line 33. The user is now presented with a screen that has the following on the first line:

```
SIR, YOUR TERM ID IS = xxxx
```

The CICS task has ended completely and unconditionally.

5.5 A PROGRAM TO DISCONNECT A TERMINAL FROM CICS OR TO ACQUIRE IT IF IT IS NOT CONNECTED

Suppose a terminal with ID D918 is acquired to CICS. You can force it out of CICS by issuing the following command on a blank screen:

```
BNKL/D918
```

If no task is active on the terminal, it will get logged off CICS. If there is a task active on it, e.g., CEMT, the terminal will get logged off when that task ends.

Now suppose a terminal with ID A102 is not acquired to CICS. If you issue BNKL/A102 on a blank screen, this terminal will get acquired to CICS and the good morning message screen will be displayed on it.

Procedure for Installing This Facility

Step 1. Enter the program shown in Figure 5.10 in a source PDS as member BNKLPGM.

Step 2. Now assemble and link this program using the JCL given in Section B. 1 in Appendix B. This job will create load module BNKLPGM in your load library. This load library must be included under DDname DFHRPL in the CICS start-up procedure or job.

Step 3. Define the following resources in CICS tables:

Definition of Program in the PPT

```
PROGRAM     BNKLPGM
GROUP       CICSBOOK
LANGUAGE    COBOL
```

Other parameters for this program in the PPT should be the same as those for sample program BNPROG1 given in Section 1.6.

Definition of Transaction in the PCT

```
TRANSACTION    BNKL
GROUP          CICSBOOK
PROGRAM        BNKLPGM
```

Other parameters for this transaction in the PCT should be the same as those for sample transaction BNC1 given in Section 1.6.

Step 4. Make sure the facility given in Section 2.3 in Chapter 2 is installed according to installation instructions given there. This is because program BNKLPGM starts transaction BKN2 which was installed in Section 2.3. Entering BKN2 on a blank screen will result in your terminal being logged off CICS.

Explanation of Program BNKLPGM

Suppose the user enters BNKL/A108 on a blank screen, where A108 is the ID of a valid terminal. Control then flows to line 51 in the program of Figure 5.10, which is the first executable statement in the procedure division. On line 54, we receive the data entered on the terminal and store it in WS-DATA-IN. So in this example, after line 54 has executed, IN-TERM will contain A108. On line 60, we execute the START command to start transaction BKN2 on the specified terminal, which in this example is A108. Next, on line 64, we send the content of WS-OUT-MSG-4 to the terminal. This is followed by return to CICS on line 67. The task has now ended, and the user is presented with a screen that has the following message on line 1:

```
DESIRED ACTION WILL BE TAKEN ON TERMINAL: A108
```

In what way can this program be useful? This program is an example of a simple command-level COBOL program. It can be helpful if a person you do not like is using CICS and you want to log him off. This will probably help you in releasing your pent-up emotions. But the main use of this program is in helping beginning CICS command-level programmers learn the technique of writing similar programs that use the START command to start any valid CICS transaction on any specified terminal after any specified time interval.

5.6 A FACILITY TO EXECUTE SPECIFIED CEMT TRANSACTIONS AT CICS START-UP TIME

Suppose you have eight CICS regions, two for system and program development and testing, two for training the users, and four for running the production systems. Suppose you want transaction ABC1 to be disabled when the second

```
***************************************************************
 1        IDENTIFICATION DIVISION.
 2        PROGRAM-ID.    BNKLPGM.
 3       *AUTHOR: BARRY K. NIRMAL.
 4       *=========================================================
 5       * THIS PROGRAM IS ASSOCIATED WITH TRANSACTION ID BNKL.
 6       * IT STARTS TRANSACION BKN2 ON THE SPECIFIED TERMINAL.
 7       *=========================================================
 8       * ISSUING BNKL/D903 WILL LOG TERMINAL ID D903  OFF THE CICS
 9       * SYSTEM ON WHICH THIS TRANSACTION WAS ISSUED.
10       *=========================================================
11       * IF YOU ISSUED BNKL/ABCD, AND IF ABCD IS NOT A VALID TERM. ID
12       * AN ERROR MESSAGE WILL BE DISPLAYED BECAUSE WHEN START COMMAND
13       * IS EXECUTED, CICS WILL RETURN AN ABNORMAL RETURN CODE.
14       *=========================================================
15       * IF YOU ISSUED BNKL/ABCD, AND TERM ABCD IS NOT ACQUIRED TO CICS,
16       * THE EFFECT OF THIS TRANS. WILL BE THAT TERM. ABCD WILL BE
17       * ACQUIRED TO CICS AND THE GOOD MORNING MSG FOR THE CICS SYSTEM
18       * WILL BE DISPLAYED ON THAT TERMINAL, WHEN IT BECOMES AVAILABLE.
19       *=========================================================
20        ENVIRONMENT DIVISION.
21        DATA DIVISION.
22        WORKING-STORAGE SECTION.
23        01  WS-OUT-MSG-1.
24            05 FILLER                 PIC X(80) VALUE
25            'AN ERROR OF SOME KIND HAS OCCURRED IN PROGRAM BNKLPGM.
26            05 FILLER                 PIC X(80) VALUE
27            'USE CEDF TO DEBUG. NOW PRESS CLEAR KEY TO CONTINUE.
28        01  WS-OUT-MSG-2.
29            05 FILLER                .PIC X(80) VALUE
```

274

```
30         'SIR, ERROR IN INPUT DATA HAS BEEN DETECTED.
31         05 FILLER                PIC X(80) VALUE
32         'THIS TRANSACTION HAS BEEN TERMINATED. SORRY.
33      01 WS-OUT-MSG-3.
34         05 FILLER                     PIC X(80) VALUE
35         'STOP FOOLING AROUND WITH ME, OR ELSE I WILL SCREAM.
36      01 WS-OUT-MSG-4.
37         05 FILLER               PIC X(42) VALUE
38         'DESIRED ACTION WILL BE TAKEN ON TERMINAL: '.
39         05 MSG4-TERM            PIC X(04).
40      01 WS-DATA-IN.
41         05 FILLER               PIC X(4).
42         05 IN-DELIM             PIC X.
43         05 IN-TERM              PIC X(4).
44      01 LEN-9                   PIC 9(4) COMP VALUE 9.
45
46      PROCEDURE DIVISION.
47      ******IF EIBTRMID = 'CA30'
48      *     NEXT SENTENCE
49      *     ELSE
50      ****** PERFORM SORRY-SIR.
51         EXEC CICS IGNORE CONDITION LENGERR END-EXEC.
52         EXEC CICS HANDLE CONDITION ERROR(ERRORS)
53         END-EXEC.
54         EXEC CICS RECEIVE INTO(WS-DATA-IN) LENGTH(LEN-9)
55         END-EXEC.
56         IF IN-DELIM NOT = '/'
57             PERFORM INPUT-ERROR-RTN
```

Figure 5.10. Source code of program BNKLPGM

```
58          ELSE
59              MOVE IN-TERM TO MSG4-TERM.
60          EXEC CICS START TRANSID('BKN2')
61              INTERVAL(000001)
62              TERMID(MSG4-TERM)
63          END-EXEC.
64          EXEC CICS SEND FROM(WS-OUT-MSG-4)
65              LENGTH(46)
66              ERASE END-EXEC.
67          EXEC CICS RETURN END-EXEC.
68          GOBACK.
69      ERRORS.
70          EXEC CICS SEND FROM (WS-OUT-MSG-1)
71              LENGTH(160)
72              END-EXEC.
73          EXEC CICS RETURN END-EXEC.
74      INPUT-ERROR-RTN.
75          EXEC CICS SEND FROM (WS-OUT-MSG-2)
76              LENGTH(160)
77              END-EXEC.
78          EXEC CICS RETURN END-EXEC.
79      SORRY-SIR.
80          EXEC CICS SEND FROM (WS-OUT-MSG-3)
81              LENGTH(80)
82              ERASE
83              END-EXEC.
84          EXEC CICS RETURN END-EXEC.
```

Figure 5.10. continued.

test region comes up, and that file VPPA be opened when the second production region comes up. You have two alternatives. One is to manually issue the CEMT transactions after the CICS regions have been started. This can be done either by the systems programmer or by an operator. The other alternative is to use the facility described here to have CICS automatically issue the CEMT transactions for you. The second alternative saves you both time and money, because it automates a manual process and eliminates the errors inherent in any manual process.

How does this facility work? It works like this. You allocate a partitioned dataset with logical record length of 80. This dataset will have one member for each of your CICS regions, e.g., member CICSTST1 will be for the first test region, member CICSTRN1 for the first training region, and member CICSPRD2 for the second production region. In member CICSTST1 of this PDS, you can insert the following line if you want to have CICS disable transaction ABC1 on the first test region after it comes up:

```
CEMT S TRAN(ABC1) DISABLE
```

Each CEMT command starts in position 1 and can continue up to position 72. Positions 73 to 80 of each record are ignored. You can have as many CEMT commands in this dataset as you like, but each command must be on a separate line. So, if you want CICS to issue 10 CEMT commands, you should have 10 lines in the dataset. The CEMT commands present in the dataset follow the same syntax as the CEMT command you issue on a terminal. (CEMT transaction is described in the *CICS Supplied Transactions* manual.) CICS will read the dataset and execute each command in its post-initialization phase. This scheme is definitely better than asking the operators to manually enter the commands after CICS has come up.

Procedure for Installing This Facility

Step 1. Enter the program shown in Figure 5.11 in a source PDS as member BNCEMTPG.

Step 2. Now assemble and link this program using the JCL given in Section B.2 in Appendix B. This job will create load module BNCEMTPG in your load library. This load library must be included under DDname DFHRPL in the CICS start-up procedure or job.

Step 3. Define the following resources in CICS tables:

Definition of Program in the PPT

```
PROGRAM   BNCEMTPG
GROUP     CICSBOOK
LANGUAGE  ASSEMBLER
```

Other parameters for this program in the PPT should be the same as those for sample program BNPROG1 given in Section 1.6.

Definition of Transaction in the PCT

```
TRANSACTION  NEMT
GROUP        CICSBOOK
PROGRAM      BNCEMTPG
```

Other parameters for this transaction in the PCT should be the same as those for sample transaction BNC1 given in Section 1.6.

Definitions for extra-partition queue AUTC the DCT

```
DFHDCT TYPE=EXTRA,                              X
       DESTID=AUTC,                             X
       DSCNAME=BNCEMT
(Other TYPE=EXTRA entries go here)
DFHDCT TYPE=SDSCI,                              X
       BLKSIZE=3200,                            X
       BUFNO=1,                                 X
       DSCNAME=BNCEMT,                          X
       RECSIZE=80,                              X
       RECFORM=FIXUNB,                          X
       TYPFLE=INPUT                             X
```

In the start-up procedure or job for CICS, the following must be present:

```
//BNCEMT DD DISP=SHR,DSN=pds.name(memname)
```

where pds.name must be replaced by the name of the PDS and memname must be replaced by the member name that is for this CICS region and that contains CEMT commands. This PDS and the content of its members was described above.

Definition of program BNCEMTPG in the post-initialization program list table (PLT):

```
DFHPLT TYPE=ENTRY, PROGRAM=BNCEMTPG
- - - -
DFHPLT TYPE=FINAL
```

Now assemble and link the DCT and the PLT, and install the definition of program and transaction using the CEDA INSTALL command.

```
**************************************************************************
   1  CEMTEXEC DFHEIENT CODEREG=9,DATAREG=10,EIBREG=11
   2  **************************************************************************
   3  * THIS PROGRAM SHOULD BE PRESENT IN THE PROGRAM LIST TABLE (PLT) SO
   4  * THAT IT CAN BE EXECUTED AT CICS INITIALIZATION TIME. IT DOES NOT
   5  * PERFORM ANY TERMINAL INPUT/OUTPUT BECAUSE IT IS NORMALLY NOT STARTED
   6  * FROM A TERMINAL. BUT YOU CAN EXECUTE THIS PROGRAM BY ENTERING ITS
   7  * TRANSACTION ID ON A TERMINAL. WHEN THE PROGRAM ENDS, YOUR
   8  * TERMINAL WILL BECOME FREE. THIS PROGRAM WILL EXECUTE EACH COMMAND
   9  * PRESENT IN INTRAPARTITION QUEUE 'AUTC' WHICH SHOULD BE OPEN ON CICS
  10  * FOR INPUT. NOTE: THIS PROGRAM CLOSES THE QUEUE AND THEN OPENS IT.
  11  * THIS IS TO ENSURE THAT ALL RECORDS IN THE DATA SET WILL BE READ AND
  12  * PROCESSED, EVEN THOUGH THIS DATA SET MIGHT HAVE BEEN READ TO THE END
  13  * PREVIOUSLY BY SOME OTHER CICS APPLICATION PROGRAM.
  14  **************************************************************************
  15         EXEC CICS HANDLE CONDITION ERROR(RETURN)
  16         EXEC CICS LINK PROGRAM('DFHEMTP') COMMAREA(CMD1) LENGTH(80)
  17         EXEC CICS LINK PROGRAM('DFHEMTP') COMMAREA(CMD2) LENGTH(80)
  18  LOOP   EQU  *
  19         EXEC CICS READQ TD QUEUE('AUTC') INTO(COMMAND) LENGTH(QLENGTH)
  20         EXEC CICS LINK PROGRAM('DFHEMTP') COMMAREA(COMMAND) LENGTH(80)
  21         B    LOOP
  22  RETURN EXEC CICS RETURN
  23  CMD1   DC   CL80'CEMT S Q(AUTC) CLOSED'
  24  CMD2   DC   CL80'CEMT S Q(AUTC) OPEN ENABLED'
  25  QLENGTH DC  H'80'
  26         DFHEISTG
  27  COMMAND DS  CL80
  28         END
**************************************************************************
```

Figure 5.11. Source code of program BNCEMTPG

Explanation of This Facility

Because program BNCEMTPG is present in the post-initialization PLT (PLTPI), CICS gives control to it after CICS has been initialized. So, control flows to line 1 in Figure 5.11. Here we execute the entry logic. On line 16, we link to program DFHEMTP, passing it the 80-byte area at CMD1 defined on line 23. So the CEMT command to close queue AUTC is executed. On line 17, we link to DFHEMTP, passing it the command at CMD2. This opens and enables queue AUTC. Now the pointer is positioned at the beginning of the sequential dataset that contains CEMT commands. In the loop formed by lines 18 and 21, we read each record from the extrapartitioned queue AUTC and pass it on to program DFHEMTP for execution. This way, each CEMT command present in the dataset is executed. Finally, when the READQ command on line 19 will get executed, an end of file condition will be raised. Because of the HANDLE command executed on line 15, control would flow to label RETURN on line 22. Here the execution of the RETURN command will return control to CICS.

Read the comments in Figure 5.11. They explain that there is no real need to associate this program with any transaction. But defining a transaction in the PCT and associating it with this program has the benefit that at any time while CICS is up, you can enter the ID of that transaction on a blank screen to execute this program. Every time this program is executed, it reads each record of queue AUTC from the beginning and executes the CEMT command present there.

5.7   A FACILITY TO ISSUE ANY MVS OR JES COMMAND INCLUDING THE MASTER TERMINAL TRANSACTION (CEMT) IN BATCH

The facility presented in Section 2.11 and discussed in Sections 2.11, 2.12, and 2.13 in Chapter 2 can be used to issue any MVS or JES command, including the Modify Command containing any master terminal transaction (CEMT) in a batch job. You are urged to read and understand these sections thoroughly.

5.8   A PROGRAM TO DISPLAY THE AUTOMATIC INITIATE DESCRIPTIONS (AID) AND THE REASON FOR THEIR EXISTENCE

Figures 5.12, 5.13, 5.14, and 5.15 show the various components of a facility that allows you to do the following:

Display the automatic initiate descriptors (AID) present in the CICS system and the reason for their existence

Start any transaction at any terminal after a specified interval of time

Purge a task initiation request that has not yet expired. Expired task initiation requests cannot be purged using this program.

Display the list of all terminals that are presently acquired to CICS

Display what is currently on a CRT-type terminal that is acquired to CICS but on which no task is active

All these functions are present in program BNUTL02 shown in Figure 5.13, which is a multi-function program. In this section, we will concentrate on that feature of the program that displays the automatic initiate descriptors present in the system. To display all the AIDs present in the system and the reason for their existence, you can issue the following transaction on a blank screen:

BNU2/D A

The program will display a screen that resembles the one shown in Figure 5.16. After this screen has been displayed, the task has ended completely and unconditionally, i.e., without specifying anything under the TRANSID option of the RETURN command. But on this screen, you can press the Enter key to refresh the information. This is because the top left corner of the screen displayed already contains the string 'BNU2 D A'. So, there is no need for you to clear the screen and reenter the command.

The following are the salient features of this facility:

1. On line 2 of the screen, this program will display the total number of AIDs present in the system. If all of them do not fit on one screen, only the first n of them will be displayed. The remaining AIDs will not be displayed.

2. The sample display shown in Figure 5.16 was obtained after sending a printout of a program on GENER/OL to a printer that did not have the CRE attribute. It indicates that on terminal ID D917, transaction CSPG is waiting to start. The operator ID for the terminal is PRT. This is a BMS Request type of AID. The Request ID is X'5C5CFD0000AAD600'. The status of terminal D917 is 'REL NOCRE', i.e., it is released from CICS and its attribute is NOCRE. The NOCRE attribute prevents this terminal from being acquired to CICS so that transaction CSPG can become active on this terminal. It is this kind of situation where this utility is most helpful, i.e., in displaying why a printer is not printing a report that was sent to it.

3. Only task initiation requests that have expired are displayed by this program. Unexpired task initiation requests can be displayed using a CICS monitor such as The Monitor for CICS (The Cross System Monitor), with which you should select Storage Display, followed by CICS Control Block, followed by Interval Control Elements (ICE).

```
************************************************************************
1    UASS01 TITLE 'UASS01 - GET CICS SCREEN AND STORE IN TEMP. STORAGE'
2    *---------------------------------------------------------------
3    * THIS IS A COMMAND LEVEL PROGRAM CODED IN ASSEMBLER.
4    * TRANSACTION ID ASSOCIATED WITH THIS PROGRAM: UTR1
5    * AUTHOR: BARRY K. NIRMAL
6    *---------------------------------------------------------------
7           COPY REGDEF
8    TCTTEAR EQU  9
9           COPY DFHCSADS
10          DFHTCA CICSYST=YES
11          COPY DFHTCTTE
12          COPY DFHEICDS
13   DFHEISTG DSECT
14   TSQID   DS   0CL8
15   QID     DS   CL4
16   QTERM   DS   CL4
17   CICSLEN DS   H
18   SAVESCRN DS  CL2400
19   UASS01  CSECT
20           L    R8,TCASYAA      TCASYAA CONTAINS TCA SYSTEM AREA ADDRESS
21           USING DFHTCADY,R8
22           L    R9,TCATCUCN     TCATCUCN CONTAINS ADDRESS OF TCTTE
23           MVC  CICSLEN(2),=H'2400'
24   ****  I MUST CAPTURE SCREEN BUFFER OF TERMINAL ON WHICH I AM RUNNING.
25           EXEC CICS IGNORE CONDITION LENGERR
```

```
26          EXEC CICS RECEIVE INTO(SAVESCRN) LENGTH(CICSLEN) BUFFER     X
27               MAXLENGTH(2400) ASIS
28          EXEC CICS SEND CONTROL FREEKB
29     L    R1,CICSLEN            LOAD R1 WITH LENGTH OF SCREEN BUFFER
30     LTR  R1,R1                 IS SCREEN BUFFER LENGTH = ZERO?
31     BZ   HOWEXIT               IF YES, NO NEED TO WRITE T.S. QUEUE
32     MVC  QID,=CL4'SPYZ'
33     MVC  QTERM,EIBTRMID
34          EXEC CICS WRITEQ TS QUEUE(TSQID) FROM(SAVESCRN)             X
35               LENGTH(CICSLEN)
36 *** TCTTETC HAS TERMINAL TRANSACTION CODE
37 *** TCTTEEIA HAS EXEC. INTERFACE PARM. ADDRESS
38 HOWEXIT OC   TCTTETC,TCTTETC    CHECK IF TCTTETC CONTAINS ZERO
39     BNZ  CHECK1                IF NOT, BRANCH TO CHECK1
40          EXEC CICS RETURN
41 CHECK1  OC   TCTTEEIA,TCTTEEIA  CHECK IF TCTTEEIA CONTAINS ZERO
42     BNZ  HAVECOMM              IF NOT, BRANCH TO HAVECOMM
43          EXEC CICS RETURN TRANSID(TCTTETC)
44 HAVECOMM L    R5,TCTTEEIA   LOAD R5 WITH EXEC. INTERFACE PARM. ADDRESS
45     USING DFHEICDS,R5
46          EXEC CICS RETURN TRANSID(TCTTETC) COMMAREA(EICDBA)          X
47               LENGTH(EICLL)
48     LTORG
49     END
```
****

Figure 5.12.   Source code of program UASSO1

```
*****************************************************************
1  *****************************************************************
2  * THIS IS A MULTI-PURPOSE PROGRAM:
3  *****************************************************************
4  * DATE    | DESCRIPTION OF CHANGE
5  *---------|--------------------------------
6  *YY/MM/DD| NEW PROGRAM
7  *****************************************************************
8  * THE BUILDING OF TERMINAL TABLE ITEMS IN THE TEMPORARY STORAGE,
9  * DISPLAYING THE FIRST ITEM AND SCROLLING OF SCREENS ARE ALL DONE IN
10 * CONVERSATIONAL MODE. ONLY WHEN THE USER SELECTS A TERMINAL, WE
11 * DISPLAY THAT TERMINAL'S BUFFER AND THEN END THE TASK.
12 *===============================================================
13 * THE MEANINGS OF THREE STATUS FLAGS ARE AS FOLLOWS:
14 * LOGODISP: LOGO (INITIAL SCREEN) WAS DISPLAYED.
15 * NONTBLDS: SCREEN BUFFER FROM SPIED TERMINAL HAS BEEN DISPLAYED BUT
16 *           IN NON-TABLE MODE.
17 * TRMTBLDS: SCREEN CONTAINING TABLE OF TERMINALS WAS DISPLAYED, OR
18 *           SCREEN BUFFER FROM SPIED TERMINAL WAS DISPLAYED AFTER
19 *           DISPLAYING TABLE OF TERMINALS.
20 *****************************************************************
21          COPY REGDEF
22          COPY DFHAID
23          COPY  DFHCSADS
24          COPY  DFHTCTFX
25          DFHTCTZE CICSYST=YES
26          COPY  DFHAIDDS
27 DISPREC  DSECT
28 DISPTERM DS   CL4
29 DISPFIL1 DS   CL1
```

```
30  DISPTRAN DS    CL4
31  DISPFIL2 DS    CL1
32  DISPOPER DS    CL3
33  DISPFIL3 DS    CL1
34  DISPAIDT DS    CL9
35  DISPFIL4 DS    CL1
36  DISPRQID DS    CL16
37  DISPFIL5 DS    CL1
38  DISPSTAT DS    CL20
39  DISPFIL6 DS    19C
40  DISPHDR  DSECT
41  DISPHFL1 DS    CL32
42  DISPTOT  DS    CL5
43  DISPHFL2 DS    CL43
44  DFHEISTG DSECT               DYNAMIC STORAGE AREA STARTS HERE
45  COMMAREA DS    0CL9
46  ITEMNO   DS    H             CURRENT ITEM (SCREEN) NUMBER BEING DISPLAYED
47  ITEMMAX  DS    H             MAXIMUM NUMBER OF TERM. TABLE SCREENS
48  CURRSTAT DS    C             INDICATES WHERE WE ARE AT ANY TIME
49  TERMDISP DS    CL4           TERMINAL ID BEING PROCESSED
50  *-------------------------------------------------------------
51  TRANID   DS    CL4
52  CVDA     DS    F
53  CVDA1    DS    F
54  WSLEN1   DS    H
55  TSQID    DS    0CL8
56  QID      DS    CL4
57  QTERM    DS    CL4
```

Figure 5.13. Source code of program BNUTLO2

```
58 SCREEN   DS    CL2400
59          ORG   SCREEN
60 DISP     DS    CL1920
61          ORG   SCREEN+1840
62 SYSMSG   DS    CL80
63          ORG
64          COPY  BNU2S1
65          COPY  BNU2S2
66 NONTBLDS EQU   X'01'
67 LOGODISP EQU   X'02'
68 TRMTBLDS EQU   X'03'
69 *=================================================*
70 COMM01   DS    0F              FORCE ALIGNMENT ON A FULL WORD
71 ADDRIN   DS    F
72 ADDROUT  DS    F
73 LENSMALL DS    H
74 CODE     DS    C
75 *-------------------
76 LEN1920  DC    H'1920'
77 INPUTREQ DS    CL16
78 PURGEID  DS    CL8
79 XTRAN    DS    CL4
80 XTERM    DS    CL4
81 XTIME    DS    PL4
82 *-------------------
83 PACKL8   DS    0D
84          DS    CL5
85 PACKL3   DS    CL3
86 CHARL5   DS    CL5
87 SAVEREG  DS    16F
```

```
 88  *---------------------------
 89  AIDCBAR   EQU  8
 90  TCTPFBAR  EQU  8
 91  TCTTEAR   EQU  9
 92  REGCSA    EQU  9
 93  REGBASE1  EQU  10
 94  REGBASE2  EQU  11
 95  REGDSA    EQU  12
 96  REGEIB    EQU  13
 97  REGBAL    EQU  14
 98  *---------------------------
 99  BNUTL02   DFHEIENT CODEREG=(REGBASE1,REGBASE2),DATAREG=REGDSA,     X
                        EIBREG=REGEIB
100
101            EXEC CICS IGNORE CONDITION LENGERR
102            EXEC CICS HANDLE CONDITION ERROR(ERROR)
103            CLC  EIBCALEN(2),=H'0'       NO COMM AREA PASSED?
104            BE   NOCOMMA                 YES, BRANCH
105            CLC  EIBCALEN(2),=H'9'       COMM AREA LENGTH        FOR VIEWRTN
106            BE   VIEWRTN
107            MVC  SYSMSG,ERROR2           DISPLAY MESSAGE, END PROGRAM
108            B    DMSGEPGM
109  *** WE COME HERE IF NO COMMA AREA HAS BEEN RECEIVED.
110  NOCOMMA   EQU  *
111            MVC  LEN1920(2),=H'1920'
112            EXEC CICS RECEIVE INTO(SCREEN) LENGTH(LEN1920)
113            CLC  DISP+4(4),=C'/D A'                  DISPLAY AID?
114            BE   DISPAID
115            CLC  DISP+4(4),=C'/P A'              PURGE AID?
```

Figure 5.13. continued.

```
116        BE    PURGEAID
117        CLC   DISP+4(4),=C'/H S'      HELP WITH START TRANS?
118        BE    HLPSTART
119        CLC   DISP+4(4),=C'/H P'      HELP WITH PURGE AID?
120        BE    HLPPURGE
121        CLC   DISP+4(3),=C'/S '       START A TRANS?
122        BE    STARTIT
123        CLC   DISP+4(5),=C'/VIEW'     VIEW SCREEN BUFFER?
124        BE    VIEWRTN
125 ** NOW MOVE QUESTION MARK TO FIRST 12 LINES OF SCREEN
126        LA    R2,DISP
127        LA    R3,960
128        LA    R4,*
129        SR    R5,R5
130        O     R5,=X'6F000000'
131        MVCL  R2,R4
132        B     DMSGEPGM
133 HLPSTART EQU  *
134        LA    R2,DISP
135        LA    R3,L'DISP
136        LA    R4,DISPDAT1
137        LA    R5,L'DISPDAT1
138        O     R5,=X'40000000'
139        MVCL  R2,R4
140        B     DMSGEPGM
141 HLPPURGE EQU  *
142        LA    R2,DISP
143        LA    R3,L'DISP
144        LA    R4,DISPDAT2
145        LA    R5,L'DISPDAT2
```

```
146        0      R5,=X'40000000'
147        MVCL   R2,R4
148        B      DMSGEPGM
149 STARTIT EQU   *
150        MVC    XTRAN,DISP+7
151        TR     XTRAN,TRTABLE        CONVERT TO UPPER-CASE
152        MVC    XTERM,DISP+12
153        TR     XTERM,TRTABLE        CONVERT TO UPPER-CASE
154        PACK   XTIME(4),DISP+17(6)
155        NI     XTIME+3,B'11110000'  CHANGE 2ND NIBBLE TO 0000
156        OI     XTIME+3,B'00001100'  CHANGE 2ND NIBBLE TO 1100  (C)
157        EXEC   CICS START TRANSID(XTRAN) INTERVAL(XTIME) TERMID(XTERM)
158        MVC    SYSMSG,SYSMSG2
159        B      DMSGEPGM
160 PURGEAID EQU  *
161        MVC    INPUTREQ,DISP+9
162        TR     INPUTREQ,TRTABLE        CONVERT TO UPPER-CASE
163        LA     R1,INPUTREQ
164        ST     R1,ADDRIN
165        LA     R1,PURGEID
166        ST     R1,ADDROUT
167        MVC    LENSMALL(2),=H'8'
168        MVI    CODE,C'B'
169        EXEC   CICS LINK PROGRAM('BNSUB01') COMMAREA(COMM01) LENGTH(11)
170 * BNSUB01 HAS PLACED PROPER DATA IN 8-BYTE FIELD PURGEID.
171        EXEC   CICS CANCEL REQID(PURGEID)
172        MVC    SYSMSG,SYSMSG1
173        B      DMSGEPGM
```

Figure 5.13. continued.

```
174   ************************************************************
175   * ROUTINE TO DISPLAY AUTOMATIC INITIATE DESCRIPTORS FOLLOW.
176   ************************************************************
177   DISPAID  EQU   *
178            LA    R2,DISP
179            LA    R3,L'DISP
180            LA    R4,HDR
181            LA    R5,L'HDR
182            O     R5,=X'40000000'
183            MVCL  R2,R4               MOVE HEADER TO SCREEN AREA
184            LA    R3,L'HDR
185            LA    R6,DISP
186            AR    R6,R3
187            USING DISPREC,R6
188            SR    R5,R5               CLEAR REGISTER 5
189            EXEC CICS ADDRESS CSA(REGCSA)
190            USING DFHCSADS,REGCSA
191            L     TCTPFBAR,CSATCTBA   LOAD ADDRESS OF TCT PREFIX
192            N     TCTPFBAR,=X'00FFFFFF'    CLEAR HIGH ORDER BYTE
193            USING DFHTCTFX,TCTPFBAR
194            DROP  REGCSA
195            L     TCTTEAR,TCTVSEBA    LOAD ADDR OF FIRST SYSTEM TERM ENTRY
196            N     TCTTEAR,=X'00FFFFFF'    CLEAR HIGH ORDER BYTE
197            USING DFHTCTTE,TCTTEAR
198            DROP  TCTPFBAR
199   POINT10  C     TCTTEAR,=F'0'       IS THERE A SYSTEM ENTRY?
200            BE    POINT40             ..NO, BRANCH TO POINT40
201            LA    R7,TCSEAID          SIGNIFIES END OF CHAIN
202            L     AIDCBAR,TCSESUSF    GET FIRST AID ADDRESS
203            N     AIDCBAR,=X'00FFFFFF'    CLEAR HIGH ORDER BYTE
```

```
204           USING DFHAIDDS,AIDCBAR
205   POINT20 CR    R7,AIDCBAR                  ARE THERE ANY MORE AID ??
206           BE    POINT30                     NO, BRANCH
207           BAL   REGBAL,POINT49              GO, PROCESS THIS A.I.D.
208           L     AIDCBAR,AIDCHNF             LOAD FORWARD ADDRESS
209           N     AIDCBAR,=X'00FFFFFF'        CLEAR HIGH ORDER BYTE
210           B     POINT20
211   POINT30 L     TCTTEAR,TCSENEXT    LOAD ADDR OF NEXT SYSTEM TERM. ENTRY
212           N     TCTTEAR,=X'00FFFFFF'        CLEAR HIGH ORDER BYTE
213           B     POINT10                        LOOP BACK
214   POINT40 LA    R3,DISP+80
215           USING DISPHDR,R3
216           CVD   R5,PACKL8
217           UNPK  CHARL5,PACKL3
218           MVZ   CHARL5+4(1),CHARZERO
219           MVC   DISPTOT,CHARL5
220           DROP  R3
221           MVC   LEN1920(2),=H'1920'
222           EXEC CICS SEND FROM(DISP) LENGTH(LEN1920) ERASE
223           EXEC CICS RETURN
224   *-----------------------------------------------------------
225   * IN ROUTINE BELOW, WE WILL PROCESS THE CURRENT A.I.D.
226   *-----------------------------------------------------------
227   POINT49 A     R5,=F'1' INCREMENT R5 THAT CONTAINS TOTAL A.I.D IN SYSTEM
228           LA    R2,SCREEN+1920
229           CR    R6,R2    ANY ROOM LEFT ON SCREEN FOR THIS A.I.D. ?
230           BNLR  REGBAL   NO, RETURN TO CALLER
231           MVC   DISPTRAN,AIDTRNID
```

Figure 5.13. continued.

```
232         TR    DISPTRAN,TRTABLE
233         MVC   DISPTERM,AIDTRMID
234         TR    DISPTERM,TRTABLE
235         LA    R1,AIDRQID
236         ST    R1,ADDRIN
237         LA    R1,DISPRQID
238         ST    R1,ADDROUT
239         MVC   LENSMALL(2),=H'8'
240         MVI   CODE,C'A'
241         STM   0,15,SAVEREG
242         EXEC CICS LINK PROGRAM('BNSUB01') COMMAREA(COMM01) LENGTH(11)
243 *---------------------------------------------------------------------
244 * BNSUB01 HAS PLACED PROPER DATA IN 16-BYTE FIELD DISPRQID. THIS FIELD
245 * NOW HAS ONLY CHARACTERS 0-9,A,B,C,D,E,F.
246 *---------------------------------------------------------------------
247 EXAMINE1 EQU   *
248         LM    0,15,SAVEREG
249         TM    AIDTYPE,AIDPUT
250         BNO   POINT61
251         MVC   DISPAIDT,=C'I C P PUT'
252         B     POINT70
253 POINT61 TM    AIDTYPE,AIDINT
254         BNO   POINT62
255         MVC   DISPAIDT,=C'I C P INT'
256         B     POINT70
257 POINT62 TM    AIDTYPE,AIDTDP
258         BNO   POINT63
259         MVC   DISPAIDT,=C'T D P REQ'
260         B     POINT70
261 POINT63 TM    AIDTYPE,AIDBMS
```

```
262          BNO   POINT64
263          MVC   DISPAIDT,=C'B M S REQ'
264          B     POINT70
265 POINT64  TM    AIDTYPE,AIDISC
266          BNO   POINT65
267          MVC   DISPAIDT,=C'I S C REQ'
268          B     POINT70
269 POINT65  TM    AIDTYPE,AIDCRRD
270          BNO   POINT66
271          MVC   DISPAIDT,=C'TR/TS REM'
272          B     POINT70
273 POINT66  MVC   DISPAIDT,=C'???????'
274 POINT70  LR    R3,TCTTEAR        SAVE TCTTEAR INTO R3
275          L     TCTTEAR,AIDTCTA   GET TCTTE ADDRESS INTO TCTTEAR
276          N     TCTTEAR,=X'00FFFFFF'   CLEAR HIGH ORDER BYTE
277          C     TCTTEAR,=F'0'     IS THE TCTTE ADDRES ZERO ?
278          BE    POINT99
279          MVC   DISPOPER,TCTTEOI
280          TR    DISPOPER,TRTABLE
281          LA    R4,DISPSTAT
282          TM    TCTTETS,TCTTESAT
283          BO    POINT92
284          MVC   0(5,R4),=C'NOATI'
285          A     R4,=F'6'
286 POINT92  TM    TCTTETS,TCTTESOS+TCTTESPO
287          BNO   POINT93
288          MVC   0(3,R4),=C'OUT'
289          A     R4,=F'4'
```

Figure 5.13. continued.

293

```
290 POINT93  TM    TCTIVTAM,TCTEVTAM
291          BNO   POINT99
292          TM    TCTEILOS,TCTENIS
293          BO    POINT94
294          MVC   0(3,R4),=C'REL'
295          A     R4,=F'4'
296 POINT94  TM    TCTESEST,TCTESLGI
297          BO    POINT99
298          MVC   0(5,R4),=C'NOCRE'
299 POINT99  A     R6,=F'80'
300          LR    TCTTEAR,R3            RESTORE CONTENT OF TCTTEAR
301          BR    REGBAL               RETURN TO CALLER
302 *-------------------------------------------------------------
303 VIEWERR  EQU   *
304          EXEC CICS SEND FROM(ERROR1) LENGTH(80) ERASE
305          B     EXITPGM
306 ERROR    EQU   *
307          MVC   SYSMSG,ERROR1
308 DMSGEPGM EQU   *
309          EXEC CICS SEND FROM(DISP) LENGTH(1920) ERASE
310          EXEC CICS RETURN
311 *-------------------------------------------------------------
312 VIEWRTN  EQU   *
313 ***** REGISTER 7 IS AVAILABLE FOR USE IN THIS ROUTINE.
314          EXEC CICS HANDLE CONDITION ERROR(VIEWERR)
315          EXEC CICS HANDLE AID CLEAR(CLEARKEY)
316          MVC   MAP1M010(40),BLANKS  BLANK OUT ERROR MSG
317          MVC   MAP1M020(40),BLANKS  BLANK OUT ERROR MSG
318          CLC   EIBCALEN(2),=H'0'    FIRST TIME IN THIS PROGRAM?
319          BE    INITIAL              YES, DISPLAY MAP
```

```
320          L     R6,DFHEICAP              SAVE COMM AREA  IN MY OWN AREA
321          MVC   COMMAREA(9),0(R6)
322          CLI   CURRSTAT,NONTBLDS        WERE WE AT NON TABLE DISPLAY?
323          BNE   POINT00                  NO , BRANCH
324          CLI   EIBAID,DFHENTER          PRESSED ENTER?
325          BNE   INITIAL                  NO, REDISPLAY INITIAL SCREEN
326          MVC   REQTERMI,TERMDISP        ...
327          B     REDISP1                  REDISPLAY SCREEN
328 INITIAL  EXEC CICS SEND MAP('BNU2M1') MAPSET('BNU2S1') MAPONLY            X
329          ERASE FREEKB
330          MVI   CURRSTAT,LOGODISP        INDICATE FIRST SCREEN DISPLAYED
331          MVC   TERMDISP,LOWVALS         ZEROISE TERMID IN COMMAREA
332          EXEC CICS RETURN COMMAREA(COMMAREA) LENGTH(9) TRANSID('BNU2')
333 POINT00  CLI   CURRSTAT,TRMTBLDS        WAS TABLE OF TERMINALS DISPLAYED?
334          BNE   POINT01                  NO, BRANCH
335          CLI   EIBAID,DFHENTER  ENTER KEY PRESSED ON SPIED SCREEN?
336          BE    REFRESH2
337          MVC   COMMAREA+5(4),LOWVALS    UNSET TERMID IN COMMAREA
338          B     POINT02                     DISPLAY TABLE OF TERMINALS
339 REFRESH2 EQU   *
340          MVC   REQTERMI,COMMAREA+5
341          B     REDISP1
342 POINT01  EXEC CICS RECEIVE MAP('BNU2M1') MAPSET('BNU2S1')                 X
343          INTO(BNU2M1I)
344          CLC   REQTERML(2),=X'0000'       TERM ID ENTERED?
345          BNE   REDISP1                    YES, BRANCH
346          B     ROUTINE1                   NO, DISPLAY TBL OF TERM
347 REDISP1  EXEC CICS HANDLE CONDITION TERMIDERR(NEXT300)
```

Figure 5.13. continued.

```
348  ***  INQUIRE ON REQUESTED TERM ID.
349        CLC   REQTERMI,EIBTRMID
350        BE    YOURTERM
351        MVC   TRANID,BLANKS
352        EXEC  CICS INQUIRE TERMINAL(REQTERMI) TRANSACTION(TRANID)    X
353              ACQSTATUS(CVDA) TTISTATUS(CVDA1)
354        CLC   CVDA(4),=F'69'            TERM ACQD TO CICS
355        BNE   NOTACQD
356        CLC   CVDA1(4),=F'78'     NO   TTI
357        BE    NOTTI           YES, LOOP BACK
358 NEXT200 CLC  TRANID,=CL4' '      TASK ACTIVE?
359        BE    STARTRAN        NO, OK
360 TASKACT MVC  MAP1M010,ERRMSG1    YES, DISPLAY ERROR
361        B     NEXT400
362 NOTACQD MVC  MAP1M010(40),ERRMSG2
363        B     NEXT400
364 YOURTERM MVC MAP1M010(40),ERRMSG3A
365        B     NEXT400
366 NOTTI   MVC  MAP1M010(40),ERRMSG2A
367        B     NEXT400
368 NEXT300 MVC  MAP1M010,ERRMSG3       TERM NOT IN TCT
369 NEXT400 CLI  CURRSTAT,TRMTBLDS      TERM TBL BEING PROCESSED?
370        BE    NEXT450           YES, BRANCH
371        MVI   CURRSTAT,LOGODISP      SET LOGO JUST DISPLAYED
372        MVC   COMMAREA+5(4),LOWVALS  NULLIFY TERMID IN COMMAREA
373        EXEC  CICS SEND MAP('BNU2M1') MAPSET('BNU2S1') ERASE        X
374              ALARM FREEKB
375        EXEC  CICS RETURN COMMAREA(COMMAREA) LENGTH(9) TRANSID('BNU2')
376 NEXT450 MVC  MAP2M010,MAP1M010      SET ERROR MESSAGE IN SECOND MAP X
377        EXEC  CICS SEND MAP('BNU2M2') MAPSET('BNU2S2') ERASE        X
```

```
378            ALARM  FREEKB
379        B   READHIM                    CONTINUE TBL PROCESSING
380 ****** EVERYTHING OK - CAPTURE SCREEN BUFFER FROM TARGET TERMINAL
381 STARTRAN EQU  *
382        MVC  QID,=CL4'SPYZ'
383        MVC  QTERM,REQTERMI
384        EXEC CICS HANDLE CONDITION QIDERR(NOPROB)
385        EXEC CICS DELETEQ TS QUEUE(TSQID)
386 NOPROB EXEC CICS START TRANSID('UTR1') TERMID(REQTERMI)
387 ** ATTEMPT TO READ TS QUEUE CREATED BY STARTED TASK. MAKE 9 ATTEMPTS.
388        LA   R5,9                 NUMBER OF ATTEMPTED READS.
389        EXEC CICS HANDLE CONDITION QIDERR(TSQMISS)
390 TRYAGAIN LA R6,2400
391        STH  R6,WSLEN1
392        EXEC CICS READQ TS QUEUE(TSQID) INTO(SCREEN) LENGTH(WSLEN1)
393        EXEC CICS DELETEQ TS QUEUE(TSQID)
394        EXEC CICS SEND CONTROL CURSOR(0) ERASE
395 * SEND SCREEN BUFFER TO TERMINAL FOR HIS/HER VIEWING PLEASURE.
396        EXEC CICS SEND FROM(SCREEN) LENGTH(WSLEN1)
397        B    BUFFSENT  EXIT
398 * WAIT ONE SECOND BEFORE ATTEMPTING TO READ THE T.S. QUEUE.
399 TSQMISS EXEC CICS DELAY INTERVAL(1)
400        BCT  R5,TRYAGAIN  GO TO TRYAGAIN IF LESS THAN 9 ATTEMPTS MADE
401        MVC  MAP1MO1O,ERRMSG1A
402        B    NEXT400
403 *****************************************************************
404 BUFFSENT MVC COMMAREA+5(4),REQTERMI
405        CLI  CURRSTAT,TRMTBLDS    TERMINAL TBL PROCESSED?
```

Figure 5.13. continued.

```
406             BE      GETOUT          YES, BRANCH
407             MVI     CURRSTAT,NONTBLDS
408  GETOUT     EXEC CICS RETURN TRANSID('BNU2') COMMAREA(COMMAREA) LENGTH(9)
409  *********************************************************************
410  * WE COME HERE IF CLEAR KEY WAS PRESSED BY THE USER, BUT NOT ON SPIED
411  * SCREEN, BUT ON ONE OF THE TWO MAPS DISPLAYED BY THIS PROGRAM.
412  *********************************************************************
413  CLEARKEY   EXEC CICS IGNORE CONDITION QIDERR
414             MVC     QID,=CL4'SPYT'  CLEAN UP THE T.S. QUEUE BEFORE EXITING
415             MVC     QTERM,EIBTRMID
416             EXEC CICS DELETEQ QUEUE(TSQID)
417             EXEC CICS SEND FROM(BLANKS) LENGTH(1) ERASE
418             EXEC CICS RETURN
419  *********************************************************************
420  ROUTINE1   MVI     CURRSTAT,TRMTBLDS      INDICATE PROCESSING TERM. TABLE
421             LA      R6,32
422             LA      R5,TERM10
423             MVI     BNU2M20,X'00'
424             MVC     BNU2M20+1(256),BNU2M20
425             MVC     BNU2M20+257(256),BNU2M20+256
426             MVC     BNU2M20+513(256),BNU2M20+512
427             MVC     BNU2M20+769(256),BNU2M20+768
428             MVC     BNU2M20+1025(256),BNU2M20+1025
429  * BROWSE THE TCT
430             EXEC CICS INQUIRE TERMINAL START
431             EXEC CICS HANDLE CONDITION END(YY100)
432             SR      R3,R3           R3 WILL CONTAIN NUMBER OF ITEMS STORED
433  * READ NEXT TERM IN TCT
434  YY020      MVC     TRANID,BLANKS
435             EXEC CICS INQUIRE TERMINAL(0(R5)) USERID(11(R5)) NEXT         X
```

```
436              OPERID(26(R5)) ACQSTATUS(CVDA) TRANSACTION(TRANID)     X
437              TTISTATUS(CVDA1)
438        CLC   CVDA,=F'69'    TERMINAL IS ACQUIRED?
439        BNE   YY020          NO, LOOP BACK
440        LA    R5,36(R5)
441        BCT   R6,YY020
442  YY040 MVC   MAP2M010,CONTMSG     INDICATE ANOTHER SCREEN TO COME
443        MVC   QID,=CL4'SPYT'       WRITE NEXT TS RECORD
444        MVC   QTERM,EIBTRMID
445        LA    R3,1(R3)             INCREMENT R3 BY 1
446        EXEC CICS WRITEQ TS QUEUE(TSQID) FROM(BNU2M20)               X
447              LENGTH(MAPLNGTH+2)
448        MVI   BNU2M20,X'00'        BLANK OUT ENTIRE SECOND MAP, BARRY
449        MVC   BNU2M20+1(256),BNU2M20
450        MVC   BNU2M20+257(256),BNU2M20+256
451        MVC   BNU2M20+513(256),BNU2M20+512
452        MVC   BNU2M20+769(256),BNU2M20+768
453        MVC   BNU2M20+1025(256),BNU2M20+1024
454        LA    R6,32     MAX. OF 32 TERMINALS ON SECOND SCREEN POSSIBLE
455        LA    R5,TERM10
456        B     YY020          CONTINUE BROWSING
457  *** WE COME HERE WHEN END OF TCT ENCOUNTERED ON EXEC CICS INQUIRE.
458  YY100 LA    R3,1(R3)
459        STH   R3,ITEMMAX
460        MVC   0(4,R5),LOWVALS
461        MVC   11(8,R5),LOWVALS
462        MVC   26(3,R5),LOWVALS
463        MVC   QID,=CL4'SPYT'            WRITE TS RECROD
```

Figure 5.13. continued.

```
464           MVC   QTERM,EIBTRMID
465           EXEC CICS WRITEQ TS QUEUE(TSQID) FROM(BNU2M2O)            X
466                LENGTH(MAPLNGTH+2)
467  *** STORING OF DATA FINISHED. DISPLAY THE FIRST ITEM STORED IN T.S.
468           LA    R6,1               SET ITEM NUMBER TO 1
469           STH   R6,ITEMNO
470  POINT02  EQU   *
471           EXEC CICS HANDLE AID PF7(GOBACK) PF19(GOBACK) PF8(GOAHEAD) X
472                PF20(GOAHEAD)
473  *** READ THE DESIRED ITEM FROM T.S. QUEUE.
474  YY130    MVC   QID,=CL4'SPYT'     READ RELEVANT TS Q REC
475           MVC   QTERM,EIBTRMID
476           EXEC CICS READQ TS QUEUE(TSQID) INTO(BNU2M2O) ITEM(ITEMNO) X
477                LENGTH(MAPLNGTH+2)
478  * DISPLAY THE SCREEN CONTAINING ARRAY OF TERMINALS.
479  YY135    EXEC CICS SEND MAP('BNU2M2') MAPSET('BNU2S2') ERASE FREEKB X
480  READHIM  EXEC CICS RECEIVE MAP('BNU2M2') MAPSET('BNU2S2')
481           LH    R5,EIBCPOSN        VALIDATE CURSOR POSITION
482           SH    R5,=H'324'
483           BM    INVPOS
484           CH    R5,=H'1280'
485           BNH   LOOKSOK
486  INVPOS   MVC   MAP2M01O,ERRMSG5
487  TELLHIM  EXEC CICS SEND MAP('BNU2M2') MAPSET('BNU2S2') DATAONLY    X
488                FREEKB ALARM
489           B     READHIM
490  LOOKSOK  SR    R4,R4
491           D     R4,=F'40'
492           CH    R4,=H'3'
493           BH    INVPOS
```

```
494           M     R4,=F'36'
495           LA    R6,TERM10(R5)
496           MVC   REQTERMI,0(R6)
497           CLC   REQTERMI,LOWVALS
498           BE    INVPOS
499           B     REDISP1
500  ** ROUTINE TO BROWSE BACKWARD THROUGH THE TERMINAL TABLE.
501  GOBACK   EQU   *
502           LH    R6,ITEMNO
503           SH    R6,=H'1'
504           CH    R6,=H'0'
505           BH    NOPROB1
506           MVC   MAP2M010,ERRMSG6
507           B     TELLHIM
508  NOPROB1  STH   R6,ITEMNO
509           B     YY130
510  ** ROUTINE TO BROWSE FORWARD THROUGH THE TERMINAL TABLE.
511  GOAHEAD  EQU   *
512           LH    R6,ITEMNO
513           AH    R6,=H'1'
514           CH    R6,ITEMMAX
515           BNH   NOPROB2
516           MVC   MAP2M010,ERRMSG6
517           B     TELLHIM
518  NOPROB2  STH   R6,ITEMNO
519           B     YY130
520  MAPLNGTH DC    A(BNU2M2E-BNU2M20)
521  LOWVALS  DC    XL8'0000000000000000'
```

Figure 5.13. continued.

```
522  ERRMSG1   DC  CL40'A TASK IS ACTIVE ON THIS TERM.  CHECK IT.'
523  ERRMSG1A  DC  CL40'SEEMS UTR1 IS STILL WAITING TO START....'
524  ERRMSG2   DC  CL40'TERMINAL IS NOT ACQUIRED BY THIS CICS.'
525  ERRMSG2A  DC  CL40'THIS TERMINAL SEEMS TO BE A PRINTER.'
526  ERRMSG3   DC  CL40'THIS TERMINAL ID IS NOT KNOWN TO CICS.'
527  ERRMSG3A  DC  CL40'THIS IS YOUR OWN TERMINAL- NOT ALLOWED.'
528  ERRMSG5   DC  CL40'INVALID CURSOR POSITION - TRY AGAIN.'
529  ERRMSG6   DC  CL40'SCROLLING LIMIT HAS BEEN REACHED.......'
530  CONTMSG   DC  CL40'MORE TERMINALS ARE YET TO BE SHOWN......'
531  *------------------------------------------------------------
532  DISPDAT1  DS  0CL480
533            DC  CL50'BNU2/S TRAN TERM HHMMSS'
534            DC  CL30' '
535            DC  CL50'**** JUST OVERTYPE ON THE FIRST LINE AND PRESS ENT'
536            DC  CL30'ER KEY'
537            DC  CL80' '
538            DC  CL50'    TRAN  = TRANSACTION TO BE STARTED'
539            DC  CL30' '
540            DC  CL50'    TERM  = TARGET TERMINAL'
541            DC  CL30' '
542            DC  CL50'    HHMMSS= INTERVAL AFTER WHICH TRAN. WILL BE ST'
543            DC  CL30'ARTED'
544  DISPDAT2  DS  0CL400
545            DC  CL50'BNU2/P A=XXXXXXXXXXXXXXXX'
546            DC  CL30' '
547            DC  CL50'**** JUST OVERTYPE ON THE FIRST LINE AND PRESS ENT'
548            DC  CL30'ER KEY'
549            DC  CL80' '
550            DC  CL50'    X-X = 16 BYTE FIELD IN HEX CHARACTERS ONLY SP'
551            DC  CL30'ECIFYING UNEXPIRED ICP REQ ID.'
```

```
552            DC    CL50'             TO BE PURGED.  GET THIS FROM THE MONITOR'
553            DC    CL30'  (INTERVAL, CNTL ELEMENT)'
554  ERROR1    DC    CL50'AN ERROR OF SOME KIND DETECTED IN BNUTL02.  PHONE '
555            DC    CL30'BARRY NIRMAL FOR ASSISTANCE.'
556  ERROR2    DC    CL50'COMM AREA OF LENGTH OTHER THAN 9 WAS PASSED TO PRO'
557            DC    CL30'GRAM BNUTL02.  REJECTED.'
558  SYSMSG1   DC    CL50'CANCEL HAS BEEN ISSUED. HOPEFULLY IT WILL WORK. IF'
559            DC    CL30' NOT, CONTACT BARRY NIRMAL.'
560  SYSMSG2   DC    CL50'REQUESTED TRANS ID WILL BE STARTED ON REQUESTED TE'
561            DC    CL30'RM. AFTER SPECIFIED INTERVAL'
562  HDR       DS    0CL400
563            DC    '*************'1234567890123456789012345678901234567890123'
564            DC    C'BNU2/D A  *** AUTOMATIC INITIATE DESCRIPTORS CURRENTL'
565            DC    C'Y IN THIS CICS SYSTEM ***'
566            DC    C'*** TOTAL A.I.D. IN THE SYSTEM: 00000 SOME OF THEM MA'
567            DC    C'Y NOT BE DISPLAYED BELOW.'
568            DC    C'================================================='
569            DC    C'================================================='
570            DC    C'TERM TRAN OPR   A.I.D.        REQUEST ID.   STATUS OF TER'
571            DC    C'MINAL'
572            DC    C' ID.  ID.  ID.                 TYPE'
573            DC    C' '
574  CHARZERO  DC    C'0'
575  BLANKS    DC    CL40' '
576            DC    '************' 0123456789ABCDEF ****************************
577  TRTABLE   DC    C'................',        00-0F
578            DC    C'................',        10-1F
579            DC    C'................',        20-2F
```

Figure 5.13. continued.

303

```
580        DC    C'.........................'        30-3F
581        DC    C'.......¢.<(+|'                     40-4F
582 ** NOTE TWO AMPERSANDS TELL ASSEMBLER TO REPLACE THEM BY ONE AMPERSAND.
583        DC    C'&&.........!$*);¬'                 50-5F
584        DC    C'-/.......,%_>?'                    60-6F
585        DC    C'.........:#@.="'                   70-7F
586        DC    C'.ABCDEFGHI......'                  80-8F
587        DC    C'.JKLMNOPQR......'                  90-9F
588        DC    C'..STUVWXYZ......'                  A0-AF
589        DC    C'................'                  B0-BF
590        DC    C'{ABCDEFGHI......'                  C0-CF
591        DC    C'}JKLMNOPQR......'                  D0-DF
592        DC    C'.STUVWXYZ......'                   E0-EF
593        DC    C'0123456789......'                  F0-FF
594        ORG
595        END
596 *=======================================================================
   *************************************************************************
```

Figure 5.13. continued.

```
****************************************************************
 1 BNU2S1   DFHMSD TYPE=&SYSPARM,MODE=INOUT,CTRL=FREEKB,TIOAPFX=YES,  X
 2                 STORAGE=AUTO,EXTATT=YES
 3 BNU2M1   DFHMDI SIZE=(24,80)
 4          DFHMDF POS=(05,01),LENGTH=36,ATTRB=ASKIP,COLOR=BLUE,       X
 5                 INITIAL='** A WARM WELCOME TO THE FACILITY TO'
 6          DFHMDF POS=(05,38),LENGTH=36,ATTRB=(ASKIP),COLOR=BLUE,     X
 7                 INITIAL='VIEW THE CONTENT OF ANY DISPLAY (CRT'
 8          DFHMDF POS=(06,01),LENGTH=46,ATTRB=(ASKIP),COLOR=BLUE,     X
 9                 INITIAL='TYPE) TERMINAL CURRENTLY ATTACHED TO THIS CICS'
10          DFHMDF POS=(06,48),LENGTH=07,ATTRB=(ASKIP),COLOR=BLUE,     X
11                 INITIAL='SYSTEM.'
12          DFHMDF POS=(10,01),LENGTH=46,ATTRB=ASKIP,COLOR=BLUE,       X
13                 INITIAL='ENTER THE FOUR-CHARACTER CICS TERMINAL ID HERE'
14          DFHMDF POS=(10,48),LENGTH=4,ATTRB=(ASKIP,BRT),INITIAL=' ===>'
15 REQTERM  DFHMDF POS=(10,53),LENGTH=4,ATTRB=(IC,FSET)
16          DFHMDF POS=(10,58),LENGTH=1,ATTRB=(PROT,DRK)
17          DFHMDF POS=(11,01),LENGTH=42,ATTRB=ASKIP,COLOR=BLUE,       X
18                 INITIAL='(LEAVE IT BLANK TO DISPLAY LIST OF CURRENT'
19          DFHMDF POS=(11,44),LENGTH=20,ATTRB=ASKIP,COLOR=BLUE,       X
20                 INITIAL='USERS OF THE SYSTEM)'
21          DFHMDF POS=(17,01),LENGTH=46,ATTRB=ASKIP,COLOR=BLUE,       X
22                 INITIAL='WHEN YOU OBTAIN THE TARGET SCREEN, PRESS ENTER'
23          DFHMDF POS=(17,48),LENGTH=28,ATTRB=ASKIP,COLOR=BLUE,       X
24                 INITIAL='TO UPDATE THE VIEWED SCREEN;'
25          DFHMDF POS=(18,01),LENGTH=34,ATTRB=ASKIP,COLOR=BLUE,       X
26                 INITIAL='PRESS ANY OTHER KEY TO RETURN HERE'
27          DFHMDF POS=(19,10),LENGTH=5,ATTRB=ASKIP,COLOR=BLUE,        X
```

Figure 5.14. Source code of mapset BNU2S1

305

```
28              INITIAL='PRESS'
29     DFHMDF POS=(19,16),LENGTH=05,ATTRB=(ASKIP,BRT),          X
30              INITIAL='CLEAR'
31     DFHMDF POS=(19,22),LENGTH=30,ATTRB=ASKIP,COLOR=BLUE,     X
32              INITIAL='KEY TO TERMINATE THIS FACILITY'
33 MAP1M01 DFHMDF POS=(23,19),LENGTH=40,ATTRB=(ASKIP,BRT)
34 MAP1M02 DFHMDF POS=(24,19),LENGTH=40,ATTRB=(ASKIP,BRT)
35     DFHMSD TYPE=FINAL
36     END
```

****

Figure 5.14. continued.

```
************************************************************************
 1 BNU2S2  DFHMSD TYPE=&SYSPARM,MODE=INOUT,CTRL=FREEKB,TIOAPFX=YES,     X
 2                STORAGE=AUTO,EXTATT=YES
 3 BNU2M2  DFHMDI SIZE=(24,80),COLOR=GREEN
 4         DFHMDF POS=(1,05),LENGTH=44,ATTRB=ASKIP,COLOR=TURQUOISE,     X
 5                INITIAL='FACILITY TO VIEW THE CONTENT OF ANY CRT TYPE'
 6         DFHMDF POS=(1,50),LENGTH=26,ATTRB=ASKIP,COLOR=TURQUOISE,     X
 7                INITIAL='TERMINAL CONNECTED TO CICS'
 8         DFHMDF POS=(3,3),LENGTH=25,ATTRB=(ASKIP,BRT),COLOR=NEUTRAL,  X
 9                INITIAL='TERM ID    USER ID    OP ID'
10         DFHMDF POS=(3,43),LENGTH=25,ATTRB=(ASKIP,BRT),COLOR=NEUTRAL, X
11                INITIAL='TERM ID    USER ID    OP ID'
12 TERM1   DFHMDF POS=(5,4),LENGTH=4,ATTRB=(UNPROT,IC,FSET)
13         DFHMDF POS=(5,9),LENGTH=1,ATTRB=PROT
14 USER1   DFHMDF POS=(5,12),LENGTH=8,ATTRB=(PROT,FSET)
15 OPER1   DFHMDF POS=(5,24),LENGTH=3,ATTRB=(PROT,FSET)
16 TERM2   DFHMDF POS=(5,44),LENGTH=4,ATTRB=(UNPROT,FSET)
17         DFHMDF POS=(5,49),LENGTH=1,ATTRB=PROT
18 USER2   DFHMDF POS=(5,52),LENGTH=8,ATTRB=(PROT,FSET)
19 OPER2   DFHMDF POS=(5,64),LENGTH=3,ATTRB=(PROT,FSET)
20 TERM3   DFHMDF POS=(6,4),LENGTH=4,ATTRB=(UNPROT,FSET)
21         DFHMDF POS=(6,9),LENGTH=1,ATTRB=PROT
22 USER3   DFHMDF POS=(6,12),LENGTH=8,ATTRB=(PROT,FSET)
23 OPER3   DFHMDF POS=(6,24),LENGTH=3,ATTRB=(PROT,FSET)
24 TERM4   DFHMDF POS=(6,44),LENGTH=4,ATTRB=(UNPROT,FSET)
25         DFHMDF POS=(6,49),LENGTH=1,ATTRB=PROT
26 USER4   DFHMDF POS=(6,52),LENGTH=8,ATTRB=(PROT,FSET)
27 OPER4   DFHMDF POS=(6,64),LENGTH=3,ATTRB=(PROT,FSET)
```

Figure 5.15.   Source code of mapset BNU2S2

```
28  TERM5    DFHMDF POS=(7,4),LENGTH=4,ATTRB=(UNPROT,FSET)
29           DFHMDF POS=(7,9),LENGTH=1,ATTRB=PROT
30  USER5    DFHMDF POS=(7,12),LENGTH=8,ATTRB=(PROT,FSET)
31  OPER5    DFHMDF POS=(7,24),LENGTH=3,ATTRB=(PROT,FSET)
32  TERM6    DFHMDF POS=(7,44),LENGTH=4,ATTRB=(UNPROT,FSET)
33           DFHMDF POS=(7,49),LENGTH=1,ATTRB=PROT
34  USER6    DFHMDF POS=(7,52),LENGTH=8,ATTRB=(PROT,FSET)
35  OPER6    DFHMDF POS=(7,64),LENGTH=3,ATTRB=(PROT,FSET)
36  TERM7    DFHMDF POS=(8,4),LENGTH=4,ATTRB=(UNPROT,FSET)
37           DFHMDF POS=(8,9),LENGTH=1,ATTRB=PROT
38  USER7    DFHMDF POS=(8,12),LENGTH=8,ATTRB=(PROT,FSET)
39  OPER7    DFHMDF POS=(8,24),LENGTH=3,ATTRB=(PROT,FSET)
40  TERM8    DFHMDF POS=(8,44),LENGTH=4,ATTRB=(UNPROT,FSET)
41           DFHMDF POS=(8,49),LENGTH=1,ATTRB=PROT
42  USER8    DFHMDF POS=(8,52),LENGTH=8,ATTRB=(PROT,FSET)
43  OPER8    DFHMDF POS=(8,64),LENGTH=3,ATTRB=(PROT,FSET)
44  TERM9    DFHMDF POS=(9,4),LENGTH=4,ATTRB=(UNPROT,FSET)
45           DFHMDF POS=(9,9),LENGTH=1,ATTRB=PROT
46  USER9    DFHMDF POS=(9,12),LENGTH=8,ATTRB=(PROT,FSET)
47  OPER9    DFHMDF POS=(9,24),LENGTH=3,ATTRB=(PROT,FSET)
48  TERM10   DFHMDF POS=(9,44),LENGTH=4,ATTRB=(UNPROT,FSET)
49           DFHMDF POS=(9,49),LENGTH=1,ATTRB=PROT
50  USER10   DFHMDF POS=(9,52),LENGTH=8,ATTRB=(PROT,FSET)
51  OPER10   DFHMDF POS=(9,64),LENGTH=3,ATTRB=(PROT,FSET)
52  TERM11   DFHMDF POS=(10,4),LENGTH=4,ATTRB=(UNPROT,FSET)
53           DFHMDF POS=(10,9),LENGTH=1,ATTRB=PROT
54  USER11   DFHMDF POS=(10,12),LENGTH=8,ATTRB=(PROT,FSET)
55  OPER11   DFHMDF POS=(10,24),LENGTH=3,ATTRB=(PROT,FSET)
56  TERM12   DFHMDF POS=(10,44),LENGTH=4,ATTRB=(UNPROT,FSET)
57           DFHMDF POS=(10,49),LENGTH=1,ATTRB=PROT
```

```
58   USER12   DFHMDF POS=(10,52),LENGTH=8,ATTRB=(PROT,FSET)
59   OPER12   DFHMDF POS=(10,64),LENGTH=3,ATTRB=(PROT,FSET)
60   TERM13   DFHMDF POS=(11,04),LENGTH=4,ATTRB=(UNPROT,FSET)
61            DFHMDF POS=(11,09),LENGTH=1,ATTRB=PROT
62   USER13   DFHMDF POS=(11,12),LENGTH=8,ATTRB=(PROT,FSET)
63   OPER13   DFHMDF POS=(11,24),LENGTH=3,ATTRB=(PROT,FSET)
64   TERM14   DFHMDF POS=(11,44),LENGTH=4,ATTRB=(UNPROT,FSET)
65            DFHMDF POS=(11,49),LENGTH=1,ATTRB=PROT
66   USER14   DFHMDF POS=(11,52),LENGTH=8,ATTRB=(PROT,FSET)
67   OPER14   DFHMDF POS=(11,64),LENGTH=3,ATTRB=(PROT,FSET)
68   TERM15   DFHMDF POS=(12,04),LENGTH=4,ATTRB=(UNPROT,FSET)
69            DFHMDF POS=(12,09),LENGTH=1,ATTRB=PROT
70   USER15   DFHMDF POS=(12,12),LENGTH=8,ATTRB=(PROT,FSET)
71   OPER15   DFHMDF POS=(12,24),LENGTH=3,ATTRB=(PROT,FSET)
72   TERM16   DFHMDF POS=(12,44),LENGTH=4,ATTRB=(UNPROT,FSET)
73            DFHMDF POS=(12,49),LENGTH=1,ATTRB=PROT
74   USER16   DFHMDF POS=(12,52),LENGTH=8,ATTRB=(PROT,FSET)
75   OPER16   DFHMDF POS=(12,64),LENGTH=3,ATTRB=(PROT,FSET)
76   TERM17   DFHMDF POS=(13,4),LENGTH=4,ATTRB=(UNPROT,FSET)
77            DFHMDF POS=(13,9),LENGTH=1,ATTRB=PROT
78   USER17   DFHMDF POS=(13,12),LENGTH=8,ATTRB=(PROT,FSET)
79   OPER17   DFHMDF POS=(13,24),LENGTH=3,ATTRB=(PROT,FSET)
80   TERM18   DFHMDF POS=(13,44),LENGTH=4,ATTRB=(UNPROT,FSET)
81            DFHMDF POS=(13,49),LENGTH=1,ATTRB=PROT
82   USER18   DFHMDF POS=(13,52),LENGTH=8,ATTRB=(PROT,FSET)
83   OPER18   DFHMDF POS=(13,64),LENGTH=3,ATTRB=(PROT,FSET)
84   TERM19   DFHMDF POS=(14,04),LENGTH=4,ATTRB=(UNPROT,FSET)
85            DFHMDF POS=(14,09),LENGTH=1,ATTRB=PROT
```

Figure 5.15. continued.

```
 86 USER19  DFHMDF POS=(14,12),LENGTH=8,ATTRB=(PROT,FSET)
 87 OPER19  DFHMDF POS=(14,24),LENGTH=3,ATTRB=(PROT,FSET)
 88 TERM20  DFHMDF POS=(14,44),LENGTH=4,ATTRB=(UNPROT,FSET)
 89         DFHMDF POS=(14,49),LENGTH=1,ATTRB=PROT
 90 USER20  DFHMDF POS=(14,52),LENGTH=8,ATTRB=(PROT,FSET)
 91 OPER20  DFHMDF POS=(14,64),LENGTH=3,ATTRB=(PROT,FSET)
 92 TERM21  DFHMDF POS=(15,04),LENGTH=4,ATTRB=(UNPROT,FSET)
 93         DFHMDF POS=(15,09),LENGTH=1,ATTRB=PROT
 94 USER21  DFHMDF POS=(15,12),LENGTH=8,ATTRB=(PROT,FSET)
 95 OPER21  DFHMDF POS=(15,24),LENGTH=3,ATTRB=(PROT,FSET)
 96 TERM22  DFHMDF POS=(15,44),LENGTH=4,ATTRB=(UNPROT,FSET)
 97         DFHMDF POS=(15,49),LENGTH=1,ATTRB=PROT
 98 USER22  DFHMDF POS=(15,52),LENGTH=8,ATTRB=(PROT,FSET)
 99 OPER22  DFHMDF POS=(15,64),LENGTH=3,ATTRB=(PROT,FSET)
100 TERM23  DFHMDF POS=(16,04),LENGTH=4,ATTRB=(UNPROT,FSET)
101         DFHMDF POS=(16,09),LENGTH=1,ATTRB=PROT
102 USER23  DFHMDF POS=(16,12),LENGTH=8,ATTRB=(PROT,FSET)
103 OPER23  DFHMDF POS=(16,24),LENGTH=3,ATTRB=(PROT,FSET)
104 TERM24  DFHMDF POS=(16,44),LENGTH=4,ATTRB=(UNPROT,FSET)
105         DFHMDF POS=(16,49),LENGTH=1,ATTRB=PROT
106 USER24  DFHMDF POS=(16,52),LENGTH=8,ATTRB=(PROT,FSET)
107 OPER24  DFHMDF POS=(16,64),LENGTH=3,ATTRB=(PROT,FSET)
108 TERM25  DFHMDF POS=(17,4),LENGTH=4,ATTRB=(UNPROT,FSET)
109         DFHMDF POS=(17,9),LENGTH=1,ATTRB=PROT
110 USER25  DFHMDF POS=(17,12),LENGTH=8,ATTRB=(PROT,FSET)
111 OPER25  DFHMDF POS=(17,24),LENGTH=3,ATTRB=(PROT,FSET)
112 TERM26  DFHMDF POS=(17,44),LENGTH=4,ATTRB=(UNPROT,FSET)
113         DFHMDF POS=(17,49),LENGTH=1,ATTRB=PROT
114 USER26  DFHMDF POS=(17,52),LENGTH=8,ATTRB=(PROT,FSET)
115 OPER26  DFHMDF POS=(17,64),LENGTH=3,ATTRB=(PROT,FSET)
```

```
116 TERM27  DFHMDF POS=(18,04),LENGTH=4,ATTRB=(UNPROT,FSET)
117         DFHMDF POS=(18,09),LENGTH=1,ATTRB=PROT
118 USER27  DFHMDF POS=(18,12),LENGTH=8,ATTRB=(PROT,FSET)
119 OPER27  DFHMDF POS=(18,24),LENGTH=3,ATTRB=(PROT,FSET)
120 TERM28  DFHMDF POS=(18,44),LENGTH=4,ATTRB=(UNPROT,FSET)
121         DFHMDF POS=(18,49),LENGTH=1,ATTRB=PROT
122 USER28  DFHMDF POS=(18,52),LENGTH=8,ATTRB=(PROT,FSET)
123 OPER28  DFHMDF POS=(18,64),LENGTH=3,ATTRB=(PROT,FSET)
124 TERM29  DFHMDF POS=(19,04),LENGTH=4,ATTRB=(UNPROT,FSET)
125         DFHMDF POS=(19,09),LENGTH=1,ATTRB=PROT
126 USER29  DFHMDF POS=(19,12),LENGTH=8,ATTRB=(PROT,FSET)
127 OPER29  DFHMDF POS=(19,24),LENGTH=3,ATTRB=(PROT,FSET)
128 TERM30  DFHMDF POS=(19,44),LENGTH=4,ATTRB=(UNPROT,FSET)
129         DFHMDF POS=(19,49),LENGTH=1,ATTRB=PROT
130 USER30  DFHMDF POS=(19,52),LENGTH=8,ATTRB=(PROT,FSET)
131 OPER30  DFHMDF POS=(19,64),LENGTH=3,ATTRB=(PROT,FSET)
132 TERM31  DFHMDF POS=(20,04),LENGTH=4,ATTRB=(UNPROT,FSET)
133         DFHMDF POS=(20,09),LENGTH=1,ATTRB=PROT
134 USER31  DFHMDF POS=(20,12),LENGTH=8,ATTRB=(PROT,FSET)
135 OPER31  DFHMDF POS=(20,24),LENGTH=3,ATTRB=(PROT,FSET)
136 TERM32  DFHMDF POS=(20,44),LENGTH=4,ATTRB=(UNPROT,FSET)
137         DFHMDF POS=(20,49),LENGTH=1,ATTRB=PROT
138 USER32  DFHMDF POS=(20,52),LENGTH=8,ATTRB=(PROT,FSET)
139 OPER32  DFHMDF POS=(20,64),LENGTH=3,ATTRB=(PROT,FSET)
140 MAP2M01 DFHMDF POS=(21,16),LENGTH=40,ATTRB=(ASKIP,BRT)
141         DFHMDF POS=(22,1),LENGTH=45,ATTRB=ASKIP,COLOR=BLUE,        X
142         INITIAL='PLACE CURSOR UNDER DESIRED TERMINAL, AND PRESS'    X
143         DFHMDF POS=(22,47),LENGTH=18,ATTRB=ASKIP,COLOR=BLUE,
```

Figure 5.15. continued.

```
144             INITIAL='ENTER TO SELECT IT'
145     DFHMDF POS=(23,1),LENGTH=32,ATTRB=(ASKIP),COLOR=BLUE,        X
146             INITIAL='ON VIEWED SCREEN, PRESS ENTER TO'
147     DFHMDF POS=(23,34),LENGTH=39,ATTRB=(ASKIP),COLOR=BLUE,       X
148             INITIAL='UPDATE IT, ANY OTHER KEY TO RETURN HERE'
149     DFHMDF POS=(24,10),LENGTH=46,ATTRB=(ASKIP,BRT),COLOR=NEUTRAL, X
150             INITIAL='CLEAR: TERMINATE    PF7/19: BACK    PF8/20: FWD ',
151     DFHMSD TYPE=FINAL
152     END
```

****

Figure 5.15. continued.

```
BNU2/D A  *** AUTOMATIC INITIATE DESCRIPTORS CURRENTLY IN THIS CICS SYSTEM ***
*** TOTAL A.I.D. IN THE SYSTEM: 00001 SOME OF THEM MAY NOT BE DISPLAYED BELOW.
=================================================================================
TERM TRAN OPR  A.I.D.      REQUEST ID.  STATUS OF TERMINAL
 ID.  ID.  ID.  TYPE
D917 CSPG PRT B M S REQ  5C5CFD0000AAD600 REL NOCRE
```

Figure 5.16. A sample screen displaying information about AIDs in the CICS system

Steps For Testing This Facility

Step 1. Install the complete facility, following the step-by-step procedure given later in this section.

Step 2. Enter BNU2/H S on a blank screen. The program will display a help screen where you can simply change the first line and press Enter to start any transaction. Suppose terminal CA04 is a CRT-type terminal defined on your CICS system. Change the first line to the following and press Enter to start transaction CSSN after 30 minutes on this terminal:

```
BNU2/S CSSN CA04 003000
```

Make sure the system responds by sending you the message: "REQUESTED TRANS WILL BE STARTED ON REQUESTED TERM. AFTER SPECIFIED INTERVAL."

Step 3. Right after completing Step 2, enter 'BNU2/D A' to display the AIDs. The transaction initiated in Step 2 above is not shown on the display. This is because the time interval for task initiation has not yet expired. But it will be shown by The Monitor for CICS (The Cross System Monitor) when you display the Interval Control Elements (ICEs), as described above.

Step 4. Suppose you want to purge the task initiation request made in Step 2 above. To do this, obtain the Request ID by displaying the Interval Control Elements using The Monitor for CICS, or some other CICS monitor. Suppose the Request ID is 'DF000190'. Enter 'BNU2/H P' to obtain the help screen for purging unexpired task initiation requests. Then change the first line to the following and press Enter to perform the purge:

```
BNU2/P A = C4C6F0F0F0F0F1F9F0
```

Make sure the program sends you a message confirming that the purge will be carried out. Remember, expired task initiation requests that are displayed by 'BNU2/D A' can not be purged by using BNU2 transaction. Only unexpired task initiation requests can be purged with this transaction.

Step 5. Using The Monitor for CICS, display Interval Control Elements. The task initiation request made in Step 2 above will not be present now, because it was purged in Step 4 above.

Step 6. Now suppose there is a CRT type terminal with terminal ID CA05 that is defined to this CICS but is presently busy with another application, e.g., TSO. Initiate a transaction such as CSSN on it, specifying an interval of 1 second, by entering 'BNU2/H S' and then changing the first line to the following:

```
BNU2/S CSSN CA05 000001
```

Step 7. At least two seconds after executing Step 6, if you enter 'BNU2/D A' to display all the AIDs (Quotation marks are not entered), you will find that the task initiation request made in Step 6 will be shown on AIDs display. The AID type will be 'ICP INT', i.e., it was initiated by Interval Control Program. The Terminal status of CA05 will show as Released, indicating that this task cannot run on this terminal because it is released from this CICS and cannot be immediately acquired, probably because it is being used by some other application.

Procedure for Installing This Facility

Step 1. Enter the program shown in Figure 5.12 in a source PDS as member UASS01. Enter the program in Figure 5.13 in the same source PDS as member BNUTL02.

Step 2. Enter the mapset shown in Figure 5.14 in a source PDS as member BNU2S1. Enter the mapset shown in Figure 5.15 in the same source PDS as member BNU2S2.

Step 3. Now assemble mapset BNU2S1 using the JCL given in Section B.4 in Appendix B. Let us suppose that the name of the load library where the load module for this map will be created is P1BKN.LOADLIB, and the name of the macro (copybook) library where the copybook for the map will be created is P1BKN.MACLIB. So after you have run the job given in Section B.4, it will create load module BNU2S1 in P1BKN.LOADLIB and copybook member BNU2S1 in P1BKN.MACLIB. This load library must be included under DDname DFHRPL in the CICS start-up procedure or job.

Step 4. Now assemble mapset BNU2S2 using the JCL given in Section B.4 in Appendix B. When you run this job, it will create load module BNU2S2 in your load library, and copybook member BNU2S2 in your macro (copybook) library. This load library must be included under DDname DFHRPL in the CICS start-up procedure or job.

Step 5. Now assemble and link program UASS01 using the JCL given in Section B.2 in Appendix B. This job will create load module UASS01 in your load library. This load library must be included under DDname DFHRPL in the CICS start-up procedure or job.

Step 6. Now assemble and link program BNUTL02 using the JCL given in Section B.2 in Appendix B. This job will create load module BNUTL02 in your load library. This load library must be included under DDname DFHRPL in the CICS start-up procedure or job.

Step 7. Define the following resources in CICS tables:

Definition of Mapset BNU2S1 in the PPT

```
MAPSET BNU2S1
```

```
GROUP   CICSBOOK
RSL     00
STATUS  ENABLED
```

Definition of Mapset BNU2S2 in the PPT

```
MAPSET  BNU2S2
GROUP   CICSBOOK
RSL     00
STATUS  ENABLED
```

Definition of Program UASS01 in the PPT

```
PROGRAM   UASS01
GROUP     CICSBOOK
LANGUAGE  Assembler
```

Other parameters for this program in the PPT should be the same as those for sample program BNPROG1 given in Section 1.6.

Definition of Transaction UTR1 in the PCT

```
TRANSACTION  UTR1
GROUP        CICSBOOK
PROGRAM      UASS01
```

Other parameters for this transaction in the PCT should be the same as those for sample transaction BNC1 given in Section 1.6. Its security level must be 1, which makes it unprotected.

Definition of Program BNUTL02 in the PPT

```
PROGRAM   BNUTL02
GROUP     CICSBOOK
LANGUAGE  Assembler
```

Other parameters for this program in the PPT should be the same as those for sample program BNPROG1 given in Section 1.6.

Definition of Transaction BNU2 in the PCT

```
TRANSACTION  BNU2
GROUP        CICSBOOK
PROGRAM      BNUTL02
```

Other parameters for this transaction in the PCT should be the same as those for sample transaction BNC1 given in Section 1.6. Its security level must not be 1, which makes it protected.

Explanation of That Section of Program BNUTL02 Which Displays Aids:

Let us suppose the user enters the following on a blank screen:

```
BNU2/D A
```

CICS checks the PCT and finds that this transaction is associated with program BNUTL02. So, it loads this program into storage, if it is not already there, and transfers control to the first executable statement. So, control flows to line 99 in Figure 5.13. On line 103, we are testing if any communication area was passed to the program. In this example, no communication area was passed; so, control would flow to label NOCOMMA on line 110. In this case, the test being made on line 113 would be true; so control would flow to label DISPAID on line 177.

The code that follows scans the CICS control blocks and stores information about AIDs in the 1920-byte area named DISP defined on line 60. (A 3270 screen of 24 lines and 80 columns requires 1920 (80 × 24) bytes of area to store all the data that will fit on 24 lines.) The last 80 bytes of this area is reserved for message to be displayed by the program. (See label SYSMSG on line 62.) Program BNSUB01 is invoked to convert 8-byte request ID obtained from CICS control block into 16-byte area containing printable hexadecimal characters. (See line 242). BNSUB01 is given in Section C.3 in Appendix C.

Finally, on line 222, we send 1920 bytes starting at DISP to the terminal, after erasing whatever might be present on the screen. This is followed by the execution of the RETURN command on line 223. This ends the task. The user is now presented with a screen that resembles the one shown in Figure 5.16. The user can clear the screen and enter any valid or invalid CICS transaction, or he can simply press Enter to obtain a refreshed AIDs information screen.

5.9 A PROGRAM TO START FROM YOUR TERMINAL ANY TRANSACTION ON ANY TERMINAL DEFINED TO CICS

The facility installed in Section 5.8 above is a multi-purpose facility. The main transaction of this facility, BNU2 can be used to start any valid transaction at any terminal defined to CICS. First, enter BNU2/H S on a blank screen to display the help screen for starting tasks. Then simply change the first line to suit your needs and press Enter. Make sure you receive a message confirming that the task will be started. If the transaction ID you specified is not valid or some other error exists, a suitable message will be displayed.

See Step 2 of STEPS TO TEST THIS FACILITY in Section 5.8 above to find out how any transaction can be initiated at any terminal after any specified interval.

Explanation of That Section of Program BNUTL02 Which Starts a Transaction

Let us suppose the user enters the following on a blank screen to start transaction CSSN on terminal CA04 after 1 second:

```
BNU2/S CSSN CA04 000001
```

CICS transfers control to the first executable statement in BNUTL02. So, control flows to line 99 in Figure 5.13. On line 103, we are testing if any communication area was passed to the program. In this example, no communication area was passed; so, control would flow to label NOCOMMA on line 110. In this case, the test being made on line 121 would be true; so control would flow to label STARTIT on line 149.

On line 157, we would execute the START command to start transaction CSSN on terminal CA04 after one second. Assuming that no error condition arose in executing the START command, we would then branch to label DMSGEPGM on line 308. On line 309, we would send to the terminal the content of 1920 bytes of storage starting at DISP. On line 310 we would execute the RETURN command to unconditionally and completely end this task. The user can now clear the screen and enter any valid or invalid CICS transaction.

5.10   A PROGRAM TO PURGE A TASK INITIATION REQUEST THAT HAS NOT YET EXPIRED

The facility installed in Section 5.8 above is a multi-purpose facility. The main transaction of this facility, BNU2 can be used to purge a task initiation request that has not yet expired. First, enter BNU2/H P on a blank screen to display the help screen for purging task initiation requests. Then simply change the 16 Xs on the first line to the request ID of the task initiation request that you want purged, and press Enter. Make sure you receive a message confirming that the cancellation request has been issued. If an error condition arises, a suitable message will be displayed.

See Step 4 of STEPS TO TEST THIS FACILITY in Section 5.8 above to find out how unexpired task initiation requests can be purged.

Explanation of That Section of Program BNUTL02 Which Purges a Task Initiation Request

Let us suppose the user enters the following on a blank screen to purge a task initiation request that has the request ID of X'C4C6F0F0F0F1F9F0':

```
BNU2/P A=C4C6F0F0F0F1F9F0
```

CICS transfers control to the first executable statement in BNUTL02. So, control flows to line 99 in Figure 5.13. On line 103, we are testing if any communication area was passed to the program. In this example, no communication area was passed; so, control would flow to label NOCOMMA on line 110. In this case, the test being made on line 115 would be true; so control would flow to label PURGEAID on line 160.

On line 169, we would LINK to program BNSUB01 to convert the 16-byte request ID received from the terminal into an 8-byte field and store it at PURGEID. On line 171, we would execute the CANCEL command to cancel the task initiation request whose request ID is at PURGEID. Assuming that no error condition arose in executing the CANCEL command, we would then branch to label DMSGEPGM on line 308. On line 309, we would send to the terminal the content of 1920 bytes of storage starting at DISP. On line 310, we would execute the RETURN command to unconditionally and completely end this task. The user can now clear the screen and enter any valid or invalid CICS transaction.

5.11 A PROGRAM TO DISPLAY THE TERMINALS THAT ARE ACQUIRED TO CICS AND THE USERS SIGNED ON TO THEM

Program BNUTL02 shown in Figure 5.13 is a multi-purpose program. This program is the heart of a facility whose installation instructions were given in Section 5.8 above. This program is the driver for transaction BNU2. To display information about all terminals that are currently acquired to CICS, enter the following on a blank CICS screen:

```
BNU2/VIEW
```

The program will display a screen that looks like the one shown in Figure 5.17. On this screen, do not enter anything in the Terminal ID field. Just press the Enter key. A screen resembling the one shown in Figure 5.18 will be displayed. This screen will display a maximum of 32 terminals that are acquired to CICS, including printers. For any terminal, if a user is currently signed on to it, the User ID and the three-character Operator ID of the user will also be shown. If no user is currently signed on to a terminal, the User ID and the Operator ID fields will be blank. For example, Figure 5.18 shows that on terminal S203, no user is currently signed on, while on terminal S210, the user ID of the user signed on is BKN1 and the user's Operator ID is BKN.

If more than 32 terminals are acquired to CICS, the message "MORE TERMINALS ARE YET TO BE SHOWN. . . ." will appear on the message line, which is line 21 on the screen. If this message appears, you can press PF8 to scroll forward, in which case you will see the next set of 32 (or less) terminals that are acquired to CICS. On any screen, press PF7 to scroll backward, and press PF8 to scroll forward. If there is no more screen to display (in either direction), e.g., if you pressed PF7 on the screen that shows the first 32 ter-

** A WARM WELCOME TO THE FACILITY TO VIEW THE CONTENT OF ANY DISPLAY (CRT
TYPE) TERMINAL CURRENTLY ATTACHED TO THIS CICS SYSTEM.

ENTER THE FOUR-CHARACTER CICS TERMINAL ID HERE ===>
(LEAVE IT BLANK TO DISPLAY LIST OF CURRENT USERS OF THE SYSTEM)

WHEN YOU OBTAIN THE TARGET SCREEN, PRESS ENTER TO UPDATE THE VIEWED SCREEN;
PRESS ANY OTHER KEY TO RETURN HERE
         PRESS CLEAR KEY TO TERMINATE THIS FACILITY

Figure 5.17. The screen displayed when user enters BNU2/VIEW on a blank
CICS screen

```
FACILITY TO VIEW THE CONTENT OF ANY CRT TYPE TERMINAL CONNECTED TO CICS

TERM ID    USER ID    OP ID              TERM ID    USER ID    OP ID

                                          S210       BKN1       BKN

S203       BKN1       BKN
S315                  BKN


PLACE CURSOR UNDER DESIRED TERMINAL AND PRESS ENTER TO SELECT IT
ON VIEWED SCREEN, PRESS ENTER TO UPDATE IT, ANY OTHER KEY TO RETURN HERE
       CLEAR: TERMINATE    PF7/19: BACK    PF8/20: FWD
```

Figure 5.18. The screen displayed when user leaves Term ID field blank and presses Enter on the screen of Figure 5.17.

minals, the message "SCROLLING LIMIT HAS BEEN REACHED . . ." would appear on the message line, which is on line 21.

So, by using this facility in this manner, you can display information about all the terminals that are currently acquired to CICS.

Salient features of this facility are as follows: When you press Enter on the first screen without entering anything in the Terminal ID field, the program scans the TCT and builds a terminal table that has one entry for each terminal that is acquired to CICS. This table is stored in temporary storage with queue ID of 'SPYTtttt' where tttt is replaced by your terminal ID. This queue has as many items as there are pages of screen shown in Figure 5.18. This means that if there are 60 terminals acquired to CICS, the first queue item will have the screen image with information about the first 32 terminals, and the second queue item will have the screen image of the second page with information about the remaining 28 terminals. The program will then display the first screen page. After that, if you pressed PF8, the program would read the second item of the queue 'SPYTtttt' and display it as the second page. So, if a terminal on the second page has logged off since the time when the queue was built, it will still appear on the second page. So, to refresh information, you should press the Clear key on the screen of Figure 5.18. This will end the task completely and unconditionally. You should then enter BNU2/VIEW again.

As indicated by the message at the bottom of both Figures 5.17 and 5.18, pressing Clear on any of these two screens terminates this facility. But note that pressing Clear when you are viewing the screen image of the spied terminal will take you either to the screen of Figure 5.17 or to that of Figure 5.18, depending on where you came from.

The program in Figure 5.13 does not display a count of the total number of terminals acquired to CICS. But counting the terminals displayed, and remembering that there are 32 terminals on a full screen, will give you the total number of terminals. You are advised to study program BNUTL02 shown in Figure 5.13, understand it, and then modify it so it displays the total number of terminals acquired on each page of the screen shown in Figure 5.18.

When you enter BNU2/VIEW on a blank screen, control flows first to line 99 in Figure 5.13. The test made on line 123 is found true, and hence control flows to label VIEWRTN on line 312. The logic that follows displays the screens shown in Figures 5.17 and 5.18.

5.12 A PROGRAM TO DISPLAY THE CONTENT OF ANY TERMINAL'S SCREEN ON YOUR TERMINAL

Program BNUTL02, shown in Figure 5.13, is a multi-purpose program. This program is the heart of a facility whose installation instructions were given in Section 5.8 above. This program is the driver for transaction BNU2. To display on your terminal what is on the screen of any CRT-type terminal currently logged on to CICS, enter the following on a blank CICS screen:

BNU2/VIEW

The program will display a screen that looks like the one shown in Figure 5.17. Now you have two choices:

> If you know that a terminal is currently logged on to CICS, you can enter its terminal ID and press Enter to view what is on the screen of that terminal, or
>
> You may not enter anything in the Terminal ID field and simply press the Enter key to display a screen that resembles the one shown in Figure 5.18.

If you selected the first choice, the target terminal's screen content will be displayed on your terminal. On the viewed screen, press Enter to refresh it, and press any other key to return to the previous screen, i.e., to the one of Figure 5.17. This is written at the bottom of Figure 5.17.

If you selected the second choice, you will receive a screen that will display a maximum of 32 terminals that are acquired to CICS, including printers. For any terminal, if a user is currently signed on to it, the User ID and the three-character Operator ID of the user will also be shown. If no user is currently signed on to a terminal, the User ID and the Operator ID fields will be blank. To see the content of any terminal, take the cursor under the terminal ID field, and press Enter. If it is CRT-type terminal, its screen content will be displayed. If it is a printer, you will receive a message to this effect on the message line, which is line 21 in Figure 5.18. If a task is currently active on a terminal, its screen buffer cannot be displayed and a message to this effect will appear. On the viewed screen, press Enter to refresh it, and press any other key to return to the previous screen, i.e., to the one in Figure 5.18. This is written at the bottom of Figure 5.18.

Read the information in Section 5.11 above to understand further the working of this facility. Here it is probably good to point out the mechanism of how screen capture and display facility works. When you select a terminal for display, either on the screen of Figure 5.17 or on that of Figure 5.18, program BNUTL02 checks that the specified terminal is not your own terminal, and it is not a printer, and, further, that it is acquired to CICS and there is no active task running on it. Only when all these conditions are met, does it start transaction UTR1 on the target terminal after one second. After that, it tries to read temporary storage queue with ID 'SPYZtttt' where tttt represents the target terminal's ID. If this queue is not found, it delays execution by one second and again attempts to read this queue. It makes a maximum of nine such attempts. If the queue is successfully read, it is assumed to contain the target terminal's buffer and is used to display it on your terminal. After that, the task is ended after specifying that BNU2 is to be started the next time the user presses any key.

However, if even after nine attempts queue 'SPYZtttt' is not read, the following message is displayed on the message line of Figure 5.17 or 5.18:

SEEMS UTR1 IS STILL WAITING TO START. . . .

This message tells you that UTR1 was started but for some reason it has not run on the target terminal, or that it ran but BNUTL02 was not able to read the temporary storage queue 'SPYZtttt' created by UTR1, even after nine attempts.

5.13   A PROGRAM TO WRITE A TEMPORARY STORAGE QUEUE OF DESIRED NAME WITH SPECIFIED NUMBER OF RECORDS IN MAIN OR AUXILIARY STORAGE

In Figure 5.19 is the listing of program BNWTPGM. This program is associated with transaction BNWT in the PCT. To use it, you can issue the following transaction on a blank screen:

BNWT/qqqqqqqq/d/nnnn

where qqqqqqqq should be replaced by the eight-character-long name of the temporary storage queue to be created and d should be replaced by M if the queue is to be created in main storage and by A if it is to be created in auxiliary storage, i.e., on DASD. nnnn is to be replaced by a four-digit number that stands for the number of records that are to be written in this queue. Leading zeros are required. Each record will be of 80 bytes and will contain the string 'BARRY NIRMAL' followed by spaces.

> **Note:** Positions 5, 14, and 16 of the command must contain a slash as shown above and in the example below.

Example 1: You want to write 100 records in a temporary storage queue with ID equal to ABCD1234 in main storage. You can simply enter the following on a blank screen:

BNWT/ABCD1234/M/0100

This program will create 100 records in the specified queue and display the following confirmation message on your screen:

MISSION SUCCESSFUL

If an error occurred during program execution, a suitable message will be displayed on your screen.

```
***************************************************************
*  THIS PGM WILL WRITE SPECIFIED NUMBER OF RECORDS UNDER SPECIFIED
*  QUEUE ID. IN MAIN OR AUXILIARY TEMPORARY STORAGE AS DESIRED.
***************************************************************
*  THE FOLLOWING IS ONE EXAMPLE OF EXECUTING THIS PROGRAM:
*  ENTER ON A BLANK SCREEN===>>>   BNWT/ABCDEFGH/M/0050
*  THIS WILL WRITE 50 RECORDS IN MAIN TEMPORARY STORAGE UNDER
*  QUEUE ID = ABCDEFGH
***************************************************************
IDENTIFICATION DIVISION.
PROGRAM-ID. BNWTPGM.
ENVIRONMENT DIVISION.
DATA DIVISION.
WORKING-STORAGE SECTION.
01  WS-DATA-IN.
    05  FILLER              PIC X(4).
    05  IN-DELIM-1          PIC X.
    05  IN-Q-NAME           PIC X(8).
    05  IN-DELIM-2          PIC X.
    05  IN-DEST             PIC X.
    05  IN-DELIM-3          PIC X.
    05  IN-COUNT            PIC 9(4).
    LEN-20                  PIC 9(4).   COMP VALUE 20.
01  WS-REC-AREA          PIC X(80)  VALUE 'BARRY NIRMAL'.
01  WS-OUT-MSG-1.
    05  FILLER                 PIC X(80) VALUE
    'AN ERROR OF SOME KIND HAS OCCURRED IN PROGRAM BNWTPGM    '.
```

Figure 5.19.   Source code of program BNWTPGM

325

```
28      05  FILLER                      PIC X(80) VALUE
29          'USE CEDF TO DEBUG. NOW PRESS CLEAR KEY TO CONTINUE.            '.
30  01  WS-OUT-MSG-2.
31      05  FILLER                      PIC X(80) VALUE
32          'BARRY, NO SPACE CONDITION ENCOUNTERED WHEN WRITING REC #
33      05  REC-NUMBER                  PIC 9(5) VALUE ZERO.
34      05  FILLER                      PIC X(75) VALUE SPACES.
35  01  WS-OUT-MSG-3.
36      05  FILLER                      PIC X(80) VALUE
37          'MISSION SUCCESSFUL.                                           '.
38  01  WS-OUT-MSG-4.
39      05  FILLER                      PIC X(80) VALUE
40          'ERROR IN INPUT DATA DETECTED. TRANSACTION TERMINATED.         '.
41  01  WS-OUT-MSG-5.
42      05  FILLER                      PIC X(80) VALUE
43          'STOP FOOLING AROUND WITH ME, OR ELSE I WILL SCREAM.           '.
44
45  PROCEDURE DIVISION.
46  * TO RESTRICT ACCESS TO THIS PROGRAM, DO AS SHOWN BY COMMENTED
47  * LINES BELOW:
48  **** IF EIBTRMID = 'D915' OR 'CA20'
49  *        NEXT SENTENCE
50  *    ELSE
51  *****    PERFORM SORRY-SIR.
52      EXEC CICS IGNORE CONDITION LENGERR END-EXEC.
53      EXEC CICS HANDLE CONDITION
54          ERROR(ERROR-COND)
55          NOSPACE(OUT-OF-SPACE)
56      END-EXEC.
57      EXEC CICS RECEIVE INTO(WS-DATA-IN) LENGTH(LEN-20)
```

```
58              END-EXEC.
59          IF IN-DELIM-1 NOT = '/' OR IN-DELIM-2 NOT = '/' OR
60             IN-DELIM-3 NOT = '/' OR
61             (IN-Q-NAME = SPACES OR LOW-VALUES) OR
62             (IN-COUNT NOT NUMERIC OR
63              IN-COUNT = ZERO) OR
64             (IN-DEST NOT = 'M' AND IN-DEST NOT = 'A')
65                  PERFORM INPUT-ERROR
66          ELSE
67                  PERFORM MAIN-RTN.
68          GOBACK.
69      MAIN-RTN.
70          IF IN-DEST = 'M'
71              PERFORM WRITE-TS-QUEUE-M IN-COUNT TIMES
72          ELSE
73              PERFORM WRITE-TS-QUEUE-A IN-COUNT TIMES.
74          EXEC CICS SEND FROM (WS-OUT-MSG-3)
75              LENGTH(80)
76          END-EXEC.
77          EXEC CICS RETURN END-EXEC.
78      ***************************************************************
79      WRITE-TS-QUEUE-M.
80          ADD 1 TO REC-NUMBER.
81          EXEC CICS WRITEQ TS QUEUE(IN-Q-NAME) FROM(WS-REC-AREA)
82              MAIN
83              LENGTH(80) END-EXEC.
84      ***************************************************************
85      WRITE-TS-QUEUE-A.
```

Figure 5.19. continued.

327

```
86              ADD 1 TO REC-NUMBER.
87              EXEC CICS WRITEQ TS QUEUE(IN-Q-NAME) FROM(WS-REC-AREA)
88                   AUXILIARY
89                   LENGTH(80) END-EXEC.
90     ****************************************************************
91     ERROR-COND.
92              EXEC CICS SEND FROM (WS-OUT-MSG-1)
93                   LENGTH(160)
94                   END-EXEC.
95              EXEC CICS RETURN END-EXEC.
96     SORRY-SIR.
97              EXEC CICS SEND FROM (WS-OUT-MSG-5)
98                   LENGTH(80)
99                   ERASE
100                  END-EXEC.
101             EXEC CICS RETURN END-EXEC.
102    INPUT-ERROR.
103             EXEC CICS SEND FROM (WS-OUT-MSG-4)
104                  LENGTH(80)
105                  END-EXEC.
106             EXEC CICS RETURN END-EXEC.
107    OUT-OF-SPACE.
108             EXEC CICS SEND FROM (WS-OUT-MSG-2)
109                  LENGTH(160)
110                  END-EXEC.
111             EXEC CICS RETURN END-EXEC.
112             GOBACK.
       ****************************************************************
```

Figure 5.19. continued.

In what way can this program be useful? This program can be useful for creating data in temporary storage queues. Also, it serves as a sample program for the beginning CICS command-level programmers who can understand it easily and thereby learn the technique of writing similar programs. It can also be used in production systems.

Procedure for Installing This Facility

Step 1. Enter the program shown in Figure 5.19 in a source PDS as member BNWTPGM.

Step 2. Now compile and link this program using the JCL given in Section B.1 in Appendix B. This job will create load module BNWTPGM in your load library. This load library must be included under DDname DFHRPL in the CICS start-up procedure or job.

Step 3. Define the following resources in CICS tables:

Definition of Program BNWTPGM in the PPT

```
PROGRAM   BNWTPGM
GROUP     CICSBOOK
LANGUAGE  COBOL
```

Other parameters for this program in the PPT should be the same as those for sample program BNPROG1 given in Section 1.6.

Definition of Transaction BNWT in the PCT

```
TRANSACTION  BNWT
GROUP        CICSBOOK
PROGRAM      BNWTPGM
```

Other parameters for this transaction in the PCT should be the same as those for sample transaction BNC1 given in Section 1.6.

Explanation of Program BNWTPGM

Let us suppose the user enters the following on a blank screen:

```
BNWT/ABCDEFGH/M/0100
```

CICS checks the PCT and finds that this transaction is associated with program BNWTPGM. So, it loads this program into storage, if it is not already there, and transfers control to the first statement in the procedure division. So, control flows to line 52 in Figure 5.19. On line 57, we receive whatever was entered on the screen into WS-DATA-IN. Next, we edit the content of WS-DATA-IN. In this example, everything would be found clean; so, control would flow to line 67 where MAIN-RTN would be performed.

In MAIN-RTN, because in this example IN-DEST is M, we would execute line 71, where WRITE-TS-QUEUE-M would be performed 100 times, because IN-COUNT in this example would have a value of 100. This will result in 100 records being written into a main storage temporary storage queue with queue ID of 'ABCDEFGH'. On line 74, we would send the content of WS-OUT-MSG-3 to the terminal. This would be followed by the execution of the RETURN command on line 77. This ends the task. The user is now presented with a screen that has the following on line 1:

```
BNWT/ABCDEFGH/M/0100MISSION SUCCESSFUL
```

The user can now clear the screen and enter any valid or invalid CICS transaction.

5.14 A PROGRAM TO WRITE SPECIFIED NUMBER OF RECORDS IN A TRANSIENT QUEUE OF SPECIFIED NAME

In Figure 5.20 is the listing of program BNWQPGM, which can be used to write any number of records in an intrapartition queue whose ID you specify. (It can also write to an extrapartition queue that is open for output.) The length of each record written is to be specified on the command. For intrapartition queues, you can specify any length up to 2048. But for an extrapartition queue, the record length you specify on the command must match the record length of the output sequential file. This program is associated with transaction BNWQ in the PCT. To use it, you can issue the following transaction on a blank screen:

```
BNWQ/qqqq/nnnn/llll
```

```
where qqqq  should be replaced by the four-character queue ID of the
            intrapartition or extrapartition transient data queue
            in which records are to be written.
      nnnn  is to be replaced by a four-digit number that stands for
            the number of records that are to be written in this
            queue. Leading zeros are required. Each record will be
            of fixed length and will contain the string ' BARRY
            NIRMAL', if the record length is 13. If record length is
            less than 13, each record will contain the first part of
            ' BARRY NIRMAL'. If the record length is more than 13,
            each record will contain ' BARRY NIRMAL' followed by
            one or more spaces.
      llll  is to be replaced by a four-digit number that stands for
            the length of each record to be written to the queue.
            Leading zeros are required.
```

```
*****************************************************************************
*****************************************************************
1    *
2    *  THIS PROGRAM WILL WRITE SPECIFIED NUMBER OF RECORDS IN A
3    *  TRANSIENT DATA QUEUE WHOSE NAME YOU SPECIFY ON THE COMMAND.
4    *  TO EXECUTE THIS PROGRAM, ENTER ON SCREEN: BNWQ/QQQQ/NNNN/LLLL
5    *  FOR EXAMPLE, SUPPOSE YOU ENTER: BNWQ/BARY/0050/0080
6    *  THIS WILL WRITE 50 RECORDS, EACH 80 BYTES LONG IN T.D. QUEUE
7    *  WITH ID = BARY. THE QUEUE CAN BE INTRA-PARTITION OR EXTRA-
8    *  PARTITION. IF EXTRA-PARTITION, THE QUEUE MUST BE OPEN ON
9    *  CICS FOR OUTPUT AND THE LENGTH YOU SPECIFY ON THE TRANSACTION
10   *  MUST BE SAME AS THAT IN THE DESTINATION CONTROL TABLE.
11   *****************************************************************
12   IDENTIFICATION DIVISION.
13   PROGRAM-ID. BNWQPGM.
14   ENVIRONMENT DIVISION.
15   DATA DIVISION.
16   WORKING-STORAGE SECTION.
17   01  WS-DATA-IN.
18       05  FILLER            PIC X(4).
19       05  IN-DELIM-1        PIC X.
20       05  IN-Q-NAME         PIC X(4).
21       05  IN-DELIM-2        PIC X.
22       05  IN-COUNT          PIC 9(4).
23       05  IN-DELIM-3        PIC X.
24       05  IN-RECLEN         PIC 9(4).
25   01  CICS-LENGTH           PIC S9(4) COMP.
26   01  WS-REC-AREA           PIC X(2048) VALUE ' BARRY NIRMAL'.
27   01  WS-OUT-MSG-1.
```

Figure 5.20.   Source code of program BNWQPGM

331

```
28    05 FILLER                    PIC X(80) VALUE
29       'AN ERROR OF SOME KIND HAS OCCURRED IN PROGRAM BNWQPGM.     '.
30    05 FILLER                    PIC X(80) VALUE
31       'USE CEDF TO DEBUG. NOW PRESS CLEAR KEY TO CONTINUE.        '.
32 01 WS-OUT-MSG-2.
33    05 FILLER                    PIC X(80) VALUE
34       'BARRY, NO SPACE CONDITION ENCOUNTERED WHEN WRITING REC #
35    05 REC-NUMBER                PIC 9(5) VALUE ZERO.
36    05 FILLER                    PIC X(75) VALUE SPACES.
37 01 WS-OUT-MSG-3.
38    05 FILLER                    PIC X(80) VALUE
39       'MISSION SUCCESSFUL.
40 01 WS-OUT-MSG-4.
41    05 FILLER                    PIC X(80) VALUE
42       'ERROR IN INPUT DATA DETECTED. TRANSACTION TERMINATED.      '.
43 01 WS-OUT-MSG-5.
44    05 FILLER                    PIC X(80) VALUE
45       'STOP FOOLING AROUND WITH ME, OR ELSE I WILL SCREAM.        '.
46 PROCEDURE DIVISION.
47 ****************************************************************
48 * UNCOMMENT THE CODE BELOW TO ACTIVATE RESTRICTING THE USE OF
49 * THIS PROGRAM TO TERMINAL ID'S D915 AND CA20.
50 *** IF EIBTRMID = 'D915' OR 'CA20'
51 *       NEXT SENTENCE
52 *    ELSE
53 *****   PERFORM SORRY-SIR.
54       EXEC CICS IGNORE CONDITION LENGERR END-EXEC.
55       EXEC CICS HANDLE CONDITION
56          ERROR(ERROR-COND)
57          NOSPACE(OUT-OF-SPACE)
```

```
58          END-EXEC.
59          MOVE 80 TO CICS-LENGTH.
60          EXEC CICS RECEIVE INTO(WS-DATA-IN) LENGTH(CICS-LENGTH)
61          END-EXEC.
62          IF (IN-DELIM-1 NOT = '/' OR IN-DELIM-2 NOT = '/' OR
63              IN-DELIM-3 NOT = '/') OR
64             (IN-Q-NAME = SPACES OR LOW-VALUES) OR
65             (IN-COUNT NOT NUMERIC OR IN-COUNT = ZERO) OR
66             (IN-RECLEN NOT NUMERIC OR IN-RECLEN = ZERO OR
67              IN-RECLEN GREATER THAN 2048)
68              PERFORM INPUT-ERROR
69          ELSE
70              PERFORM MAIN-RTN.
71          GOBACK.
72      MAIN-RTN.
73          PERFORM WRITE-TD-QUEUE IN-COUNT TIMES.
74          EXEC CICS SEND FROM (WS-OUT-MSG-3)
75              LENGTH(80)
76          END-EXEC.
77          EXEC CICS RETURN END-EXEC.
78      ***********************************************************
79      WRITE-TD-QUEUE.
80          MOVE IN-RECLEN TO CICS-LENGTH.
81          ADD 1 TO REC-NUMBER.
82          EXEC CICS WRITEQ TD QUEUE(IN-Q-NAME) FROM(WS-REC-AREA)
83              LENGTH(CICS-LENGTH) END-EXEC.
84      ***********************************************************
85      ERROR-COND.
```

Figure 5.20. continued.

```
 86          EXEC CICS SEND FROM (WS-OUT-MSG-1)
 87              LENGTH(160)
 88          END-EXEC.
 89          EXEC CICS RETURN END-EXEC.
 90      SORRY-SIR.
 91          EXEC CICS SEND FROM (WS-OUT-MSG-5)
 92              LENGTH(80)
 93              ERASE
 94          END-EXEC.
 95          EXEC CICS RETURN END-EXEC.
 96      INPUT-ERROR.
 97          EXEC CICS SEND FROM (WS-OUT-MSG-4)
 98              LENGTH(80)
 99          END-EXEC.
100      OUT-OF-SPACE.
101          EXEC CICS SEND FROM (WS-OUT-MSG-2)
102              LENGTH(160)
103          END-EXEC.
104          EXEC CICS RETURN END-EXEC.
105          GOBACK.
```

Figure 5.20. continued.

334

Note: Positions 5, 10, and 15 of the input command must contain a slash as shown above and in the examples below.

Example 1: You want to write 100 records in an extrapartition transient data queue with ID equal to ABCD. The record length is to be 80, because the dataset used for this queue has record length of 80. This queue, when viewed using command CEMT I Q(ABCD), displays the following:

```
Que(ABCD)  Ext  Enabled  Open
```

You can simply enter the following on a blank screen:

```
BNWQ/ABCD/0100/0080
```

This program will create 100 records in the specified queue and display the following confirmation message on your screen:

```
MISSION SUCCESSFUL
```

If an error occurred during program execution, a suitable message will be displayed on your screen.

Example 2: You want to write five records in an intrapartition transient data queue with ID equal to E931. The record length can be anything up to and including 2048, because in program BNWQPGM the maximum record length supported is 2048. This queue, when viewed using command 'CEMT I Q(E931)', displays the following:

Que(E931) Tigger-Level(010) Intra Enabled Trans(XREQ) Dest(E931).
You can simply enter the following on a blank screen:

```
BNWQ/E931/0005/0075
```

This program will create five records in the specified queue, where each record will be 75 bytes long. It will display the following confirmation message on your screen:

```
MISSION SUCCESSFUL
```

If an error occurred during program execution, a suitable message will be displayed on your screen.

In what way can this program be useful?   This program can be useful for creating data in transient queues, whether intrapartition or extrapartition. Also, it serves as a sample program for the beginning CICS command-level programmers who can understand it easily and thereby learn the technique of writing similar programs.

Procedure for Installing This Facility

Step 1. Enter the program shown in Figure 5.20 in a source PDS as member BNWQPGM.

Step 2. Now compile and link this program using the JCL given in Section B.1 in Appendix B. This job will create load module BNWQPGM in your load library. This load library must be included under DDname DFHRPL in the CICS start-up procedure or job

Step 3. Define the following resources in CICS tables:

Definition of Program BNWQPGM in the PPT

```
PROGRAM   BNWQPGM
GROUP     CICSBOOK
LANGUAGE  COBOL
```

Other parameters for this program in the PPT should be the same as those for sample program BNPROG1 given in Section 1.6.

Definition of Transaction BNWQ in the PCT

```
TRANSACTION BNWQ
GROUP       CICSBOOK
PROGRAM     BNWQPGM
```

Other parameters for this transaction in the PCT should be the same as those for sample transaction BNC1 given in Section 1.6.

Explanation of Program BNWQPGM

Let us suppose the user enters the following on a blank screen:

```
BNWQ/ABCD/0100/0080
```

CICS checks the PCT and finds that this transaction is associated with program BNWQPGM. So, it loads this program into storage, if it is not already there, and transfers control to the first statement in the procedure division. So, control flows to line 54 in Figure 5.20. On line 60, we receive whatever was entered on the screen into WS-DATA-IN. Next, we edit the content of WS-DATA-IN. In this example, everything would be found clean; so, control would flow to line 70 where MAIN-RTN would be performed.

In MAIN-RTN we would execute line 73, where WRITE-TD-QUEUE would be performed 100 times. This would result in 100 records being written into a transient data queue with ID equal to ABCD. On line 74, we would send the content of WS-OUT-MSG-3 to the terminal. This would be followed by the execution of the RETURN command on line 77. This ends the task. The user is now presented with a screen that has the following on line 1:

```
BNWQ/ABCD/0100/0080MISSION SUCCESSFUL
```

The user can now clear the screen and enter any valid or invalid CICS transaction.

5.15 A PROGRAM TO DELETE ALL RECORDS FROM A TRANSIENT QUEUE OF SPECIFIED NAME

In Figure 5.21 is the listing of program BNDQPGM, which can be used to read all records present in an intrapartition queue whose ID you specify. Because of the way CICS is designed, when all records are read from an intrapartition queue, they are also purged from the queue. This program is associated with transaction BNDQ in the PCT. To use it, you can issue the following transaction on a blank screen:

```
BNDQ/qqqq
```

> where qqqq should be replaced by the four-character long ID of the intrapartition transient data queue from which records are to be purged.

Note: Position 5 of the command must contain a slash, as shown above and in the example below.

Example 1: Suppose you wrote some records to intrapartition queue with ID E931 using transaction BNWQ given in the previous section. You now want to read and hence purge all records from this intrapartition transient data queue. This queue, when viewed using command 'CEMT I Q(E931)', displays the following:

```
Que(E931) Tigger-Level(010) Intra Enabled Trans(XREQ) Dest(E931)
```

You can simply enter the following on a blank screen:

```
BNDQ/E931
```

This program will display the following message confirming the number of records that were read and hence purged from the queue:

```
BARRY, NUMBER OF ITEMS READ FROM TD QUEUE: E931 = nnnnn
```

```
****************************************************************
       IDENTIFICATION DIVISION.
       PROGRAM-ID. BNDQPGM.
      *=========================================================*
      * THIS PGM WILL READ ALL RECORDS IN AN INTRA Q AND TELL HOW HOW
      * MANY IT READ FROM QUEUE. IT WILL NOT DO ANYTHING WITH THE DATA
      * READ FROM THE TD QUEUE. THIS PROGRAM IS USEFUL WHEN YOU HAVE
      * WRITTEN RECORDS TO AN INTRA QUEUE AND YOU WANT TO GET RID OF
      * THOSE RECORDS, BUT WANT TO KNOW HOW MANY RECORDS YOU GOT RID OF.
      * TO EXECUTE ENTER: BNDQ/QQQQ WHERE QQQQ= ID OF T.D. QUEUE.
      *=========================================================*
       ENVIRONMENT DIVISION.
       DATA DIVISION.
       WORKING-STORAGE SECTION.
       01  WS-DATA-IN.
           05 FILLER                 PIC X(4).
           05 IN-DELIM               PIC X.
           05 IN-Q-NAME              PIC X(4).
       01  CICS-LENGTH               PIC S9(4) COMP.
       01  TD-Q-IN                   PIC X(2048).
       01  WS-OUT-MSG-1.
           05 FILLER                 PIC X(80) VALUE
           'AN ERROR OF SOME KIND HAS OCCURRED IN PROGRAM BNDQPGM.    '.
           05 FILLER                 PIC X(80) VALUE
           'USE CEDF TO DEBUG. NOW PRESS CLEAR KEY TO CONTINUE.    '.
       01  WS-OUT-MSG-2.
           05 FILLER                 PIC X(38) VALUE
           'NUMBER OF RECORDS READ FROM TD QUEUE: '.
           05 TD-Q-NAME              PIC X(4).
           05 FILLER                 PIC X(3)  VALUE ' = '.
           05 CNT-TD-READ            PIC 9(5)  VALUE ZERO.
```

338

```cobol
31          05  FILLER                        PIC X(30) VALUE SPACES.
32      01  WS-OUT-MSG-3.
33          05  FILLER                        PIC X(80) VALUE
34          'SIR, ERROR IN INPUT DATA HAS BEEN DETECTED.            '.
35          05  FILLER                        PIC X(80) VALUE
36          'THIS TRANSACTION HAS BEEN TERMINATED. SORRY.          '.
37      01  WS-OUT-MSG-4.
38          05  FILLER                        PIC X(80) VALUE
39          'STOP FOOLING AROUND WITH ME, OR ELSE I WILL SCREAM.    '.
40      PROCEDURE DIVISION.
41  ****  IF EIBTRMID = 'D915' OR 'CA20'
42  *         NEXT SENTENCE
43  *     ELSE
44  *****     PERFORM SORRY-SIR.
45          EXEC CICS IGNORE CONDITION LENGERR END-EXEC.
46          EXEC CICS HANDLE CONDITION ERROR(ERRORS)
47                                     QZERO(ENDA) END-EXEC.
48          MOVE 80   TO CICS-LENGTH.
49          EXEC CICS RECEIVE INTO(WS-DATA-IN) LENGTH(CICS-LENGTH)
50          END-EXEC.
51          IF IN-DELIM NOT = '/' OR IN-Q-NAME = SPACES OR
52          IN-Q-NAME = LOW-VALUES
53              PERFORM INPUT-ERROR-RTN
54          ELSE
55          MOVE IN-Q-NAME TO TD-Q-NAME
56          PERFORM MAIN-RTN.
57          GOBACK.
58      MAIN-RTN.
```

Figure 5.21. Source code of program BNDQPGM

```
59          MOVE 2048 TO CICS-LENGTH.
60          EXEC CICS READQ TD INTO(TD-Q-IN)
61                LENGTH(CICS-LENGTH)
62                QUEUE(IN-Q-NAME) END-EXEC.
63          ADD 1 TO CNT-TD-READ.
64          GO TO MAIN-RTN.
65      ERRORS.
66          EXEC CICS SEND FROM (WS-OUT-MSG-1)
67                LENGTH(160)
68                END-EXEC.
69          EXEC CICS RETURN END-EXEC.
70      INPUT-ERROR-RTN.
71          EXEC CICS SEND FROM (WS-OUT-MSG-3)
72                LENGTH(160)
73                END-EXEC.
74          EXEC CICS RETURN END-EXEC.
75      SORRY-SIR.
76          EXEC CICS SEND FROM (WS-OUT-MSG-4) ERASE
77                LENGTH(80) END-EXEC.
78          EXEC CICS RETURN END-EXEC.
79      ENDA.
80          EXEC CICS SEND FROM (WS-OUT-MSG-2) ERASE
81                LENGTH(80) END-EXEC.
82          EXEC CICS RETURN END-EXEC.
83          GOBACK.
```

****

Figure 5.21. continued.

where nnnnn would be 00010, if for example, 10 records were read from the queue. If an error occurred during program execution, a suitable message will be displayed on your screen. After this, if you issue the above BNDQ command again, the program will confirm that zero records were read from the queue. This is because the prior execution of BNDQ had deleted all records from this intrapartition transient queue.

In what way can this program be useful?   This program can be useful for removing all the data present in an intrapartition transient data queue. It also serves as a useful sample program for the beginning CICS command-level programmers who can understand it easily and thereby learn the technique of writing similar programs.

Procedure for Installing This Facility

Step 1. Enter the program shown in Figure 5.21 in a source PDS as member BNDQPGM.

Step 2. Now compile and link this program using the JCL given in Section B.1 in Appendix B. This job will create load module BNDQPGM in your load library. This load library must be included under DDname DFHRPL in the CICS start-up procedure or job.

Step 3. Define the following resources in CICS tables:

Definition of Program BNDQPGM in the PPT

```
PROGRAM    BNDQPGM
GROUP      CICSBOOK
LANGUAGE   COBOL
```

Other parameters for this program in the PPT should be the same as those for sample program BNPROG1 given in Section 1.6.

Definition of Transaction BNDQ in the PCT

```
TRANSACTION  BNDQ
GROUP        CICSBOOK
PROGRAM      BNDQPGM
```

Other parameters for this transaction in the PCT should be the same as those for sample transaction BNC1 given in Section 1.6.

Explanation of Program BNDQPGM

Let us suppose the user enters the following on a blank screen:

BNDQ/ABCD

CICS checks the PCT and finds that this transaction is associated with program BNDQPGM. So, it loads this program into storage, if it is not already there, and transfers control to the first statement in the procedure division. So, control flows to line 45 in Figure 5.21. On line 49, we receive whatever was entered on the screen into WS-DATA-IN. Next, we edit the content of WS-DATA-IN. In this example, everything would be found clean; so, control would flow to line 56 where MAIN-RTN would be performed.

In MAIN-RTN, we would execute line 58 and then branch back to execute this line again. So, the READQ TD command on line 60 would be executed repeatedly, until QZERO condition occurred. This condition would send control to line 79 with label ENDA, where we would send the content of WS-OUT-MSG-2 to the terminal. This would be followed by the execution of the RETURN command on line 82. This would end the task completely and unconditionally.

Exercises

1. Test if program BNDQPGM given in Section 5.15 can be used to read all records that have not yet been read from an extrapartition transient data queue that is open on CICS for input. Make any suitable changes to the program so it can do so. Can the reading of all unread records from an extrapartition queue be useful to a programmer in real life?

2. Program BNUTL02 shown in Figure 5.13 does the following:

> Before starting transaction UTR1, temporary storage queue 'SPYZtttt' is deleted, if it is present. Under what conditions might this queue be present?

> If temporary storage queue 'SPYZtttt' cannot be read even after nine attempts, the program says that transaction UTR1 has not been able to successfully run on the terminal within a short interval. Under what conditions would UTR1 not be able to run on the target terminal, even though it was successfully started by program BNUTL02?

References

1. Stephen Hopkins, Displaying Automatic Initiate Descriptors, CICS Update (Berkshire, England, Issue 42, May 1989), pp. 17–23.
2. Geraint Waters, CICS Screen Capture and Display Facility, CICS Update (Berkshire, England, Issue 41, April 1989), pp. 13–22.

6

Commonly Asked Questions Regarding System Programming Answered

In this chapter we answer some questions that are commonly asked by the system programmer. But the concepts discussed here are of great interest to the application programmer as well, especially if he or she has the desire to move into system programming or understand the causes of problems that occur in the CICS systems that affect his or her application. The author was asked most of these questions by system and application programmers, data processing managers, application systems managers, and others during the course of his work as a consulting CICS specialist at corporations in Canada and Saudi Arabia.

6.1 WHY DOES CICS SIGN ME OFF AUTOMATICALLY AFTER A CERTAIN INTERVAL, AND HOW CAN I CONTROL IT?

Suppose you are using a transaction that is pseudo-conversational and it is a secured transaction, meaning that its security key in the PCT is greater than 1. Since you are using a secured transaction, you must have signed on to CICS using the CSSN transaction. What makes a task pseudo-conversational? It means that this transaction displays a map and then returns to CICS specifying the same (or some other) transaction on the TRANSID parameter of the EXEC CICS RETURN command. Suppose you do not use the terminal for a certain period of time. When you press a key, rather than receiving a screen displayed by the transaction, you will receive a message from CICS at the bottom of the screen, informing you that you have not signed on. This means that CICS has signed you off this terminal. You will have to sign on again using the CSSN transaction before using a secured transaction. Here's why:

In the TCT, there is an entry for every terminal. One parameter specifies TYPETERM, or the terminal type. So suppose in your terminal's TCT, TY-

PETERM is coded as IBMCRT2. So, on the DFHCSD file, there must be an entry for TYPETERM named IBMCRT2. Note: TYPETERM is a resource type just like program, mapset, transaction, profile, and terminal. TYPETERM entry has a parameter called SIGNOFF, which can have the value YES, NO, or LOGOFF. If its value is YES, the terminal will get signed off if the time-out limit for the user specified in the SNT (sign-on table) is exceeded. The value NO means the terminal will not get signed off, even if the time-out value has been exceeded.

So, since you are getting signed off, the SIGNOFF parameter for your TYPTERM must have the value YES. Now examine the entry in the SNT for the user name and password you are using. It has a parameter named TI-MEOUT. Suppose it is coded as 10 (i.e., TIMEOUT = 10). This means that the time-out value for this user is 10 minutes. If you code a value for TIMEOUT, any terminal that has SIGNOFF coded as YES in its TCT entry will get signed off if a transaction has not started on that terminal within the specified number of minutes after the previous transaction has completed and freed that terminal. If TIMEOUT is not specified in the SNT entry for a user, that user will not get signed off.

Now suppose you have signed on to CICS using the CSSN transaction. Your user ID has a TIMEOUT value of 10 minutes in the sign-on table. Suppose you enter a transaction that is not secured, that is, its security key is 1. This transaction displays a map and then returns to CICS specifying the same transaction under TRANSID option of the EXEC CICS RETURN command. You do not press a key on your terminal for 12 minutes. So, CICS will sign you off. But when you press a key, the transaction will start successfully, because it is unsecured. You will not receive a message informing you that you have not signed on, because you are using an unsecured transaction.

6.2   CAN I REFRESH DL/I DBD OR PSB WHILE CICS IS UP?

While CICS is up, if you assemble and link a new version of a DBD (Data Base definition) or a PSB (Program Specification Block), it will not become effective. There is no facility to refresh a new version of DBD or PSB. You will have to bring down CICS and restart it in order the make the new version of DBD or PSB effective.

6.3   WHAT IS THE ADVANTAGE OF DEFINING A VSAM FILE AS (ENABLED, CLOSED) IN THE FCT?

There are many advantages to this. In Release 1.7, CICS uses a new approach to opening data sets. CICS no longer opens all data sets during start-up. Normally, a data set is opened at first reference by an application program, unless it has OPENED under the FILSTAT operand in the file control table, in which case CICS opens it immediately after start-up.

So, the initial state of a dataset is controlled by the FILSTAT parameter specified in the file control table. The ENABLED and DISABLED operands only control the dataset at a cold start. The ENABLED, UNENABLED, or DISABLED state of a dataset at CICS termination is retained across a warm or emergency start.

A file that has FILSTAT = (ENABLED,CLOSED) in the file control table, either explicitly specified or assumed by default, is not opened by CICS after start-up. It will be opened when a program refers to the dataset for the first time. The benefit of this scheme is that if a dataset is not used during the entire time CICS is up, it will remain closed, thus not requiring any storage for opening it. Also, it will remain unallocated to CICS (provided it is not present in the start-up JCL), thereby facilitating access to the dataset by some other task such as a batch job that might delete the dataset, redefine, and reload it.

Only if a file has OPENED specified under FILSTAT operand in the file control table will it get opened after CICS is initialized. This will require storage for control blocks needed for opening it. But it may not be accessed by any program during the entire time CICS is up. So, the virtual storage space used for opening it is wasted. (Even though the storage is virtual and not real, you can't waste it, because you don't have an unlimited supply of it.)

Therefore, it is recommended that all files be defined in the FCT with FILSTAT = (ENABLED,CLOSED) coded explicitly or implicitly by omitting the FILSTAT operand.

6.4 WHY DO I GET ABEND APCP WHEN I EXECUTE A PROGRAM AFTER RELINKING IT, AND HOW CAN I RESOLVE THIS PROBLEM?

Sometimes, when you get abend APCP, you can solve the problem by relinking the module and refreshing it by issuing the newcopy command: CEMT S PROG(program) NEWCOPY. But what if this does not resolve the problem? The circumstance is usually as follows.

CICS is started and the DDname DFHRPL is opened for the extents of the load libraries allocated to it. Usually, multiple libraries are allocated to DFHRPL. So, suppose dataset CICS.SYSPROG.LOAD is one of the datasets allocated to DFHRPL, and at the time of CICS start-up, it has three extents. Later, program P1 is linked into this library, and it forces a new secondary extent. So, P1 is linked into the fourth extent. The user issues the newcopy command to refresh this program. When CICS attempts to load the module from the new extent, which in this example is the fourth extent in CICS.SYSPROG.LOAD, an IOERROR condition is returned by the operating system. So, CICS will abend the task on abend code AKCP, any time CICS attempts to read from an extent that is not described in the DEB (Data Extent Block) known to CICS.

What are the solutions to this problem? The long-term and proper solution to this problem is to allocate enough tracks for the primary extent of any load library where many programs are linked during the course of the day. This way, such a dataset will not go into too many extents. Also, all such load libraries with high activity should be compressed on a daily or weekly basis. So, if a data set has 30 primary tracks allocated to it, after compressing it, it's good if all the load modules are stored in the first 10 primary tracks. If new load modules are stored into it during the course of the day, hopefully they will all get stored in the primary extent alone.

But if AKCP starts occurring while CICS is up, you can solve it by bringing down CICS, reallocating and/or compressing the library that is giving you trouble, and then restarting CICS.

6.5 I AM RUNNING SHORT OF STORAGE IN THE DYNAMIC STORAGE AREA. WILL IT HELP IF I USE CICS MODULE FROM THE LINK PACK AREA (LPA)? WHAT ARE THE BENEFITS OF USING MODULES FROM THE LPA?

Yes. Placing selected CICS modules in the Link Pack Area (LPA) of MVS is always a good strategy, especially if you are running the non-XA version of MVS. After placing the modules in the LPA, you should start CICS with LPA=YES in the SIT or SIT override dataset. If the size of the modules placed in the LPA is 500K, and you started CICS with LPA=YES, then the dynamic storage area (DSA) that is part of the CICS address space has 500K more storage than it would have if you started CICS with LPA=NO, meaning, CICS modules are not to be used from the LPA. The following are the benfits of using CICS modules from the LPA:

1. INTEGRITY: Since LPA is key 0 protected, all CICS modules placed there are automatically protected against overwriting by other programs in the CICS region. It is almost impossible to modify the contents of programs placed in the LPA. Note that CICS also provides a similar facility for protecting CICS modules within the region. You need to code a Nucleus Load Table (NLT) with PROTECT=YES parameter specified for those nucleus modules that are to be protected. This facility is only available for nucleus modules and not for user application (PPT) programs.

2. VIRTUAL STORAGE CONSTRAINT RELIEF: Using modules from the LPA decreases the storage requirement in the private area, thereby giving you a larger dynamic storage area (DSA).

3. SHARING: Modules in the LPA can be shared by two or more CICS regions in the same processor. This results in overall reduction in the

total working set. If multiple CICS regions are executing the same releases of CICS, each address space requires access to the CICS nucleus modules. These modules can be loaded into each of the address spaces or shared in the LPA. Using LPA to share the nucleus modules can reduce the working set and therefore the demand for real storage and paging. Less paging means better performance.

The disadvantage of placing too many modules in the LPA is that the common area of the operating system may become too large. Since the division between the common and the private area is on a segment boundary, this means that in the MVS/XA (Extended Architecture) environment, the common line may move down by 1 megabyte. The aim should be to use LPA wisely and derive the optimum benefit from using LPA modules. You should also utilize the unused storage in the common area created by rounding to the next segment boundary.

6.6 I HAVE CHANGED ONE PARAMETER FOR A VSAM FILE IN THE FCT. DO I NEED TO COLD-START CICS TO PICK UP THIS CHANGE?

If you have added a new DFHFCT TYPE = DATASET entry or removed an existing DFHFCT TYPE = DATASET entry from the file control table, there is no need to perform a cold start to pick up the change. The change will get picked up on a warm start. Changing the DDname (i.e., value of the DATASET option) is equivalent to deleting an existing file and adding a new file. So, changing the DDname also does not need a cold start. Changing the dataset name (i.e., value of the DSNAME option) of an existing file also does not need a cold start. However, if you have changed some other parameter(s), you are advised to cold start the CICS so that the change will get picked up, even though experimentation might reveal that a change to a particular option does not need a cold start of CICS.

6.7 DO I NEED TO COLD-START CICS AFTER ADDING A NEW FILE OR DELETING AN EXISTING FILE FROM THE FILE CONTROL TABLE?

Adding a new DFHFCT TYPE = DATASET entry or deleting an existing DFHFCT TYPE = DATASET entry from the file control table does not require cold start of CICS in order for the change to become effective. Since changing the DDname of an existing file entry in the file control table is tantamount to (i.e., equivalent to) deleting an existing file and adding a new one, this also does not need a cold start.

6.8 EXPLAIN HOW I CAN USE THE SYSTEM RECOVERY TABLE (SRT) TO TELL CICS NOT TO CRASH WHEN AN 806 (PROGRAM NOT FOUND) ABEND OCCURS?

Let us suppose your SRT is coded as follows:

```
DFHSRT TYPE=INITIAL, SUFFIX=A1
DFHSRT TYPE=SYSTEM,                                              X
     ABCODE=(106,306,406,706,806,906,A06),                      X
     ROUTINE=DFHSRTRR
DFHSRT TYPE=FINAL
END,
```

(Note: X shown at the end of two lines must be coded in column 72 and words DFHSRT should start in column 10. Continued lines must start in column 16.)

This table specifies that when system abend code 806 (or one of the other codes specified in the table) occurs, CICS should use routine DFHSRTRR to recover from it. This routine is provided by IBM as part of CICS package. So, if abend 806 takes place during the course of CICS operation, CICS will not end abnormally but will recover from it. Apart from the system abend codes specified in the table above, a number of system abend codes such as 001, 013, D37, B37, etc., are automatically recovered by CICS. They need not be present in the SRT. A list of these abend codes is given in the CICS *Resource Definition (Macro)* manual under DFHSRT.

Now suppose you want the system to end abnormally rather than recover any time that system abend D37 occurs. You must add the following line after the fourth line in the SRT given above:

```
DFHSRT TYPE=SYSTEM,ABCODE=(D37)
```

Here, by omitting the ROUTINE operand, we are specifying that no recovery should be attempted when system abend D37 occurs. For further information about how the system recovery table works, read the information under DFHSRT in the CICS *Resource Definition (Macro)* manual.

6.9 WHEN USER ENTERS 'PAY' ON THE SCREEN WITH MY COMPANY LOGO, HE GETS LOGGED ON TO CICSPRD1. EXPLAIN HOW THIS WORKS. HOW CAN I CHANGE THINGS SO 'PAY' WILL ACCESS CICSPRD2?

There is a table in VTAM called USSTAB. Suppose the VTAM application ID of CICSPRD1 is CMVSPRD1. Since entering PAY on the screen with the company logo logs you to the job or started task named CICSPRD1, you must have an entry for PAY in the USS table which is similar to the following:

```
PAY   USSCMD CMD=PAY,REP=LOGON,FORMAT=BAL
      USSPARM PARM=APPLID,DEFAULT=CMVSPRD1
      USSPARM PARM=LOGMODE
      USSPARM PARM=DATA
```

What this entry is basically specifying is that when the user enters PAY on the screen, this should be interpreted as a command to log on to VTAM application with application ID CMVSPRD1.

So, if you want PAY to log you on to CICSPRD2, you have to do the following:

1. Find the VTAM application ID of CICSPRD2. We'll say it is CMVSPRD2.
2. Change the entry for PAY in the source of USS table so that instead of using the application ID of CICSPRD1, it uses that of CICSPRD2. In the above example of USS table, you would change the second line to the following:

```
USSPARM PARM=APPLID,DEFAULT=CMVSPRD2
```

3. Rename USSTAB in the VTAM load library to USSTABX. The load library is the one used in the VTAM start-up procedure.
3. Assemble and link the USS table as member USSTAB in VTAM load library.
4. After the next initialization of VTAM, the new USS table should be the one in use.
5. Test that entering PAY on native VTAM screen logs you on to job CICSPRD2.
6. If the test is not successful, find the cause of the problem and solve it.

6.10 HOW CAN I ENSURE THAT CERTAIN JOBS SUBMITTED DURING THE DAY ONLY EXECUTE AFTER ALL CICS REGIONS HAVE BEEN SHUT DOWN?

Under MVS, assign to all such jobs a job class whose initiator is stopped during the day when all CICS regions are up, and that is started immediately after all CICS regions have been completely brought down. Due to the fact that the initiator for such a class is never started during the entire period when all CICS regions are up, all such jobs will never run when CICS is up. Proper operations procedures need to be established to achieve this.

6.11 AT THE END OF THE DAY, CERTAIN TASKS PREVENT THE SYSTEM FROM COMING DOWN IN RESPONSE TO 'CEMT P SHUT'. HOW CAN I ENSURE THAT THE SYSTEM WILL COME DOWN QUICKLY AS A RESULT OF THIS COMMAND?

At the end of the day, when the operator issues the CEMT P SHUT command, if one or more tasks are present in the system, the system will not come down. So, you can ask the operator to follow this procedure for bringing down the system:

Step 1: From the system console, issue CEMT I TASK to display all tasks in the system.

Step 2. From the console, issue the following command to forcibly close VTAM:

```
CEMT S VTAM FORCECLOSE
```

This will cause the tasks to be terminated, and the VTAM sessions will be ended. He or she should receive the message VTAM ACB IS CLOSED on the system log. Now, if the operator issues command CEMT I TASK, he will find that no tasks are active.

Step 3. Issue CEMT P SHUT to shut down the system normally. The system will come down normally. So, if in your SIT the START option is set to AUTO, the next start-up of CICS will be warm.

Step 4. If the system does not come down completely within a reasonable period of time (e.g., seven minutes) after issuing CEMT P SHUT, issue CEMT P SHUT IMMEDIATE, which should bring down the system.

Step 5. If this also does not bring down the system, issue the cancel command to cancel the CICS region with a dump. The dump will be analyzed by the system programmer the next day to determine why the CICS region had to be cancelled.

6.12 AN ENTRY IS DEFINED IN THE DFHCSD FILE, BUT I DON'T KNOW IN WHICH GROUPS. IS THERE AN EASY WAY TO VIEW OR ALTER SUCH AN ENTRY?

Yes, there is. Let us explain the technique by assuming that the entry is a program, even though the discussion below is applicable to any type of resource, such as a transaction or a terminal. Suppose you want to know which groups contain program P1. Issue one of the following commands on a blank screen:

```
CEDA VIEW PROGRAM(P1) GROUP(*)
CEDA ALTER PROG(P1) G(*)
```

If this program is in one group only, the view of the alter panel showing information about the program will be displayed. However; if this program is present in more than one group, you will receive a panel listing the name of each group that contains this program. On this panel, you can take the cursor to the right of the group name and enter V, if you want to view, or ALT, if you want to alter this entry in that group.

So, the point is that if the entry is in only one group, your search has ended because that is the proper group for it. But if it is present in multiple groups, you must determine the proper group for the program, which is normally the one included in the LIST for CICS. For example, suppose program P1 is in groups G1 and G2. In the SIT for CICS, suppose GRPLIST = L1 and list L1 contains group G1 and not G2. This means that group G1 is the proper group for program P1. So you should enter the following on the CEDA command line to alter the definition of program P1 in group G1:

```
ALTER PROGRAM(P1) GROUP(G1)
```

6.13 THE USER SENDS A PRINTOUT TO A PRINTER, WHICH IS OCCUPIED WITH ANOTHER APPLICATION. EVEN AFTER THE PRINTER BECOMES FREE FROM THAT APPLICATION, THE PRINTOUT SENT BY CICS NEVER PRINTS. WHY? SOMETIMES A PRINTER REFUSES TO PRINT A REPORT GENERATED THROUGH CICS ON-LINE PRINT (CSPG TRANSACTION). HOW CAN I SOLVE THIS PROBLEM?

A printer that is not being used on CICS should have the following attributes when displayed using the CEMT I TERM(termid) command:

```
AUT INS ATI REL CRE
```

INS means the terminal is in-service. OUT means it is out of service. A terminal, whether a printer or a 3270-type terminal, must be in service in order to work properly.

ATI means automatic transaction initiation is allowed on this terminal. NOATI means that automatic transaction is not allowed. Automatic transaction initiation means initiating a transaction on a terminal without the user entering it.

REL means this terminal is released from CICS. ACQ means it is acquired to CICS.

CRE means that this terminal can be acquired to CICS if a transaction is initiated for this terminal, e.g., through the interval control START command. This means that an internally generated log-on is allowed for this terminal. NOCRE means the opposite.

```
=============================================================
IDENTIFICATION DIVISION.
PROGRAM-ID. FIXTERM.
AUTHOR. BARRY K. NIRMAL.
ENVIRONMENT DIVISION.
DATA DIVISION.
WORKING-STORAGE SECTION.
01  LENGTH-160          PIC S9(4) COMP SYNC VALUE +160.
01  WS-DATA-IN          PIC X(160).
01  CEMT-CMD.
    05 FILLER           PIC X(12) VALUE 'CEMT S TERM('.
    05 WS-TERM-ID       PIC X(4).
    05 FILLER           PIC X(17) VALUE ') INS ATI CRE ACQ'.
    05 FILLER           PIC X(47) VALUE SPACES.
01  WS-MSG              PIC X(80).
01  WS-MSG-1            PIC X(80) VALUE
    'COMMAREA PASSED TO FIXTERM IS NOT OF 4 BYTES. NO ACTION TAKEN'.
01  WS-MSG-2            PIC X(80) VALUE
    'SOME ERROR OCCURRED IN FIXTERM. USE CEDF TO DEBUG THE ERROR'.
LINKAGE SECTION.
01  DFHCOMMAREA.
    10 LS-TERM-ID       PIC X(4).
```

352

```
PROCEDURE DIVISION.
    EXEC CICS HANDLE CONDITION ERROR(ERROR-RTN) END-EXEC.
    IF EIBCALEN NOT = 4
        MOVE WS-MSG-1 TO WS-MSG
        PERFORM SEND-MSG-END-PGM.
    MOVE LS-TERM-ID TO WS-TERM-ID.
    EXEC CICS LINK PROGRAM('DFHEMTP') COMMAREA(CEMT-CMD)
        LENGTH(80) END-EXEC.
    EXEC CICS RETURN END-EXEC.
ERROR-RTN.
    MOVE WS-MSG-2 TO WS-MSG.
SEND-MSG-END-PGM.
    EXEC CICS IGNORE CONDITION ERROR END-EXEC.
    EXEC CICS SEND FROM(WS-MSG) LENGTH(80) ERASE END-EXEC.
    EXEC CICS RECEIVE INTO(WS-DATA-IN) LENGTH(LENGTH-160) END-EXEC.
    EXEC CICS RETURN END-EXEC.
```

==

Figure 6.1. Complete listing of program FIXTERM to change attributes of a
printer

So, if a printer is not printing, even though you sent a printout to it, find out its four-character CICS terminal ID, and issue CEMT I TERM(termid) to display its status. It should show as REL. Change the attributes to INS, ATI, and CRE. All of these should be present. Now the printer should get acquired to CICS and start printing. Now it should show as ACQ instead of REL and the name of the transaction, e.g., CSPG, that is doing the printing, should also show on the CEMT panel.

If it still does not print, the printer could be defined incorrectly in the terminal control table, or there might be something wrong with the printer's hardware or the cable connecting it to the local controller. If it is a remote printer, the line connecting it to the host computer might be down.

It has been the author's experience that many times a printer would not print simply because it had NOCRE attribute. Changing it to CRE or changing REL to ACQ on the CEMT panel would fix the problem and the printer would start printing. (The transaction, e.g., CSPG, would show as active on the terminal on the CEMT I TERM display.) So, I wrote a small routine called FIX-TERM that could be invoked from an application program. This routine is shown in Figure 6.1. It sets the attributes of any specified terminal to INS ATI ACQ and CRE. The application program would LINK to this routine before writing report lines to a printer. The terminal ID of the printer is passed to the routine in the COMMAREA. For example, suppose an application program written in command-level COBOL prints report lines to a printer with terminal ID D917. So, prior to writing the lines, it would do the following:

```
MOVE 'D917' TO TERMID.
EXEC CICS LINK PROGRAM ('FIXTERM') COMMAREA(TERMID) LENGTH(4).
```

where TERMID is defined in the working storage as a field with PIC X(4).

6.14 CAN I OPEN A FILE THAT IS A PATH FOR AN AUXILIARY INDEX CLUSTER THAT IS EMPTY?

Suppose you have a base cluster, and you have defined an auxiliary index cluster for it. You have also defined the path, but have not loaded the auxiliary index cluster yet using the BLDINDEX command of IDCAMS. So, the auxiliary index cluster is empty. The path is defined in the CICS file control table. CICS will not be able to open such a path, and when you try to open it explicitly, using the CEMT transaction or the BEMT transaction described in Section 2.15, it is going to abend with code AFCI. There might also be a problem with the CICS region that might necessitate bringing down the entire region.

You may ask, "If the base cluster is empty, how can I build the auxiliary index, since there is no record in the base cluster?" In this case, you can load the base cluster with a dummy record whose key consists of all 9's. Then you can build the auxiliary index.

So, the point to remember is that even though an empty base cluster can be opened by CICS, an empty auxiliary index cluster cannot be opened. So, the proper procedure to follow is as follows:

1. Define the base cluster using IDCAMS DEFINE CLUSTER command, and load the base cluster with one or more records.
2. Define the auxiliary index cluster using IDCAMS DEFINE ALTER-NATEINDEX command, and define the path using IDCAMS DEFINE PATH command.
3. Load the auxiliary index cluster using the BLDINDEX command of IDCAMS.

Also, read Section 3.21 in this book and refer to the section headed *Creating an Alternate Index in VSAM Administration Guide* (IBM manual number GC26-4151).

6.15 A VSAM KSDS DOES NOT OPEN ON FIRST REFERENCE AFTER CICS START-UP. IT IS DEFINED IN THE FCT AS (CLOSED, ENABLED). WHY?

In CICS Release 1.7, a file that is specified as CLOSED (under FILSTAT operand) in the file control table is not opened at the time of CICS initialization. It is opened at first reference, i.e., when an application program refers to it for the first time. CICS initiates transaction CSFU for opening the file. The CSFU task is processed in parallel with other tasks in the system. The priority of CSFU in the PCT should be 255, which is the maximum allowed, or it should be equal to or greater than the highest priority of any transaction that refers to a file that is closed and needs to be opened through the CSFU transaction.

For example, if the highest priority of any transaction in the system that might access a file is p, then make sure that the priority of CSFU is p or greater. If CSFU has a lower priority than the transaction it services, problems can occur.

Once, the author encountered the following situation: Transaction ACS1 had a priority of 100 and CSFU had a priority of 1. When ACS1 requested access to a file, CICS started CSFU to open the file. The CSFU task made an open request, and because its priority was lower than that of ACS1, it gave control to ACS1 task. CSFU had enqueued on the file for open, and now the ACS1 task enqueued on the same file. This resulted in a DTIMOUT deadlock. Because in the PCT entry for ACS1 we had DTIMOUT=10, ACS1 task was abended by CICS on abend code AKCS. But the FCT open in progress bits (FCTDSOPX and FCTDSOPI) were left on, and the CSFU task never got started again. So, we had a file hung in the process of being opened. The author was able to purge the task and open the file using the CEMT transaction. This way, the problem was solved. But right after that, we increased the priority of CSFU to 255 to prevent recurrence of the problem.

```
//============================================================
//jobname  PROC   CLASS=1        IT WILL PROCESS ONLY THOSE JOBS THAT HAVE
//***                            SYSOUT CLASS=1 ON JES SPOOL
//*************************************************************
//* DUMP SYSOUT FROM JES SPOOL INTO A TAPE OR DASD DATA SET
//*************************************************************
//STEP01   EXEC PGM=IASXWROO,PARM='P&CLASS',REGION=20K
//IEFRDER  DD DSN=full.name.of.data.set,DISP=(NEW,CATLG,DELETE),
//         UNIT=TAPE,
//         DCB=(RECFM=FBA,LRECL=133,BLKSIZE=13300)
//SYSABEND DD SYSOUT=X
//============================================================
```

Figure 6.2. Complete listing of procedure EXTWTR1 that is an external writer

356

6.16 HOW CAN I TRANSFER A HUGE SYSOUT FROM JES2 SPOOL TO A DATA SET ON TAPE OR DISK?

The following step-by-step procedure should be followed.

Step 1. In a system procedure library, create member EXTWTR1 as shown in Figure 6.2. In this procedure, enter the name of the tape dataset under DSN parameter on line 7. If you want to place the output in a disk dataset, you must delete line 8 that has UNIT=TAPE and enter proper values for UNIT and SPACE parameters after line 7. This procedure processes all outputs in class 1. You may change this to some other value by changing the value assigned to CLASS on line 1.

Step 2. Change the sysout class of the job on output queue to 1 or to a value specified on line 1 in procedure EXTWTR1.

Step 3. Issue the following MVS command to start the external writer:

```
S EXTWTR1
```

Step 4. The external writer will ask the operator to mount a tape if you are creating a tape data set. It will process all jobs on the output queue that have the specified SYSOUT class (which is 1, in this example) and after all the jobs have been processed, they will be purged from JES spool and will disappear from the output queue.

Step 5. Find out the address of the unit (tape drive or DASD) where the external writer created the output dataset. On the DA screen of SDSF, you can see the unit under STEPNAME for the external writer started task.

Step 6. Issue the following command to purge the external writer:

```
P jobname.uuu
```

where jobname is to be replaced by the job name of the external writer, and uuu is to be replaced by the unit address determined in Step 5. The system should respond by displaying messages on the system log to the effect that the external writer job ended and that it was purged.

Step 7. Now the tape or the DASD dataset specified in the procedure for EXTWTR1 should be cataloged. You can browse it using the ISPF Browse option.

6.17 HOW CAN I CHANGE THE DEFINITION OF A TERMINAL OR ADD A NEW TERMINAL DEFINITION TO CICS ON THE RUNNING SYSTEM?

Follow the step-by-step procedure given on the next page.

1. If this is a new terminal, go to Step 4, or make sure the terminal whose definition is being changed does not have an active task on it. You can issue CEMT I TERM(term) to display this. But, remember, this command will also put a lock on the TCTTE. So, after issuing this command, press PF3 to terminate CEMT.

2. Make sure there are no outstanding ATIs (Automatic Transaction Initiations) for the terminal. Use the program given in Section 5.8 to display expired automatic task initiation requests that are present in the system.

3. Change the terminal status by issuing the following:

   ```
   CEMT S TERM(term) REL OUT NOATI
   ```

4. Create the new terminal's definition or the new definition of an existing terminal in group TEMPNIRM or any other temporary group, and ensure that this group does not contain any other entry.

5. Issue CEDA INSTALL GROUP(TEMPNIRM) to install the terminal definition present in TEMPNIRM on the running system.

6. Now command CEMT INQ TERM(term) should show the terminal as released, in service, and with ATI attribute.

7. Test that the terminal is usable. It may not be if its definition in the TCT does not match its physical characteristics. If the terminal is working, go to Step 8, or find out why it is not working and then go to Step 1.

8. Using CEDA, copy the terminal's definition from group TEMPNIRM to the proper group where it belongs. The proper group is the one included in the list.

6.18 HOW CAN I CHANGE A DEFINITION OR ADD A NEW DEFINITION OF A RESOURCE ON THE RUNNING SYSTEM?

If the resource is a terminal, follow the procedure outlined in Section 6.17. For other types of resources, such as programs, transactions, profiles, and TYPETERMs that are defined using RDO (Resource Definition On-Line), follow this procedure:

1. Create the new resource's definition or the new definition of an existing resource in group TEMPNIRM or any other temporary group and ensure that this group does not contain any other entry.

2. Issue CEDA INSTALL GROUP(TEMPNIRM) to install the definition present in TEMPNIRM on the running system. If the resource is currently being used by a task, the installation might not succeed, in which case you would have to wait until that task has ended before issuing the command again.

3. Issue CEMT INQUIRE resource-type (resource-name) to inquire about the resource. The display should reflect the new definition.

4. Using CEDA, copy the resource's definition from group TEMPNIRM to the proper group where it belongs. The proper group is the one included in the list.

6.19 AFTER INSTALLING A NEW RELEASE OF CICS, "INVALID SIGN-ON ATTEMPT" MESSAGE APPEARS WITH VALID USER AND PASSWORD. HOW DO I SOLVE THIS PERPLEXING PROBLEM?

The scenario surrounding this kind of problem is usually as follows. In the CICS start-up procedure or job, there is a DDname called DFHRPL, to which more than one datasets are normally allocated. For example, suppose one CICS system has the following:

```
//DFHRPL DISP = SHR,DSN = CICS.RELXXX.LOADLIB2
//       DISP = SHR,DSN = CICS.RELXXX.LOADLIB
//       DISP = SHR,DSN = CICS.RELXXX.TEST.TABLES
//       DISP = SHR,DSN = CICS.TEST.SYSPROG.LOAD
//       DISP = SHR,DSN = CICS.TEST.APPLPROG.LOAD
```

Suppose you compile and link a new version of the sign-on table DFHSNT into CICS.RELXXX.TEST.TABLES and bring up the system. Now, suppose that DFHSNT also resides in CICS.RELXXX.LOADLIB, which was created at CICS installation time and contains load modules supplied by IBM. So, when CICS is started, it will search all datasets allocated under DFHRPL. The first dataset to be searched will be

```
CICS.RELXXX.LOADLIB2
```

the next to be searched will be

```
CICS.RELXXX.LOADLIB
```

and so on, because this is the order in which they are allocated under DFHRPL. So, CICS, finding DFHSNT in CICS.RELXXX.LOADLIB, will load it into virtual storage and use it for validating the user name and password entered by the user on the CSSN panel. (The reason it is there is because this dataset was created by downloading what was on the installation tape, and it contained DFHSNT supplied by IBM.) So, even though you linked a new version of DFSNT into CICS.RELXXX.TEST. TABLES, it would not be used.

The solution in this case is to rename DFHSNT in CICS.RELXXX.LOADLIB to DFHSNTXX, and then restart the system. Note that while other tables such as DFHFCT and DFHDCT have two-character suffixes at the end of the load module name, (e.g., DFHFCTA1 or DFHDCTA2) the sign-on table must not have any suffix. This is partly the cause of the problem described above.

6.20 CAN YOU SUGGEST A GOOD SCHEME FOR ASSEMBLING A NEW VERSION OF A CICS TABLE SUCH AS FCT AND JCT?

A good scheme that has proved to be highly beneficial to the author is as follows. Allocate two load libraries and two source libraries for each CICS region to contain load and source modules, respectively, of tables only. To store tables, for example, for CICSTST1, you may allocate the following libraries:

```
CICS.RELXXX.TST1.TEMPTBLS.LOAD
CICS.RELXXX.TST1.TABLES.LOAD
CICS.RELXXX.TST1.TEMPTBLS.SOURCE
CICS.RELXXX.TST1.TABLES.SOURCE
```

The two load libraries should be allocated under DDname DFHRPL in the CICS start-up procedure or JCL. In the concatenation, the TEMPTBLS library should be ahead of TABLES. For example, one test CICS region may have the following:

```
//DFHRPL DISP=SHR,DSN=CICS.RELXXX.LOADLIB2
//       DISP=SHR,DSN=CICS.RELXXX.LOADLIB
//       DISP=SHR,DSN=CICS.RELXXX.TST1. TEMPTBLS.LOAD
//       DISP=SHR,DSN=CICS.RELXXX.TST1.TABLES.LOAD
//       DISP=SHR,DSN=CICS.TEST.SYSPROG.LOAD
//       DISP=SHR,DSN=CICS.TEST.APPLPROG.LOAD
```

The TABLES load library will contain all load modules of tables that have been tested, and the TEMPTBLS load library will contain load modules that have not yet been tested. Similarly, the TABLES source library will contain source of tables that have been tested, and the TEMPTBLS source library will contain source modules that have not yet been tested.

Now, suppose you want to make a change to a table, e.g., the file control table. You should copy the source (e.g., DFHFCTA1) from TABLES source library into TEMPTBLS source library. Then you can make the change to the table in TEMPTBLS source library. You can then assemble the new version of the table in TEMPTBLS library as member DFHFCTA1 and leave the old version in TABLES dataset as member DFHFCTA1. (Note the suffixes in member names in both the dataset of TEMPTBLS and TABLES are the same. So, there is no need to change the SIT or the SIT override dataset, which specifies FCT=A1.) When the system is started, it will load DFHFCTA1 from TEMPTBLS. If the new version of FCT is found to be working properly for a day or two, you should migrate it to production by doing the following:

Move the source of the table from TEMTBLS source dataset into TABLES source dataset. Note: This is Move, not Copy.

Move the load module of the table from TEMPTBLS load library into TABLES load library. Note: This is Move, not Copy.

But, if the new version of the table is found to be defective, or for some reason you want to discard the changes made to it, you can simply revert back to the old version, which was the stable and tested version, by doing the following:

Delete the source of the table from TEMPTBLS source dataset.

Delete the load module of the table from TEMPTBLS load library.

The scheme described here is also applicable for managing application programs. But for application programs, it would not be advisable to allocate two load libraries and two source libraries for each CICS region. You can have just one load library for all test regions and another load library for all production regions. Similarly, you can have just one source library for all test regions and another source library for all production regions.

6.21 CAN I USE THE SAME DFHCSD DATASET ON TEST AND PRODUCTION CICS REGIONS?

Yes, you can, but it is not advisable. The production regions should share a common DFHCSD dataset, while test and training systems should share another dataset. So the scheme of having one dataset for the production regions and another for test and training regions is a good scheme. Why should production regions not share the DFHCSD dataset with test regions? The reason is so we can isolate production regions from the test regions.

Suppose group GENEROL exists on both test and production datasets. To install a new release of GENER/OL, you can make changes to group GENEROL on the test dataset and bring up the new release of GENER/OL for testing. The production regions are not affected by this change; they are stable and are executing the old release of GENER/OL. If you shared the same dataset with test and production regions, a change to group GENEROL would also affect the production regions, which you definitely do not want. So, in this case, you would have to create another group and copy the content of old group GENEROL into it for use by production regions. Why not avoid all this unnecessary work and problems by isolating production regions from test and training regions?

At one shop where the author was working in Saudi Arabia, one gentleman was put in charge of CICS, even though he had no prior knowledge of CICS or application systems. Somehow he found merit in having all CICS regions share a common DFHCSD dataset. Probably he thought he could make a change on the test system and not have to make the same change on the production system. His ill-conceived scheme may have saved him some effort, but it created many problems in production regions by coupling them with test regions. After he resigned, the author took his position, and he set up one DFHCSD dataset for production regions and another for test and training regions. This scheme was found to be a good one.

6.22 SOMETIMES THE USER CLOSES MANY FILES DURING THE DAY AND DOES NOT REOPEN THEM BEFORE CICS COMES DOWN. HOW CAN I ENSURE THAT THESE FILES WILL BE OPENED AUTOMATICALLY AFTER CICS STARTS THE NEXT MORNING?

Let us assume that the files are defined in the file control table as (ENABLED, CLOSED) under the FILSTAT operand, as all files generally should be. So, when the user closes the files during the day, their status becomes CLOSED and UNENABLED, or, if the user also disables them, their status becomes CLOSED and DISABLED. Upon a warm start, their status will remain CLOSED and UNENABLED, or CLOSED and DISABLED. This means that these files will not be automatically opened by CICS at first reference by application programs. So you have two choices:

1. Cold start the CICS every morning. This will make all files CLOSED and ENABLED, and the files will be automatically opened when application programs access them for the first time.

2. Start CICS with START-AUTO in the SIT, but right after CICS has been initialized, issue one or more CEMT commands to set the status of specific files to ENABLED. So, suppose the files with DDnames starting with LK and FK are the ones closed by the user during the day. You would have to execute the following commands:

```
CEMT S DA(LK*) ENABLED
CEMT S DA(FK*) ENABLED
```

You do not have to execute these transactions manually. You can use the facility presented in Section 5.6 to execute them automatically after CICS has been initialized.

The second choice is recommended, because it allows CICS to be started in warm mode, which means less time required in CICS initialization, apart from other benefits.

6.23 HOW CAN I BE SURE THAT A CICS SYSTEM IS INDEED LOOPING, OR IS UNUSABLE AND NEEDS TO BE CANCELLED.

First, use a terminal that is defined in the TCT of the CICS region and try to log on to CICS. If you cannot log on to CICS from any terminal within a reasonable period of time, this indicates that the system is unusable. You may be able to log on to CICS, but when you enter transactions, they may abend or you may not receive any response. These conditions also indicate that the system is not well.

Now, using the CICS monitor you have, especially the cross-system monitor, you may be able to isolate the task that is looping or is causing the problem, purge such a task, and revive the system. If you do not have a powerful CICS monitor, issue the CEMT I TASK for the CICS region in trouble and see if you get any response. If you get a response, try to purge the task that has the lowest task number because most likely that task created the problem. See if you are able to purge the task. Were you able to purge the task? Probably not. Did it revive the system? If not, display tasks again and purge the lowest priority task. Did it revive the system? If so, your mission is fulfilled.

But if you are not able to identify or purge the offending task, either through a monitor or through the CEMT commands issued from the console, and the system is still unusable after a reasonable period of time, you may have to cancel the CICS with dump. Analyze the dump and try to find the cause of the problem. Make necessary changes to rectify the problem, and then restart the CICS. Without finding and rectifying the root cause of the problem, if you restart CICS, the problem is likely to reoccur. But sometimes you may not be in a position to keep the system down while you are reading the dump, because the users cannot sit with their hands folded for that long.

6.24 WHAT ARE THE FOUR LEADING FACTORS THAT CAUSE PROBLEMS IN PRODUCTION OR TEST CICS SYSTEMS?

The four main factors that cause problems in CICS, MVS, or other software systems are as follows.

1. Making a change without thoroughly understanding the implications of the change. One should not make a change if he or she does not understand it. For example, if someone does not understand how to generate the DBD's (Data Base Definitions) for DL/I databases, and if he or she does not understand the DBD parameters, he or she should not make a change to a DBD or run a job to assemble it. The golden rule to follow here is:

   "If something is working and you don't know how it works, leave it alone."

2. Making a change in haste. This means not spending the time required to make the change, e.g., not checking job output to make sure that the assembly of a program or table ran successfully. The time required to make a change depends on the skills and abilities of the person making the change. A system programmer should never rush things. He or she should spend the required amount of time to ensure that the work he or she is doing is done well.

3. Making a change in production system without first testing it on a test system. Every CICS shop has one ore more test regions that are used by both system and application programmers to test installations of and changes to software. In addition to the test systems, there should be one CICS region for the exclusive testing of system programmers. This will allow the system programmers to carry out their testing without affecting the application programmers. Usually, a system programming manager who does not understand the need for setting up such a test region is one who has not "dirtied" his or her hands with real system programming work for a long time, or one who is a political appointee rather than one who was appointed on the basis of his or her technical and managerial skills.

So a system programmer should first test a change on the system programmer's test region, and then test it on the regular test region. Only if these tests have been successful should the change be implemented on production systems.

4. Assuming that something works in a certain way. There is no place for assumptions in system programming. The golden rule here is:
   "Do not assume; be sure."
Anything done on the basis of assumption is bound to malfunction. My system programming manager at SCECO East in Saudi Arabia, Max Seirawan, once told us this joke: "You know what the word 'assume' stands for? It means when you assume, you make an ass of both 'U' and me."

How can you be sure? You make sure by reading IBM manuals, books, and program product manuals and by consulting a member of the systems programming group, or a person outside your division, department, or company, who has the knowledge.

6.25 WHAT ARE THE FOUR GUIDELINES TO FOLLOW TO MINIMIZE PROBLEMS IN CICS PRODUCTION OR TEST SYSTEMS?

The four guidelines are as follows. These should be followed by everyone who supports any kind of software system, whether of system programming or application programming nature.

1. Any work you do, do it well. Plan the work in detail before doing it. Write down the plan, which should follow a step-by-step order. When you are doing a job, concentrate on it, and do not let anyone disturb your concentration.

2. Do not think that the work you are doing is minor or unimportant. The grass always looks greener on the other side of the fence. When a person thinks that the work he or she is doing is of less importance than the work being done by someone else or that it is boring, he or she is more likely to not do it well.

3. Attempt to prevent problems from occurring in the systems rather than reacting to them after they have occurred. To prevent problems, spend a sufficient amount of time checking the work done. This includes checking the output of table assemblies and installation jobs to ensure that condition codes of all job steps are either zero or indicate absence of error. If you encounter a system message, do not ignore or overlook it; rather, look it up in the messages manual to be sure it is not a symptom of a serious error.

4. Do not assume; be sure.

6.26 CAN YOU SUGGEST A SAMPLE FORM TO KEEP TRACK OF PROBLEMS OCCURING IN CICS SYSTEMS?

Every time a problem occurs in any CICS region, especially a production region, the system programmer should document it. This documentation is very important, because it makes the system programmer's work organized. Whether the problem is solved or remains pending, the problem report can be filed in a binder that provides a history of problems occurring in the CICS regions. Figure 6.3 shows a form that should be used to describe the problem. Figure 6.4 shows a form where the results of investigations, diagnostic tests performed, and solutions to problems can be recorded.

CICS PROBLEM REPORT – PART I

NAME: CICS _____   DATE: ___ / ___ / ___   TIME: ___ / ___

JOB/TASK NUMBER _____

PROBLEM NUMBER: _____ of 19   RESOLVED? (YES/NO) _____

DESCRIPTION OF PROBLEM (Attach additional sheets, if required)

Figure 6.3. A form to record problems in CICS Systems.

CICS PROBLEM REPORT – PART II

PROBLEM NUMBER: _____ of 19

RESULTS OF INVESTIGATION CARRIED OUT AND TESTS PERFORMED

368

Figure 6.4. A form to record investigations carried out to resolve a CICS problem.

Commonly Asked Questions Regarding CICS Performance and Tuning

In this chapter we present answers to questions regarding CICS performance and tuning that are commonly asked by or crop up in the minds of system programmers.

7.1 WHAT INFORMATION MUST I RECORD EACH DAY TO HELP ME MONITOR AND TUNE A CICS SYSTEM? CAN YOU SUGGEST A FORM?

The information that should be recorded is shown in Figures 7.1, 7.2, and 7.3. Let us see where each item is obtained.

CICS Name: This is the name of the CICS region, which can be the name of the started task or job. PRD1 represents the first production region, TRN1 the first training region, and TST1 the first test region. You should enter the actual name of your CICS regions in the place of PRD1, PRD2, etc.

Started task/job number: This can be obtained from the MVS system log, or from SDSF (Spool Display and Search Facility) display.

Region size: This is the value of the REGION= parameter on the EXEC card used to execute program DFHSIP, which is the CICS initialization program. Here is an example:

```
//MAIN EXEC PGM=DFHSIP,REGION=4000K,PARM=SYSIN,TIME=1440
```

Subpool in kilobytes: This is the value displayed by CICS at system initialization time. The last subpool size displayed prior to the following message is to be recorded:

DATE: ____/____/____						
CICS Name	Started Task/Job No.	Region Size	Subpool in Kilobytes	DSA in Kilobytes	Max. DSA Percentage Used	Oscor size in Kilobytes
PRD1						
PRD2						
PRD3						
TRN1						
TST1						
TST2						

Figure 7.1. CICS Data Collected - Part 1 of 3

TIME: _____/_____/_____

Max. Oscor Percentage Used	Total Number of Files	Number of Files that are Open	Number of Terminals Using System	Value of MXT	Value of AMXT

DATE: ___/___ TIME: ___/___							
CICS Name	Peak No. of Tasks	Number of Times at Max. Task	Total Number of Tasks	Max. Active Tasks Reached	Average Response Time	Number of Program Compressions	Elapsed Time H – M
PRD1							
PRD2							
PRD3							
TRN1							
TST1							
TST2							

Figure 7.2. CICS Data Collected - Part 2 of 3

| Max. RPL Posted | Number of Times Reached Max. | Total Waits for Strings | FOR LSR POOL #1 | | | | Total Batch Sharing D.B. |
			Total Strings	Total String Waits	Max. Concurrent Strings	Total Buffer Waits	

DATE: _____/_____/_____	
CICS NAME	OBSERVATIONS /
PRD1	
PRD2	
PRD3	
TRN1	
TST1	
TST2	

Figure 7.3. CICS Data Collected - Part 3 of 3

TIME: _____/_____/_____

COMMENTS

CONTROL IS BEING GIVEN TO CICS

This is the amount of storage available for servicing the storage requirements of the tasks.

DSA in kilobytes: This is the size of the dynamic storage area. You may need a CICS monitor, such as The Monitor for CICS or CICSPARS, to obtain DSA size.

Maximum DSA percentage used: This is the maximum percentage of DSA used during the life of CICS. This gives an idea of the utilization of the dynamic storage area and whether the DSA size is too low or too high. You may need to use a CICS monitor to obtain this value.

OSCOR size in kilobytes: This is the size of OSCOR, as specified in the SIT or the SIT override dataset in OSCOR= parameter. So, if your SIT has OS-COR=300000, this means your OSCOR size is roughly 300K.

Maximum OSCOR percentage used: This is the maximum percentage of OSCOR storage used during the life of CICS. This gives an idea of the utilization of OSCOR, and whether OSCOR size specified is too low or too high. You may need to use a CICS monitor to obtain this value.

Total number of files: This is the total number of files defined in the FCT. You can obtain this value by using command: CEMT I DA(*) and counting the files displayed. Alternatively, you can use the facility given in Section 2.15 in Chapter 2. Enter the following to display all files:

```
YOUR WISH (I,S,R) :I
RESOURCE TYPE :DA
RESOURCE NAME :*
```

The program will display the first page containing a list of files. Press Enter to obtain the next page and keep pressing the Enter key. Finally, you will receive the main panel where you entered the inquire command. On this panel, the total number of files will be shown.

Number of files that are open: This is the number of files that are open at the time the data was recorded. You can obtain this by issuing CEMT I DA(*) and counting the files that are open.

Number of terminals using the system: This is the count of the terminals that are connected to CICS at the time of taking the reading. Some of these terminals may not be using any CICS transaction, i.e., they may be idle.

But this gives you an idea of the number of terminals using the system at a particular time. You can obtain this by using the facility given in Section 5.11 in Chapter 5.

Value of MXT: This is the value of the MXT operand in the SIT or the SIT override dataset. You can obtain this by using the CEMT inquire command.

Value of AMXT: This is the value of the AMXT operand in the SIT or the SIT override dataset. You can obtain this, as well as other system parameters, by using the CEMT Inquire command.

Peak number of tasks: This is the maximum number of tasks concurrently in the system at any time during the life of CICS. This is shown at the top of CICS statistics printed when CICS is brought down normally.

Number of times at max. task: This is the number of times CICS reached the maximum task level, which is specified in the SIT in the MXT operand. This value is printed at the top of CICS shutdown statistics.

Total number of tasks: This is the total number of tasks processed during the entire life of CICS. This is shown at the top of CICS shutdown statistics.

Maximum active tasks reached: This is the maximum number of tasks that have been dispatched at least once and are waiting but not suspended (for example, they are doing file I/O). This is shown at the top of CICS shutdown statistics.

Average response time: You may have to use a CICS monitor to obtain this value.

Number of program compressions: This is the number of times a phenomenon known as program compression occurred in the CICS system. The maximum number of times any program was loaded, as shown in shutdown statistics, is very close to the number of program compressions that occurred.

Look at the program statistics under the heading "NUMBER OF TIMES FETCHED," and locate the program that has the highest number of fetches during that life of CICS. (Ignore programs specified as RELOAD = YES or as USAGE = MAP in the PPT.) This is the number of times that this program was loaded, and the number of program compressions was at least that high.

If program compressions occur more than once every 15 minutes (at peak workloads), this will adversely affect overall performance.

Elapsed time: Obtain it from CICS shutdown statistics, where it is recorded right in the beginning.

Maximum RPL posted and number of times reached maximum: Obtained from VTAM statistics in CICS shutdown statistics.

Total number of waits for strings: In the shutdown statistics, there is an area for file statistics. For each file, there is "Wait-on-string total" and "Wait-on-string highest." At the end, there is the sum of "Wait-on-string total" for all datasets. It is this sum that should be recorded.

LSR pool #1 items: Obtained from shutdown statistics, which contain information about each local shared resources pool.

Total batch jobs sharing databases: Obtained from shutdown statistics.

7.2 WHY DOES CICS DISPLAY THE MESSAGE "SHORT ON STORAGE—SYSTEM UNDER STRESS"? HOW CAN I RESOLVE THIS PROBLEM?

This message indicates shortage of Dynamic Storage Area (DSA). To understand how to solve this problem, you must understand what DSA is and what it is used for.

The CICS dynamic storage area is used to supply CICS tasks with the storage needed to execute the user transactions. The amount of storage in the DSA is what is left after CICS has allocated all the other areas.

Too little DSA results in the SOS (short on storage) condition reflected by the CICS issuing message "Short on Storage—System Under Stress." This results in program compression, or even more seriously, stall purge abends when program compression is not sufficient to alleviate the problem.

The CICS dynamic storage area is a single contiguous block of virtual storage in the CICS region, from which all requests (i.e., CICS GETMAIN requests) for dynamic storage are satisfied during normal execution. The DSA size is determined by what is left in the CICS region after the CICS system is initialized. Initialization involves allocation of OSCOR, loading of CICS resident programs and tables, and initial opening of datasets and the terminal network.

To alleviate the shortage of DSA, you may take one or more of these actions.

1. Increase region size, keeping OSCOR value the same. This will increase the size of the DSA.

2. Revise the use of options such as MXT (Maximum Number of Tasks), primed storage, and making heavily used programs resident, to keep down the overall requirement for DSA storage. This, however, may limit task throughput.

3. Divide your CICS system, possibly by splitting it into two regions, or

possibly by use of facilities such as CICS multiregion operation (MRO), described in the *CICS/OS/VS Intercommunication Facilities Guide*.

Refer to *CICS/OS/VS Performance Guide* for more information about related topics.

7.3 SOMETIMES A VSAM KSDS WOULD NOT OPEN WHEN OPENED USING CEMT. MY MONITOR SHOWS SHORT ON OSCOR STORAGE. HOW CAN I SOLVE THIS PROBLEM?

This is a symptom of a lack of OSCOR storage or its fragmentation. If OSCOR storage is too little, or when it gets fragmented after a certain time, datasets may not open. In this case, you may have to bring down the CICS system, possibly increase the OSCOR value in the SIT or the SIT override dataset, and then restart the system. This is the surest way to solve this problem.

The part of the CICS address space called OSCOR is the storage available to the MVS operating system to perform region-related services in response to an operating system macro or an SVC. For example, operating system components such as VSAM issue OS GETMAIN requests to obtain storage in which to build control blocks, and these requests are satisfied from OSCOR.

OSCOR is used to contain control blocks and data areas used for opening datasets and for other operating system functions, as well as program modules for access method routines not already resident in the LPA and shared routines for the COBOL and PL/I programs.

The amount of OSCOR is specified in the OSCOR = operand in the SIT. This specification must be enough to satisfy the requests for storage during the entire life of the CICS region. You should use a CICS monitor or a program to monitor the use of OSCOR and thereby tune the value specified under the OSCOR operand in the SIT. The aim should be never to run out of OSCOR but not to overallocate it either.

Due to the dynamic nature of a CICS system, the demands on OSCOR will vary during the day, depending on the number of tasks or datasets that are opened and closed. Also, because of the dynamic nature of OSCOR, fragmentation will occur, and one must allow for additional storage to compensate for this.

7.4 WHAT IS THE DIFFERENCE BETWEEN DSA AND OSCOR? EXPLAIN ANY INTERRELATIONSHIP BETWEEN THE TWO.

To understand the difference between OSCOR and DSA, take a look at Figure 7.4, which depicts the private area of the CICS address space (in MVS/370 or MVS/XA) right after CICS has been initialized.

OS Free Storage (OSCOR)—Area 7

This is the storage that remains free out of the initial OSCOR specification

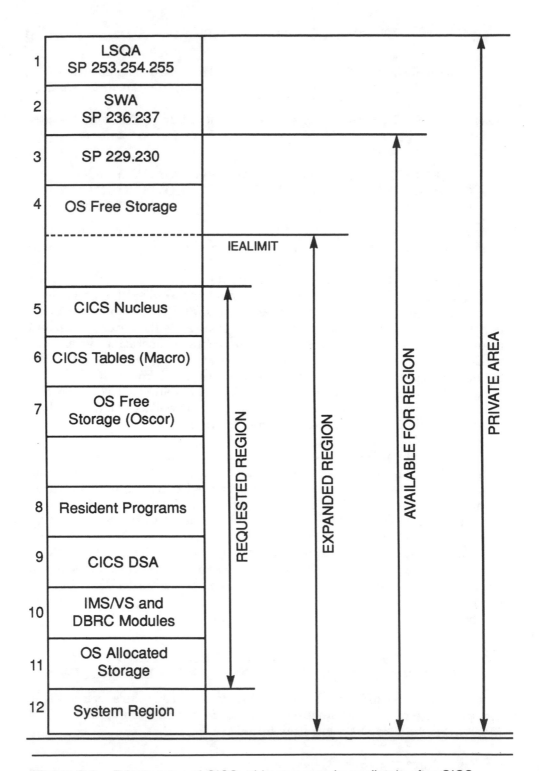

Figure 7.4. Private area of CICS address space immediately after CICS initialization.

in the SIT. Opening of files is the major contributor to usage of this area. For more information about this area, see Section 7.3 above.

OS Allocated Storage—Area 11

The storage allocated for the control blocks and buffers to support the CICS address space and access methods is conceptually presented in Figure 7.4 as OS Allocated Storage.

CICS Dynamic Storage Area (DSA)—Area 9

This is a single contiguous block of statically allocated storage from which all CICS GETMAIN requests will be satisfied during CICS execution. CICS DSA is statically allocated during initialization, but the use of storage within the DSA is very dynamic. For further information about DSA, see Section 7.2 above.

So, we have examined the difference between DSA and OSCOR storage areas. As regards the interrelationship between them, it can be understood as follows.

If all factors in a CICS system are kept constant, increasing the region size, in most cases, gives an increase in the DSA. Keeping all factors constant, increasing OSCOR specification in the SIT gives a smaller DSA, and decreasing OSCOR specification gives a bigger DSA.

Whereas the size of OSCOR is specified by the system programmer under the OSCOR operand in the SIT, the size of DSA cannot be specified. The size of DSA is calculated by CICS at initialization time.

7.5 WHAT IS THE BENEFIT OF PLACING AN FCT ENTRY IN THE LSR POOL?

A file in the FCT is defined as an NSR file by specifying LSRPOOL = NONE in the DFHFCT macro. Omitting this operand makes the file use LSR pool number 1 by default. The benefit of using an LSR pool for a file can be understood through an analogy.

Suppose a company has 100 employees and a fleet of 30 cars. Employees use company cars to go out on business trips. At any one time, not more than 20 employees are allowed to go out of the office. So, rather than permanently assigning cars to a selected 30 employees, thereby denying cars to 70 employees, management can place its fleet of cars in a car pool. When an employee needs a car, he or she can be assigned one of the 20 cars. This scheme would result in better utilization of the fleet of cars. It also will not deny any employee the use of a company car.

Similarly, using the LSR pool for an FCT file has the following advantages:

More efficient use of virtual storage because buffers and strings are shared.

Better performance because of better buffer look-aside, which can reduce I/O operations.

Self-tuning because more buffers are allocated to busy files, and frequently referenced index control intervals are kept in its buffers.

Better read integrity because there is only one copy of a control interval in storage.

Refer to *CICS/OS/VS Performance Guide* for more information about related topics.

7.6 HOW CAN I TUNE THE LSR POOL PARAMETERS SPECIFIED IN THE FCT?

Tuning the LSR pool parameters specified through the DFHFCT TYPE = SHRCTL statement in the FCT is done by examining the VSAM shared resources section in the CICS shutdown statistics. You should consider the following points:

Maximum number of concurrent active file control strings is the maximum number of strings that were active during CICS execution. You can reduce the value of STRNO specified on the TYPE = SHRCTL statement so that it is closer to the maximum number of concurrent active file control strings.

Number of successful look-asides is the number of read requests that VSAM was able to satisfy without initiating an I/O operation. This means that the requested record, whether index or data, was already present in one of the buffer resident control intervals. No physical I/O had to be done to place the control interval from the VSAM file into the buffer. You can either increase the number of buffers of a particular CI size until the ratio of look-asides to READs stops increasing significantly or, conversely, reduce the number of buffers until the ratio of look-asides to READs begins to drop significantly.

Total number of requests that had to wait for a buffer is given for each LSR file. It is the total number of requests for a buffer that had to wait because all buffers in the LSR pool were in use. If wait-on-buffers are occurring, examine the TYPE = SHRCTL,BUFFER operand, along with the LISTCAT information for the file, which will give you the control interval size for the data (and index, if used) component. If no buffers of the CI size are specified on the TYPE = SHRCTL statement, specify some buffers of that size. Otherwise, the next larger size buffers will have been used, resulting in a waste of storage. In this case, you should increase the number of buffers of that size.

Highest number of requests waited for string is the highest number of requests that were queued at one time because all the strings in the pool were in use. You may increase the number of strings specified on TYPE = SHRCTL statement so that this value is zero or a low value. Remember, for best performance, wait-on-buffers must not occur, whereas wait-on-strings of a low value may be tolerable.

7.7 HOW CAN I TUNE THE STRNO (STRING NUMBER) PARAMETER FOR A FILE IN THE FCT?

If access to a file is read only with no browsing, there is no need to have a large number of strings; just one may suffice. However, where some browsing or updates are used, STRNO should be set to 2 or 3 initially, and you should check the file statistics in CICS shutdown statistics regularly to find the number of wait-on-strings. Wait-on-strings up to 5 percent of the number of file accesses are permissible. With NSR files you should not try to keep wait-on-strings permanently zero.

Note that a file can "wait-on-string" for an LSR pool string also. This type of wait is not included in the wait-on-string totals in file statistics; they are included in LSR pool statistics. While setting the STRNO operand in the DFHFCT TYPE = DATASET macro, you should use the "highest number of wait-on-strings" value in the file statistics.

The higher the STRNO value you choose, the more VSAM buffers will be required, and hence, more virtual storage. Consequently, more real storage will be required. When storage is limited, the "wait-on-strings" can be reduced by controlling the number of concurrent tasks. This can be done, for example, by setting CMXT to a smaller value.

7.8 WHICH PPT MODULES SHOULD BE MADE RESIDENT?

As a general rule, strike a balance between resident and nonresident programs. Most used programs should be resident and less used programs should be nonresident.

Application modules that are rarely needed should generally be made nonresident. If the most frequently used programs and mapsets are made resident, making additional programs resident, in most cases, becomes counterproductive, because the size of the CICS dynamic storage area (DSA) falls below a minimum acceptable amount. This leads to an increased number of program compressions, and, consequently, an increased number of program reloads. The tuning aim should be to reduce the total number of reloads.

If program compressions are occurring, examine the shutdown statistics and see if there are any programs with low use counts and zero fetch counts. This would mean that such programs could probably be made nonresident. Also, look for programs that have high use counts and high fetch counts. They could probably be made resident.

7.9 WHAT IS PROGRAM COMPRESSION? HOW CAN I MINIMIZE IT?

Nonresident programs are loaded in the CICS dynamic storage area (DSA). Program storage is allocated from the top of the DSA down, while other storage is allocated from the bottom of the DSA up. This is done so that there is enough room to load large programs. Storage allocated for nonresident programs is not freed at task end, even if there are no tasks to use it. This is done in the anticipation that a task may soon arrive that would need the program. But to prevent endless accumulation of program storage, a process known as "program compression" is periodically carried out.

Program compression is used in the event that one of these conditions occurs:

A request for storage (CICS GETMAIN) cannot be satisfied due to lack of available storage.

A request for storage is successful, but it results in fewer storage pages in the DSA than the threshhold specified in the SIT as the storage cushion.

The process of program compression consists of the following steps:

Storage of all programs that are currently not in use are freed up (FREE-MAIN).

Programs that are loaded so low in the DSA that they are mixed with, or near, nonprogram storage are marked for deletion.

Why is program compression considered bad from the performance point of view? This is because the first of the two steps given above can consume many processor cycles and take several seconds. Also, programs purged from storage may be needed and loaded right after program compression has finished. Several tasks may need programs that were purged from storage. Because CICS uses BSAM to load programs and because there is only one I/O block associated with the data control block for the program library, this process is serialized and causes delay in the processing of tasks.

If the size of the DSA is not sufficiently large and the number of concurrent tasks in the system is large, program compressions can occur more frequently. In fact, it is quite normal for program compression to occur to prevent the short-on-storage condition from arising. However, if program compressions are occurring more frequently than once every 15 minutes, this will adversely affect performance and result in intolerably long response times at the terminals.

To reduce the number of program compressions, you can take one or more of the following actions:

1. Make more storage available in the DSA by increasing the region size and/or reducing OSCOR size.

2. Make frequently used programs resident and infrequently used programs nonresident. (See Section 7.8 to find out how.)

3. Tune the system so as to make more storage available in the DSA to load nonresident programs. Follow the recommendations given under various items of the Virtual Storage Checklist given in CICS/OS/VS Performance Guide. (Refer to the chapter entitled Performance Checklists.)

4. Reduce the workload by lowering MXT, AMXT, and/or CMXT parameters in the SIT. This will reduce CICS throughput and may result in bad response times on some terminals.

7.10 WHAT ARE THE ADVANTAGES AND DISADVANTAGES OF COMBINING TWO CICS TEST REGIONS INTO A SINGLE REGION?

Two regions that were functioning properly under MVS/370 may need to be combined into one region to function under MVS/XA. Under MVS/370, sometimes one region is split into two regions to provide virtual storage constraint relief. Unless the operating system is migrated to MVS/XA, these two regions should not be combined into one.

The benefits of combining two CICS test regions into one region under MVS/XA is as follows:

1. The combined test region will take on the average less real storage at any one time compared to the two regions before combining. This is because the CICS/VS and IMS/VS control programs and some control blocks are in two regions before combining, whereas they will be in only one region after combining.

2. The CPU cycles requirement of the combined region will be less compared to that of the two regions before combining. This is because the CICS/VS control programs are in two regions before combining, whereas they will be in a single region after combining.

3. Computer operations division will have to start and stop only one region after combining, rather than two regions before combining. This will result in better management and handling of CICS on their part.

4. The system programming group will have to maintain and support only one region after combining, rather than two before combining. This will result in better management of CICS on their part.

The disadvantages of combining two test regions into one region are as follows:

1. Suppose a test region supports only one application system before combining. If the project leader responsible for that application wants

to keep his system down, he simply instructs the operations division not to start that region, or to bring it down if it is already started. If we combine this test region with another region, the impact will be as follows. The combined region will be started at a fixed time every day. If the project leader wants to keep his application down, he will have to do the following:

Disable all the transactions for his application.

Close and deallocate all the files for his application from the combined region.

Take any other action, such as closing user journals, for the application.

When the project leader wants to bring up his application, he will have to do the following:

Allocate and open all the files for the application.

Take any other action, such as opening any user journals, for the application.

Finally, enable all the transactions for the application. It is evident that combining two regions into one makes it more difficult to keep an application down until it is ready to be brought up on the CICS region.

2. Sometimes, before combining, a test region would go into "endless loop," and the only remedy would be to cancel the region, resolve the problem causing the loop, and then restart it. This would not affect the other test regions. But after combining, when the combined test region starts to loop, and when it is cancelled, this would affect all the applications that are on the region. This means that the loss of availability of the CICS region would be felt by a greater number of users.

7.11 EXPLAIN THE SIGNIFICANCE OF KEYLEN PARAMETER IN THE SHRCTL MACRO, ESPECIALLY AS IT RELATES TO CICS START-UP TIME.

If the KEYLEN parameter is missing from the SHRCTL macro in your FCT, CICS will search all the catalogs that contain VSAM files using LSR pool, defined in the FCT, to figure out the largest key for building the LSR pool. Obviously, this can take a long time and may result in longer CICS start-up time. But when you code the KEYLEN parameter, CICS is spared this search and the building of the LSR pool takes considerably less time.

How do you decide the value for the KEYLEN parameter? Look at the CICS shutdown statistics, find out the maximum key length used in your LSR pool, and code this value under KEYLEN parameter.

8

Problem Determination Techniques for the Systems Programmer

In this chapter we present some problem determination techniques useful for the systems programmers. Solving problems that arise with systems software on CICS systems is an important duty of system programmers. Hence, the importance of this chapter is obvious.

8.1 HOW DO YOU FIND OUT THE CAUSE OF AN ASRA ABEND IN A MACRO LEVEL ASSEMBLER PROGRAM?

When the failing program is written under command level, whether in COBOL or Assembler, you can use the CICS Execution Debugging Facility (CEDF) to diagnose the problem. But in case of macro-level programs, CEDF can't be used. So, let us illustrate the technique of finding out the cause of an ASRA (or any other) abend in a macro-level program:

Step 1. Obtain the PSW from the dump. In this example, it is the following:

```
078D0000 003A8268 00040007 00000000
```

So, the address of the next sequential instruction (NSI) to be executed when the abend occurred is X'003A8268'.

Step 2. The dump indicates that the program storage is from X'003A8008' to X'003A87CF' for a length of X'07C8'. So, calculate the offset within the program of the next sequential instruction:

```
        003A8268
Minus   003A8008
-------------------
Result  00000260
```

Step 3. Look at the assembly listing of the program. In this example, it is as follows:

```
PACK TDOUBLE, TTOTREC
CVB  R5, TDOUBLE
L    R7, TLASTNUM
```

The last instruction is at offset X'260'. This means that the problem occurred while executing the CVB instruction. Most likely, TDOUBLE does not have a proper number in the packed format. This means that TTOTREC does not have all numeric characters. It is defined as follows:

```
TTOTREC DS CL4
```

In the dump, if we look at the content of TTOTREC, we find that it does not contain a valid number in the display format. So, we have determined the exact cause of the ASRA abend. This method can be used to diagnose other kinds of abends as well.

Sometimes, you can use the trace entries in the CICS dump to figure out the address in the program where CICS macros were issued. For example, a trace entry may have the following:

```
Time of Day:    016:03:12.829664
ID:             F5
Register 14:    503A8190
Task Number:    01584
Resource:       XXCIV009
Trace Type:     FCP GET
```

This trace entry indicates that FCP GET was issued at address X'3A8190' in the program. The task number was 1584. The dump also tells us the starting address of the program. From this, the offset in the program where FCP GET was issued can be determined. This will locate the instruction in the program source where FCP GET was issued.

8.2 HOW DO YOU FIND OUT WHICH TASK IS IN AN ENDLESS LOOP AND CAUSING THE WHOLE CICS REGION TO HANG?

Suppose that CICS is looping or is so "sick" that the only way out is to cancel it. So, you cancel the region with the dump option, so as to obtain a region (partition) dump. From this region dump, you must figure out which task was looping or was active, and why. Below is given a step-by-step procedure to determine the CICS task that was active when the CICS region was cancelled.

Step 1. Find the CSA (Common System Area) in the partition dump. Unless the code being executed is in an access method routine, Register 13 addresses either the CSA or a save area that contains the address of the CSA at offset X'4'. However, the following method of finding the CSA will always work.

The CSA can be recognized in a partition dump by the presence of a DFHVM expansion beginning '*DFHCSAxx*' and a copyright notice, followed by a short piece of code to handle AICA transaction abends and the string 'STORAGE'. The CSA itself begins at the next doubleword boundary.

Step 2. The address of the current task's user TCA (Task Control Area) is at CSA plus X'4C'. The address of the current task's System TCA can be calculated as the address of the User TCA minus X'190'.

Step 3. The address of the Facility Control Area (FCA) is at User TCA plus X'8'. Go to the Facility Control Area. The first four characters are the CICS terminal ID if this task was issued from a terminal.

Step 4. The address of the initiating PCT entry can be found at System TCA plus X'14'. Go to the initiating PCT entry. The first four characters represent the transaction ID of the task that was active.

Step 5. The address of the current PPT entry can be found at System TCA plus X'34'. Go to the current PPT entry. The first eight characters represent the program ID of the program that was being executed at the time CICS was cancelled.

Step 6. At System TCA plus X'F0' is the suffixed name of the most recently loaded BMS mapset.

Refer to *CICS Data Areas* manual for the layout of various control blocks, such as CSA, TCA, etc. This will help you in finding other information helpful in diagnosing and solving this as well as other kinds of problems.

9

Interesting CICS Applications and Facilities

In this chapter we present two very interesting facilities that run under CICS. The first is the Humor Storage and Retrieval Facility (HSRF) that can be used to store humor or quotations and then display one item at a time on the screen in random order. The second is a CICS monitor that is simple yet quite powerful. This monitor can be used to display important information about the running system, as well as active and suspended task chains. You can also use it to display any area of virtual storage.

Both these facilities are complete and ready to install and run. The explanations that accompany each facility and program will enable you to understand these facilities so that you can either modify them or develop similar facilities to meet your unique needs.

9.1 HUMOR STORAGE AND RETRIEVAL FACILITY (HSRF)

Figures 9.1 through 9.4 present various components of this facility, which allows you to store humor/quotation items on a VSAM key-sequenced dataset and to display the humor/quotations one by one in random order on your terminal. The fact that items from the file are displayed in random order makes this facility an interesting one, especially if you have stored a large number of items on the file. To help you get started quickly with this facility, we are providing some humor/quotations in Appendix A. You can store these items on the VSAM file and start to use this facility quickly.

9.1.1 Procedure for Installing This Facility

Step 1. Enter the mapset shown in Figure 9.1 in member BNMSGS2 of a source PDS. Enter the program shown in Figure 9.2 in member MSGPROG2

```
       ***********************************************************************  X
     1       PRINT NOGEN
     2 BNMSGS2 DFHMSD TYPE=&SYSPARM,MODE=INOUT,CTRL=(FREEKB,FRSET),              X
     3              LANG=COBOL,TIOAPFX=YES
     4 BNMSGM2 DFHMDI SIZE=(24,80)
     5       DFHMDF POS=(03,01),LENGTH=03,ATTRB=(ASKIP,BRT),INITIAL='L0:'
     6 L0    DFHMDF POS=(03,05),LENGTH=75,ATTRB=(UNPROT,IC)
     7       DFHMDF POS=(04,01),LENGTH=01,ATTRB=ASKIP
     8       DFHMDF POS=(05,01),LENGTH=03,ATTRB=(ASKIP,BRT),INITIAL='L1:'
     9 L1    DFHMDF POS=(05,05),LENGTH=75,ATTRB=UNPROT
    10       DFHMDF POS=(06,01),LENGTH=01,ATTRB=ASKIP
    11       DFHMDF POS=(07,01),LENGTH=03,ATTRB=(ASKIP,BRT),INITIAL='L2:'
    12 L2    DFHMDF POS=(07,05),LENGTH=75,ATTRB=UNPROT
    13       DFHMDF POS=(08,01),LENGTH=01,ATTRB=ASKIP
    14       DFHMDF POS=(09,01),LENGTH=03,ATTRB=(ASKIP,BRT),INITIAL='L3:'
    15 L3    DFHMDF POS=(09,05),LENGTH=75,ATTRB=UNPROT
    16       DFHMDF POS=(10,01),LENGTH=01,ATTRB=ASKIP
    17       DFHMDF POS=(11,01),LENGTH=03,ATTRB=(ASKIP,BRT),INITIAL='L4:'
    18 L4    DFHMDF POS=(11,05),LENGTH=75,ATTRB=UNPROT
    19       DFHMDF POS=(12,01),LENGTH=01,ATTRB=ASKIP
```

```
20          DFHMDF  POS=(13,01),LENGTH=03,ATTRB=(ASKIP,BRT),INITIAL='L5:'
21  L5      DFHMDF  POS=(13,05),LENGTH=75,ATTRB=UNPROT
22          DFHMDF  POS=(14,01),LENGTH=01,ATTRB=ASKIP
23          DFHMDF  POS=(15,01),LENGTH=03,ATTRB=(ASKIP,BRT),INITIAL='L6:'
24  L6      DFHMDF  POS=(15,05),LENGTH=75,ATTRB=UNPROT
25          DFHMDF  POS=(16,01),LENGTH=01,ATTRB=ASKIP
26          DFHMDF  POS=(17,01),LENGTH=03,ATTRB=(ASKIP,BRT),INITIAL='L7:'
27  L7      DFHMDF  POS=(17,05),LENGTH=75,ATTRB=UNPROT
28          DFHMDF  POS=(18,01),LENGTH=01,ATTRB=ASKIP
29          DFHMDF  POS=(19,01),LENGTH=03,ATTRB=(ASKIP,BRT),INITIAL='L8:'
30  L8      DFHMDF  POS=(19,05),LENGTH=75,ATTRB=UNPROT
31          DFHMDF  POS=(20,01),LENGTH=01,ATTRB=ASKIP
32          DFHMDF  POS=(21,01),LENGTH=03,ATTRB=(ASKIP,BRT),INITIAL='L9:'
33  L9      DFHMDF  POS=(21,05),LENGTH=75,ATTRB=UNPROT
34          DFHMDF  POS=(22,01),LENGTH=01,ATTRB=ASKIP
35          DFHMSD  TYPE=FINAL
36          END
```

****

Figure 9.1.   Source code of mapset BNMSGS2

```
****************************************************************************
 1        IDENTIFICATION DIVISION.
 2        PROGRAM-ID.      MSGPROG2.
 3        AUTHOR.          BARRY NIRMAL.
 4        DATE-WRITTEN.    YY/MM/DD.
 5        DATE-COMPILED.
 6    ************************************************************************
 7    * THIS PROGRAM ACCESSES FILE MSGFILE1.                                *
 8    ************************************************************************
 9    *  HISTORY OF CHANGES TO THIS PROGRAM:                                *
10    *-------------------------------------------------------------        *
11    *VERSION    DATE    DESCRIPTION OF CHANGE                             *
12    *-------   --------  -------------------------------------------------*
13    * 0        YY/MM/DD NEW PROGRAM.                                       *
14    ************************************************************************
15        ENVIRONMENT DIVISION.
16        DATA DIVISION.
17        WORKING-STORAGE SECTION.
18        01  IX                      PIC S9(04) COMP.
19        01  IY                      PIC S9(04) COMP.
20        01  IZ                      PIC S9(04) COMP.
21        01  ANY-RECORD-WRITTEN      PIC X(01) VALUE 'N'.
22        01  WS-FILE-KEY.
23            05  FILLER              PIC X(03) VALUE 'MSG'.
24            05  FK-REC-NUM          PIC 9(04).
25            05  FK-REC-SEQ-NUM      PIC 9(01).
26            05  FILLER              PIC X(04) VALUE '$$$$'.
27        01  WS-FILE-RECORD.
28            05  FR-KEY              PIC X(12).
29            05  FR-DATA.
```

396

```
30          10  FILLER OCCURS 75 TIMES.
31              15  CHAR-IN.
32                  20  FR-DATA-CHAR      PIC X(01).
33      05  FILLER  REDEFINES FR-DATA.
34          10  FR-LAST-REC-NUM      PIC 9(04).
35          10  FILLER               PIC X(71).
36  01  CHAR-HOLD                    PIC X(01).
37  01  WS-NEW-REC-NUM               PIC 9(04).
38  01  WS-COMM-AREA.
39      05  CA-TRANS-ID                  PIC X(04)  VALUE 'BNMG'.
40  01  WS-OUT-MSG                       PIC X(80).
41  01  WS-OUT-MSG-R  REDEFINES WS-OUT-MSG.
42      05  TEXT1                        PIC X(14).
43      05  REC-NUM-WRITTEN              PIC ZZZ9.
44      05  TEXT2                        PIC X(40).
45  01  WS-OUT-MSG-1                     PIC X(80)  VALUE
46      '** INPUT DATA NOT PROPERLY ENTERED- TRANSACTION TERMINATED'.
47  01  WS-OUT-MSG-2                     PIC X(80)  VALUE
48      '* THE FILE HAS 9999 MESSAGE RECORDS- MESSAGE NOT PROCESSED'.
49  01  WS-OUT-MSG-3                     PIC X(80)  VALUE
50      'CONDITION LENGERR HAS OCCURED. THIS NEEDS LOOKING INTO. '.
51  01  WS-OUT-MSG-4                     PIC X(80)  VALUE
52      'NO DATA ENTERED ON THIS SCREEN. HENCE NO RECORD WRITTEN. '.
53  01  WS-OUT-MSG-5                     PIC X(80)  VALUE
54      'AN ERROR HAS OCCURRED IN MSGPROG2. USE CEDF TO DEBUG. '.
55  01  CICS-LENGTHS.
56      05  LEN-INPUT-FILE-RECORD     PIC S9(04)  COMP SYNC.
57      COPY BNMSGS2.
```

Figure 9.2. Source code of program MSGPROG2

397

```
58   01  BNMSGM2R REDEFINES BNMSGM2I.
59       05 FILLER                    PIC X(12).
60       05 MAP-DETAIL-LINE OCCURS 10 TIMES.
61          10 FILLER                 PIC X(03).
62          10 LXI                    PIC X(75).
63   COPY DFHAID.
64   LINKAGE SECTION.
65   01  DFHCOMMAREA.
66       05 LS-AREA                          PIC X(04).
67       05 LS-AREA-1 REDEFINES LS-AREA.
68          10 LS-TRANS-ID               PIC X(04).
69   PROCEDURE DIVISION.
70       EXEC CICS HANDLE CONDITION ERROR (ERROR-PROCESS) END-EXEC.
71   1000-MAINLINE.
72       IF EIBCALEN = 0
73          PERFORM 2000-FIRST-TIME-PROCESS THRU 2000-EXIT.
74       IF LS-TRANS-ID = 'BNMG'
75          PERFORM 2100-RETURNING THRU 2100-EXIT
76       ELSE
77          MOVE 'ILLEGAL ENTRY INTO BNMSGP02' TO WS-OUT-MSG
78          PERFORM 9000-ABEND-RTN THRU 9000-EXIT.
79       GOBACK.
80   1000-EXIT.
81       EXIT.
82   2000-FIRST-TIME-PROCESS.
83       EXEC CICS SEND MAP ('BNMSGM2')
84          MAPSET ('BNMSGS2')
85          ERASE
86          MAPONLY
87       END-EXEC.
```

```
88          EXEC CICS RETURN
89              TRANSID ('BNMG')
90              COMMAREA (WS-COMM-AREA)
91              LENGTH (4)
92              END-EXEC.
93  2000-EXIT.
94      EXIT.
95  2100-RETURNING.
96      IF EIBAID = DFHENTER
97          PERFORM 3000-ENTER-PROCESS THRU 3000-EXIT.
98      IF EIBAID = DFHCLEAR
99          PERFORM 3100-CLEAR-PROCESS THRU 3100-EXIT.
100     MOVE 'ILLEGAL KEY PRESSED - TRANSACTION TERMINATED' TO
101         WS-OUT-MSG.
102     PERFORM 9000-ABEND-RTN THRU 9000-EXIT.
103 2100-EXIT.
104     EXIT.
105
106 3000-ENTER-PROCESS.
107     EXEC CICS HANDLE CONDITION MAPFAIL (3010-MAPFAIL) END-EXEC.
108     EXEC CICS RECEIVE
109         MAP ('BNMSGM2')
110         MAPSET ('BNMSGS2')
111         INTO (BNMSGM2I)
112         END-EXEC.
113
114     GO TO 3020-PROCEED.
115
```

Figure 9.2. continued.

```
116   3010-MAPFAIL.
117       MOVE WS-OUT-MSG-1 TO WS-OUT-MSG.
118       PERFORM 9000-ABEND-RTN THRU 9000-EXIT.
119
120   3020-PROCEED.
121       IF L0I = LOW-VALUES
122           MOVE WS-OUT-MSG-1 TO WS-OUT-MSG
123           PERFORM 9000-ABEND-RTN THRU 9000-EXIT.
124       MOVE SPACES TO WS-FILE-RECORD.
125       EXEC CICS HANDLE CONDITION LENGERR(LENGTH-ERROR) END-EXEC.
126       MOVE 'MSG00000$$$' TO WS-FILE-KEY.
127       MOVE +87 TO LEN-INPUT-FILE-RECORD.
128       EXEC CICS READ
129           DATASET ('MSGFILE1')
130           RIDFLD (WS-FILE-KEY)
131           LENGTH (LEN-INPUT-FILE-RECORD)
132           INTO (WS-FILE-RECORD)
133           END-EXEC.
134   NEXT01.
135       IF FR-LAST-REC-NUM EQUAL TO 9999
136           MOVE WS-OUT-MSG-2 TO WS-OUT-MSG
137           PERFORM 9000-ABEND-RTN THRU 9000-EXIT.
138
139       ADD +1 TO FR-LAST-REC-NUM.
140       MOVE FR-LAST-REC-NUM TO WS-NEW-REC-NUM.
141
142       MOVE 'N' TO ANY-RECORD-WRITTEN.
143       PERFORM 4000-WRITE-RECORD-RTN THRU 4000-EXIT
144           VARYING IX FROM 1 BY 1 UNTIL IX GREATER THAN 10.
145
```

```
146         IF ANY-RECORD-WRITTEN = 'N'
147             MOVE 'WS-OUT-MSG-4' TO WS-OUT-MSG
148             PERFORM 9000-ABEND-RTN THRU 9000-EXIT.
149
150         EXEC CICS HANDLE CONDITION LENGERR(LENGTH-ERROR) END-EXEC.
151         MOVE SPACES TO WS-FILE-RECORD.
152         MOVE 'MSG00000$$$' TO WS-FILE-KEY.
153         MOVE +87 TO LEN-INPUT-FILE-RECORD.
154         EXEC CICS READ
155             DATASET ('MSGFILE1')
156             RIDFLD (WS-FILE-KEY)
157             UPDATE
158             LENGTH (LEN-INPUT-FILE-RECORD)
159             INTO (WS-FILE-RECORD)
160             END-EXEC.
161     NEXT02.
162         EXEC CICS HANDLE CONDITION LENGERR(LENGTH-ERROR) END-EXEC.
163         MOVE +87 TO LEN-INPUT-FILE-RECORD.
164         ADD +1 TO FR-LAST-REC-NUM.
165         EXEC CICS REWRITE
166             DATASET ('MSGFILE1')
167             FROM (WS-FILE-RECORD)
168             LENGTH (LEN-INPUT-FILE-RECORD)
169             END-EXEC.
170
171     NEXT03.
172         MOVE SPACE TO WS-OUT-MSG.
173         MOVE 'RECORD NUMBER ' TO TEXT1.
```

Figure 9.2. continued.

401

```
174        MOVE WS-NEW-REC-NUM TO REC-NUM-WRITTEN.
175        MOVE ' HAS BEEN SUCCESSFULLY WRITTEN ONTO FILE' TO TEXT2.
176
177        EXEC CICS SEND FROM (WS-OUT-MSG)
178                  LENGTH (80)
179                  ERASE
180                  END-EXEC.
181        EXEC CICS RETURN END-EXEC.
182
183    3000-EXIT.
184        EXIT.
185
186    3100-CLEAR-PROCESS.
187        MOVE SPACES TO WS-OUT-MSG.
188        EXEC CICS SEND FROM (WS-OUT-MSG)
189                  LENGTH (01)
190                  ERASE
191                  END-EXEC.
192
193        EXEC CICS RETURN
194                  END-EXEC.
195
196    3100-EXIT.
197        EXIT.
198
199    4000-WRITE-RECORD-RTN.
200        IF LXI (IX) = LOW-VALUES OR LXI(IX) = SPACES
201            GO TO 4000-EXIT.
202
203        MOVE LXI (IX) TO FR-DATA.
```

```
204        MOVE WS-NEW-REC-NUM TO FK-REC-NUM.
205        SUBTRACT 1 FROM IX GIVING IY.
206        MOVE IY TO FK-REC-SEQ-NUM.
207        MOVE WS-FILE-KEY TO FR-KEY.
208        PERFORM 5000-SWAP-RTN THRU 5000-SWAP-EXIT VARYING
209            IY FROM 2 BY 2 UNTIL IY > 74.
210        PERFORM 5010-TRAN-RTN THRU 5010-TRAN-EXIT VARYING
211            IY FROM 1 BY 1 UNTIL IY > 75.
212        PERFORM 5020-SWAP2-RTN THRU 5020-SWAP2-EXIT VARYING
213            IY FROM 1 BY 1 UNTIL IY = 38.
214        EXEC CICS HANDLE CONDITION LENGERR(LENGTH-ERROR) END-EXEC.
215        MOVE +87 TO LEN-INPUT-FILE-RECORD.
216        EXEC CICS WRITE
217            FROM (WS-FILE-RECORD)
218            DATASET ('MSGFILE1')
219            LENGTH (LEN-INPUT-FILE-RECORD)
220            RIDFLD (WS-FILE-KEY)
221            END-EXEC.
222        MOVE 'Y' TO ANY-RECORD-WRITTEN.
223
224    4000-EXIT.
225        EXIT.
226
227    5000-SWAP-RTN.
228        ADD 1, IY GIVING IZ.
229        MOVE FR-DATA-CHAR (IY) TO CHAR-HOLD.
230        MOVE FR-DATA-CHAR (IZ) TO FR-DATA-CHAR (IY).
231        MOVE CHAR-HOLD TO FR-DATA-CHAR (IZ).
```

Figure 9.2. continued.

403

```cobol
232
233
234     5000-SWAP-EXIT.
235         EXIT.
236     5010-TRAN-RTN.
237         IF CHAR-IN (IY) = 'A'
238             MOVE 'B' TO CHAR-IN (IY)
239             GO TO 5010-TRAN-EXIT.
240         IF CHAR-IN (IY) = 'B'
241             MOVE 'C' TO CHAR-IN (IY)
242             GO TO 5010-TRAN-EXIT.
243         IF CHAR-IN (IY) = 'C'
244             MOVE 'D' TO CHAR-IN (IY)
245             GO TO 5010-TRAN-EXIT.
246         IF CHAR-IN (IY) = 'D'
247             MOVE 'E' TO CHAR-IN (IY)
248             GO TO 5010-TRAN-EXIT.
249         IF CHAR-IN (IY) = 'E'
250             MOVE 'F' TO CHAR-IN (IY)
251             GO TO 5010-TRAN-EXIT.
252         IF CHAR-IN (IY) = 'F'
253             MOVE 'G' TO CHAR-IN (IY)
254             GO TO 5010-TRAN-EXIT.
255         IF CHAR-IN (IY) = 'G'
256             MOVE 'H' TO CHAR-IN (IY)
257             GO TO 5010-TRAN-EXIT.
258         IF CHAR-IN (IY) = 'H'
259             MOVE 'I' TO CHAR-IN (IY)
260             GO TO 5010-TRAN-EXIT.
261         IF CHAR-IN (IY) = 'I'
```

```
262        MOVE 'J' TO CHAR-IN (IY)
263        GO TO 5010-TRAN-EXIT.
264    IF CHAR-IN (IY) = 'J'
265        MOVE 'K' TO CHAR-IN (IY)
266        GO TO 5010-TRAN-EXIT.
267    IF CHAR-IN (IY) = 'K'
268        MOVE 'L' TO CHAR-IN (IY)
269        GO TO 5010-TRAN-EXIT.
270    IF CHAR-IN (IY) = 'L'
271        MOVE 'M' TO CHAR-IN (IY)
272        GO TO 5010-TRAN-EXIT.
273    IF CHAR-IN (IY) = 'M'
274        MOVE 'N' TO CHAR-IN (IY)
275        GO TO 5010-TRAN-EXIT.
276    IF CHAR-IN (IY) = 'N'
277        MOVE 'O' TO CHAR-IN (IY)
278        GO TO 5010-TRAN-EXIT.
279    IF CHAR-IN (IY) = 'O'
280        MOVE 'P' TO CHAR-IN (IY)
281        GO TO 5010-TRAN-EXIT.
282    IF CHAR-IN (IY) = 'P'
283        MOVE 'Q' TO CHAR-IN (IY)
284        GO TO 5010-TRAN-EXIT.
285    IF CHAR-IN (IY) = 'Q'
286        MOVE 'R' TO CHAR-IN (IY)
287        GO TO 5010-TRAN-EXIT.
288    IF CHAR-IN (IY) = 'R'
289        MOVE 'S' TO CHAR-IN (IY)
```

Figure 9.2. continued.

```
290         GO TO 5010-TRAN-EXIT.
291     IF CHAR-IN (IY) = 'S'
292         MOVE 'T' TO CHAR-IN (IY)
293         GO TO 5010-TRAN-EXIT.
294     IF CHAR-IN (IY) = 'T'
295         MOVE 'U' TO CHAR-IN (IY)
296         GO TO 5010-TRAN-EXIT.
297     IF CHAR-IN (IY) = 'U'
298         MOVE 'V' TO CHAR-IN (IY)
299         GO TO 5010-TRAN-EXIT.
300     IF CHAR-IN (IY) = 'V'
301         MOVE 'W' TO CHAR-IN (IY)
302         GO TO 5010-TRAN-EXIT.
303     IF CHAR-IN (IY) = 'W'
304         MOVE 'X' TO CHAR-IN (IY)
305         GO TO 5010-TRAN-EXIT.
306     IF CHAR-IN (IY) = 'X'
307         MOVE 'Y' TO CHAR-IN (IY)
308         GO TO 5010-TRAN-EXIT.
309     IF CHAR-IN (IY) = 'Y'
310         MOVE 'Z' TO CHAR-IN (IY)
311         GO TO 5010-TRAN-EXIT.
312     IF CHAR-IN (IY) = 'Z'
313         MOVE 'A' TO CHAR-IN (IY)
314         GO TO 5010-TRAN-EXIT.
315     IF CHAR-IN (IY) = ','
316         MOVE '.' TO CHAR-IN (IY)
317         GO TO 5010-TRAN-EXIT.
318     IF CHAR-IN (IY) = '.'
319         MOVE '+' TO CHAR-IN (IY)
```

```
320             GO TO 5010-TRAN-EXIT.
321         IF CHAR-IN (IY) = '?'
322             MOVE '=' TO CHAR-IN (IY)
323             GO TO 5010-TRAN-EXIT.
324         IF CHAR-IN (IY) = '='
325             MOVE '<' TO CHAR-IN (IY)
326             GO TO 5010-TRAN-EXIT.
327         IF CHAR-IN (IY) = '-'
328             MOVE '>' TO CHAR-IN (IY)
329             GO TO 5010-TRAN-EXIT.
330         IF CHAR-IN (IY) = '*'
331             MOVE '$' TO CHAR-IN (IY)
332             GO TO 5010-TRAN-EXIT.
333     5010-TRAN-EXIT.
334         EXIT.
335
336     5020-SWAP2-RTN.
337         COMPUTE IZ = 76 - IY.
338         MOVE CHAR-IN (IY) TO CHAR-HOLD.
339         MOVE CHAR-IN (IZ) TO CHAR-IN (IY).
340         MOVE CHAR-HOLD TO CHAR-IN (IZ).
341
342     5020-SWAP2-EXIT.
343         EXIT.
344
345     9000-ABEND-RTN.
346         EXEC CICS SEND FROM (WS-OUT-MSG)
347             LENGTH (80)
```

Figure 9.2. continued.

```
348              ERASE
349          END-EXEC.
350      EXEC CICS RETURN
351          END-EXEC.
352
353
354  9000-EXIT.
355      EXIT.
356
357  LENGTH-ERROR.
358      EXEC CICS SEND FROM (WS-OUT-MSG-3)
359          LENGTH (80)
360          ERASE
361          END-EXEC.
362
363      EXEC CICS RETURN
364          END-EXEC.
365  ERROR-PROCESS.
366      EXEC CICS SEND FROM (WS-OUT-MSG-5)
367          LENGTH (80)
368          ERASE
369          END-EXEC.
370
371      EXEC CICS RETURN
372          END-EXEC.
**********************************************************************
```

Figure 9.2. continued.

```
      **********************************************************************
    1 *         DATA SET MSGPROG1    AT LEVEL 001
    2           TITLE 'MSGPROG1- DISPLAY RECORDS FROM MESSAGE FILE'
    3 *****************************************************************
    4 *REMEMEBER THIS IS NOT A COBOL PROGRAM. HENCE BE CAREFUL WHEN MODIFYING
    5 *IT SO THAT IT ALWAYS REMAINS QUASI-REENTRANT.
    6 * THIS PROGRAM READS FILE MSGFILE1, WHICH HAS VARIABLE LENGTH RECORDS.
    7 *****************************************************************
    8 * DATE    |PGMR-ID |     DESCRIPTION OF CHANGE                 *
    9 *--------|--------|-----------------------------------------*
   10 * YY/MM/DD| BKN    | NEW PRPGRAM                              *
   11 *****************************************************************
   12           SPACE 1
   13 R0        EQU   0
   14 R1        EQU   1
   15 R2        EQU   2
   16 R3        EQU   3
   17 PICABAR   EQU   3
   18 R4        EQU   4
   19 R5        EQU   5
   20 R6        EQU   6
   21 R7        EQU   7
   22 TSIOABAR  EQU   7
   23 R8        EQU   8
   24 PGMBASE   EQU   8
   25 R9        EQU   9
   26 FWACBAR   EQU   9
   27 R10       EQU   10
```

Figure 9.3. Source code of program MSGPROG1

409

```
28   TCTTEAR   EQU   10
29   R11       EQU   11
30   TIOABAR   EQU   11
31   R12       EQU   12
32   R13       EQU   13
33   R14       EQU   14
34   R15       EQU   15
35   PGMBAL    EQU   15
36             PRINT OFF
37             COPY  DFHTCTTE
38             PRINT ON
39             COPY  DFHTSIOA
40   LASTNUM   DS    CL4
41             DS    CL1
42   LASTREC   DS    CL4
43             DS    CL1
44   TOTREC    DS    CL4
45             PRINT OFF
46             COPY  DFHCSADS
47             COPY  DFHTCADS
48             PRINT ON
49   *************************************
50   *   T W A   STARTS HERE
51   *************************************
52   TDOUBLE   DS    D
53   TRANDOM   DS    CL4
54   TLASTNUM  DS    CL4
55   TLASTREC  DS    CL4
56   TTOTREC   DS    CL4
57   *
```

```
58  TFILEKEY  DS   0CL12
59  TRECTYPE  DS   CL3
60  TRECNUM   DS   CL4
61  TSEQNUM   DS   C
62  TFILLER   DS   CL4
63  *
64  TRECAVL   DS   C
65  TSAVE     DS   C
66  *
67  TSNAME    DS   CL8
68  *==== END OF TWA ==============================================================
69            COPY DFHFWADS
70  *=============================================================================
71  * THE LLBB FIELD BELOW IS ONLY REQUIRED IF THE FILE IS VARIABLE LENGTH
72  * FILE. IF IT IS FIXED LENGTH, COMMENT OUT THE LLBB LINE BELOW.
73  *=============================================================================
74  LLBB      DS   CL4          LLBB FIELD FOR VARIABLE LEN FILE
75  FKEY      DS   0CL12        RECORD KEY
76  FRECTYPE  DS   CL3
77  FRECNUM   DS   CL4
78  FSEQNUM   DS   C
79  FFILLER   DS   CL4
80  FDATA     DS   0CL75        RECORD DATA
81  FMAXREC#  DS   CL4
82            ORG  FDATA
83  FMSGTXT   DS   CL75         MESSAGE TEXT
84  *====== END OF RECORD LAYOUT =================================================
85            COPY DFHTIOA
```

Figure 9.3. continued.

411

```
                 COPY  DFHAID
         *=======================================================================
                 EJECT
         MSGPROG1 CSECT
                 USING MSGPROG1,PGMBASE
                 LR    PGMBASE,R14
                 B     START
                 DS    0D
                 DC    CL40'**** PROGRAM MSGPROG1 STARTS HERE ****'   ALIGN FOR DUMP
         START   EQU   *
                 L     TCTTEAR,TCAFCAAA          ESTABLISH ADDRESSIBILITY WITH TCT
                 L     PICABAR,TCTTECIA          LOAD ADDRESS OF TCT USER AREA
                 CLI   TCTTEAID,DFHCLEAR
                 BNE   NOTCLEAR
                 DFHSC TYPE=GETMAIN,CLASS=TERMINAL,NUMBYTE=01,INITIMG=40
                 L     TIOABAR,TCASCSA          LOAD TIOABAR
                 ST    TIOABAR,TCTTEDA          PUT ADDRESS AT TCTTEDA
                 MVC   TIOATDL(2),=H'01'
                 MVI   TIOADBA,X'40'
                 DFHTC TYPE=(ERASE,WRITE)
                 DFHPC TYPE=RETURN
         *=======================================================================
         NOTCLEAR EQU   *
                 CLI   TCTTEAID,DFHPF1
                 BE    PF1KEY
                 CLI   TCTTEAID,DFHPF13
                 BE    PF13KEY
                 CLI   TCTTEAID,DFHENTER
                 BNE   SORRY
         *=======================================================================
```

```
116 ENTERKEY EQU     *
117 *================================================================
118 ****        CLC    TCTTEOI,=C'BKN'
119 ****        BNE    REJECT
120             B      ALRIGHT
121 ***         CLC    TCTTETI,=C'CA25'
122 ***         BE     ALRIGHT
123 *================================================================
124 REJECT  EQU     *
125 SENDMSG1 EQU    *
126         DFHSC  TYPE=GETMAIN,CLASS=TERMINAL,NUMBYTE=50,INITIMG=40
127         L      TIOABAR,TCASCSA              LOAD TIOABAR
128         ST     TIOABAR,TCTTEDA       PUT ADDRESS AT TCTTEDA
129         MVC    TIOATDL(2),=H'50'
130         MVC    TIOADBA(50),MSG001
131         DFHTC  TYPE=(ERASE,WRITE)
132         DFHPC  TYPE=RETURN
133 *================================================================
134 *
135 ALRIGHT     EQU     *
136             L      TIOABAR,TCTTEDA       SET ADDRESS TO TIOA
137             CLI    TIOADBA+4,X'E0'
138             BNE    SORRY
139             CLI    TIOADBA+9,X'E0'
140             BNE    SORRY
141             CLI    TIOADBA+5,X'D8'
142             BNE    SORRY
143             CLI    TIOADBA+6,X'C1'
```

Figure 9.3. continued.

413

```
144          BNE     SORRY
145          CLI     TIOADBA+7,X'D7'
146          BNE     SORRY
147          CLI     TIOADBA+8,X'C1'
148          BNE     SORRY
149          B       GOAHEAD
150 SORRY    EQU     *
151 SENDMSG2 EQU     *
152          DFHSC   TYPE=GETMAIN,CLASS=TERMINAL,NUMBYTE=50,INITIMG=40
153          L       TIOABAR,TCASCSA         LOAD TIOABAR
154          ST      TIOABAR,TCTTEDA         PUT ADDRESS AT TCTTEDA
155          MVC     TIOATDL(2),=H'50'
156          MVC     TIOADBA(50),MSG002
157          DFHTC   TYPE=(ERASE,WRITE)
158          DFHPC   TYPE=RETURN
159 #===================================================================
160 GOAHEAD  EQU     *
161 #================================================================= #
162 # USER HAS ENTERED THIS TRANSACTION INITIALLY ON A BLANK SCREEN.  #
163 # HE  HAS PASSED ALL CHECKING. PROCEED TO SERVICE THIS USER.     #
164 #================================================================= #
165 # NOW READ T-S QUEUE. AND DETERMINE IF IT IS THERE OR NOT.       #
166 #================================================================= #
167          MVC     TSNAME(4),TCTTETI
168          MVC     TSNAME+4(4),=C'BNDP'
169          DFHTS   TYPE=GET,DATAID=TSNAME,NORESP=TSISOK
170          MVC     TLASTNUM,=F'8193'
171          B       NEXT05
172 TSISOK   EQU     *
173          L       TSIOABAR,TCATSDA
```

414

```
174          SH      TSIOABAR,=H'8'
175          MVC     TLASTNUM,LASTNUM
176 NEXT05   EQU     *
177          DFHFC   TYPE=GET,DATASET=MSGFILE1,RDIDADR=CKEY,NORESP=GOTCNTL
178 SENDMSG3 EQU     *
179          DFHSC   TYPE=GETMAIN,CLASS=TERMINAL,NUMBYTE=50,INITIMG=40
180          L       TIOABAR,TCASCSA            LOAD TIOABAR
181          ST      TIOABAR,TCTTEDA       PUT ADDRESS AT TCTTEDA
182          MVC     TIOATDL(2),=H'50'
183          MVC     TIOADBA(50),MSG004
184          DFHTC   TYPE=(ERASE,WRITE)
185          DFHPC   TYPE=RETURN
186 *==========================================================
187 GOTCNTL  EQU     *
188          L       FWACBAR,TCAFCAA     GET REC POINTER
189          MVC     TTOTREC,FMAXREC#
190          B       PROCEED
191 *##############################################################
192 PF1KEY   EQU     *
193 PF13KEY  EQU     *
194          MVC     TSNAME(4),TCTTETI
195          MVC     TSNAME+4(4),=C'BNDP'
196          DFHTS   TYPE=GET,DATAID=TSNAME,NORESP=NEXT10
197 SENDMSG4 EQU     *
198          DFHSC   TYPE=GETMAIN,CLASS=TERMINAL,NUMBYTE=50,INITIMG=40
199          L       TIOABAR,TCASCSA            LOAD TIOABAR
200          ST      TIOABAR,TCTTEDA       PUT ADDRESS AT TCTTEDA
201          MVC     TIOATDL(2),=H'50'
```

Figure 9.3. continued.

415

```
202         MVC   TIOADBA(50),MSG005
203         DFHTC TYPE=(ERASE,WRITE)
204         DFHPC TYPE=RETURN
205  *=============================================================
206  NEXT10  EQU   *
207         L     TSIOABAR,TCATSDA
208         SH    TSIOABAR,=H'8'
209         MVC   TLASTNUM,LASTNUM
210         MVC   TTOTREC,TOTREC
211  PROCEED EQU   *
212  *#############################################################
213  * FOLLOWING CODE GENERATES A RANDOM NUMBER BETWEEN 0 AND (FMAXREC#-1)
214  *#############################################################
215         PACK  TDOUBLE,TTOTREC
216         CVB   R5,TDOUBLE
217         L     R7,TLASTNUM
218         M     R6,=F'65541'
219         ST    R7,TLASTNUM          STORE IN TWA
220         LR    R0,R7
221  *#############
222         LPR   R7,R0
223         M     R4,=F'2'
224         MR    R4,R7
225         LR    R0,R4
226  *##### R0 NOW CONTAINS A NUMBER BETWEEN 0 AND (FMAXREC# - 1)
227  *#############################################################
228         LR    R6,R0
229         LA    R6,1(R6)
230  *##### R6 NOW CONTAINS A NUMBER BETWEEN 1 AND FMAXREC#
231         CVD   R6,TDOUBLE
```

```
232     UNPK    TRANDOM(4),TDOUBLE+5(3)
233     OI      TRANDOM+3,X'F0'
234     MVC     TRECTYPE,=CL3'MSG'
235     MVC     TRECNUM,TRANDOM
236     MVC     TFILLER,=CL4'$$$$'              MOVE DOLLARS TO FILLER
237     MVI     TSEQNUM,C'0'
238 ***************************************************************
239 * INITIALIZE TIOA TO BLANKS
240 *=============================================================
241     DFHSC   TYPE=GETMAIN,CLASS=TERMINAL,NUMBYTE=809,INITIMG=40
242     L       TIOABAR,TCASCSA                LOAD TIOABAR
243     ST      TIOABAR,TCTTEDA                PUT ADDRESS AT TCTTEDA
244     MVC     TIOADBA(5),=X'11C2E31DE8'
245     MVC     TIOADBA+80(5),=X'11C3F31DE8'
246     MVC     TIOADBA+160(5),=X'11C5C31DE8'
247     MVC     TIOADBA+240(5),=X'11C6D31DE8'
248     MVC     TIOADBA+320(5),=X'11C7E31DE8'
249     MVC     TIOADBA+400(5),=X'11C8F31DE8'
250     MVC     TIOADBA+480(5),=X'114AC31DE8'
251     MVC     TIOADBA+560(5),=X'114BD31DE8'
252     MVC     TIOADBA+640(5),=X'114CE31DE8'
253     MVC     TIOADBA+720(5),=X'114DF31DE8'
254     MVC     TIOADBA+800(09),=X'114F401DC8114FC113'
255     MVC     TIOATDL(2),=H'809'
256 +++++++++++++++++++++++++++++++++++++++++++++++++++++++++++++++
257     MVI     TRECAVL,C'Y'
258     BAL     PGMBAL,GETREC
259     CLI     TRECAVL,C'Y'
```

Figure 9.3. continued.

417

```
260         BE    GOTRECO
261 ERROR   EQU   *
262 SENDMSG5 EQU  *
263         DFHSC TYPE=GETMAIN,CLASS=TERMINAL,NUMBYTE=50,INITIMG=40
264         L     TIOABAR,TCASCSA          LOAD TIOABAR
265         ST    TIOABAR,TCTTEDA          PUT ADDRESS AT TCTTEDA
266         MVC   TIOATDL(2),=H'50'
267         MVC   TIOADBA(50),MSG003
268         MVC   TIOADBA+18(4),TRECNUM
269         DFHTC TYPE=(ERASE,WRITE)
270         DFHPC TYPE=RETURN
271 *=================================================================
272 *
273 GOTRECO EQU   *
274         MVC   TIOADBA+5(75),FMSGTXT
275         MVI   TSEQNUM,C'1'
276         BAL   PGMBAL,GETREC
277         CLI   TRECAVL,C'N'
278         BE    THATSIT
279 GOTREC1 EQU   *
280         MVC   TIOADBA+085(75),FMSGTXT
281         MVI   TSEQNUM,C'2'
282         BAL   PGMBAL,GETREC
283         CLI   TRECAVL,C'N'
284         BE    THATSIT
285 GOTREC2 EQU   *
286         MVC   TIOADBA+165(75),FMSGTXT
287         MVI   TSEQNUM,C'3'
288         BAL   PGMBAL,GETREC
289         CLI   TRECAVL,C'N'
```

```
290          BE     THATSIT
291 GOTREC3  EQU    *
292          MVC    TIOADBA+245(75),FMSGTXT
293          MVI    TSEQNUM,C'4'
294          BAL    PGMBAL,GETREC
295          CLI    TRECAVL,C'N'
296          BE     THATSIT
297 GOTREC4  EQU    *
298          MVC    TIOADBA+325(75),FMSGTXT
299          MVI    TSEQNUM,C'5'
300          BAL    PGMBAL,GETREC
301          CLI    TRECAVL,C'N'
302          BE     THATSIT
303 GOTREC5  EQU    *
304          MVC    TIOADBA+405(75),FMSGTXT
305          MVI    TSEQNUM,C'6'
306          BAL    PGMBAL,GETREC
307          CLI    TRECAVL,C'N'
308          BE     THATSIT
309 GOTREC6  EQU    *
310          MVC    TIOADBA+485(75),FMSGTXT
311          MVI    TSEQNUM,C'7'
312          BAL    PGMBAL,GETREC
313          CLI    TRECAVL,C'N'
314          BE     THATSIT
315 GOTREC7  EQU    *
316          MVC    TIOADBA+565(75),FMSGTXT
317          MVI    TSEQNUM,C'8'
```

Figure 9.3. continued.

419

```
318          BAL    PGMBAL,GETREC
319          CLI    TRECAVL,C'N'
320          BE     THATSIT
321 GOTREC8  EQU    *
322          MVC    TIOADBA+645(75),FMSGTXT
323          MVI    TSEQNUM,C'9'
324          BAL    PGMBAL,GETREC
325          CLI    TRECAVL,C'N'
326          BE     THATSIT
327 GOTREC9  EQU    *
328          MVC    TIOADBA+725(75),FMSGTXT
329 *===============================================================
330 THATSIT  EQU    *
331 *===============================================================
332 * NOW WRITE OR REWRITE THE T-S RECORD.
333 *===============================================================
334          DFHTS  TYPE=RELEASE,DATAID=TSNAME
335          DFHSC  TYPE=GETMAIN,CLASS=TEMPSTRG,NUMBYTE=18
336          L      TSIOABAR,TCASCSA
337          MVC    TSIOAVRL,=AL2(18)      4 BYTES MORE THAN LENGTH OF T-S
338          MVC    LASTNUM,TLASTNUM
339          MVC    LASTREC,TRECNUM
340          MVC    TOTREC,TTOTREC
341          DFHTS  TYPE=PUT,DATAID=TSNAME,TSDADDR=TSIOAVRL,NORESP=EXIT99,  X
342                 STORFAC=MAIN
343 SENDMSG6 EQU    *
344          DFHSC  TYPE=GETMAIN,CLASS=TERMINAL,NUMBYTE=50,INITIMG=40
345          L      TIOABAR,TCASCSA           LOAD TIOABAR
346          ST     TIOABAR,TCTTEDA           PUT ADDRESS AT TCTTEDA
347          MVC    TIOATDL(2),=H'50'
```

```
348          MVC   TIOADBA(50),MSG005
349          DFHTC TYPE=(ERASE,WRITE)
350          DFHPC TYPE=RETURN
351 *=================================================================
352 EXIT99 EQU   *
353          DFHTC TYPE=(ERASE,WRITE),CTLCHAR=C2
354          DFHPC TYPE=RETURN,TRANSID=BNDP
355 *=================================================================
356 GETREC EQU   *
357          DFHFC TYPE=GET,DATASET=MSGFILE1,RDIDADR=TFILEKEY,NORESP=RECFND
358          MVI   TRECAVL,C'N'
359          BR    PGMBAL
360 RECFND EQU   *
361          L     FWACBAR,TCAFCAA
362          CLC   FRECNUM,TRECNUM
363          BE    RECOK
364          MVI   TRECAVL,C'N'
365          BR    PGMBAL
366 RECOK  EQU   *
367 *=================================================================
368 START1 LA    R1,FMSGTXT
369          LA    R2,FMSGTXT+74
370          LA    R3,FMSGTXT+37
371 LOOP1  EQU   *
372          MVC   TSAVE,0(R1)
373          MVC   0(1,R1),0(R2)
374          MVC   0(1,R2),TSAVE
375 *=================================================================
```

Figure 9.3. continued.

421

```
376           LA    R1,1(R1)
377           SH    R2,=H'1'
378           CR    R1,R3
379           BL    LOOP1
380 #=================================================
381 FINIT1    EQU   *
382 START2    TR    FMSGTXT(75),TABLE
383 FINIT2    EQU   *
384 START3    LA    R1,FMSGTXT+1
385           LA    R2,FMSGTXT+2
386           LA    R3,FMSGTXT+75
387 LOOP3     EQU   *
388           MVC   TSAVE,0(R1)
389           MVC   0(1,R1),0(R2)
390           MVC   0(1,R2),TSAVE
391 #=================================================
392           LA    R1,2(R1)
393           LA    R2,2(R2)
394           CR    R1,R3
395           BL    LOOP3
396 +++++++++++++++++++++++++++++++++++++++++++++++++
397           BR    PGMBAL
398 #=================================================
399 CKEY      DC    CL12'MSG00000$$$$'
400 MSGANY    DC    CL50'HERE ANY MESSAGE TO BE SENT TO USER CAN BE PLACED.'
401 MSG001    DC    CL50'==> INVALID OPERATOR OR TERMINAL.'
```

```
402   MSG002   DC     CL50'==> DATA OR KEY PRESSED IS NOT RIGHT.'
403   MSG003   DC     CL50'==> RECORD NUMBER XXXX NOT FOUND ON FILE MSGFILE1 '
404   MSG004   DC     CL50'==> ERROR HAS OCCURRED ON ACCESSING FILE MSGFILE1 '
405   MSG005   DC     CL50'==> ERROR HAS OCCURRED ON ACCESSING T-S QUEUE.'
406            DS     0D
407   TABLE    DC     X'000102030405060708090A0B0C0D0E0F'
408            DC     X'101112131415161718191A1B1C1D1E1F'
409            DC     X'202122232425262728292A2B2C2D2E2F'
410            DC     X'303132333435363738393A3B3C3D3E3F'
411            DC     X'404142434445464748494A4B4C4D4E4F'
412            DC     X'505152535455565758595A5B5C5D5E5F'
413            DC     X'606162636465666768696A6B6C6D6E6F'
414            DC     X'707172737475767778797A7B7C7D7E7F'
415            DC     X'808182838485868788898A8B8C8D8E8F'
416            DC     X'909192939495969798999A9B9C9D9E9F'
417            DC     X'A0A1A2A3A4A5A6A7A8A9AAABACADAEAF'
418            DC     X'B0B1B2B3B4B5B6B7B8B9BABBBCBDBEBF'
419            DC     X'C0C1C2C3C4C5C6C7C8C9CACBCCCDCECF'
420            DC     X'D0D1D2D3D4D5D6D7D8D9DADBDCDDDEDF'
421            DC     X'E0E1E2E3E4E5E6E7E8E9EAEBECEDEEEF'
422            DC     X'F0F1F2F3F4F5F6F7F8F9FAFBFCFDFEFF'
423            LTORG
424            END
```

Figure 9.3. continued.

423

```
**************************************************************
1   //jobname   JOB CARD
2   //*=========================================================*
3   //*  DEFINE THE VSAM FILE THAT WILL CONTAIN MESSAGES.      *
4   //*=========================================================*
5   //STEP01 EXEC PGM=IDCAMS
6   //SYSPRINT DD SYSOUT=*
7   //SYSIN DD *
8      DEFINE -
9        CLUSTER ( NAME (vsam.cluster.name) -
10         UNIQUE -
11         TRK (1 1) -
12         FSPC ( 0 0 ) -
13         KEYS ( 12 0 ) -
14         SHR(2 3) -
15         RECSZ( 87 256 ) -
16         VOLUMES(CICS01)) -
17       DATA -
18         (NAME (vsam.data.component.name) -
19         CISZ (2048) ) -
20       INDEX -
21         (NAME (vsam.index.component.name) -
22         CISZ( 512) )
**************************************************************
```

Figure 9.4. JCL to define VSAM file to contain humour/quotation items

in a source PDS, and enter the program shown in Figure 9.3 in member MSGPROG1 in the same source PDS.

Step 2. Assemble and link mapset BNMSGS2 using the JCL given in Section B.4 in Appendix B. This job will create member BNMSGS2 in your copybook library and load module BNMSGS2 in your load library. This copybook is used on COPY statement in Figure 9.2 on line 57. The load library containing BNMSGS2 must be included under DDname DFHRPL in the CICS start-up procedure or job.

Step 3. Compile and link program MSGPROG2 using the JCL given in Section B.1 in Appendix B. This job will create load module MSGPROG2 in your load library. This load library must be included under DDname DFHRPL in the CICS start-up procedure or job.

Step 4. Compile and link program MSGPROG1 using the JCL given in Section B.3 in Appendix B. This job will create load module MSGPROG1 in your load library. This load library must be included under DDname DFHRPL in the CICS start-up procedure or job.

Step 5. Next you should define a VSAM key-sequenced dataset (KSDS) using IDCAMS which has variable-length records. The average record length is 87, and the maximum record length is 256. Note that this facility (HSRF) always stores records that are 87 bytes long, with the first 12 bytes of each record containing the key and the remaining 75 bytes containing data, i.e., the text of humor/quotations. Defining this file as a variable-length file means that records for some other application or facility can also be stored on the same file.

Use the sample JCL shown in Figure 9.4 for defining this file. Replace line 1 with a valid job card. Replace names in lower case on lines 9, 18, and 21 by proper names. On line 16, replace CICS01 with the volume ID of the DASD where you want the file defined. Then submit the job and make sure the file was successfully defined.

Step 6. USING the REPRO command of IDCAMS, load the VSAM file with a record that is 87 bytes long and that has the following in the first 16 bytes:

```
MSG00000$$$$0000
```

This is the control record. Four zeros in positions 13 thru 16 of the record is indicating that currently there are no (i.e., zero) items on the file. After writing the first item, this record will be updated to contain 0001 in positions 13 through 16, to indicate that there is one item on the file. Note that an item of humor/quotation can consist of up to 10 lines.

Step 7. Ask your CICS system programmer to define DDname MSGFILE1 in the CICS FCT as a VSAM file with variable-length records, which has all options in the SERVREQ parameter. The dataset name is what you chose when you defined the file in Step 5 above. Use the definition of file BASCLUST given in Section 1.6 as a guide.

Step 8. Define the following in CICS tables, in addition to defining file MSGFILE1 in the FCT as described above:

Definition of Mapset BNMSGS2 in the PPT

```
MAPSET  BNMSGS2
GROUP   CICSBOOK
RSL     00
STATUS  ENABLED
```

Definition of Program MSGPROG1 in the PPT

```
PROGRAM   MSGPROG1
GROUP     CICSBOOK
LANGUAGE  ASSEMBLER
```

Definition of Program MSGPROG2 in the PPT

```
PROGRAM   MSGPROG2
GROUP     CICSBOOK
LANGUAGE  COBOL
```

Other parameters for MSGPROG1 and MSGPROG2 in the PPT should be the same as those for sample program BNPROG1 given in Section 1.6.

Definition of Transaction BNMG in the PCT

```
TRANSACTION  BNMG
GROUP        CICSBOOK
PROGRAM      MSGPROG2
```

Other parameters for BNMG in the PCT should be the same as those for sample transaction BNC1 given in Section 1.6.

Definition of Transaction BNDP in the PCT

```
TRANSACTION  BNDP
GROUP        CICSBOOK
PROGRAM      MSGPROG1
TWASIZE      50
```

Other parameters for BNDP in the PCT should be the same as those for sample transaction BNC1 given in Section 1.6.

9.1.2 Layout of the VSAM File Containing Humor/Quotation Items

Let us now consider how data is stored on the humor/quotation file. A humor/quotation item can consist of up to 10 lines. Each line contains 75 characters and is stored on one record on the file. (The VSAM record has 12 bytes for the key and 75 bytes for the data, giving 87 bytes as the record length.) When you use transaction BNDP to display an item from the file, each record read from the file is displayed on one line on the screen after decrypting its content. So, a maximum of 10 lines can be displayed for each humor/quotation item. Suppose you want to display an item in this way:

```
          DO NOT SPIT IN THE WELL
               BECAUSE
   ONE DAY YOU MAY HAVE TO DRINK FROM IT!
```

When you store this item using the BNMG transaction, you should enter these three lines on the map in the same way you want them to appear on the screen when you display them. This means that each line you enter should have the proper number of spaces in the beginning and at the end.

As regards the layout of records on the file, the very first record is a control record. Its key is MSG00000$$$$. It has a four-byte number in positions 13 through 16 of the record, indicating the number of items stored on the file at any time. (The content in positions 17 through 87 of the control record is never used.) After adding the next humor/quotation item consisting of up to 10 lines on the file, the control record on the file is updated after incrementing by one the number in positions 13 through 16 of the record.

Other records have this layout:

FROM	TO	LENGTH	TYPE	CONTENTREMARKS
1	3	3	Character	Constant: MSG
4	7	4	Numeric	Item Number (also called Record Number in the programs.) It Can be from 0001 thru 9999.
8	8	1	Numeric	Record Sequence Number. Can be from 0 thru 9.
9	12	4	Character	Constant: $$$$
13	87	75	Character	Text of message in encrypted form

This layout means that no more than 9999 items can be stored on the file. If you want to store more records, you may consider revising the record layout and changing the programs and the VSAM file definition.

Suppose the first item you store on this file consists of three lines as follows:

```
         DO NOT SPIT IN THE WELL
                BECAUSE
ONE DAY YOU MAY HAVE TO DRINK FROM IT!
```

So, this item will be stored on the file as three records whose keys are as follows:

```
MSG00010$$$$
MSG00011$$$$
MSG00012$$$$
```

The data portion of each record will contain a message in encrypted form. This is done so that when someone dumps the file, he will not be able to read the messages stored. However, the program that reads the file and displays the messages on the screen has the logic to decrypt the messages so that they are displayed in readable form. This means that if you deny someone access to the source code of the two programs, he will not be able to figure out the logic for encrypting or decrypting messages. And if you deny him the use of the two transactions of this facility, he will also not be able to store records on the file or display them. This can be very helpful when you do not want anyone, especially your boss, to use this facility, or even to know about its existence. Because if your boss knows that you use this facility, he might think that you spend most of your time playing with it, even though this might be far from the truth.

9.1.3   Procedure for Storing A Humor/Quotation Item on the VSAM File

Enter BNMG on a blank screen. A map will be displayed without any heading. There will be 10 unprotected fields on 10 lines on the screen with captions L0, L1, and so on up to L9. You can enter the text of your humor/quotation on these lines. After entering all lines of the item, press the Enter key to write a new set of records on the file.

You must enter something, even spaces, on the first line on the map. Not doing so will cause rejection of all data by the program, and you would receive the following message:

```
** INPUT DATA NOT PROPERLY ENTERED—TRANSACTION TERMINATED
```

If you did not enter anything on a line, or entered only spaces, that line will be ignored while storing text on the file. If no lines have even non-blank text, no record will be written to the file, and a message to this effect will be displayed. If you entered text in at least one line on the map, one or more records will be written to the file. The records written will be assigned an item number that is one more than the highest item number stored in the control record. The counter on the control record will also be updated after incrementing it by one. You will receive a message informing you of the item number that was written to the file.

9.1.4 Procedure for Displaying Humor/Quotation Items from the File

Enter the following on a blank screen and press the Enter key:

```
BNDP\QAPA\
```

(Note: The back slash character '\' in EBCDIC is equivalent to Hexadecimal 'E0'.)

Program MSGPROG1 will generate a random number between 1 and the maximum number of items on the file, which is in positions 13 through 16 of the control record. It will then read all records for this item and display them on the screen. After you have read the messages on the screen, you can either press the PF1 or the PF13 key to display the next item from the file on a random basis, or you can press the Clear key to terminate the transaction and obtain a blank screen. Once the next set of records is displayed, press PF1 or PF13 to display the text for the next humor/quotation item on a random basis, and continue pressing PF1 or PF13 to entertain yourself. You can press the Clear key at any time to terminate the transaction.

9.1.5 Explanation of the Message Display Program

Program MSGPROG1 displays messages from the file. Let us understand this macro-level CICS program by examining what happens when a user enters BNDP\QAPA\ on a blank screen. CICS checks the program control table and finds that transaction BNDP is associated with program MSGPROG1. So CICS loads this program into virtual storage if it is not already there and transfers control to the first executable statement in it.

So execution starts with line 91 in Figure 9.3. On line 98, we are checking if the Clear key was pressed. In this example, this would not be the case; so control would flow to label NOTCLEAR on line 108. On lines 109 through 114, we are checking which key was pressed. Since the Enter key was pressed, control would flow to line 116 and then to label ALRIGHT on line 135. On lines 137 through 148, we are checking if the user entered \QAPA\ after transaction ID BNDP. If not, control would flow to label SORRY. But since we are assuming that the user entered BNDP\QAPA\ on the screen, control flows to label GOAHEAD on line 160. On line 169, we are reading a temporary storage queue whose eight-character ID consists of user's four-character terminal ID followed by BNDP. Supposing that this is the first time the user is using this transaction, this queue would not be found. So, control would not flow to label TSISOK but would flow to line 170, and then to label NEXT05.

On line 177, we would read the control record from the file. Because of NORESP = GOTCNTL on the DFHFC macro, assuming that the control record was successfully read, control would flow to label GOTCNTL on line 187. On line 189, we would store in variable TTOTREC the counter present on the control record. This represents the maximum number of humor/quotation items present on the file. Next we would branch to label PROCEED.

Let us see what we do at label PROCEED on line 211. As the comments indicate, we calculate a random number between 0 and (FMAXREC# -1), where FMAXREC# was on control record, and store the random number in Register 6. On line 229, we increment the content of Register 6. So, Register 6 now contains a random number between 1 and FMAXREC#. The content of Register 6 will be used in record key for reading records from the file. On line 241, we obtain 809 bytes of storage and initialize them with blanks (INITIMG = 40). Next we insert control characters in the storage so that the text will be displayed at proper positions on the 3270 screen.

On line 258, we execute routine GETREC. So, control flows to line 357 where we read the first record for the item from the file, decrypt the text, and then, on line 397, we return back to the caller. So, control flows to line 259 and then to label GOTREC0. (For any humor/quotation item, there can be up to 10 records on the file, and they will be handled at labels GOTREC0, GOTREC1, and so on, up to GOTREC9.) This way, we will read each record for that item, decrypt the text, and store the decrypted text in the 809-byte storage area obtained previously. (Decryption of the 75-byte text on each file record is done by the code between lines 367 and 396.) Finally, control would flow to label THATSIT. On line 341, we will write the temporary storage queue with ID equal to terminal ID followed by BNDP. Assuming that the DFHTS macro on line 341 was successful, control would flow to label EXIT99 on line 352. Here we would write the 809 bytes of storage area consisting of message text and control characters on the screen, and then, on line 354, we would return to CICS with BNDP in the TRANSID option. This means that the next time the user pressed any key, transaction BNDP would be started.

Now let us suppose that the user read the messages on his screen and then pressed the PF1 key. So, CICS would pass control to line 91 in this program again. Control would then flow to labels START, NOTCLEAR, and PF1KEY, in that order. On line 196, we would successfully read the temporary storage queue because it was written last time. So, control would flow to label NEXT10 on line 206. Here we would again calculate a random number between 1 and FMAXREC#, where FMAXREC# was obtained in the previous cycle from the control record and stored in the temporary storage queue. We would store the random number in Register 6. After line 229 has been executed, Register 6 would contain a random number between 1 and FMAXREC#. Next, we will again read all the records for this item from the file and store the decrypted message text in the 809-byte storage area. So, after line 229 has executed, the processing would be similar to that described above.

Hopefully, this explanation clarifies the flow of control in the program associated with transaction BNDP and helps you to understand this program fully. This will also help you understand other macro-level CICS programs written in Assembler.

9.1.6 Explanation of the Message Store Program

Program MSGPROG2 is used to store humor/quotation items on the VSAM file. The layout of this file was given above, under LAYOUT OF THE VSAM FILE CONTAINING HUMOR/QUOTATION ITEMS. Now let us understand how this command-level COBOL program works. Suppose the user enters BNMG on a blank screen. CICS checks the program control table, and, finding that transaction BNMG is associated with program MSGPROG2, it loads this program into virtual storage, if it is not already there, and then transfers control to it.

So execution starts with the first statement in the procedure division. i.e., line 70 in Figure 9.2. On line 72, we are checking if the length of the communication area passed to the program is zero. This would be true in this example. So, the PERFORM statement on line 73 would be executed. In the 2000-FIRST-TIME-PROCESS routine we send map BNMSGM2 from mapset BNMSGS2 (shown in Figure 9.1) and then return to CICS, specifying BNMG as the next transaction to be started, and passing out four bytes at WS-COMM-AREA as the communication area to be made available to the program in the next cycle.

So, the user is now sitting with a map where 10 lines of 75 characters each are available for him to enter text of his humor or quotation. Suppose the user enters the following on lines 1 and 2 (L0 and L1 fields) on the map and then presses the Enter key:

```
MARRIAGE IS LIKE STRONG HORSERADISH
YOU CAN ENJOY IT AND STILL HAVE TEARS IN YOUR EYES.
```

CICS then starts transaction BNMG, which means that control again flows to line 70 in Figure 9.2. But this time the length of the communication area will be 4. So, line 73 will not get executed. The condition tested on line 74 would be true. So, the PERFORM on line 75 would be executed. Routine 2100-RE-TURNING would be executed, sending control to line 96. Because the user pressed the Enter key, the condition tested on line 96 would be true. Routine 3000-ENTER-PROCESS would be executed, sending control to line 107. On line 108, we would receive the data entered by the user and store it in fields under group item BNMSGM2I in the working storage.

Next, control flows to line 120. On line 128, we would read the control record from the file. After this, the maximum number of items present on the file would be in field FR-LAST-REC-NUM. Let us suppose that it is 97. On line 139, we would increment it by 1, so it becomes 98. The new item to be written to the file would be assigned this item number, i.e., 98. Then on line

```
**************************************************************
 1           COPY REGDEF
 2  CSACBAR  EQU  13
 3  DCACBAR  EQU  6
 4  **** TCACBAR IS ALREADY EQUATED TO 12, AS PART OF IBM MACRO EXPANSION.
 5           COPY DFHAID
 6           COPY DFHCSADS
 7           DFHTCA CICSYST=YES
 8           COPY DFHDCADS
 9  BNINFP1  DFHEIENT CODEREG=(8,9),DATAREG=10,EIBREG=11
10           EXEC CICS IGNORE CONDITION LENGERR
11           EXEC CICS HANDLE CONDITION ERROR(ERRCOND)
12  INITIAL  EQU  *
13           CLI  EIBAID,DFHCLEAR
14           BE   CLEARKEY
15           CLI  EIBAID,DFHPF1
16           BE   PF1KEY
17           EXEC CICS ASSIGN APPLID(SYSID0)
18           MVC  TERMID0,EIBTRMID
19           EXEC CICS ADDRESS CSA(CSACBAR)
20           TM   CSASSI2,CSAMXTON
21           BO   MXTON
22           MVI  MXTSWO,C'N'
23           B    NEXT01
24  MXTON    MVI  MXTSWO,C'Y'
25  NEXT01   EQU  *
26           MVC  OKOUNT,=X'40202020'
27           ED   OKOUNT,CSAKCMT
28           MVC  MXTO(3),OKOUNT+1
29           SR   R1,R1
```

432

```
30          LH    R1,CSAMAXT
31          CVD   R1,DOUBLE
32          UNPK  AMXTO(3),DOUBLE(8)
33          OI    AMXTO+2,X'F0'
34          SR    R1,R1
35          L     R1,CSAKCMTC
36          CVD   R1,DOUBLE
37          UNPK  TMXTO(6),DOUBLE(8)
38          OI    TMXTO+5,X'F0'
39  SENDMAP EQU   *
40          EXEC  CICS SEND MAP('BNINFM1') MAPSET('BNINFS1') ERASE
41          EXEC  CICS RETURN TRANSID('BNI1')
42  *===========================================================*
43  PF1KEY  EQU   *
44          MVI   EIBAID,DFHENTER
45          EXEC  CICS XCTL PROGRAM('BNINFP2')
46  *===========================================================*
47  CLEARKEY EQU  *
48          EXEC  CICS SEND FROM(BLANKS) LENGTH(1) ERASE
49          EXEC  CICS RETURN
50  ERRCOND EQU   *
51          EXEC  CICS HANDLE CONDITION ERROR(GETOUT)
52          EXEC  CICS SEND FROM(ERRMSG01) LENGTH(74) ERASE
53  GETOUT  EXEC  CICS RETURN
54  *===========================================================*
55  BLANKS  DC    CL10' '
56  LENG8   DC    H'8'
57  ERRMSG01 DS   0CL74
```

Figure 9.5. Source code of program BNINFP1

433

```
58              DC      CL44'ERROR CONDITION DETECTED. USE CEDF TO DEBUG '
59              DC      CL30'                              '
60      *==================================================================*
61              DFHEISTG
62              COPY BNINFS1
63      OKOUNT  DS      CL4     ZZZZ
64      DOUBLE  DS      D
65              END
************************************************************
```

Figure 9.5. continued.

```
****************************************************************
 1   BNINFS1  DFHMSD TYPE=&SYSPARM,MODE=INOUT,CTRL=(FREEKB,FRSET),     *
 2                   LANG=ASM,TIOAPFX=YES,EXTATT=MAPONLY,COLOR=GREEN
 3   BNINFM1  DFHMDI SIZE=(24,80)                                      *
 4            DFHMDF POS=(01,01),LENGTH=10,                            *
 5                   INITIAL='SYSTEM ID:'
 6   SYSID    DFHMDF POS=(01,12),LENGTH=8,ATTRB=(ASKIP,BRT)            *
 7            DFHMDF POS=(01,21),LENGTH=08,                            *
 8                   INITIAL='TERM ID:'
 9   TERMID   DFHMDF POS=(01,30),LENGTH=4,ATTRB=(ASKIP,BRT)            *
10            DFHMDF POS=(01,35),LENGTH=13,                            *
11                   INITIAL='MAX TASK ON ?'
12   MXTSW    DFHMDF POS=(01,49),LENGTH=1,ATTRB=(ASKIP,BRT)            *
13            DFHMDF POS=(01,51),LENGTH=4,                             *
14                   INITIAL='MXT='
15   MXT      DFHMDF POS=(01,56),LENGTH=3,ATTRB=(ASKIP,BRT)            *
16            DFHMDF POS=(01,60),LENGTH=5,                             *
17                   INITIAL='AMXT='
18   AMXT     DFHMDF POS=(01,66),LENGTH=3,ATTRB=(ASKIP,BRT)            *
19            DFHMDF POS=(02,01),LENGTH=22,                            *
20                   INITIAL='# OF TIMES AT MAX TASK'
21   TMXT     DFHMDF POS=(02,24),LENGTH=6,ATTRB=(ASKIP,BRT)            *
22            DFHMDF POS=(23,01),LENGTH=24,                            *
23                   INITIAL='CLEAR=END, ENTER=REFRESH'
24            DFHMDF POS=(23,26),LENGTH=33,                            *
25                   INITIAL='PF1=ACT'
26            DFHMSD TYPE=FINAL
27            END
****************************************************************
```

Figure 9.6. Source code of mapset BNINFS1

```
**********************************************************************
1   *---------------------------------------------------------------*
2   * NOTE: BNINFP2 AND BNINFP3 ARE SIMILAR. THE BASE PGM IS BNINFP2.*
3   *---------------------------------------------------------------*
4   * TO CREATE BNINFP3, COPY THIS MEMBER INTO BNINFP3, THEN MAKE THE*
5   * FOLLOWING CHANGES:                                             *
6   *---------------------------------------------------------------*
7   * CHANGE FROM              CHANGE TO                             *
8   *---------------------------------------------------------------*
9   * CSAACTBA                 CSASUSBA                              *
10  * CSAACTOF                 CSASUSOF                              *
11  * 'ACT'                    'SUS'                                 *
12  * XCTL PROGRAM('BNINFP3')  XCTL PROGRAM('BNINFP2')              *
13  * RETURN TRANSID('BNI2')   RETURN TRANSID('BNI3')               *
14  * PGM=BNINFP2              PGM=BNINFP3                           *
15  *---------------------------------------------------------------*
16  * THIS PROGRAM IS NEVER PASSED A COMMUNICATION AREA.            *
17  *---------------------------------------------------------------*
18            COPY REGDEF
19  CSACBAR   EQU  13
20  EIBREG    EQU  11
21  DCACBAR   EQU  6
22  *** TCACBAR IS ALREADY EQUATED TO 12, AS PART OF IBM MACRO EXPANSION.
23            COPY DFHAID
24            COPY DFHCSADS
25            DFHTCA CICSYST=YES
26            COPY DFHDCADS
27  BNINFP2   DFHEIENT CODEREG=(8,9),DATAREG=10,EIBREG=11
28            EXEC CICS IGNORE CONDITION LENGERR
29            EXEC CICS HANDLE CONDITION ERROR(ERRCOND)
30            EXEC CICS ADDRESS EIB(EIBREG)
```

```
31 INITIAL  EQU   *
32          CLI   EIBAID,DFHCLEAR
33          BE    CLEARKEY
34          CLI   EIBAID,DFHPF1
35          BE    PF1KEY
36          CLI   EIBAID,DFHPF2
37          BE    PF2KEY
38          CLI   EIBAID,DFHPF3
39          BE    PF3KEY
40          EXEC  CICS ASSIGN APPLID(SYSIDO)
41          EXEC  CICS ADDRESS CSA(CSACBAR)
42          ST    CSACBAR,FIELD4
43 *** CALLING BNSUB01 STARTS ***
44          LA    R1,FIELD4
45          ST    R1,INADDR
46          LA    R1,FIELD8
47          ST    R1,OUTADDR
48          MVI   CODE,C'A'
49          MVC   LENSMALL(2),=H'4'
50          EXEC  CICS LINK PROGRAM('BNSUB01') COMMAREA(INADDR)      X
51                LENGTH(11)
52          CLI   CODE,C'S'
53          BNE   ERROR1
54 *** CALLING BNSUB01 FINISHED ***
55          MVC   ADDRCSAO,FIELD8+2
56          L     DCACBAR,CSAACTBA
57          LA    R2,TASK10
58          SR    R3,R3
```

Figure 9.7. Source code of program BNINFP2

```
59          LA    R3,20
60          MVC   TASTYPEO,=CL3'ACT'
61          UNPK  FIELD6(6),EIBTIME(4)
62          OI    FIELD6+5,X'F0'
63          MVC   TIMEO(2),FIELD6
64          MVI   TIMEO+2,C':'
65          MVC   TIMEO+3(2),FIELD6+2
66          MVI   TIMEO+5,C':'
67          MVC   TIMEO+6(2),FIELD6+4
68 SCANACT  EQU   *
69          LA    1,CSAACTOF
70          CR    1,DCACBAR
71          BE    FINISHED
72          BAL   14,CHKTASK
73          L     DCACBAR,DCAKCBA
74          BCT   R3,SCANACT
75          B     SENDMAP
76 FINISHED EQU   *
77          B     SENDMAP
78 CHKTASK  EQU   *
79          ST    R14,SAVEREG
80          L     TCACBAR,DCATCAA
81          ST    TCACBAR,ADDRUTCA
82          L     TCACBAR,TCASYAA-DFHTCADS(TCACBAR)
83          DROP  TCACBAR
84          USING DFHSYTCA,TCACBAR
85          CLC   TCAKCOID,=C'JNL2'
86          BER   R14
87          CLC   TCAKCOID,=C'CVST'
88          BER   R14
```

```
 89          CLC     TCAKCOID,=C'CSNC'
 90          BER     R14
 91          CLC     TCAKCOID,=C'CSSY'
 92          BER     R14
 93          CLC     TCAKCOID,=X'D1D1D100'
 94          BER     R14
 95          TM      TCAKCTTA+2,X'0C'
 96          BNOR    R14
 97  * NOW BUILD TASK NUM ON THE MAP AREA.
 98          MVC     OKOUNT,=X'402020202020202020'
 99          ED      OKOUNT,TCAKCTTA
100          MVC     0(6,R2),OKOUNT+1
101          MVC     TRANSID,TCAKCOID
102          L       TCACBAR,ADDRUTCA
103          DROP    TCACBAR
104          USING DFHUSTCA,TCACBAR
105  * NOW BUILD TERM  ID ON THE MAP AREA.
106          LA      R2,9(R2)
107          L       R1,TCAFCAAA
108          MVC     0(4,R2),0(R1)
109  * NOW BUILD TRANS ID ON THE MAP AREA.
110          LA      R2,7(R2)
111          MVC     0(4,R2),TRANSID
112  * NOW BUILD DCI ON THE MAP AREA.
113          LA      R2,7(R2)
114          MVC     DCI,TCAICEI
115  *** CALLING BNSUB01 STARTS ***
116          LA      R1,DCI
```

Figure 9.7. continued.

```
117          ST    R1,INADDR
118          LA    R1,DCICHAR
119          ST    R1,OUTADDR
120          MVI   CODE,C'A'
121          MVC   LENSMALL(2),=H'1'
122          EXEC  CICS LINK PROGRAM('BNSUB01') COMMAREA(INADDR)     X
123                LENGTH(11)
124          CLI   CODE,C'S'
125          BNE   ERROR1
126   *** CALLING BNSUB01 FINISHED ***
127          MVC   0(2,R2),DCICHAR
128   * NOW BUILD ECB ADDRESS ON THE MAP AREA.
129          LA    R2,5(R2)
130          MVC   FIELD4(4),TCATCEA
131          LA    R1,FIELD4
132          ST    R1,INADDR
133          LA    R1,FIELD8
134          ST    R1,OUTADDR
135          MVI   CODE,C'A'
136          MVC   LENSMALL(2),=H'4'
137          EXEC  CICS LINK PROGRAM('BNSUB01') COMMAREA(INADDR)     X
138                LENGTH(11)
139          CLI   CODE,C'S'
140          BNE   ERROR2
141          MVC   0(8,R2),FIELD8
142   * NOW FIND OUT FACILITY CONTROL AREA ADDRESS.....
143          LA    R2,11(R2)
144          MVC   FIELD4(4),TCAFCAAA
145          LA    R1,FIELD4
146          ST    R1,INADDR
```

```
147         LA    R1,FIELD8
148         ST    R1,OUTADDR
149         MVI   CODE,C'A'
150         MVC   LENSMALL(2),=H'4'
151         EXEC  CICS LINK PROGRAM('BNSUB01') COMAREA(INADDR)    X
152               LENGTH(11)
153         CLI   CODE,C'S'
154         BNE   ERROR2
155         MVC   0(8,R2),FIELD8
156 * NOW GET READY TO RETURN.
157         L     R14,SAVEREG
158         LA    R2,11(R2)                R2 POINTS TO NEXT TASK NUMBER
159         BR    R14
160 SENDMAP EQU   *
161         EXEC  CICS SEND MAP('BNINFM2') MAPSET('BNINFS2') ERASE
162         EXEC  CICS RETURN TRANSID('BNI2')
163 *=================================================================*
164 CLEARKEY EQU  *
165         EXEC  CICS SEND FROM(BLANKS) LENGTH(1) ERASE
166         EXEC  CICS RETURN
167 PF1KEY  EQU   *
168 *=================================================================*
169 * REMEMBER WHEN CONTROL IS TRANSFERRED TO THE NEW PROGRAM, THE VALUE OF
170 * EIBAID WILL STILL BE DFHPF1 UNLESS YOU CHANGE IT PRIOR TO EXECUTING
171 * THE XCTL COMMAND.
172 *=================================================================*
173         MVI   EIBAID,DFHENTER
174         EXEC  CICS XCTL PROGRAM('BNINFP3')
```

Figure 9.7. continued.

```
175 PF2KEY   EQU   *
176          EXEC CICS RECEIVE MAP('BNINFM2') MAPSET('BNINFS2')       X
177               INTO(BNINFM2I)
178 *** SHOULD VALIDATE THE ADDRESS ENTERED ON THE SCREEN.
179          MVI   EIBAID,DFHENTER
180          MVI   COMM01,C'F'           INDICATE TO BNINFP4- FIRST TIME
181          MVC   COMM01+1(6),ADDRI
182          EXEC CICS XCTL PROGRAM('BNINFP4') COMMAREA(COMM01) LENGTH(7)
183 *==========================================================*
184 PF3KEY   EQU   *
185 *==========================================================*
186 * REMEMBER WHEN CONTROL IS TRANSFERRED TO THE NEW PROGRAM, THE VALUE OF
187 * EIBAID WILL STILL BE DFHPF3 UNLESS YOU CHANGE IT PRIOR TO EXECUTING
188 * THE XCTL COMMAND.
189 *==========================================================*
190          MVI   EIBAID,DFHENTER
191          EXEC CICS XCTL PROGRAM('BNINFP1')
192 ERRCOND  EQU   *
193          EXEC CICS HANDLE CONDITION ERROR(GETOUT)
194          EXEC CICS SEND FROM(ERRMSG00) LENGTH(74)  ERASE
195          B     GETOUT
196 ERROR1   EQU   *
197          EXEC CICS HANDLE CONDITION ERROR(GETOUT)
198          EXEC CICS SEND FROM(ERRMSG01) LENGTH(74)  ERASE
199          B     GETOUT
200 ERROR2   EQU   *
201          EXEC CICS HANDLE CONDITION ERROR(GETOUT)
202          EXEC CICS SEND FROM(ERRMSG02) LENGTH(74)  ERASE
203          B     GETOUT
204 ERROR3   EQU   *
```

```
205          EXEC CICS HANDLE CONDITION ERROR(GETOUT)
206          EXEC CICS SEND FROM(ERRMSG03) LENGTH(74) ERASE
207          B    GETOUT
208 GETOUT   EXEC CICS RETURN
209 *===============================================================*
210 BLANKS   DC   CL10' '
211 ERRMSG00 DS   0CL74
212          DC   CL44'ERROR CONDITION DETECTED. USE CEDF TO DEBUG '
213          DC   CL30' '
214 ERRMSG01 DS   0CL74
215          DC   CL44'RETURN CODE FROM BNSUB01 IS NOT S. REFER TO '
216          DC   CL30'LABEL ERROR1 IN PGM=BNINFP2 '
217 ERRMSG02 DS   0CL74
218          DC   CL44'RETURN CODE FROM BNSUB01 IS NOT S. REFER TO '
219          DC   CL30'LABEL ERROR2 IN PGM=BNINFP2 '
220 ERRMSG03 DS   0CL74
221          DC   CL44'RETURN CODE FROM BNSUB01 IS NOT S. REFER TO '
222          DC   CL30'LABEL ERROR3 IN PGM=BNINFP2 '
223 *===============================================================*
224          DFHEISTG
225          COPY BNINFS2
226 INADDR   DS   F
227 OUTADDR  DS   F
228 LENSMALL DS   H
229 CODE     DS   CL1
230 COMM01   DS   CL12
231 OKOUNT   DS   CL7    ZZZZZZZ
232 DOUBLE   DS   D
```

Figure 9.7. continued.

443

```
233    ADDRUTCA    DS    F
234    TRANSID     DS    CL4
235    DCI         DS    CL1
236    DCICHAR     DS    CL2
237    SAVEREG     DS    F
238    FIELD6      DS    CL6
239    FIELD4      DS    F
240    FIELD8      DS    D
241                END
```

****

Figure 9.7. continued.

```
       ***********************************************************************
     1 BNINFS2 DFHMSD TYPE=&SYSPARM,MODE=INOUT,CTRL=(FREEKB,FRSET),         *
     2              LANG=ASM,TIOAPFX=YES,EXTATT=MAPONLY,COLOR=GREEN
     3 BNINFM2 DFHMDI SIZE=(24,80)
     4 SYSID   DFHMDF POS=(01,01),LENGTH=08,ATTRB=(ASKIP,BRT)
     5 ADDR    DFHMDF POS=(01,10),LENGTH=06,ATTRB=(UNPROT,BRT,IC),          X
     6              INITIAL=;
     7         DFHMDF POS=(01,17),LENGTH=07,INITIAL='A(CSA):'
     8 ADDRCSA DFHMDF POS=(01,25),LENGTH=06,ATTRB=(ASKIP,BRT)
     9 TASTYPE DFHMDF POS=(01,40),LENGTH=03,ATTRB=(ASKIP,BRT)
    10         DFHMDF POS=(01,66),LENGTH=05,                                *
    11              INITIAL='TIME:'
    12 TIME    DFHMDF POS=(01,72),LENGTH=08,ATTRB=(ASKIP,BRT)
    13         DFHMDF POS=(02,01),LENGTH=42,                                *
    14              INITIAL=' TASK   TERM   TRAN   DCI   A(ECB)   A(FCA) '
    15 *----------------------------------------------------------------------*
    16 TASK1   DFHMDF POS=(03,01),LENGTH=06,ATTRB=(ASKIP,BRT)
    17 TERM1   DFHMDF POS=(03,09),LENGTH=04,ATTRB=(ASKIP,BRT)
    18 TRAN1   DFHMDF POS=(03,15),LENGTH=04,ATTRB=(ASKIP,BRT)
    19 DCI1    DFHMDF POS=(03,21),LENGTH=02,ATTRB=(ASKIP,BRT)
    20 ECBA1   DFHMDF POS=(03,25),LENGTH=08,ATTRB=(ASKIP,BRT)
    21 FCAA1   DFHMDF POS=(03,35),LENGTH=08,ATTRB=(ASKIP,BRT)
    22 *----------------------------------------------------------------------*
    23 TASK2   DFHMDF POS=(04,01),LENGTH=06,ATTRB=(ASKIP,BRT)
    24 TERM2   DFHMDF POS=(04,09),LENGTH=04,ATTRB=(ASKIP,BRT)
    25 TRAN2   DFHMDF POS=(04,15),LENGTH=04,ATTRB=(ASKIP,BRT)
    26 DCI2    DFHMDF POS=(04,21),LENGTH=02,ATTRB=(ASKIP,BRT)
```

Figure 9.8. Source code of mapset BNINFS2

```
27  ECBA2    DFHMDF  POS=(04,25),LENGTH=08,ATTRB=(ASKIP,BRT)
28  FCAA2    DFHMDF  POS=(04,35),LENGTH=08,ATTRB=(ASKIP,BRT)
29  *-------------------------------------------------------*
30  TASK3    DFHMDF  POS=(05,01),LENGTH=06,ATTRB=(ASKIP,BRT)
31  TERM3    DFHMDF  POS=(05,09),LENGTH=04,ATTRB=(ASKIP,BRT)
32  TRAN3    DFHMDF  POS=(05,15),LENGTH=04,ATTRB=(ASKIP,BRT)
33  DCI3     DFHMDF  POS=(05,21),LENGTH=02,ATTRB=(ASKIP,BRT)
34  ECBA3    DFHMDF  POS=(05,25),LENGTH=08,ATTRB=(ASKIP,BRT)
35  FCAA3    DFHMDF  POS=(05,35),LENGTH=08,ATTRB=(ASKIP,BRT)
36  *-------------------------------------------------------*
37  TASK4    DFHMDF  POS=(06,01),LENGTH=06,ATTRB=(ASKIP,BRT)
38  TERM4    DFHMDF  POS=(06,09),LENGTH=04,ATTRB=(ASKIP,BRT)
39  TRAN4    DFHMDF  POS=(06,15),LENGTH=04,ATTRB=(ASKIP,BRT)
40  DCI4     DFHMDF  POS=(06,21),LENGTH=02,ATTRB=(ASKIP,BRT)
41  ECBA4    DFHMDF  POS=(06,25),LENGTH=08,ATTRB=(ASKIP,BRT)
42  FCAA4    DFHMDF  POS=(06,35),LENGTH=08,ATTRB=(ASKIP,BRT)
43  *-------------------------------------------------------*
44  TASK5    DFHMDF  POS=(07,01),LENGTH=06,ATTRB=(ASKIP,BRT)
45  TERM5    DFHMDF  POS=(07,09),LENGTH=04,ATTRB=(ASKIP,BRT)
46  TRAN5    DFHMDF  POS=(07,15),LENGTH=04,ATTRB=(ASKIP,BRT)
47  DCI5     DFHMDF  POS=(07,21),LENGTH=02,ATTRB=(ASKIP,BRT)
48  ECBA5    DFHMDF  POS=(07,25),LENGTH=08,ATTRB=(ASKIP,BRT)
49  FCAA5    DFHMDF  POS=(07,35),LENGTH=08,ATTRB=(ASKIP,BRT)
50  *-------------------------------------------------------*
51  TASK6    DFHMDF  POS=(08,01),LENGTH=06,ATTRB=(ASKIP,BRT)
52  TERM6    DFHMDF  POS=(08,09),LENGTH=04,ATTRB=(ASKIP,BRT)
53  TRAN6    DFHMDF  POS=(08,15),LENGTH=04,ATTRB=(ASKIP,BRT)
54  DCI6     DFHMDF  POS=(08,21),LENGTH=02,ATTRB=(ASKIP,BRT)
55  ECBA6    DFHMDF  POS=(08,25),LENGTH=08,ATTRB=(ASKIP,BRT)
56  FCAA6    DFHMDF  POS=(08,35),LENGTH=08,ATTRB=(ASKIP,BRT)
```

```
57   *-----------------------------------------------------------------------*
58   TASK7   DFHMDF POS=(09,01),LENGTH=06,ATTRB=(ASKIP,BRT)
59   TERM7   DFHMDF POS=(09,09),LENGTH=04,ATTRB=(ASKIP,BRT)
60   TRAN7   DFHMDF POS=(09,15),LENGTH=04,ATTRB=(ASKIP,BRT)
61   DCI7    DFHMDF POS=(09,21),LENGTH=02,ATTRB=(ASKIP,BRT)
62   ECBA7   DFHMDF POS=(09,25),LENGTH=08,ATTRB=(ASKIP,BRT)
63   FCAA7   DFHMDF POS=(09,35),LENGTH=08,ATTRB=(ASKIP,BRT)
64   *-----------------------------------------------------------------------*
65   TASK8   DFHMDF POS=(10,01),LENGTH=06,ATTRB=(ASKIP,BRT)
66   TERM8   DFHMDF POS=(10,09),LENGTH=04,ATTRB=(ASKIP,BRT)
67   TRAN8   DFHMDF POS=(10,15),LENGTH=04,ATTRB=(ASKIP,BRT)
68   DCI8    DFHMDF POS=(10,21),LENGTH=02,ATTRB=(ASKIP,BRT)
69   ECBA8   DFHMDF POS=(10,25),LENGTH=08,ATTRB=(ASKIP,BRT)
70   FCAA8   DFHMDF POS=(10,35),LENGTH=08,ATTRB=(ASKIP,BRT)
71   *-----------------------------------------------------------------------*
72   TASK9   DFHMDF POS=(11,01),LENGTH=06,ATTRB=(ASKIP,BRT)
73   TERM9   DFHMDF POS=(11,09),LENGTH=04,ATTRB=(ASKIP,BRT)
74   TRAN9   DFHMDF POS=(11,15),LENGTH=04,ATTRB=(ASKIP,BRT)
75   DCI9    DFHMDF POS=(11,21),LENGTH=02,ATTRB=(ASKIP,BRT)
76   ECBA9   DFHMDF POS=(11,25),LENGTH=08,ATTRB=(ASKIP,BRT)
77   FCAA9   DFHMDF POS=(11,35),LENGTH=08,ATTRB=(ASKIP,BRT)
78   *-----------------------------------------------------------------------*
79   TASK10  DFHMDF POS=(12,01),LENGTH=06,ATTRB=(ASKIP,BRT)
80   TERM10  DFHMDF POS=(12,09),LENGTH=04,ATTRB=(ASKIP,BRT)
81   TRAN10  DFHMDF POS=(12,15),LENGTH=04,ATTRB=(ASKIP,BRT)
82   DCI10   DFHMDF POS=(12,21),LENGTH=02,ATTRB=(ASKIP,BRT)
83   ECBA10  DFHMDF POS=(12,25),LENGTH=08,ATTRB=(ASKIP,BRT)
84   FCAA10  DFHMDF POS=(12,35),LENGTH=08,ATTRB=(ASKIP,BRT)
```

Figure 9.8. continued.

```
 85  *------------------------------------------------------------*
 86  TASK11   DFHMDF  POS=(13,01),LENGTH=06,ATTRB=(ASKIP,BRT)
 87  TERM11   DFHMDF  POS=(13,09),LENGTH=04,ATTRB=(ASKIP,BRT)
 88  TRAN11   DFHMDF  POS=(13,15),LENGTH=04,ATTRB=(ASKIP,BRT)
 89  DCI11    DFHMDF  POS=(13,21),LENGTH=02,ATTRB=(ASKIP,BRT)
 90  ECBA11   DFHMDF  POS=(13,25),LENGTH=08,ATTRB=(ASKIP,BRT)
 91  FCAA11   DFHMDF  POS=(13,35),LENGTH=08,ATTRB=(ASKIP,BRT)
 92  *------------------------------------------------------------*
 93  TASK12   DFHMDF  POS=(14,01),LENGTH=06,ATTRB=(ASKIP,BRT)
 94  TERM12   DFHMDF  POS=(14,09),LENGTH=04,ATTRB=(ASKIP,BRT)
 95  TRAN12   DFHMDF  POS=(14,15),LENGTH=04,ATTRB=(ASKIP,BRT)
 96  DCI12    DFHMDF  POS=(14,21),LENGTH=02,ATTRB=(ASKIP,BRT)
 97  ECBA12   DFHMDF  POS=(14,25),LENGTH=08,ATTRB=(ASKIP,BRT)
 98  FCAA12   DFHMDF  POS=(14,35),LENGTH=08,ATTRB=(ASKIP,BRT)
 99  *------------------------------------------------------------*
100  TASK13   DFHMDF  POS=(15,01),LENGTH=06,ATTRB=(ASKIP,BRT)
101  TERM13   DFHMDF  POS=(15,09),LENGTH=04,ATTRB=(ASKIP,BRT)
102  TRAN13   DFHMDF  POS=(15,15),LENGTH=04,ATTRB=(ASKIP,BRT)
103  DCI13    DFHMDF  POS=(15,21),LENGTH=02,ATTRB=(ASKIP,BRT)
104  ECBA13   DFHMDF  POS=(15,25),LENGTH=08,ATTRB=(ASKIP,BRT)
105  FCAA13   DFHMDF  POS=(15,35),LENGTH=08,ATTRB=(ASKIP,BRT)
106  *------------------------------------------------------------*
107  TASK14   DFHMDF  POS=(16,01),LENGTH=06,ATTRB=(ASKIP,BRT)
108  TERM14   DFHMDF  POS=(16,09),LENGTH=04,ATTRB=(ASKIP,BRT)
109  TRAN14   DFHMDF  POS=(16,15),LENGTH=04,ATTRB=(ASKIP,BRT)
110  DCI14    DFHMDF  POS=(16,21),LENGTH=02,ATTRB=(ASKIP,BRT)
111  ECBA14   DFHMDF  POS=(16,25),LENGTH=08,ATTRB=(ASKIP,BRT)
112  FCAA14   DFHMDF  POS=(16,35),LENGTH=08,ATTRB=(ASKIP,BRT)
113  *------------------------------------------------------------*
114  TASK15   DFHMDF  POS=(17,01),LENGTH=06,ATTRB=(ASKIP,BRT)
```

```
115   TERM15   DFHMDF  POS=(17,09),LENGTH=04,ATTRB=(ASKIP,BRT)
116   TRAN15   DFHMDF  POS=(17,15),LENGTH=04,ATTRB=(ASKIP,BRT)
117   DCI15    DFHMDF  POS=(17,21),LENGTH=02,ATTRB=(ASKIP,BRT)
118   ECBA15   DFHMDF  POS=(17,25),LENGTH=08,ATTRB=(ASKIP,BRT)
119   FCAA15   DFHMDF  POS=(17,35),LENGTH=08,ATTRB=(ASKIP,BRT)
120   *-----------------------------------------------------*
121   TASK16   DFHMDF  POS=(18,01),LENGTH=06,ATTRB=(ASKIP,BRT)
122   TERM16   DFHMDF  POS=(18,09),LENGTH=04,ATTRB=(ASKIP,BRT)
123   TRAN16   DFHMDF  POS=(18,15),LENGTH=04,ATTRB=(ASKIP,BRT)
124   DCI16    DFHMDF  POS=(18,21),LENGTH=02,ATTRB=(ASKIP,BRT)
125   ECBA16   DFHMDF  POS=(18,25),LENGTH=08,ATTRB=(ASKIP,BRT)
126   FCAA16   DFHMDF  POS=(18,35),LENGTH=08,ATTRB=(ASKIP,BRT)
127   *-----------------------------------------------------*
128   TASK17   DFHMDF  POS=(19,01),LENGTH=06,ATTRB=(ASKIP,BRT)
129   TERM17   DFHMDF  POS=(19,09),LENGTH=04,ATTRB=(ASKIP,BRT)
130   TRAN17   DFHMDF  POS=(19,15),LENGTH=04,ATTRB=(ASKIP,BRT)
131   DCI17    DFHMDF  POS=(19,21),LENGTH=02,ATTRB=(ASKIP,BRT)
132   ECBA17   DFHMDF  POS=(19,25),LENGTH=08,ATTRB=(ASKIP,BRT)
133   FCAA17   DFHMDF  POS=(19,35),LENGTH=08,ATTRB=(ASKIP,BRT)
134   *-----------------------------------------------------*
135   TASK18   DFHMDF  POS=(20,01),LENGTH=06,ATTRB=(ASKIP,BRT)
136   TERM18   DFHMDF  POS=(20,09),LENGTH=04,ATTRB=(ASKIP,BRT)
137   TRAN18   DFHMDF  POS=(20,15),LENGTH=04,ATTRB=(ASKIP,BRT)
138   DCI18    DFHMDF  POS=(20,21),LENGTH=02,ATTRB=(ASKIP,BRT)
139   ECBA18   DFHMDF  POS=(20,25),LENGTH=08,ATTRB=(ASKIP,BRT)
140   FCAA18   DFHMDF  POS=(20,35),LENGTH=08,ATTRB=(ASKIP,BRT)
141   *-----------------------------------------------------*
142   TASK19   DFHMDF  POS=(21,01),LENGTH=06,ATTRB=(ASKIP,BRT)
```

Figure 9.8. continued.

449

```
143   TERM19    DFHMDF  POS=(21,09),LENGTH=04,ATTRB=(ASKIP,BRT)
144   TRAN19    DFHMDF  POS=(21,15),LENGTH=04,ATTRB=(ASKIP,BRT)
145   DCI19     DFHMDF  POS=(21,21),LENGTH=02,ATTRB=(ASKIP,BRT)
146   ECBA19    DFHMDF  POS=(21,25),LENGTH=08,ATTRB=(ASKIP,BRT)
147   FCAA19    DFHMDF  POS=(21,35),LENGTH=08,ATTRB=(ASKIP,BRT)
148   *-----------------------------------------------------------*
149   TASK20    DFHMDF  POS=(22,01),LENGTH=06,ATTRB=(ASKIP,BRT)
150   TERM20    DFHMDF  POS=(22,09),LENGTH=04,ATTRB=(ASKIP,BRT)
151   TRAN20    DFHMDF  POS=(22,15),LENGTH=04,ATTRB=(ASKIP,BRT)
152   DCI20     DFHMDF  POS=(22,21),LENGTH=02,ATTRB=(ASKIP,BRT)
153   ECBA20    DFHMDF  POS=(22,25),LENGTH=08,ATTRB=(ASKIP,BRT)
154   FCAA20    DFHMDF  POS=(22,35),LENGTH=08,ATTRB=(ASKIP,BRT)
155   *-----------------------------------------------------------*
156             DFHMDF  POS=(24,01),LENGTH=37,                    *
157             INITIAL='CLEAR=END, ENTER=REFRESH,  PF1=ACT/SUS'
158             DFHMDF  POS=(24,39),LENGTH=41,                    *
159             INITIAL='PF2=STOR DISP,  PF3=MAIN INFO
160             DFHMSD TYPE=FINAL
161             END
```

****

Figure 9.8.   continued.

```
*****************************************************************
 1    *-----------------------------------------------------------*
 2    * NOTE: BNINFP2 AND BNINFP3 ARE SIMILAR. THE BASE PGM IS BNINFP2.
 3    *-----------------------------------------------------------*
 4    * THIS PROGRAM IS NEVER PASSED A COMMUNICATION AREA.
 5    *-----------------------------------------------------------*
 6           COPY  REGDEF
 7    CSACBAR   EQU   13
 8    EIBREG    EQU   11
 9    DCACBAR   EQU   6
10    *** TCACBAR IS ALREADY EQUATED TO 12, AS PART OF IBM MACRO EXPANSION.
11           COPY  DFHAID
12           COPY  DFHCSADS
13           DFHTCA CICSYST=YES
14           COPY  DFHDCADS
15    BNINFP2  DFHEIENT CODEREG=(8,9),DATAREG=10,EIBREG=11
16           EXEC CICS IGNORE CONDITION LENGERR
17           EXEC CICS HANDLE CONDITION ERROR(ERRCOND)
18           EXEC CICS ADDRESS EIB(EIBREG)
19    INITIAL   EQU   *
20           CLI   EIBAID,DFHCLEAR
21           BE    CLEARKEY
22           CLI   EIBAID,DFHPF1
23           BE    PF1KEY
24           CLI   EIBAID,DFHPF2
25           BE    PF2KEY
26           CLI   EIBAID,DFHPF3
27           BE    PF3KEY
```

Figure 9.9.   Source code of program BNINFP3

451

```
28            EXEC  CICS ASSIGN APPLID(SYSIDO)
29            EXEC  CICS ADDRESS CSA(CSACBAR)
30            ST    CSACBAR,FIELD4
31       ***  CALLING BNSUB01 STARTS ***
32            LA    R1,FIELD4
33            ST    R1,INADDR
34            LA    R1,FIELD8
35            ST    R1,OUTADDR
36            MVI   CODE,C'A'
37            MVC   LENSMALL(2),=H'4'
38            EXEC  CICS LINK PROGRAM('BNSUB01') COMMAREA(INADDR)     X
39                  LENGTH(11)
40            CLI   CODE,C'S'
41            BNE   ERROR1
42       ***  CALLING BNSUB01 FINISHED ***
43            MVC   ADDRCSAO,FIELD8+2
44            L     DCACBAR,CSASUSBA
45            LA    R2,TASK1O
46            SR    R3,R3
47            LA    R3,20
48            MVC   TASTYPEO,=CL3'SUS'
49            UNPK  FIELD6(6),EIBTIME(4)
50            OI    FIELD6+5,X'F0'
51            MVC   TIMEO(2),FIELD6
52            MVI   TIMEO+2,C':'
53            MVC   TIMEO+3(2),FIELD6+2
54            MVI   TIMEO+5,C':'
55            MVC   TIMEO+6(2),FIELD6+4
56  SCANACT   EQU   *
57            LA    1,CSASUSOF
```

```
58                CR    1,DCACBAR
59                BE    FINISHED
60                BAL   14,CHKTASK
61                L     DCACBAR,DCAKCBA
62                BCT   R3,SCANACT
63                B     SENDMAP
64       FINISHED EQU   *
65                B     SENDMAP
66       CHKTASK  EQU   *
67                ST    R14,SAVEREG
68                L     TCACBAR,DCATCAA
69                ST    TCACBAR,ADDRUTCA
70                L     TCACBAR,TCASYAA-DFHTCADS(TCACBAR)
71                DROP  TCACBAR
72                USING DFHSYTCA,TCACBAR
73                CLC   TCAKCOID,=C'JNL2'
74                BER   R14
75                CLC   TCAKCOID,=C'CVST'
76                BER   R14
77                CLC   TCAKCOID,=C'CSNC'
78                BER   R14
79                CLC   TCAKCOID,=C'CSSY'
80                BER   R14
81                CLC   TCAKCOID,=X'D1D1D100'
82                BER   R14
83                TM    TCAKCTTA+2,X'0C'
84                BNOR  R14
85       * NOW BUILD TASK NUM ON THE MAP AREA.
```

Figure 9.9. continued.

453

```
86          MVC   OKOUNT,=X'402020202020'
87          ED    OKOUNT,TCAKCTTA
88          MVC   0(6,R2),OKOUNT+1
89          MVC   TRANSID,TCAKCOID
90          L     TCACBAR,ADDRUTCA
91          DROP  TCACBAR
92          USING DFHUSTCA,TCACBAR
93    * NOW BUILD TERM  ID ON THE MAP AREA.
94          LA    R2,9(R2)
95          L     R1,TCAFCAAA
96          MVC   0(4,R2),0(R1)
97    * NOW BUILD TRANS ID ON THE MAP AREA.
98          LA    R2,7(R2)
99          MVC   0(4,R2),TRANSID
100   * NOW BUILD DCI ON THE MAP AREA.
101         LA    R2,7(R2)
102         MVC   DCI,TCATCEI
103   *** CALLING BNSUB01 STARTS ***
104         LA    R1,DCI
105         ST    R1,INADDR
106         LA    R1,DCICHAR
107         ST    R1,OUTADDR
108         MVI   CODE,C'A'
109         MVC   LENSMALL(2),=H'1'
110         EXEC  CICS LINK PROGRAM('BNSUB01') COMMAREA(INADDR)        X
111               LENGTH(11)
112         CLI   CODE,C'S'
113         BNE   ERROR1
114   *** CALLING BNSUB01 FINISHED ***
115         MVC   0(2,R2),DCICHAR
```

454

```
116   * NOW BUILD ECB ADDRESS ON THE MAP AREA.
117          LA      R2,5(R2)
118          MVC     FIELD4(4),TCATCEA
119          LA      R1,FIELD4
120          ST      R1,INADDR
121          LA      R1,FIELD8
122          ST      R1,OUTADDR
123          MVI     CODE,C'A'
124          MVC     LENSMALL(2),=H'4'
125          EXEC    CICS LINK PROGRAM('BNSUB01') COMMAREA(INADDR)     X
126                  LENGTH(11)
127          CLI     CODE,C'S'
128          BNE     ERROR2
129          MVC     0(8,R2),FIELD8
130   * NOW FIND OUT FACILITY CONTROL AREA ADDRESS.....
131          LA      R2,11(R2)
132          MVC     FIELD4(4),TCAFCAAA
133          LA      R1,FIELD4
134          ST      R1,INADDR
135          LA      R1,FIELD8
136          ST      R1,OUTADDR
137          MVI     CODE,C'A'
138          MVC     LENSMALL(2),=H'4'
139          EXEC    CICS LINK PROGRAM('BNSUB01') COMMAREA(INADDR)     X
140                  LENGTH(11)
141          CLI     CODE,C'S'
142          BNE     ERROR2
143          MVC     0(8,R2),FIELD8
```

Figure 9.9. continued.

455

```
144  * NOW GET READY TO RETURN.
145           L     R14,SAVEREG
146           LA    R2,11(R2)              R2 POINTS TO NEXT TASK NUMBER
147           BR    R14
148  SENDMAP  EQU   *
149           EXEC  CICS SEND MAP('BNINFM2') MAPSET('BNINFS2') ERASE
150           EXEC  CICS RETURN TRANSID('BNI3')
151  *===================================================================*
152  CLEARKEY EQU   *
153           EXEC  CICS SEND FROM(BLANKS) LENGTH(1) ERASE
154           EXEC  CICS RETURN
155  PF1KEY   EQU   *
156  *===================================================================*
157  * REMEMBER WHEN CONTROL IS TRANSFERRED TO THE NEW PROGRAM, THE VALUE OF
158  * EIBAID WILL STILL BE DFHPF1 UNLESS YOU CHANGE IT PRIOR TO EXECUTING
159  * THE XCTL COMMAND.
160  *===================================================================*
161           MVI   EIBAID,DFHENTER
162           EXEC  CICS XCTL PROGRAM('BNINFP2')
163  PF2KEY   EQU   *
164           EXEC  CICS RECEIVE MAP('BNINFM2') MAPSET('BNINFS2')         X
165                 INTO(BNINFM2I)
166  *** SHOULD VALIDATE THE ADDRESS ENTERED ON THE SCREEN.
167           MVI   EIBAID,DFHENTER
168           MVI   COMM01,C'F'            INDICATE TO BNINFP4- FIRST TIME
169           MVC   COMM01+1(6),ADDRI
170           EXEC  CICS XCTL PROGRAM('BNINFP4') COMMAREA(COMM01) LENGTH(7)
171  *===================================================================*
172  PF3KEY   EQU   *
173  *===================================================================*
```

```
174  * REMEMBER WHEN CONTROL IS TRANSFERRED TO THE NEW PROGRAM, THE VALUE OF
175  * EIBAID WILL STILL BE DFHPF3 UNLESS YOU CHANGE IT PRIOR TO EXECUTING
176  * THE XCTL COMMAND.
177  *========================================================================*
178          MVI   EIBAID,DFHENTER
179          EXEC CICS XCTL PROGRAM('BNINFP1')
180  ERRCOND EQU   *
181          EXEC CICS HANDLE CONDITION ERROR(GETOUT)
182          EXEC CICS SEND FROM(ERRMSG00) LENGTH(74) ERASE
183          B    GETOUT
184  ERROR1  EQU   *
185          EXEC CICS HANDLE CONDITION ERROR(GETOUT)
186          EXEC CICS SEND FROM(ERRMSG01) LENGTH(74) ERASE
187          B    GETOUT
188  ERROR2  EQU   *
189          EXEC CICS HANDLE CONDITION ERROR(GETOUT)
190          EXEC CICS SEND FROM(ERRMSG02) LENGTH(74) ERASE
191          B    GETOUT
192  ERROR3  EQU   *
193          EXEC CICS HANDLE CONDITION ERROR(GETOUT)
194          EXEC CICS SEND FROM(ERRMSG03) LENGTH(74) ERASE
195          B    GETOUT
196  GETOUT  EXEC CICS RETURN
197  *========================================================================*
198  BLANKS  DC    CL10' '
199  ERRMSG00 DS   0CL74
200          DC    CL44'ERROR CONDITION DETECTED. USE CEDF TO DEBUG '
201          DC    CL30' '
```

Figure 9.9. continued.

```
202  ERRMSG01 DS   0CL74
203           DC   CL44'RETURN CODE FROM BNSUB01 IS NOT S. REFER TO '
204           DC   CL30'LABEL ERROR1 IN PGM=BNINFP3'
205  ERRMSG02 DS   0CL74
206           DC   CL44'RETURN CODE FROM BNSUB01 IS NOT S. REFER TO '
207           DC   CL30'LABEL ERROR2 IN PGM=BNINFP3'
208  ERRMSG03 DS   0CL74
209           DC   CL44'RETURN CODE FROM BNSUB01 IS NOT S. REFER TO '
210           DC   CL30'LABEL ERROR3 IN PGM=BNINFP3'
211  *================================================================*
212           DFHEISTG
213           COPY BNINFS2
214  INADDR   DS   F
215  OUTADDR  DS   F
216  LENSMALL DS   H
217  CODE     DS   CL1
218  COMM01   DS   CL12
219  OKOUNT   DS   CL7       ZZZZZZZ
220  DOUBLE   DS   D
221  ADDRUTCA DS   F
222  TRANSID  DS   CL4
223  DCI      DS   CL1
224  DCICHAR  DS   CL2
225  SAVEREG  DS   F
226  FIELD6   DS   CL6
227  FIELD4   DS   F
228  FIELD8   DS   D
229           END
```

****

Figure 9.9. continued.

458

```
**********************************************************************
**********************************************************************
     1  **********************************************************************
     2  * PROGRAM ID: BNINFP4
     3  * FUNCTION:    DISPLAY CICS VIRTUAL STORAGE
     4  * AUTHOR:      BARRY KUMAR NIRMAL
     5  **********************************************************************
     6          COPY REGDEF
     7  CSACBAR EQU  13
     8  EIBREG  EQU  11
     9  DCACBAR EQU  6
    10  *** TCACBAR IS ALREADY EQUATED TO 12, AS PART OF IBM MACRO EXPANSION.
    11          COPY DFHAID
    12          COPY DFHCSADS
    13          DFHTCA CICSYST=YES
    14          COPY DFHDCADS
    15  BNINFP4 DFHEIENT CODEREG=(8,9),DATAREG=10,EIBREG=11
    16          EXEC CICS IGNORE CONDITION LENGERR
    17          EXEC CICS HANDLE CONDITION ERROR(ERRCOND)
    18          EXEC CICS ADDRESS EIB(EIBREG)
    19  INITIAL EQU  *
    20          LH   R1,EIBCALEN
    21          LTR  R1,R1
    22          BZ   SORRY
    23          CLI  EIBAID,DFHCLEAR    WAS CLEAR KEY PRESSED?
    24          BE   CLEARKEY
    25          CLI  EIBAID,DFHPF1      WAS PF1 PRESSED?
    26          BE   PF1KEY
    27          CLI  EIBAID,DFHPF2      WAS PF2 PRESSED?
```

Figure 9.10. Source code of program BNINFP4

```
28              BE    PF2KEY
29 ** THE USER HAS PRESSED A KEY OTHER THAN CLEAR, PF1 AND PF2.
30              L     R4,DFHEICAP          POINT R4 TO COMM AREA
31              CLI   0(R4),C'F'      IS THIS FIRST TIME ENTRY TO THIS PGM ?
32              BE    FIRST
33              CLI   0(R4),C'N'      IS THIS NEXT TIME ENTRY TO THIS PGM ?
34              BNE   SORRY
35 *
36 NEXTTIME EQU  *
              EXEC CICS RECEIVE MAP('BNINFM3') MAPSET('BNINFS3')           X
37                   INTO(BNINFM30)
38              MVC   FIELD8+2(6),ADDRI
39              B     COMMON
40 *
41 FIRST    EQU  *
42              MVI   EIBAID,DFHENTER      FORCE ENTER KEY ON FIRST TIME.
43              MVC   FIELD8+2(6),1(R4)
              MVC   ADDRO(6),1(R4)         MOVE INCOMING ADDRESS TO MAP
44 *
45 COMMON   EQU  *
              MVI   CODE,C'B'
46              MVC   FIELD8(2),=C'00'
47              LA    R1,FIELD8
48              ST    R1,INADDR
49              LA    R1,FIELD4
50              ST    R1,OUTADDR
51              MVC   LENGTH(2),=H'4'        LENGTH OF SMALLER AREA
52              EXEC CICS LINK PROGRAM('BNSUB01') COMMAREA(INADDR)          X
53                   LENGTH(11)
54              CLI   CODE,C'S'
55              BNE   ERROR1
56              CLI   EIBAID,DFHPF8          WAS PG8 PRESSED?
57              BE    HAVEPF8                YES, BRANCH
```

```
58            CLI    EIBAID,DFHPF7      WAS PF7 PRESSED?
59            BE     HAVEPF7             YES, BRANCH
60 ** THE USER PRESSED ENTER OR SOME OTHER KEY. TREAT IT AS IF ENTER KEY
61 ** WAS PRESSED, AND DISPLAY STORAGE AT ADDRESS OBTAINED FROM 'RECEIVE
62 ** MAP' COMMAND.
63            B      PROCEED1
64 HAVEPF7    EQU    *
65            SR     R1,R1
66            L      R1,FIELD4
67            S      R1,=F'352'
68            ST     R1,FIELD4
69            B      EXPAND
70 HAVEPF8    EQU    *
71            SR     R1,R1
72            L      R1,FIELD4
73            A      R1,=F'352'
74            ST     R1,FIELD4
75            B      EXPAND
76 EXPAND     EQU    *
77            MVI    CODE,C'A'
78            LA     R1,FIELD4
79            ST     R1,INADDR
80            LA     R1,FIELD8
81            ST     R1,OUTADDR
82            MVC    LENGTH(2),=H'4'     LENGTH OF SMALLER AREA
83            EXEC CICS LINK PROGRAM('BNSUB01') COMMAREA(INADDR)         X
84            LENGTH(11)
85            CLI    CODE,C'S'
```

Figure 9.10. continued.

461

```
 86           BNE   ERROR1
 87           MVC   ADDRO(6),FIELD8+2     MOVE STORAGE ADDRESS TO MAP
 88 PROCEED1  EQU   *
 89           MVI   CODE,C'A'
 90           L     R1,FIELD4
 91           ST    R1,INADDR
 92           LA    R1,DISPAREA
 93           ST    R1,OUTADDR
 94           MVC   LENGTH(2),=H'352'   LENGTH OF SMALLER AREA
 95           EXEC  CICS LINK PROGRAM('BNSUB01') COMMAREA(INADDR)      X
 96                 LENGTH(11)
 97           CLI   CODE,C'S'
 98           BNE   ERROR2
 99 *=========================================================*
100 * MOVE DATA FROM STORAGE TO MAP.
101 *=========================================================*
102 * AFTER YOU MAKE USE OF CONTENT OF NEXTADDR OR NEXTDISP, ADVANCE IT SO
103 * IT WILL HAVE CORRECT VALUE THE NEXT TIME IT IS MADE USE OF.
104 *=========================================================*
105           LA    R5,22            THERE ARE 22 LINES ON SCREEN
106           MVC   NEXTADDR(4),INADDR   SET NEXTADDR TO CORRECT VALUE
107           LA    R3,4             4 FIELDS OF 8 BYTES EACH ON ONE LINE
108           LA    R2,DATA110
109           LA    R4,DISPAREA
110           LA    R4,32(R4)
111           ST    R4,NEXTDISP      SET NEXTDSIP TO CORRECT VALUE
112           S     R4,=F'32'        BACKTRACK R4 TO AREA FOR THIS LINE
113 LOOPX     EQU   *
114           MVC   0(8,R2),0(R4)    MOVE 8-BYTE SEGMENT TO MAP
115           LA    R2,11(R2)        ADVANCE R2 TO POINT TO NEW MAP FIELD
```

```
116          LA    R4,8(R4)                     ADVANCE R4 TO NEW SEGMENT IN DISPAREA
117          BCT   R3,LOOPX                     BRANCH TO LOOPX
118   * NOW BUILD THE TWO FIELDS OF 8 BYTES EACH
119          L     R4,NEXTADDR
120          LA    R4,16(R4)
121          ST    R4,NEXTADDR                  STORE FOR NEXT LINE ON MAP
122          S     R4,=F'16'                    BACKTRACK R4 TO AREA DESIRED
123          LA    R3,2                         R3 MUST HAVE 2 IN IT.
124   LOOPY  EQU   *
125          MVC   WORKAREA,0(R4)
126          TR    WORKAREA,TRTABLE
127          MVC   0(8,R2),WORKAREA
128          LA    R2,11(R2)                    ADVANCE R2 TO POINT TO NEW MAP FIELD
129          LA    R4,8(R4)                     ADVANCE R4 TO NEW AREA IN STORAGE
130          BCT   R3,LOOPY                     LOOP BACK
131   * NOW START WORKING ON NEXT LINE ON MAP.
132          L     R4,NEXTDISP                  POINT R4 TO CORRECT LOC IN DISPAREA
133          LA    R4,32(R4)
134          ST    R4,NEXTDISP
135          S     R4,=F'32'
136          LA    R3,4                         R3 MUST HAVE 4 IN IT.
137          BCT   R5,LOOPX                     LOOP BACK FOR NEW LINE
138   SENDMAP EQU  *
139          EXEC  CICS SEND MAP('BNINFM3') MAPSET('BNINFS3') ERASE
140          MVI   COMM01,C'N'                  INDICATE NEXT TIME
141          EXEC  CICS RETURN TRANSID('BNI4') COMMAREA(COMM01)                    X
142                LENGTH(1)
143   *========================================================================*
```

Figure 9.10. continued.

463

```
144  SORRY     EQU   *
145            EXEC  CICS SEND FROM(ERRMSG99) LENGTH(74) ERASE
146            B     GETOUT
147  CLEARKEY  EQU   *
148            MVI   COMM01,C' '
149            EXEC  CICS SEND FROM(COMM01) LENGTH(1) ERASE
150            B     GETOUT
151  PF1KEY    EQU   *
152  *=======================================================*
153  * REMEMBER WHEN CONTROL GOES TO PGM 'BNINFP2', THE VALUE OF EIBAID
154  * WILL STILL BE EQUAL TO DFHPF1 UNLESS YOU CHANGE IT PRIOR TO
155  * TRANSFERRING CONTROL TO IT.
156  *=======================================================*
157            MVI   EIBAID,DFHENTER
158            EXEC  CICS XCTL PROGRAM('BNINFP2')
159  PF2KEY    EQU   *
160            MVI   EIBAID,DFHENTER
161            EXEC  CICS XCTL PROGRAM('BNINFP1')
162  ERRCOND   EQU   *
163            EXEC  CICS HANDLE CONDITION ERROR(GETOUT)
164            EXEC  CICS SEND FROM(ERRMSG00) LENGTH(74) ERASE
165            B     GETOUT
166  ERROR1    EQU   *
167            EXEC  CICS HANDLE CONDITION ERROR(GETOUT)
168            EXEC  CICS SEND FROM(ERRMSG01) LENGTH(74) ERASE
169            B     GETOUT
170  ERROR2    EQU   *
171            EXEC  CICS HANDLE CONDITION ERROR(GETOUT)
172            EXEC  CICS SEND FROM(ERRMSG02) LENGTH(74) ERASE
173            B     GETOUT
```

```
174 GETOUT   EXEC CICS RETURN
175 *=================================================*
176 ERRMSG00 DS   0CL74
177          DC   CL44'ERROR CONDITION DETECTED IN PROGRAM BNINFP4.'
178          DC   CL30'    USE CEDF TO DEBUG.'
179 ERRMSG01 DS   0CL74
180          DC   CL44'RETURN CODE PASSED BACK BY BNSUB01 IS NOT S.'
181          DC   CL30'SEE LABEL=ERROR1 IN BNINFP4'
182 ERRMSG02 DS   0CL74
183          DC   CL44'RETURN CODE PASSED BACK BY BNSUB01 IS NOT S.'
184          DC   CL30'SEE LABEL=ERROR2 IN BNINFP4'
185 ERRMSG99 DS   0CL74
186          DC   CL44'PROGRAM BNINFP4 CAN NOT BE EXECUTED EXCEPT'
187          DC   CL30'THROUGH THE CICS MONITOR.'
188 *===============================================================*
189 *****************  0123456789ABCDEF  ***************************
190 TRTABLE  DC   C'................'          00-0F
191          DC   C'................'          10-1F
192          DC   C'................'          20-2F
193          DC   C'........¢.<(+|'            30-3F
194          DC   C'.........!$*);¬'           40-4F
195 *** NOTE TWO AMPERSANDS TELL ASSEMBLE RO REPLACE THEM BY ONE ASSEMBLER.
196          DC   C'&&.......!$*);¬'           50-5F
197          DC   C'-/......,%_>?'             60-6F
198          DC   C'.......:#@.="'             70-7F
199          DC   C'.ABCDEFGHI......'          80-8F
200          DC   C'.JKLMNOPQR......'          90-9F
201          DC   C'..STUVWXYZ......'          A0-AF
```

Figure 9.10. continued.

```
202            DC    C'................'           B0-BF
203            DC    C'{ABCDEFGHI.......'           C0-CF
204            DC    C'}JKLMNOPQR.......'           D0-DF
205            DC    C'..STUVWXYZ.......'           E0-EF
206            DC    C'0123456789.......'           F0-FF
207            DFHEISTG
208            COPY BNINFS3
209   WORKAREA DS    CL8
210   NEXTADDR DS    F
211   NEXTDISP DS    F
212   INADDR   DS    F
213   OUTADDR  DS    F
214   LENGTH   DS    H
215   CODE     DS    CL1
216   FIELD4   DS    F
217   FIELD8   DS    D
218   COMM01   DS    CL12
219   DISPAREA DS    CL704
220            END
```

****

Figure 9.10. continued.

```
************************************************************
 1  BNINFS3   DFHMSD TYPE=&SYSPARM,MODE=INOUT,CTRL=(FREEKB,FRSET),           *
 2                   LANG=ASM,TIOAPFX=YES,EXTATT=MAPONLY,COLOR=GREEN
 3  BNINFM3   DFHMDI SIZE=(24,80)
 4            DFHMDF POS=(01,01),LENGTH=09,INITIAL='ADDR(HEX)'
 5  ADDR      DFHMDF POS=(01,11),LENGTH=06,ATTRB=(BRT,UNPROT,IC,FSET)
 6  HEAD      DFHMDF POS=(01,24),LENGTH=30,ATTRB=(ASKIP,BRT)
 7  *------------------------------------------------------------*
 8            DFHMDF POS=(02,01),LENGTH=04,INITIAL='0000'
 9  DATA11    DFHMDF POS=(02,08),LENGTH=08,ATTRB=(ASKIP,BRT)
10  DATA12    DFHMDF POS=(02,17),LENGTH=08,ATTRB=(ASKIP,BRT)
11  DATA13    DFHMDF POS=(02,26),LENGTH=08,ATTRB=(ASKIP,BRT)
12  DATA14    DFHMDF POS=(02,35),LENGTH=08,ATTRB=(ASKIP,BRT)
13  DATA15    DFHMDF POS=(02,63),LENGTH=08,ATTRB=(ASKIP,BRT)
14  DATA16    DFHMDF POS=(02,72),LENGTH=08,ATTRB=(ASKIP,BRT)
15  *------------------------------------------------------------*
16            DFHMDF POS=(03,01),LENGTH=04,INITIAL='0010'
17  DATA21    DFHMDF POS=(03,08),LENGTH=08,ATTRB=(ASKIP,BRT)
18  DATA22    DFHMDF POS=(03,17),LENGTH=08,ATTRB=(ASKIP,BRT)
19  DATA23    DFHMDF POS=(03,26),LENGTH=08,ATTRB=(ASKIP,BRT)
20  DATA24    DFHMDF POS=(03,35),LENGTH=08,ATTRB=(ASKIP,BRT)
21  DATA25    DFHMDF POS=(03,63),LENGTH=08,ATTRB=(ASKIP,BRT)
22  DATA26    DFHMDF POS=(03,72),LENGTH=08,ATTRB=(ASKIP,BRT)
23  *------------------------------------------------------------*
24            DFHMDF POS=(04,01),LENGTH=04,INITIAL='0020'
25  DATA31    DFHMDF POS=(04,08),LENGTH=08,ATTRB=(ASKIP,BRT)
26  DATA32    DFHMDF POS=(04,17),LENGTH=08,ATTRB=(ASKIP,BRT)
27  DATA33    DFHMDF POS=(04,26),LENGTH=08,ATTRB=(ASKIP,BRT)
```

Figure 9.11. Source code of mapset BNINFS3

```
28  DATA34   DFHMDF  POS=(04,35),LENGTH=08,ATTRB=(ASKIP,BRT)
29  DATA35   DFHMDF  POS=(04,63),LENGTH=08,ATTRB=(ASKIP,BRT)
30  DATA36   DFHMDF  POS=(04,72),LENGTH=08,ATTRB=(ASKIP,BRT)
31  *--------------------------------------------------------------*
32           DFHMDF  POS=(05,01),LENGTH=04,INITIAL='0030'
33  DATA41   DFHMDF  POS=(05,08),LENGTH=08,ATTRB=(ASKIP,BRT)
34  DATA42   DFHMDF  POS=(05,17),LENGTH=08,ATTRB=(ASKIP,BRT)
35  DATA43   DFHMDF  POS=(05,26),LENGTH=08,ATTRB=(ASKIP,BRT)
36  DATA44   DFHMDF  POS=(05,35),LENGTH=08,ATTRB=(ASKIP,BRT)
37  DATA45   DFHMDF  POS=(05,63),LENGTH=08,ATTRB=(ASKIP,BRT)
38  DATA46   DFHMDF  POS=(05,72),LENGTH=08,ATTRB=(ASKIP,BRT)
39  *--------------------------------------------------------------*
40           DFHMDF  POS=(06,01),LENGTH=04,INITIAL='0040'
41  DATA51   DFHMDF  POS=(06,08),LENGTH=08,ATTRB=(ASKIP,BRT)
42  DATA52   DFHMDF  POS=(06,17),LENGTH=08,ATTRB=(ASKIP,BRT)
43  DATA53   DFHMDF  POS=(06,26),LENGTH=08,ATTRB=(ASKIP,BRT)
44  DATA54   DFHMDF  POS=(06,35),LENGTH=08,ATTRB=(ASKIP,BRT)
45  DATA55   DFHMDF  POS=(06,63),LENGTH=08,ATTRB=(ASKIP,BRT)
46  DATA56   DFHMDF  POS=(06,72),LENGTH=08,ATTRB=(ASKIP,BRT)
47  *--------------------------------------------------------------*
48           DFHMDF  POS=(07,01),LENGTH=04,INITIAL='0050'
49  DATA61   DFHMDF  POS=(07,08),LENGTH=08,ATTRB=(ASKIP,BRT)
50  DATA62   DFHMDF  POS=(07,17),LENGTH=08,ATTRB=(ASKIP,BRT)
51  DATA63   DFHMDF  POS=(07,26),LENGTH=08,ATTRB=(ASKIP,BRT)
52  DATA64   DFHMDF  POS=(07,35),LENGTH=08,ATTRB=(ASKIP,BRT)
53  DATA65   DFHMDF  POS=(07,63),LENGTH=08,ATTRB=(ASKIP,BRT)
54  DATA66   DFHMDF  POS=(07,72),LENGTH=08,ATTRB=(ASKIP,BRT)
55  *--------------------------------------------------------------*
56           DFHMDF  POS=(08,01),LENGTH=04,INITIAL='0060'
57  DATA71   DFHMDF  POS=(08,08),LENGTH=08,ATTRB=(ASKIP,BRT)
```

```
58  DATA72     DFHMDF  POS=(08,17),LENGTH=08,ATTRB=(ASKIP,BRT)
59  DATA73     DFHMDF  POS=(08,26),LENGTH=08,ATTRB=(ASKIP,BRT)
60  DATA74     DFHMDF  POS=(08,35),LENGTH=08,ATTRB=(ASKIP,BRT)
61  DATA75     DFHMDF  POS=(08,63),LENGTH=08,ATTRB=(ASKIP,BRT)
62  DATA76     DFHMDF  POS=(08,72),LENGTH=08,ATTRB=(ASKIP,BRT)
63  *----------------------------------------------------------*
64             DFHMDF  POS=(09,01),LENGTH=04,INITIAL='0070'
65  DATA81     DFHMDF  POS=(09,08),LENGTH=08,ATTRB=(ASKIP,BRT)
66  DATA82     DFHMDF  POS=(09,17),LENGTH=08,ATTRB=(ASKIP,BRT)
67  DATA83     DFHMDF  POS=(09,26),LENGTH=08,ATTRB=(ASKIP,BRT)
68  DATA84     DFHMDF  POS=(09,35),LENGTH=08,ATTRB=(ASKIP,BRT)
69  DATA85     DFHMDF  POS=(09,63),LENGTH=08,ATTRB=(ASKIP,BRT)
70  DATA86     DFHMDF  POS=(09,72),LENGTH=08,ATTRB=(ASKIP,BRT)
71  *----------------------------------------------------------*
72             DFHMDF  POS=(10,01),LENGTH=04,INITIAL='0080'
73  DATA91     DFHMDF  POS=(10,08),LENGTH=08,ATTRB=(ASKIP,BRT)
74  DATA92     DFHMDF  POS=(10,17),LENGTH=08,ATTRB=(ASKIP,BRT)
75  DATA93     DFHMDF  POS=(10,26),LENGTH=08,ATTRB=(ASKIP,BRT)
76  DATA94     DFHMDF  POS=(10,35),LENGTH=08,ATTRB=(ASKIP,BRT)
77  DATA95     DFHMDF  POS=(10,63),LENGTH=08,ATTRB=(ASKIP,BRT)
78  DATA96     DFHMDF  POS=(10,72),LENGTH=08,ATTRB=(ASKIP,BRT)
79  *----------------------------------------------------------*
80             DFHMDF  POS=(11,01),LENGTH=04,INITIAL='0090'
81  DATA101    DFHMDF  POS=(11,08),LENGTH=08,ATTRB=(ASKIP,BRT)
82  DATA102    DFHMDF  POS=(11,17),LENGTH=08,ATTRB=(ASKIP,BRT)
83  DATA103    DFHMDF  POS=(11,26),LENGTH=08,ATTRB=(ASKIP,BRT)
84  DATA104    DFHMDF  POS=(11,35),LENGTH=08,ATTRB=(ASKIP,BRT)
```

Figure 9.11. continued.

469

```
85   DATA105  DFHMDF  POS=(11,63),LENGTH=08,ATTRB=(ASKIP,BRT)
86   DATA106  DFHMDF  POS=(11,72),LENGTH=08,ATTRB=(ASKIP,BRT)
87   *-------------------------------------------------------*
88            DFHMDF  POS=(12,01),LENGTH=04,INITIAL='00A0'
89   DATA111  DFHMDF  POS=(12,08),LENGTH=08,ATTRB=(ASKIP,BRT)
90   DATA112  DFHMDF  POS=(12,17),LENGTH=08,ATTRB=(ASKIP,BRT)
91   DATA113  DFHMDF  POS=(12,26),LENGTH=08,ATTRB=(ASKIP,BRT)
92   DATA114  DFHMDF  POS=(12,35),LENGTH=08,ATTRB=(ASKIP,BRT)
93   DATA115  DFHMDF  POS=(12,63),LENGTH=08,ATTRB=(ASKIP,BRT)
94   DATA116  DFHMDF  POS=(12,72),LENGTH=08,ATTRB=(ASKIP,BRT)
95   *-------------------------------------------------------*
96            DFHMDF  POS=(13,01),LENGTH=04,INITIAL='00B0'
97   DATA121  DFHMDF  POS=(13,08),LENGTH=08,ATTRB=(ASKIP,BRT)
98   DATA122  DFHMDF  POS=(13,17),LENGTH=08,ATTRB=(ASKIP,BRT)
99   DATA123  DFHMDF  POS=(13,26),LENGTH=08,ATTRB=(ASKIP,BRT)
100  DATA124  DFHMDF  POS=(13,35),LENGTH=08,ATTRB=(ASKIP,BRT)
101  DATA125  DFHMDF  POS=(13,63),LENGTH=08,ATTRB=(ASKIP,BRT)
102  DATA126  DFHMDF  POS=(13,72),LENGTH=08,ATTRB=(ASKIP,BRT)
103  *-------------------------------------------------------*
104           DFHMDF  POS=(14,01),LENGTH=04,INITIAL='00C0'
105  DATA131  DFHMDF  POS=(14,08),LENGTH=08,ATTRB=(ASKIP,BRT)
106  DATA132  DFHMDF  POS=(14,17),LENGTH=08,ATTRB=(ASKIP,BRT)
107  DATA133  DFHMDF  POS=(14,26),LENGTH=08,ATTRB=(ASKIP,BRT)
108  DATA134  DFHMDF  POS=(14,35),LENGTH=08,ATTRB=(ASKIP,BRT)
109  DATA135  DFHMDF  POS=(14,63),LENGTH=08,ATTRB=(ASKIP,BRT)
110  DATA136  DFHMDF  POS=(14,72),LENGTH=08,ATTRB=(ASKIP,BRT)
111  *-------------------------------------------------------*
112           DFHMDF  POS=(15,01),LENGTH=04,INITIAL='00D0'
113  DATA141  DFHMDF  POS=(15,08),LENGTH=08,ATTRB=(ASKIP,BRT)
114  DATA142  DFHMDF  POS=(15,17),LENGTH=08,ATTRB=(ASKIP,BRT)
```

```
115  DATA143   DFHMDF POS=(15,26),LENGTH=08,ATTRB=(ASKIP,BRT)
116  DATA144   DFHMDF POS=(15,35),LENGTH=08,ATTRB=(ASKIP,BRT)
117  DATA145   DFHMDF POS=(15,63),LENGTH=08,ATTRB=(ASKIP,BRT)
118  DATA146   DFHMDF POS=(15,72),LENGTH=08,ATTRB=(ASKIP,BRT)
119  *------------------------------------------------------*
120            DFHMDF POS=(16,01),LENGTH=04,INITIAL='00E0'
121  DATA151   DFHMDF POS=(16,08),LENGTH=08,ATTRB=(ASKIP,BRT)
122  DATA152   DFHMDF POS=(16,17),LENGTH=08,ATTRB=(ASKIP,BRT)
123  DATA153   DFHMDF POS=(16,26),LENGTH=08,ATTRB=(ASKIP,BRT)
124  DATA154   DFHMDF POS=(16,35),LENGTH=08,ATTRB=(ASKIP,BRT)
125  DATA155   DFHMDF POS=(16,63),LENGTH=08,ATTRB=(ASKIP,BRT)
126  DATA156   DFHMDF POS=(16,72),LENGTH=08,ATTRB=(ASKIP,BRT)
127  *------------------------------------------------------*
128            DFHMDF POS=(17,01),LENGTH=04,INITIAL='00F0'
129  DATA161   DFHMDF POS=(17,08),LENGTH=08,ATTRB=(ASKIP,BRT)
130  DATA162   DFHMDF POS=(17,17),LENGTH=08,ATTRB=(ASKIP,BRT)
131  DATA163   DFHMDF POS=(17,26),LENGTH=08,ATTRB=(ASKIP,BRT)
132  DATA164   DFHMDF POS=(17,35),LENGTH=08,ATTRB=(ASKIP,BRT)
133  DATA165   DFHMDF POS=(17,63),LENGTH=08,ATTRB=(ASKIP,BRT)
134  DATA166   DFHMDF POS=(17,72),LENGTH=08,ATTRB=(ASKIP,BRT)
135  *------------------------------------------------------*
136            DFHMDF POS=(18,01),LENGTH=04,INITIAL='0100'
137  DATA171   DFHMDF POS=(18,08),LENGTH=08,ATTRB=(ASKIP,BRT)
138  DATA172   DFHMDF POS=(18,17),LENGTH=08,ATTRB=(ASKIP,BRT)
139  DATA173   DFHMDF POS=(18,26),LENGTH=08,ATTRB=(ASKIP,BRT)
140  DATA174   DFHMDF POS=(18,35),LENGTH=08,ATTRB=(ASKIP,BRT)
141  DATA175   DFHMDF POS=(18,63),LENGTH=08,ATTRB=(ASKIP,BRT)
```

Figure 9.11. continued.

```
142  DATA176   DFHMDF POS=(18,72),LENGTH=08,ATTRB=(ASKIP,BRT)
143  *-----------------------------------------------------------------*
144  DATA181   DFHMDF POS=(19,01),LENGTH=04,INITIAL='0110'
145  DATA181   DFHMDF POS=(19,08),LENGTH=08,ATTRB=(ASKIP,BRT)
146  DATA182   DFHMDF POS=(19,17),LENGTH=08,ATTRB=(ASKIP,BRT)
147  DATA183   DFHMDF POS=(19,26),LENGTH=08,ATTRB=(ASKIP,BRT)
148  DATA184   DFHMDF POS=(19,35),LENGTH=08,ATTRB=(ASKIP,BRT)
149  DATA185   DFHMDF POS=(19,63),LENGTH=08,ATTRB=(ASKIP,BRT)
150  DATA186   DFHMDF POS=(19,72),LENGTH=08,ATTRB=(ASKIP,BRT)
151  *-----------------------------------------------------------------*
152  DATA191   DFHMDF POS=(20,01),LENGTH=04,INITIAL='0120'
153  DATA191   DFHMDF POS=(20,08),LENGTH=08,ATTRB=(ASKIP,BRT)
154  DATA192   DFHMDF POS=(20,17),LENGTH=08,ATTRB=(ASKIP,BRT)
155  DATA193   DFHMDF POS=(20,26),LENGTH=08,ATTRB=(ASKIP,BRT)
156  DATA194   DFHMDF POS=(20,35),LENGTH=08,ATTRB=(ASKIP,BRT)
157  DATA195   DFHMDF POS=(20,63),LENGTH=08,ATTRB=(ASKIP,BRT)
158  DATA196   DFHMDF POS=(20,72),LENGTH=08,ATTRB=(ASKIP,BRT)
159  *-----------------------------------------------------------------*
160  DATA201   DFHMDF POS=(21,01),LENGTH=04,INITIAL='0130'
161  DATA201   DFHMDF POS=(21,08),LENGTH=08,ATTRB=(ASKIP,BRT)
162  DATA202   DFHMDF POS=(21,17),LENGTH=08,ATTRB=(ASKIP,BRT)
163  DATA203   DFHMDF POS=(21,26),LENGTH=08,ATTRB=(ASKIP,BRT)
164  DATA204   DFHMDF POS=(21,35),LENGTH=08,ATTRB=(ASKIP,BRT)
165  DATA205   DFHMDF POS=(21,63),LENGTH=08,ATTRB=(ASKIP,BRT)
166  DATA206   DFHMDF POS=(21,72),LENGTH=08,ATTRB=(ASKIP,BRT)
167  *-----------------------------------------------------------------*
```

```
168            DFHMDF  POS=(22,01),LENGTH=04,INITIAL='0140'
169  DATA211   DFHMDF  POS=(22,08),LENGTH=08,ATTRB=(ASKIP,BRT)
170  DATA212   DFHMDF  POS=(22,17),LENGTH=08,ATTRB=(ASKIP,BRT)
171  DATA213   DFHMDF  POS=(22,26),LENGTH=08,ATTRB=(ASKIP,BRT)
172  DATA214   DFHMDF  POS=(22,35),LENGTH=08,ATTRB=(ASKIP,BRT)
173  DATA215   DFHMDF  POS=(22,63),LENGTH=08,ATTRB=(ASKIP,BRT)
174  DATA216   DFHMDF  POS=(22,72),LENGTH=08,ATTRB=(ASKIP,BRT)
175  *----------------------------------------------------------*
176            DFHMDF  POS=(23,01),LENGTH=04,INITIAL='0150'
177  DATA221   DFHMDF  POS=(23,08),LENGTH=08,ATTRB=(ASKIP,BRT)
178  DATA222   DFHMDF  POS=(23,17),LENGTH=08,ATTRB=(ASKIP,BRT)
179  DATA223   DFHMDF  POS=(23,26),LENGTH=08,ATTRB=(ASKIP,BRT)
180  DATA224   DFHMDF  POS=(23,35),LENGTH=08,ATTRB=(ASKIP,BRT)
181  DATA225   DFHMDF  POS=(23,63),LENGTH=08,ATTRB=(ASKIP,BRT)
182  DATA226   DFHMDF  POS=(23,72),LENGTH=08,ATTRB=(ASKIP,BRT)
183  *----------------------------------------------------------*
184            DFHMDF  POS=(24,01),LENGTH=36,                          *
185            INITIAL='CLEAR=END, ENTER=REFRESH, PF1=ACTIVE'
186            DFHMDF  POS=(24,38),LENGTH=42,                          *
187            INITIAL='TASKS, PF2: MAIN INFO, PF8: FWD, PF7: BACK'
188            DFHMSD TYPE=FINAL
189            END
**********************************************************************

Figure 9.11.  continued.
```

473

143, we perform routine 4000-WRITE-RECORD-RTN 10 times. In this routine, we would first encrypt the text of messages entered on the screen and then write two records on the file with the following key:

```
MSG00980$$$$
MSG00981$$$$
```

Control would then flow to line 146. On line 154, we would read the control record for update. On line 164, we would increment the item counter on the control record, and, on line 165, we would rewrite the control record. Next, on line 177, we would send the following message to the terminal:

```
RECORD NUMBER 98 HAS BEEN SUCCESSFULLY WRITTEN ONTO FILE
```

Next, on line 181, we would return to CICS. The transaction BNMG has completely ended. The user can now clear the screen and enter any CICS transaction, including BNMG, if he wants to write another humor/quotation on the file.

9.2 A SIMPLE BUT POWERFUL CICS MONITOR

Figures 9.5 through 9.11 give the various components of a simple yet powerful CICS monitor. Let us first see how to install it, and then we will see how and when to use it.

9.2.1 Procedure for Installing the Monitor

Step 1. Enter the mapset shown in Figure 9.6 in member BNINFS1 of a source PDS. Enter the mapset shown in Figure 9.8 in member BNINFS2 of the same PDS, and enter the mapset shown in Figure 9.11 in member BNINFS3 of the same PDS.

Step 2. Assemble and link mapsets BNINFS1, BNINFS2, and BNINFS3, one by one, using the JCL given in Section B.4 in Appendix B. The first job will create member BNINFS1 in your copybook library and load module BNINFS1 in your load library. The second job will create member BNINFS2 in your copybook library and load module BNINFS2 in your load library. The third job will create member BNINFS3 in your copybook library and load module BNINFS3 in your load library. The load library containing these three mapsets must be included under DDname DFHRPL in the CICS start-up procedure or job.

Step 3. Enter the program shown in Figure 9.5 in member BNINFP1 of a source PDS. Enter the program shown in Figure 9.7 in member BNINFP2 of the same PDS, and enter the program shown in Figure 9.9 in member BNINFP3 of the same PDS. Enter the program shown in Figure 9.10 in member BNINFP4 of the same PDS.

Step 4. Compile and link programs BNINFP1, BNINFP2, BNINFP3, and BNINFP4, one by one, using the JCL given in Section B.2 in Appendix B. The first job will create load module BNINFP1 in your load library. The second job will create load module BNINFP2 in the same load library. The third job will create load module BNINFP3 in the same load library. The fourth job will create load module BNINFP4 in the same load library. The load library containing these four programs must be included under DDname DFHRPL in the CICS start-up procedure or job.

Step 5. Define the following in CICS tables:

Definition of Mapset BNINFS1 in the PPT

```
MAPSET  BNINFS1
GROUP   CICSBOOK
RSL     00
STATUS  ENABLED
```

Definition of Mapset BNINFS2 in the PPT

```
MAPSET  BNINFS2
GROUP   CICSBOOK
RSL     00
STATUS  ENABLED
```

Definition of Mapset BNINFS3 in the PPT

```
MAPSET  BNINFS3
GROUP   CICSBOOK
RSL     OO
STATUS  ENABLED
```

Definition of Program BNINFP1 in the PPT

```
PROGRAM   BNINFP1
GROUP     CICSBOOK
LANGUAGE  ASSEMBLER
```

Definition of Program BNINFP2 in the PPT

```
PROGRAM   BNINFP2
GROUP     CICSBOOK
LANGUAGE  ASSEMBLER
```

Definition of Program BNINFP3 in the PPT

```
PROGRAM   BNINFP3
GROUP     CICSBOOK
LANGUAGE  ASSEMBLER
```

Definition of Program BNINFP4 in the PPT

```
PROGRAM   BNINFP4
GROUP     CICSBOOK
LANGUAGE  ASSEMBLER
```

Other parameters for programs BNINFP1, BNINFP2, BNINFP3, and BNINFP4 in the PPT should be the same as those for sample program BNPROG1 given in Section 1.6 in Chapter 1.

Definition of Transaction BNI1 in the PCT

```
TRANSACTION  BNI1
GROUP        CICSBOOK
PROGRAM      BNINFP1
```

Definition of Transaction BNI2 in the PCT

```
TRANSACTION  BNI2
GROUP        CICSBOOK
PROGRAM      BNINFP2
```

Definition of Transaction BNI3 in the PCT

```
TRANSACTION  BNI3
GROUP        CICSBOOK
PROGRAM      BNINFP3
```

Definition of Transaction BNI4 in the PCT

```
TRANSACTION  BNI4
GROUP        CICSBOOK
PROGRAM      BNINFP4
```

Other parameters for transactions BNI1, BNI2, BNI3, and BNI4 in the PCT should be the same as those for sample transaction BNC1 given in Section 1.6 in Chapter 1.

```
SYSTEM ID: C170TST1 TERM ID: D915 MAX TASK ON ? N MXT=    20 AMXT= 020
# OF TIMES AT MAX TASK 000000
```

```
CLEAR=END,  ENTER=REFRESH  PF1=ACT
```

Figure 9.12. A sample screen showing some general information about the running CICS system.

9.2.2 Using the Monitor to Display Some General Information About the Running CICS System

On a blank screen, type BNI1 and press the Enter key. A screen resembling the one shown in Figure 9.12 will be displayed. To understand the information on this screen, let us study the content of Figure 9.12. This figure shows the following:

The VTAM application ID of this CICS system is C170TST1.

The ID of the terminal on which this display is presented is D915.

The maximum task condition is currently off (MAX TASK ON ? N). This means that the system is currently not at maximum task. If it was, you would see Y after 'MAX TASK ON ?'.

The value of MXT (maximum number of tasks allowed) in the SIT or the SIT override data set is 20, and the value of AMXT (maximum number of active tasks allowed) in the SIT or the SIT override dataset is 20.

The number of times the system has been at maximum tasks condition is zero.

Program BNINFP1 is the one that is associated with transaction BNI1, and it is this program that figures out the values displayed in Figure 9.12. The explanation of this program is given below. Most of the fields displayed by this program are obtained from the CSA (Common System Area). You can refer to the layout of the CSA and other control blocks in the *CICS Data Areas* manual. If you want to display some other information from the CSA or some other control block, you need to do these things:

Modify mapset BNINFS1 by adding additional fields and their captions. Then assemble and link BNINFS1.

Modify program BNINFP1 to determine the content of those fields. Then assemble and link BNINFP1.

Test that entering BNI1 on a blank screen displays all the fields correctly on map BNINFM1.

What are the valid keys and their functions on the map of figure 9.12? Pressing the Enter key will refresh the screen, meaning that you will receive the same map but with current and therefore possibly different values in the fields. Pressing the PF1 key will display the screen shown in Figure 9.13 where information about all the active tasks in the system is shown. Pressing the Clear key will terminate the transaction and you will receive a blank screen.

In what way can this display be useful in the day-to-day work of a system or application programmer? The display shown in Figure 9.12 is not highly useful. It shows you VTAM application ID and your own terminal ID. This can be helful while problem solving, when you can use a terminal on CICS but do not know its terminal ID or its VTAM logical unit name. This program will display the terminal ID, say tttt, and then you can issue the CEMT I TERM(tttt) command to find out its VTAM logical unit name. But, as mentioned before, once you have understood how BNINFP1 works, you can easily modify it to display those fields from CICS control blocks that are of great interest to you.

9.2.3 Using the Monitor to Display Active and Suspended Task Chain

On a blank screen, type BNI2 and press the Enter key. The active task display resembling the one shown in Figure 9.13 will be displayed. (On a blank screen, if you enter BNI3, the suspended task display resembling the one shown in Figure 9.14 will be displayed.) To understand the information on this screen, let us study the content of Figure 9.13.

First, let us analyze the first line. The first field C170TST1 is the VTAM application ID of this CICS region. The next field containing six underscore characters is where you can enter an address in hexadecimal and press PF2 to display the content of virtual storage starting at that address. The next field tells us that the address of the CSA (Common System Area) is X'007C6110'. This and all other addresses in this facility are shown in hexadecimal notation. The ACT indicates that this is the active task display, as opposed to suspended task display. The last field tells us the current time.

The second line contains field headings. TASK stands for task number in decimal; TERM stands for terminal ID on which that task is running; TRAN is the transaction ID of that task; and DCI stands for dispatch control indicator, which is a one-byte field. A(ECB) stands for address of ECB (Event Control Block), and A(FCA) stands for address of FCA (Facility Control Area).

The third line shows information about one task in the system. Task number is 2063 and it is running on terminal D915. Its transaction ID is BNI1 and its dispatch control indicator is X'20'. The address of event control block for this task is X'0000644C', and the address of facility control area is X'0122F754'. In fact, this line displays information about transaction BNI1, which was issued to display the map we are analyzing.

Lines 4 thru 22 are blank in this example because there is only one displayable active task in the system. If there were other displayable active tasks, they would have been displayed on lines 4 through 22. This is to say that a maximum of 20 active tasks can be displayed on this screen.

Program BNINFP2 is the one that is associated with transaction BNI2, and it is this program that figures out the values displayed in Figure 9.13. Similarly, program BNINFP3 is the one associated with transaction BNI3, and it is this program that figures out the values displayed in Figure 9.14. The explanations of these program are given below.

```
C170TST1 _____ A(CSA): 7C6110          ACT          TIME: 11:33:49
TASK  TERM TRAN DCI A(ECB)    A(FCA)
2063  D915 BNI1  20 0000644C  0122F754
```

CLEAR=END, ENTER=REFRESH PF1=ACT/SUS PF2=STOR DISP, PF3=MAIN INFO

Figure 9.13. A sample screen showing active tasks in the running CICS system.

```
C170TST1 _____ A(CSA): 7C6110           SUS          TIME: 11:34:41
 TASK  TERM  TRAN  DCI  A(ECB)  A(FCA)
```

CLEAR=END, ENTER=REFRESH PF1=ACT/SUS PF2=STOR DISP, PF3=MAIN INFO

Figure 9.14. A sample screen showing suspended tasks in the running CICS system.

What are the valid keys and their functions on the map of Figure 9.13? Pressing the Enter key will refresh the screen, meaning that you will receive the same map but with current and therefore possibly different values in the fields. Pressing the PF1 key will display the screen shown in Figure 9.14, where information about all the suspended tasks in the system is shown. Pressing the Clear key will terminate the transaction and you will receive a blank screen. Pressing the PF3 key will display the screen shown in Figure 9.12 containing general information about the running system.

The PF2 is the storage display key and it works like this. If you enter a valid address (in hexadecimal notation) in the second field on the first line that contains six underscores, and then press PF2, you will receive a screen resembling the one shown in Figure 9.15. This screen will show the content of virtual storage starting at the address that you entered. The storage displayed will be in both hexadecimal and characters formats.

Note the similarity between active and suspended task displays. There is a close similarity between the active and suspended task displays of Figures 9.13 and 9.14. The Clear, Enter, PF2, and PF3 keys work in identical manner on both these screens. Pressing PF1 on the active task screen will display the suspended task screen, and pressing PF1 on the suspended task screen will display the active task screen. In fact, the screens shown in Figures 9.13 and 9.14 have the same appearance except that one has ACT on the first line and the other has SUS. This is because they both use the same mapset, BNINFS2, shown in Figure 9.8. The word ACT on the first line is moved in program BNINFP2, and the word SUS is moved in program BNINFP3.

The logic of programs BNINFP2 and BNINFP3 are very similar, as shown by the comments at the beginning of BNINFP2. In fact, BNINFP3 is created by taking a copy of BNINFP2 and making a few changes, as described in the comments at the beginning of BNINFP2.

In what way can this display be useful in the day-to-day work of a system or application programmer? System programmers frequently have to display active tasks, mainly while solving problems with the system. If a task is not completing, you have to find out why. Perhaps it is waiting for a resource. The resource it is waiting for could be owned by another task. The dispatch control indicator under DCI will tell you the status of this task. The meanings of dispatch control indicator bytes are given in *CICS Problem Determination Guide* for CICS Version 1, Release 7 in Figure 14 in Chapter 1.3 entitled "Approach to Wait Problems." This figure is very helpful in determining why a task is waiting.

To investigate wait problems further, you can use the addresses given on active or suspended task display. Find out the address of its event control block under A(ECB), and then display storage at that address. This will give you an idea of the kind of control block in which the ECB lies, which will give you a clue to the reason why it might be waiting. You can then proceed to investigate the problem further.

The address of the facility control area under A(FCA) is helpful to locate the TCTTE (terminal control table terminal entry) of the terminal on which a task is running. If a task is waiting for terminal I/O, because it is conversational, its DCI will be X'13' and the addresses under A(ECB) and A(FCA) will be the same.

In any event, to view the TCTTE of the terminal on which a task is running, find the address under A(FCA), enter this address in the second field on the first line of the active or suspended task display, and press the PF2 key. The TCTTE will be displayed. From the display, you can figure out the terminal ID and other information about that terminal. You will have to refer to *CICS Data Areas* manual while using this simple but powerful CICS monitor.

9.2.4 Using the Monitor to Display Any Area of CICS Virtual Storage

Unlike other screens, you can not enter BN14 on a blank screen to receive the storage display screen. This is because the storage display program BNINFP4 expects a starting address to be passed to it in the communication area. So, to display any area of virtual storage in the CICS region, you can do the following:

Display either the active task screen of Figure 9.13 or the suspended task screen of Figure 9.14.

On either screen, enter the address in the field on the first line that has six underscores and then press the PF2 key.

You will receive a display that resembles the one shown in Figure 9.15. This figure is showing storage content starting at address X'196480'. To display storage at some other address, overtype the address after ADDR(HEX) on the first line and press the Enter key. If you don't change the starting address and press the Enter key, the screen content will be refreshed, meaning that the content displayed will be that of storage in the way it was at the time the program was executed after you pressed the Enter key.

Now let us see how to read the screen shown in Figure 9.15. The second line has 0000 in the first field. This is the offset from the starting address shown on the first line. The next four fields of eight characters each on the second line give the storage content in hexadecimal notation. (Note: Each byte of storage requires two characters to display it in hexadecimal notation. So, each line displays 16 bytes of storage.) The next two fields of 8 bytes each display the storage content in character format. Any non-displayable character is shown as a dot in this area.

```
ADDR(HEX) 196480
0000  82000040 00000000 00000040 00000000   B... ... ... ...
0010  80196480 002C6190 0000001C 05D5C9D9   ..../. ....NIR
0020  D4C141D6 00E9F3E2 C8D44040 40E2C7E3   MA.O.Z3S HM  SGT
0030  D3C9C2F1 40000000 00000000 00000000   LIB1 ...
0040  82000040 00268F50 0000005C 00000000   B...&. ..*. ...
0050  801964C0 002E7190 0000001C 002B0C70   ..{. ...
0060  D6C1F1F0 F0E9F3C1 D5C64040 40E2C7E3   OA10Z3A NF  SGT
0070  D3C9C2F1 40000000 00000000 00000000   LIB1 ...
0080  94000040 002E4000 00000000 00000000   M... ...
0090  00000000 00000000 00000001 00000000   ...
00A0  000001C2 C2E30000 40404040 40404040   ...BBT..
00B0  00000000 00000000 00000000 00000000   ...
00C0  94000040 002E4000 00000000 00000000   M...
00D0  00000000 00000000 00000001 00000000   ...
00E0  000001C2 C2E30000 40404040 40404040   ...BBT..
00F0  00000000 00000000 00000000 00000000   ...
0100  94000040 002E4000 00000000 00000000   M...
0110  00000000 00000000 00000001 00000000   ...
0120  000001C2 C2E30000 40404040 40404040   ...BBT..
0130  00000000 00000000 00000000 00000000   ...
0140  94000040 002E4000 00000000 00000000   M...
0150  00000000 00000000 00000001 00000000   ...
CLEAR=END, ENTER=REFRESH, PF1=ACTIVE TASKS, PF2: MAIN INFO, PF8: FWD, PF7: BACK
```

Figure 9.15. A sample screen showing content of virtual strage starting at address '00196480' (in hexadecimal notation).

The third line has 0010 in the first field. This is offset; so storage displayed on this line is at address X'196480' plus X'0010', that is at X'196490'. This is how the other lines are to be read. Since there are 16 bytes displayed on each line, and there are 22 lines of storage display, the total number of bytes displayed on each screen is 16 times 22, that is 352 in decimal notation and 160 in hexadecimal.

Program BNINFP4 is the one that figures out the fields to be displayed and displays the map shown in Figure 9.15. The explanation of this program is given below.

What are the valid keys and their functions on the map of Figure 9.15? Pressing the Enter key will refresh the screen, meaning that you will receive the same map but with current and therefore possibly different values in the fields. Pressing the PF1 key will display the active task screen shown in Figure 9.13 where information about all the active tasks in the system is shown. Pressing the Clear key will terminate the transaction and you will receive a blank screen. Pressing the PF2 key will display the screen shown in Figure 9.12 containing general information about the running system.

Pressing PF8 will display the next page of storage where each page consists of 352 bytes. So, on the screen of Figure 9.15, if you pressed the PF8 key, you would receive storage display with the starting address of X'196480' plus X'160', that is, X'1965E0'. Pressing PF7 will display the previous page of storage. So, on the screen of Figure 9.15, if you pressed the PF7 key, you would receive storage display with the starting address of X'196480' minus X'160', i.e., X'196320'.

In what way can this display be useful in the day-to-day work of a system or application programmer? A CICS system programmer frequently has to display content of storage in the CICS region, mainly while solving a problem, but also while investigating a problem or understanding how things work. This facility can be of indispensable help to him in his work. This facility is also used to figure out why a task is in the wait state, as described in the previous section.

9.2.5 Explanation of General Information Display Program

Let us see what happens when a user types BNI1 on a blank screen and presses the Enter key. CICS would check the PCT and find that this transaction is associated with program BNINFP1. So, CICS would load this program into storage if it not already there and then transfer control to it.

Control would flow to the first executable statement in this program, which is line 9 in Figure 9.5. On this line, the DFHEIENT macro is used to set up entry logic, using Registers 8 and 9 to address the code, Register 10 to address the data, and Register 11 to address the EIB. On line 11, we are setting up a trap so that in the event of an abnormal condition arising on the execution of any CICS command, control would be transferred to label ERRCOND. On line 13, we are checking if the Clear key was pressed. Since this would not be the case in this example, control would flow to line 15 and then to line 17. On line 17, we are obtaining the VTAM application ID of the CICS region and storing it in SYSIDO, which is a field in map BNINFM1.

On line 18, we move the terminal ID to·the field on the map. On the next line we load the address of the CSA in Register 13 (CSACBAR). So, now the fields in the CSA are addressable. In the code that follows, we take one specific field from the CSA at a time, examine it, and move proper value into a map field. On line 40, we send the map BNINFM1 after erasing whatever might be on the screen. On the next line, we return to CICS, specifying BNI1 under the TRANSID option. This means that the next time, if the user pressed any key, CICS would automatically start transaction BNI1.

So, the user is presented with a screen that resembles the one in Figure 9.12. Suppose that the user reads the screen and presses the PF1 key. Control would flow to line 9 in Figure 9.5 again. The condition tested on line 15 would be true; so control would flow to label PF1KEY on line 43. On line 45, we would transfer control to program BNINFP2, which displays active tasks.

The explanation given above will enable you to understand this program thoroughly. This will allow you to insert the necessary logic in this program to display any other desired fields from the CSA or some other control block of CICS.

9.2.6 Explanation of Active Tasks Display Program

Let us see what happens when a user types BNI2 on a blank screen and presses the Enter key. CICS would check the PCT and find that this transaction is associated with program BNINFP2. So, CICS would load this program into storage if it is not already there and then transfer control to it.

Control would flow to the first executable statement in this program, which is line 27 in Figure 9.7. On this line, the DFHEIENT macro is used to set up entry logic, using Registers 8 and 9 to address the code, Register 10 to address the data, and Register 11 to address the EIB. On line 29, we are setting up a trap so that in the event of an abnormal condition arising on the execution of any CICS command, control would be transferred to label ERRCOND. On lines 32 through 39, we are checking which key was pressed. Since in this example the Enter key was pressed, control would flow to line 40. Here we obtain the VTAM application ID of the CICS region and store it in SYSIDO, which is a field on map BNINFM2. Next, on line 41, we store the address of the CSA in Register 13 (CSACBAR). On lines 42 through 55, we translate the four-byte address of the CSA into an eight-byte field containing hexadecimal characters only, and store the last six bytes of the result in ADDRCSAO, a field on the map. The translation is done by linking to program BNSUB01, which is given in Figure C.3 in Appendix C.

Let us see how we scan the active task chain. On line 56, we load Register

6 (DCACBAR) with the four-byte field at CSAACTBA, a field in the CSA. So Register 6 now contains the address of the first DCA (dispatch control area) on the active chain. On line 69, we load Register 1 with the address of CSAAC-TOF, a datum point in the CSA. On line 70, we compare Register 1 with Register 6. If they are the same, this means that the active task chain has been completely scanned. Otherwise, before executing line 72, Register 6 contains the address of the current task's dispatch control area. On line 72, we execute routine CHKTASK to examine and report on this task. On line 73, we load Register 6 with the address of the next task's dispatch control area. Next, we conditionally branch to label SCANACT, where we will again determine if the active task has been completely scanned.

Now let us see how we build the fields on detail lines on the map. On line 59, Register 3 is loaded with 20, because a maximum of 20 tasks only can be displayed on map BNINFM2. On line 74, we branch back to SCANACT, provided Register 3 has not become zero. This means we will only scan the first 20 tasks on the active chain. (But some tasks out of the first 20 may not be eligible for displaying on the map, due to the checking that is done on lines 85 through 96. So, it would be better if we scanned the first 20 tasks that are eligible for displaying on the map. This is an enhancement that you can make to this program and to BNINFP3.)

On line 72, we execute the CHKTASK routine through the BAL instruction. In this routine, we will scan the current task, and if it is eligible for displaying, we will build the fields on one line on the map. The first thing we do in the CHKTASK routine is save the return register on line 79. Next, on lines 85 through 96, we check if this task is a system task. If so, it will not be displayed on the map. This is done by immediately branching back to the caller (see lines 86, 88, 90, 92, 94, and 96).

If this is not a system task, control will flow to line 98, and this task will be reported on the map. As the comments indicate, the code following line 97 builds the task number on the map; the code following line 105 builds the terminal ID on the map; the code that follows line 109 builds the transaction ID field on the map; and the code following line 112 builds the dispatch control indicator (DCI) field on the map. The code following line 128 builds the address of ECB on the map, and the code following line 142 builds the address of facility control area on the map. BNSUB01 is linked to at many places to convert a field such as the dispatch control indicator byte or an address into a field twice as long containing only hexadecimal characters, which are 0 through 9, A, B, C, D, E, and F. The output field is then displayed on the map.

On line 159, we return to the caller. This transfers control to line 73, where we load Register 6 with the address of the next task's dispatch control area on the active chain. If 20 tasks have not been scanned yet, **and** if a task exists on the active task, we would again execute routine CHKTASK. Otherwise, we would branch to label SENDMAP, due to the execution of line 75 or 77. After coming to label SENDMAP on line 160, we would send map BNINFM2 and then return to CICS with BNI2 in the TRANSID option. This means that after receiving the map, if the user presses any key, CICS would start transaction BNI2.

This is how this program works. The explanation given above will enable you to understand this program thoroughly. Only a good understanding of this program will enable you to modify it to display some other important information related to an active task, for example, resources a task might be owning and/or waiting for.

9.2.7 Explanation of Suspended Tasks Display Program

Program BNINFP3 is very similar to BNINFP2. In fact, BNINFP3, shown in Figure 9.9, was not coded separately. It was created by taking a copy of BNINFP2 and making some changes to it, as described in the beginning of BNINFP2 in Figure 9.7. The reasons for making these changes are as follows:

1. Instead of using field CSAACTBA in the CSA, which contains the address of the first DCA on the active chain, we have to use field CSASUSBA in the CSA, which contains the address of the first DCA on the suspend chain.

2. Instead of using the address of CSAACTOF as a datum point to determine if we have come to the end of the active chain, we have to use the address of CSASUSOF as a datum point to determine if we have come to the end of the suspend chain.

3. Since both BNINFP2 and BNINFP3 use the same map, i.e., BNINFM2, which is in mapset BNINFS2 shown in Figure 9.8, we have to move SUS on the first line of the map to indicate this is the display of suspended tasks. In program BNINFP2, we move ACT on the first map line to indicate that this is the display of active tasks.

4. When the user presses the PF1 key on the screen showing suspended tasks, we must transfer control to program BNINFP2.

5. When we return to CICS after displaying the map with suspended tasks, we must use BNI3 in the TRANSID option of the RETURN command. This means that after viewing the screen, if the user presses any key, CICS would start transaction BNI3.

9.2.8 Explanation of Virtual Storage Display Program

It was mentioned earlier that you can't execute BNINFP4 by entering BNI4 on a blank screen. To execute it, you have to enter an address on the first line of the active or suspended task display and press the PF2 key. Suppose you enter 7C6110 on the first line of the active task display and press the PF2 key. Program BNINFP2 will build a seven-byte communication area and transfer control to BNINFP4. (See lines 180 through 182 in Figure 9.7.) The communication area will have the following content in character format:

`F7Cb11D`

The first character is F, so BNINFP4 will know that this is the first time it is receiving control. Control will flow to the first executable statement in BNINFP4, i.e., line 15 in Figure 9.10. On line 20, we would load Register 1 with the length of the communication area, which in this case would be 7. On Line 21, we would check if Register 1 contains zero. This would not be the case, so control would flow to line 23, and because EIBAID contains DFHENTER (because of line 173 in BNINFP2), on to line 30. On line 31, we are checking if the first character of the communication area is F. This would be the case; so, control would flow to label FIRST on line 40.

On line 42, we would store the last six bytes of the communication area into the last six bytes of FIELD8. On the next line, we would move the same six bytes in field ADDRO on map BNINFM3. In the code on lines 45 through 55 we would link to BNSUB01 to translate the eight-byte value at FIELD8 containing hexadecimal characters only into a four-byte field, which presumably would contain a valid address. Control would then flow to line 63 and then to label PROCEED1 on line 88.

The code on lines 90 through 98 is used to translate 352 bytes of storage starting at the address stored in FIELD4, into an area 704 bytes long containing hexadecimal characters only. The output is stored in DISPAREA, which is a 704-byte field on line 219 in dynamic storage, i.e., after DFHEISTG. The code following line 104 moves the data from DISPAREA to fields on 22 lines on the map. The Translate instruction on line 126 is used to translate storage into displayable characters so that they can be placed on the last two fields of eight characters each on each line on the map. After building all 22 lines on the map, control flows to line 139 where map BNINFM3 is sent after erasing the screen. On line 141, we return to CICS, specifying BNI4 as the next transaction and a one-byte communication area that contains N.

At this point, the user is presented with a screen that resembles the one shown in Figure 9.15. After viewing the screen, he can press any key. CICS will start transaction BNI4, and control would again flow to line 15 in BNINFP4. This time the program will receive a one-byte communication area that has N in it. You can follow the logic in this program and figure out what would happen. The processing will, of course, depend on what key was pressed.

25 Humor Items for the Humor Storage and Retrieval Facility

Below we present some items that can be stored on the humor/quotation master file. The items stored on the master file can be displayed one at a time on a random basis. The humor storage and retrieval facility was presented in Section 9.1 in Chapter 9.

1. Sign on a diner wall: Don't laugh at our coffee; someday you too will be weak and old.

2. What is good breeding? It is that quality that enables a person to wait in well mannered silence while the loudmouth gets the service.

3. I love work. I can sit and look at it for hours.

4. "Tell me the secret of your great success," the ambitious young man said to the successful businessman.

   "There is no secret," was the answer. "You just have to jump at your opportunities."

   "But how will I know when these opportunities come along?" the young man asked.

   "You won't; you just have to keep jumping."

5. The formula for success, J. Paul Getty once said, is easy: Rise early, work late, and strike oil.

6. A pat on the back is just a few centimeters away from a kick in the pants.—Murphy's Law.

7. The seven ages of mankind are: Spills. . . . Drills . . . Thrills . . . Bills . . . Ills . . . Pills . . . Wills

8. Often statistics are used as a drunken man uses a lamppost—for support, rather than illumination!

9. If you would be pungent, be brief; for it is with words as with a sunbeam. The more they are condensed, the deeper they burn.—Robert Southey

10. Music washes away from the soul the dust of everyday life.—Bernard Auerbach

11. There are people who can talk sensibly about a controversial issue without taking sides; they're called humorists.—Cullen Hightown

12. A man can live well, even in a palace.—Marcus Aurelius

13. The difference between a conviction and prejudice is that you can explain a conviction without getting angry.

14. If you laugh a lot, when you get older, your wrinkles will be in the right places.—Andrew V. Mason, M.D.

15. When you lose your temper, you lose more than your temper. So, don't get into the habit of losing your temper.—Barry K. Nirmal

16. "Jimmy, I'm ashamed of you. When I was your age, I would never have thought of telling a lie.
    "How old were you when you did think of it, daddy?"

17. You are young only once, but you can be immature indefinitely.

18. If something is confidential, it will be left in the copier machine.

19. Friends come and go, but enemies accumulate.

20. What is the easiest thing to do? I vote for snoring since you can do it while asleep.

21. Nobody is rich enough to buy back his past.—Oscar Wilde

22. For every child with a spark of genius, there are at least ten others with ignition trouble.

23. The problem with being punctual is that nobody's there to appreciate it.

24. To do is to be—Nietzsche.
    To be is to do—Sartre.
    Do be do be do be—Sinatra

25. Definition of a bachelor: a man who can get into the bed from either side.

Sample JCL Decks

In this appendix we present some JCL decks that can be used to perform tasks required to install various programs and facilities given in this book. These sample JCL decks are referred to mainly in Chapters 2 and 9 of this book.

B.1 SAMPLE JCL TO COMPILE AND LINK A CICS COMMAND-LEVEL PROGRAM WRITTEN IN COBOL

Figure B.1 gives the required JCL. But before you use this JCL, you must perform the following tasks:

Step 1. Enter the content of Figure B.1 in a JCL library.

Step 2. Enter the content of procedure KIKSCOB given in Figure B.2 in a source dataset. Now, make the following changes after consulting with your CICS system programmer. Change the value of PREFIX1 on line 2. You will note that on line 23, the name of the dataset after substitution will be CICS. R170.LOADLIB, and on line 44, the name of the dataset will be CICS.R170.COBLIB. So, for example, if the name of your LOADLIB dataset is CICS170.LOADLIB, and the name of the COBLIB dataset is CICS170.COBLIB, then change line 2 to the following:

```
//  PREFIX1=CICS170
```

On line 22 in Figure B.2, the program executed is DFHECP1$. This is the translator program for COBOL. If the name of this program at your installation is something else, you must change the value of SUFFIX on line 1 accordingly. For example, if the name of the translator at your shop is DFHECP2$, then change SUFFIX=1$ on line 1 to SUFFIX=2$.

```
***********************************************************************
 1    //JOBNAME    JOB  Card                  Note 1
 2    //*================================================================*
 3    //* THIS JOB WILL COMPILE A CICS COMMAND LEVEL PROGRAM WRITTEN IN COBOL.
 4    //* KIKSCOB IS STORED IN A SYSTEM PROCEDURE LIBRARY.
 5    //*================================================================*
 6    //* CHANGE THE JOB CARD TO SUIT YOUR INSTALLATION STANDARDS. AND THEN
 7    //* CHANGE WORDS SHOWN IN SMALL LETTERS ONLY BEFORE SUBMITTING THIS JOB.
 8    //*================================================================*
 9    //STEP01  EXEC KIKSCOB
10    //GENER.SYSUT1 DD DISP=SHR,DSN=source.pds.name(memsour)   Note 2
11    //COBOL.SYSLIB DD DISP=SHR,DSN=cics.r170.coblib           Note 3
12    //          DD DISP=SHR,DSN=copybook.pds.name             Note 4
13    //LKED.SYSLIB  DD DISP=SHR,DSN=cics.r170.loadlib          Note 5
14    //          DD DISP=SHR,DSN=loadlib.pds.name              Note 6
15    //LKED.SYSLMOD DD DISP=SHR,DSN=loadlib.pds.name(memload)  Note 7
***********************************************************************
```

Figure B.1. JCL to compile and link a CICS command-level program written in COBOL

494

```
*********************************************************************
1  //KIKSCOB  PROC SUFFIX=1$,OUTC='*',REG=2048K,WORK=SYSDA,BUF=128K,
2  //         PREFIX1='CICS.R170'
3  //*=============================================================*
4  //* THIS PROCEDURE IS USED TO COMPILE AND LINK A CICS COMMAND LEVEL
5  //* PROGRAM WRITTEN IN COBOL.
6  //*=============================================================*
7  //* THIS PROCEDURE CONSISTS OF FOUR STEPS:
8  //*    1.    COPY PROGRAM SOURCE INTO A TEMPORARY DATA SET.      *
9  //*    2.    EXEC THE COBOL TRANSLATOR                           *
10 //*    3.    EXEC THE COBOL COMPILER                             *
11 //*    4.    LINK-EDIT OUTPUT FROM COBOL COMPILER               *
12 //*=============================================================*
13 //GENER      EXEC    PGM=IEBGENER
14 //SYSPRINT   DD  SYSOUT=&OUTC
15 //SYSUT2     DD  DSN=&&PGMSRCE,
16 //               DISP=(NEW,PASS),
17 //               UNIT=SYSDA,
18 //               SPACE=(TRK,(1,1)),
19 //               DCB=(RECFM=FB,LRECL=80,BLKSIZE=4000)
20 //SYSIN DD DUMMY
21 //*=============================================================*
22 //TRANSL    EXEC   PGM=DFHECP&SUFFIX,REGION=&REG
23 //STEPLIB   DD  DSN=&PREFIX1..LOADLIB,DISP=SHR
24 //SYSPRINT  DD  SYSOUT=&OUTC
25 //SYSPUNCH  DD  DSN=&&SYSCIN,DISP=(,PASS),UNIT=&WORK,
26 //              DCB=BLKSIZE=400,SPACE=(400,(400,100))
27 //SYSIN     DD DSN=&&PGMSRCE,DISP=(OLD,DELETE)
28 //*=============================================================*
```

Figure B.2. Listing of procedure KIKSCOB used in JCL of Figure B.1.

```
29  //COBOL    EXEC PGM=IKFCBL00,REGION=&REG,
30  //         PARM='NOTRUNC,OPTIMIZE,NODYNAM,LIB,SIZE=&REG,BUF=&BUF,LANGLVL(1)'
31  //SYSPRINT DD    SYSOUT=&OUTC
32  //SYSIN    DD    DSN=&&SYSCIN,DISP=(OLD,DELETE)
33  //SYSLIN   DD    DSN=&&LOADSET,DISP=(MOD,PASS),
34  //               UNIT=&WORK,SPACE=(80,(800,400))
35  //SYSUT1   DD    UNIT=&WORK,SPACE=(460,(350,100))
36  //SYSUT2   DD    UNIT=&WORK,SPACE=(460,(350,100))
37  //SYSUT3   DD    UNIT=&WORK,SPACE=(460,(350,100))
38  //SYSUT4   DD    UNIT=&WORK,SPACE=(460,(350,100))
39  //*==================================================*
40  //LKED     EXEC PGM=IEWL,REGION=&REG,PARM=(LIST,LET,MAP,XREF),
41  //               COND=(4,LT,COBOL)
42  //SYSUT1   DD    UNIT=&WORK,DCB=BLKSIZE=1024,SPACE=(1024,(500,100))
43  //SYSPRINT DD    SYSOUT=&OUTC
44  //SYSLIN   DD    DSN=&PREFIX1..COBLIB(DFHEILIC),DISP=SHR
45  //         DD    DSN=&&LOADSET,DISP=(OLD,DELETE)
    ************************************************************************
```

Figure B.2. continued.

Step 3. You may also have to change the values of OUTC and WORK on line 1 in procedure KIKSCOB. OUTC should be assigned to the TSO-held SYSOUT class, and WORK should be assigned to the unit for creating temporary work files. Your MVS system programmer will help you in this task.

Step 4. Now copy this modified procedure in a system procedure library as member KIKSCOB. There are normally two system procedure libraries. SYS1.PROCLIB normally contains procedures supplied by IBM, and SYS2.PROCLIB normally contains non-IBM procedures. Your MVS systems programmer can help you decide which procedure library to use.

You may decide to initially use procedure KIKSCOB as an in-stream procedure. If so, copy the content of procedure KIKSCOB after the job card in Figure B.1, and then insert the following line after the last line of KIKSCOB copied:

```
// PEND
```

This will indicate the end of in-stream procedure KIKSCOB.

Step 5. In the JCL of Figure B.1, make the following changes to lines that have 'Note n' at the end.
Note 1. Change this line to a valid job card. The JOB card can consist of one or more lines.
Note 2. Change 'source.pds.name' to the name of PDS, which contains the source program written in COBOL. Change 'memsour' to the member name that contains the source COBOL program.
Note 3. Change 'cics.r170.coblib' to the full name of the CICS COBLIB dataset that was created at the time of CICS installation. Your CICS system programmer will tell you the full name of the COBLIB dataset.
Note 4. Change 'copybook.pds.name' to the full name of the PDS, which contains COBOL copybooks, e.g., copybooks created by the job that assembles CICS mapsets. For example, in COBOL program BNDISPTI of Figure 2.2, you have:

```
01 BNMAPTII COPY BNMAPTI.
```

So, the COBOL compiler will search datasets allocated under DDname SYSLIB for copybook member BNMAPTI. This copybook was created by the job to assemble map BNMAPTI. Map BNMAPTI is given in Figure 2.3.
Note 5. Replace 'cics.r170.loadlib' with the name of the CICS LOADLIB dataset that was created at the time of CICS installation. Your CICS system programmer will tell you the full name of the LOADLIB dataset. This LOADLIB dataset is also used in the start-up procedure or job used to start up CICS.
Note 6. Replace 'loadlib.pds.name' with the full name of the load library that contains load modules of non-IBM routines that are invoked through the CALL verb of COBOL. For example, program BNDISPTI of Figure 2.2 invokes program BNDATE through the CALL verb. So, the linkage editor will search libraries allocated under DDname SYSLIB for load module BNDATE.

Note 7. Replace 'loadlib.pds.name' with the full name of the load library where the load module of the program being compiled and linked will be stored. Replace 'memload' with the name you want the linkage editor to assign to the load module it creates. This name will be used in the PPT entry of this program.

Step 6. Submit the JCL to perform translation, compilation, and linking of the CICS Command Level COBOL program. Make sure the job does not abend and all job steps end in condition code of zero. Make sure the desired load module was created in the desired load library. If not, find out the cause of the problem, make necessary changes to the job, and resubmit it.

B.2 SAMPLE JCL TO ASSEMBLE AND LINK A CICS COMMAND-LEVEL PROGRAM WRITTEN IN ASSEMBLER

Figure B.3 gives the required JCL deck. But before you use this JCL, you must perform the following tasks:

Step 1. Enter the content of Figure B.3 in a JCL library.

Step 2. Enter the content of procedure KIKSASM given in Figure B.4 in a source dataset. Now make the following changes after consulting with your CICS system programmer. Change the value of INDEX on line 2. You will note that on line 13, the name of the dataset after substitution will be CICS.R170.LOADLIB, and on line 31, the name of the dataset will be CICS.R170.MACLIB. So, for example, if the name of your LOADLIB dataset is CICS170.LOADLIB, and the name of the MACLIB dataset is CICS170.MACLIB, then change line 2 to the following:

```
// INDEX=CICS170
```

On line 12, in Figure B.4, the program executed is DFHEAP1$. This is the translator program for Assembler. If the name of this program at your installation is something else, you must change the value of SUFFIX on line 1 accordingly. For example, if the name of the translator at your shop is DFHEAP2$, then change SUFFIX=1$ on line 1 to SUFFIX=2$.

Step 3. You may also have to change the values of OUTC and WORK on line 1 in procedure KIKSASM. OUTC should be assigned to the TSO held SYSOUT class, and WORK should be assigned to the unit for creating temporary work files. Your MVS system programmer will help you in this task.

Step 4. Now copy this modified procedure in a system procedure library as member KIKSASM. There are normally two system procedure libraries. SYS1.PROCLIB normally contains procedures supplied by IBM, and SYS2.PROCLIB normally contains non-IBM procedures. Your MVS systems programmer can help you decide which procedure library to use.

```
**************************************************************************
1  //jobname   JOB  Card                              Note 1
2  //*===================================================================*
3  //* JCL TO ASSEMBLE AND LINK A COMMAND LEVEL CICS PROGRAM IN ASSEMBLER
4  //*===================================================================*
5  //STEP01 EXEC KIKSASM
6  //TRN.SYSIN DD DISP=SHR,DSN=source.pds.name(memsour)    Note 2
7  //ASM.SYSLIB DD DISP=SHR,DSN=cics.r170.maclib           Note 3
8  //        DD DISP=SHR,DSN=copybook.pds.name             Note 4
9  //        DD DISP=SHR,DSN=SYS1.MACLIB
10 //LKED.SYSLIB  DD DISP=SHR,DSN=cics.r170.loadlib        Note 5
11 //        DD DISP=SHR,DSN=loadlib.pds.name              Note 6
12 //LKED.SYSLMOD DD DISP=SHR,DSN=loadlib.pds.name(memload)  Note 7
**************************************************************************
```

Figure B.3. JCL to assemble and link a CICS command-level program written in Assembler.

```
**************************************************************
 1  //KIKSASM  PROC SUFFIX=1$,OUTC='*',REG=2048K,WORK=SYSDA,
 2  //              INDEX='CICS.R170'
 3  //*===========================================================*
 4  //* THIS PROCEDURE IS USED TO ASSEMBLE AND LINK A CICS COMMAND LEVEL
 5  //* PROGRAM WRITTEN IN ASSEMBLER.
 6  //*===========================================================*
 7  //* THIS PROCEDURE CONSISTS OF THREE STEPS:                   *
 8  //*       1.  EXEC THE ASSEMBLER TRANSLATOR                    *
 9  //*       2.  EXEC THE ASSEMBLER                               *
10  //*       3.  LINK-EDIT OUTPUT FROM ASSEMBLER                  *
11  //*===========================================================*
12  //TRN     EXEC PGM=DFHEAP&SUFFIX,REGION=&REG
13  //STEPLIB DD DSN=&INDEX..LOADLIB,DISP=SHR
14  //SYSPRINT DD SYSOUT=&OUTC
15  //SYSPUNCH DD DSN=&&SYSCIN,DISP=(,PASS),UNIT=&WORK,
16  //              DCB=BLKSIZE=400,SPACE=(400,(400,100))
17  //*===========================================================*
18  //ASM     EXEC PGM=IEV90,REGION=&REG,PARM='DECK,NOOBJECT,LIST'
```

```
19   //SYSUT1    DD    UNIT=&WORK,SPACE=(1700,(400,400))
20   //SYSUT2    DD    UNIT=&WORK,SPACE=(1700,(400,400))
21   //SYSUT3    DD    UNIT=&WORK,SPACE=(1700,(400,400))
22   //SYSPUNCH  DD    DSN=&&LOADSET,UNIT=&WORK,DISP=(,PASS),
23   //                SPACE=(400,(100,100,1)),DCB=(RECFM=FB,LRECL=80,BLKSIZE=400)
24   //SYSPRINT   DD    SYSOUT=&OUTC
25   //SYSIN      DD    DSN=&&SYSCIN,DISP=(OLD,PASS)
26   //*==========================================================*
27   //LKED       EXEC  PGM=IEWL,REGION=&REG,COND=(8,LT,ASM),
28   //                PARM=(LIST,LET,XREF,MAP)
29   //SYSUT1     DD    UNIT=&WORK,DCB=BLKSIZE=1024,SPACE=(1024,(200,20))
30   //SYSPRINT   DD    SYSOUT=&OUTC
31   //SYSLIN     DD    DSN=&INDEX..MACLIB(DFHEILIA),DISP=SHR,DCB=BLKSIZE=80
32   //           DD    DSN=&&LOADSET,DISP=(OLD,DELETE)
33   //           DD    DDNAME=SYSIN
     //*************************************************************
```

Figure B.4. Listing of procedure KIKSASM used in JCL of Figure B.3.

But you may decide to initially use procedure KIKSASM as an in-stream procedure. If so, copy the content of procedure KIKSASM after the job card in Figure B.3, and then insert the following line after the last line of KIKSASM copied:

```
// PEND
```

This will indicate the end of in-stream procedure KIKSASM.

Step 5. In the JCL of Figure B.3, make the following changes to lines that have 'Note n' at the end.

Note 1. Change this line to a valid job card. The JOB card can consist of one or more lines.

Note 2. Change 'source.pds.name' to the name of source PDS which contains the source program written in assembler language. Change 'memsour' to the member name that contains the source program.

Note 3. Change 'cics.r170.maclib' to the full name of the CICS MACLIB dataset that was created at the time of CICS installation. Your CICS system programmer will tell you the full name of the MACLIB dataset. CICS macros used in assembler programs come from this MACLIB dataset. For example, in program COMPBLNK shown in Figure 2.6, you find macro DFHEIENT being used on line 22. So, member DFHEIENT must be present in the CICS MACLIB dataset.

Note 4. Change 'copybook.pds.name' to the full name of the PDS, which contains assembler copybooks and macros that are not supplied by IBM as part of CICS, e.g., copybooks created by the job that assembles CICS mapsets. For example, in many command-level assembler programs, you have the following line in the beginning:

```
COPY REGDEF
```

So, the assembler (program IEV90) will search datasets allocated under DDname SYSLIB for the copybook member REGDEF.

Note 5. Replace cics.r170.loadlib with the name of the CICS LOADLIB dataset that was created at the time of CICS installation. Your CICS system programmer will tell you the full name of the LOADLIB dataset. This LOADLIB dataset is also used in the start-up procedure or job used to start up CICS.

Note 6. Replace 'loadlib.pds.name' with the full name of the load library that contains load modules of non-IBM routines that are invoked through the CALL macro.

Note 7. Replace 'loadlib.pds.name' with the full name of the load library where the load module of the program being assembled and linked will be stored. Replace 'memload' with the name you want the linkage editor to assign to the load module it creates. This name will be used in the PPT entry of this program.

Step 6. Submit the JCL to perform translation, assembly, and linking of the CICS Command Level assembler program. Make sure the job does not abend and all job steps end in condition code of zero. Make sure the desired load module was created in the desired load library. If not, find out the cause of the problem, make necessary changes to the job, and resubmit it.

B.3 SAMPLE JCL TO ASSEMBLE AND LINK A CICS MACRO-LEVEL PROGRAM OR A SUBROUTINE WRITTEN IN ASSEMBLER

Figure B. 5 gives the JCL deck to perform this task. But before you use this JCL, you must perform the following tasks:

Step 1. Enter the content of Figure B.5 in a JCL library.

Step 2. In the JCL of Figure B.5, make the following changes to lines that have 'NOTE n' at the end.
NOTE 1. Change this line to a valid job card. The JOB card can consist of one or more lines.
NOTE 2. Change 'CICS.R170.MACLIB' to the full name of the CICS MACLIB dataset that was created at the time of CICS installation. Your CICS system programmer will tell you the full name of the MACLIB dataset. CICS macros used in assembler programs come from this MACLIB dataset. For example, in the CICS macro-level program BNTERMID shown in Figure 5.9, you find macro DFHTCA being used on line 11. So, member DFHTCA must be present in the CICS MACLIB dataset.
NOTE 3. Change 'COPYBOOK.PDS.NAME' to the full name of the PDS which contains assembler copybooks and macros that are not supplied by IBM as part of CICS. For example, in program BNTERMID of Figure 5.9, and in many other assembler programs, you have:

```
COPY REGDEF
```

So, the assembler (program IEV90) will search datasets allocated under DDname SYSLIB for the copybook member REGDEF.
NOTE 4. Change 'SOURCE.PDS.NAME' to the name of source PDS which contains the source program written in assembler language. Change 'MEM-SOUR' to the member name that contains the source program.
NOTE 5. Replace CICS.R170.LOADLIB with the name of the CICS LOADLIB dataset that was created at the time of CICS installation. Your CICS system programmer will tell you the full name of the LOADLIB dataset. This LOAD-LIB dataset is also used in the start-up procedure or job used to start up CICS.
NOTE 6. Replace 'LOADLIB.PDS.NAME' with the full name of the load library that contains load modules of non-IBM routines that are invoked through the CALL macro.
NOTE 7. Replace 'LOADLIB.PDS.NAME' with the full name of the load library where the load module of the program being assembled and linked will be

```
*******************************************************************
 1   //JOBNAME   JOB CARD                                    NOTE 1
 2   //*===============================================================
 3   //* THIS JOB WILL ASSEMBLE A PROGRAM WRITTEN IN ASSEMBLER. THE PROGRAM
 4   //* CAN BE A CICS MACRO LEVEL PROGRAM OR A PROGRAM TO RUN IN 'BATCH',
 5   //* OR AN ASSEMBLER SUBROUTINE THAT CAN BE 'CALLED' FROM A COBOL OR
 6   //* ASSEMBLER PROGRAM; E.G. ROUTINE HEXCOMP.
 7   //*===============================================================
 8   //STEP01   EXEC PGM=IEV90,
 9   //              PARM='DECK,NOLOAD,XREF(SHORT)'
10   //SYSUT1    DD   DSN=&&SYSUT1,UNIT=SYSDA,SPACE=(CYL,(10,10))
11   //SYSUT2    DD   DSN=&&SYSUT2,UNIT=SYSDA,SPACE=(CYL,(10,10))
12   //SYSUT3    DD   DSN=&&SYSUT3,UNIT=SYSDA,SPACE=(CYL,(10,10))
13   //SYSPRINT  DD   SYSOUT=*
14   //SYSLIB    DD   DISP=SHR,DSN=CICS.R170.MACLIB             NOTE 2
15   //          DD   DISP=SHR,DSN=COPYBOOK.PDS.NAME           NOTE 3
16   //          DD   DSN=SYS1.MACLIB,DISP=SHR
```

```
17  //SYSPUNCH DD   DSN=&&SYSPUNCH,DISP=(NEW,PASS),
18  //             UNIT=SYSDA,
19  //             SPACE=(TRK,(5,2,)),
20  //             DCB=(RECFM=FB,LRECL=80,BLKSIZE=3120)
21  //SYSIN    DD   DISP=SHR,DSN=SOURCE.PDS.NAME(MEMSOUR)        NOTE 4
22  //*==================================================================*
23  //STEP02   EXEC PGM=IEWL,PARM=(XREF,LET,LIST),
24  //             COND=(0,LT,STEP01)
25  //SYSLIN   DD   DSN=&&SYSPUNCH,DISP=OLD
26  //SYSLIB   DD   DISP=SHR,DSN=CICS.R170.LOADLIB              NOTE 5
27  //             DISP=SHR,DSN=LOADLIB.PDS.NAME                NOTE 6
28  //SYSLMOD  DD   DISP=SHR,DSN=LOADLIB.PDS.NAME(MEMLOAD)      NOTE 7
29  //SYSUT1   DD   DSN=&&SYSUT1,UNIT=SYSDA,SPACE=(CYL,(10,10))
30  //SYSPRINT DD   SYSOUT=*
//*******************************************************************
```

Figure B.5. JCL to assemble and link a Subroutine or a CICS macro-level
program

stored. Replace 'MEMLOAD' with the name you want the linkage editor to assign to the load module it creates. This name will be used in the PPT entry of this program.

Step 3. This job uses UNIT = SYSDA and SYSOUT = * on more than one line. You may have to change these to suit your installation standards. SYSOUT should be equated to a character used for TSO-held class, and UNIT should be equated to a value used for creating temporary work files.

Step 4. Submit the JCL to perform assembly and linking of the CICS macro-level assembler program or an assembler subroutine such as BNDATE or HEXCOMP given in Appendix C. Make sure the job does not abend and all job steps end in condition code of zero. Make sure the desired load module was created in the desired load library. If not, find out the cause of the problem, make necessary changes to the job, and resubmit it.

B.4   SAMPLE JCL TO ASSEMBLE AND LINK A CICS MAPSET

Figure B.6 gives the required JCL deck. But before you use this JCL, you must perform the following tasks:

Step 1. Enter the content of Figure B.6 in a JCL library.

Step 2. Enter the content of procedure KIKSMAP given in Figure B.7 in a source dataset. Now make the following changes after consulting with your CICS system programmer. Change the value of PREFIX1 on line 1. You will note that on lines 25 and 47, the name of the dataset after substitution will be CICS.R170.MACLIB. So, for example, if the name of your MACLIB dataset is CICS170.MACLIB, then change on line 1 to PREFIX1 = CICS170

```
// PREFIX1=CICS170
```

Step 3. You may also have to change values of OUTC on line 5 and WORK on line 6 in procedure KIKSMAP. OUTC should be assigned to the TSO held SYSOUT class, and WORK should be assigned to the unit for creating temporary work files. Your MVS system programmer will help you in this task.

Step 4. Now copy this modified procedure in a system procedure library as member KIKSMAP. There are normally two system procedure libraries. SYS1.PROCLIB normally contains procedures supplied by IBM, and SYS2.PROCLIB normally contains non-IBM procedures. Your MVS systems programmer can help you decide which procedure library to use.

But you may decide to initially use procedure KIKSMAP as an in-stream procedure. If so, copy the content of procedure KIKSMAP after the job card in Figure B.6, and then insert the following line after the last line of KIKSMAP copied:

```
// PEND
```

```
****************************************************************
 1    //Jobname    JOB   Card                         Note 1
 2    //*=======================================================
 3    //* THIS JCL IS TO ASSEMBLE A CICS MAP. PROCEDURE KIKSMAP IS STORED
 4    //* IN A SYSTEM PROCEDURE LIBRARY. INSERT VALID JOB CARD IN PLACE OF
 5    //* FIRST CARD AND THEN CHANGE ONLY WORDS IN SMALL LETTERS BEFORE
 6    //* SUBMITTING THIS JOB.
 7    //*=======================================================
 8    //STEP01  EXEC KIKSMAP
 9    //GENER.SYSUT1 DD DISP=SHR,DSN=source.pds.name(memsour)       Note 2
10    //LINKMAP.SYSLMOD DD DISP=SHR,DSN=loadlib.pds.name(memload)   Note 3
11    //ASMDSECT.SYSPUNCH DD DISP=SHR,DSN=copybook.pds.name(memcopy) Note 4
****************************************************************
```

Figure B.6. JCL to assemble and link a CICS mapset

507

```
************************************************************************
 1  //KIKSMAP PROC PREFIX1='CICS.R170',    PREFIX OF CICS DATA SETS
 2  //             A=,                      A=A FOR ALIGNED MAP
 3  //             ASMBLR=IEV90,            ASSEMBLER PROGRAM NAME
 4  //             REG=256K,                REGION FOR ASSEMBLY
 5  //             OUTC='*',                PRINT SYSOUT CLASS
 6  //             WORK=SYSDA               WORK FILE UNIT
 7  //*==========================================================*
 8  //*   CREATE TEMPORARY WORK FILE                             *
 9  //*==========================================================*
10  //GENER      EXEC    PGM=IEBGENER
11  //SYSPRINT   DD   SYSOUT=&OUTC
12  //SYSUT1     DD   DUMMY
13  //SYSUT2     DD   DSN=&&MAPSRCE,
14  //                DISP=(NEW,PASS),
15  //                UNIT=SYSDA,
16  //                SPACE=(TRK,(1,1)),
17  //                DCB=(RECFM=FB,LRECL=80,BLKSIZE=4000)
18  //SYSIN DD DUMMY
19  //*==========================================================*
20  //*   ASSEMBLE MAP                                           *
21  //*==========================================================*
22  //ASMMAP     EXEC PGM=&ASMBLR,REGION=&REG,
23  //                PARM='SYSPARM(&A.MAP),DECK,NOLOAD'
24  //SYSPRINT   DD SYSOUT=&OUTC
25  //SYSLIB     DD DSN=&PREFIX1..MACLIB,DISP=SHR
26  //           DD DSN=SYS1.MACLIB,DISP=SHR
27  //SYSUT1     DD UNIT=&WORK,SPACE=(CYL,(5,5))
```

```
28  //SYSUT2    DD  UNIT=&WORK,SPACE=(CYL,(5,5))
29  //SYSUT3    DD  UNIT=&WORK,SPACE=(CYL,(5,5))
30  //SYSPUNCH  DD  DSN=&&MAP,DISP=(,PASS),UNIT=&WORK,
31  //             DCB=(RECFM=FB,LRECL=80,BLKSIZE=400),
32  //             SPACE=(400,(50,50))
33  //SYSIN     DD  DSN=&&MAPSRCE,DISP=(OLD,PASS)
34  //*==================================================*
35  //*  CREATE LOAD MODULE FOR MAP IN THE LOAD LIBRARY  *
36  //*==================================================*
37  //LINKMAP   EXEC PGM=IEWL,PARM='LIST,LET,XREF'
38  //SYSPRINT  DD  SYSOUT=&OUTC
39  //SYSUT1    DD  UNIT=&WORK,SPACE=(1024,(20,20))
40  //SYSLIN    DD  DSN=&&MAP,DISP=(OLD,DELETE)
41  //*==================================================*
42  //*  ASSEMBLE MAP AND CREATE COPYBOOK IN COPYBOOK LIBRARY  *
43  //*==================================================*
44  //ASMDSECT  EXEC PGM=&ASMBLR,REGION=&REG,
45  //             PARM='SYSPARM(&A.DSECT),DECK,NOLOAD'
46  //SYSPRINT  DD  SYSOUT=&OUTC
47  //SYSLIB    DD  DSN=&PREFIX1..MACLIB,DISP=SHR
48  //          DD  DSN=SYS1.MACLIB,DISP=SHR
49  //SYSUT1    DD  UNIT=&WORK,SPACE=(CYL,(5,5))
50  //SYSUT2    DD  UNIT=&WORK,SPACE=(CYL,(5,5))
51  //SYSUT3    DD  UNIT=&WORK,SPACE=(CYL,(5,5))
52  //SYSIN     DD  DSN=&&MAPSRCE,DISP=(OLD,DELETE)
```

Figure B.7. Listing of procedure KIKSMAP used in JCL of Figure B.6.

This will indicate the end of in-stream procedure KIKSMAP.

Step 5. In the JCL of Figure B.6, make the following changes to lines that have 'Note n' at the end.

Note 1. Change this line to a valid job card. The JOB card can consist of one or more lines.

Note 2. Change 'source.pds.name' to the name of source PDS which contains the source of the mapset coded using assembler macros. Change 'memsour' to the member name that contains the mapset. (Note: 'memsour', 'memload', and 'memcopy' should be given identical names, i.e., the name of the mapset that will be used in the PPT entry.)

Note 3. Replace 'loadlib.pds.name' with the full name of the load library where the load module of the mapset being assembled and linked will be stored. Replace 'memload' with the name you want the linkage editor to assign to the load module it creates. This name will be used in the PPT entry of this mapset.

Note 4. Change 'copybook.pds.name' to the full name of the PDS where copybook created by this job will be stored. Replace 'memcopy' with the name you want assigned to the copybook. This name should be the same as the name of the mapset.

Step 6. Submit the JCL to perform assembly and linking of the CICS mapset. Make sure the job does not abend and all job steps end in condition code of zero. Make sure the desired load module was created in the desired load library and that the desired copybook was created in the desired copybook library. If not, find out the cause of the problem, make necessary changes to the job, and resubmit it.

Subprograms and Copylib Members Used By One or More Programs

In this appendix we present those subprograms that can be invoked by any higher-level program. These subprograms are used by one or more programs in Chapters 2, 5, and 9 of this book.

C.1   DATE CONVERSION SUBPROGRAM BNDATE

This program converts dates from one format to another.

Procedure for Installing Subprogram BNDATE

Step 1. Enter this program shown in Figure C.1 in member BNDATE of a source PDS.

Step 2. Compile and link this subprogram using the JCL given in Section B.3 in Appendix B. This job will create load module BNDATE in your load library. This load library must be included under DDname SYSLIB of the job step that executes linkage editor to link any program that invokes BNDATE using the CALL statement of COBOL or the CALL macro of Assembler.

Procedure for Using This Program

See program BNDISPTI in Figure 2.2 for an example of how to call this subprogram.

```
       *****************************************************************
    1          TITLE 'BNDATE: DATE CONVERSION ROUTINE BY B.K. NIRMAL'
    2  *****************************************************************
    3  * FOLLOWING IS AN EXAMPLE OF CALLING THIS ROUTINE IN A COBOL PROGRAM:*
    4  *    CALL 'BNDATE' USING IN-TYPE OUT-TYPE IN-DATE OUT-DATE            *
    5  *                                                                    *
    6  * THE FOLLOWING VALUES OF IN-TYPE ARE CURRENTLY SUPPORTED:           *
    7  *                                                                    *
    8  * 9 :  SYSTEM DATE IS DESIRED.  THE CALLER MAY NOT SPECIFY THE FOURTH *
    9  *      PARAMETER, IN WHICH CASE THE SYSTEM DATE SHOULD BE PLACED IN   *
   10  *      IN THE DATA AREA SPECIFIED BY THE THIRD PARAMETER.            *
   11  *                                                                    *
   12  * 4 :  IN-DATE IS IN THE JULIAN FORMAT (YY.DDD).                     *
   13  *                                                                    *
   14  * THE FOLLOWING VALUES OF OUT-TYPE ARE CURRENTLY SUPPORTED:          *
   15  *                                                                    *
   16  * 3 :  OUT-DATE IS DESIRED IN THE YY/MM/DD FORMAT.                   *
   17  *                                                                    *
   18  * NOTE: WHEN IN-TYPE = 9, ONLY THE FIRST THREE PARAMETERS MAY BE     *
   19  *       SPECIFIED ON THE CALL STATEMENT.                             *
   20  *****************************************************************
   21         COPY  REGDEF
   22         TITLE 'DSECT DEFINITIONS'
   23  DSECT1  DSECT
   24  INDATE  DS    0CL8                8-BYTE DATE STRING
   25  INYY    DS    CL2                 YEAR
   26          DS    CL1                 SLASH
   27  INMM    DS    CL2                 MONTH
   28          DS    CL1                 SLASH
   29  INDD    DS    CL2                 DAY
```

```
30          ORG   INDATE
31 INJYY    DS    CL2               JULIAN YEAR (ZONED)
32 INJX     DS    CL1               C' '
33 INJDDD   DS    CL3               JULIAN DAY  (ZONED)
34 DSECT2   DSECT
35 OUTDATE  DS    0CL8              8-BYTE DATE STRING
36 OUTYY    DS    CL2               YEAR
37          DS    CL1               SLASH
38 OUTMM    DS    CL2               MONTH
39          DS    CL1               SLASH
40 OUTDD    DS    CL2               DAY
41          ORG   OUTDATE
42 OUTJYY   DS    CL2               JULIAN YEAR (ZONED)
43 OUTJX    DS    CL1               C' '
44 OUTJDDD  DS    CL3               JULIAN DAY  (ZONED)
45 BNDATE   CSECT
46          USING *,R15             R15 ADDRESSES ENTRY POINT
47          STM   R14,R12,12(R13)   SAVE REGISTERS
48          LA    R12,0(R13)        R12 = A(PREVIOUS SAVEAREA)
49          ST    R13,*+12          ESTABLISH BACKWARD CHAIN
50          BAL   R13,*+(4*19)      R13 = A(CURRENT SAVEAREA)
51          USING *,R13             SAVEAREA ADDR = BASE ADDR
52          DS    18F               SAVEAREA
53          DROP  R15               NO FURTHER NEED FOR R15
54          ST    R13,8(R12)        ESTABLISH FORWARD CHAIN
55          LM    R9,R12,0(R1)      REGS 9-12 = PARAMETER ADDRESSES
56          LTR   R11,R11           WERE ONLY 3 PARAMETERS SPECIFIED?
57          BNM   NEXT1             NO, SKIP
```

Figure C.1. Source code of Subprogram BNDATE

```
58            LR      R12,R11                    YES; SET PARM4 = PARM3
59  NEXT1     EQU     *
60            USING   INDATE,R11                 R11 = ADDRESS OF INPUT AREA
61            USING   OUTDATE,R12                R12 = ADDRESS OF OUTPUT AREA
62            L       R9,0(R9)                   R9  = FUNCTION NUMBER
63            C       R9,=F'4'                   IS FUNCTION = 4 ?
64            BE      FUNC04                     YES, BRANCH
65            C       R9,=F'9'                   IS FUNCTION = 9 ?
66            BE      FUNC09                     YES, BRANCH
67            B       ERROR1           ERROR1 IS FOR INVALID FUNCTION
68  ***** ERROR RETURN POINTS FOLLOW *****************************
69  ERROR1    MVC     OUTDATE,=C'ERROR 01'
70            B       GETOUT
71  ERROR2    MVC     OUTDATE,=C'ERROR 02'
72            B       GETOUT
73  GETOUT    DS      0H
74            L       R13,4(R13)
75            LM      R14,R12,12(R13)
76            XR      R15,R15
77            BR      R14
78  *****************************************************************
79            TITLE 'CONVERT JULIAN DATE INTO YY/MM/DD FORMAT'
80  FUNC04    EQU     *
81  * R11 ALREADY POINTS TO THE DATA AREA CONTAINING INPUT DATE IN JULIAN.
82            BAL     R14,CONVRTN3
83            B       GETOUT
84  *****************************************************************
85            TITLE 'PROVIDE SYSTEM DATE IN YY/MM/DD FORMAT'
86  FUNC09    EQU     *
87            TIME
```

514

```
88           ST    R1,SYSDATE        SYSDATE = 00YYDDDF
89           MVC   WORK1(7),=X'F021204B202020'
90           ED    WORK1(7),SYSDATE+1
91           LA    R11,WORK1+1       R11 = A(SOURCE AREA)
92           BAL   R14,CONVRTN3      CONVERT JULIAN TO YY/MM/DD
93           B     GETOUT
94 ********  CONVERT JULIAN DATE TO  YY/MM/DD FORMAT  *********
95 CONVRTN3  EQU   *
96           ST    R14,SAVEDR14      SAVE RETURN ADDRESS
97           BAL   R14,EDITJUL       VALIDATE INPUT
98           BNE   ERROR2
99           PACK  DOUBLE,INJDDD     PACK JULIAN DAY
100          CVB   R2,DOUBLE         CONVERT TO BINARY
101          STH   R2,JULDAY
102          LA    R3,26             R3 = (12 MONTHS * 2 BYTES/MONTH) + 2
103          MVC   JULTAB,JTN        INIT TABLE FOR NON-LEAP YEAR
104          TM    BINYEAR+1,3       IS IT A LEAP YEAR?
105          BNZ   FUNC03A           NO  - BRANCH
106          MVC   JULTAB,JTL        YES - INIT TABLE FOR LEAP YEAR
107          SPACE
108 FUNC03A  EQU   *                 LOOP TO FIND MONTH
109          SH    R3,=H'2'          DECREMENT POINTER
110          CH    R2,JULTAB-2(R3)   LOOK FOR LOW ENTRY IN TABLE
111          BNH   FUNC03A           KEEP LOOKING UNTIL FOUND
112          SH    R2,JULTAB-2(R3)   R2 = DAY OF MONTH
113          SRL   R3,1              R3 = MONTH OF YEAR
114          CVD   R2,DOUBLE         CONVERT DAY TO DECIMAL
115          UNPK  OUTDD,DOUBLE+6(2)
```

Figure C.1.   continued.

```
116          OI      OUTDD+1,C'0'        OUTPUT IS ZONED DECIMAL
117          CVD     R3,DOUBLE           CONVERT MONTH TO DECIMAL
118          UNPK    OUTMM,DOUBLE+6(2)
119          OI      OUTMM+1,C'0'        OUTPUT IS ZONED DECIMAL
120          MVI     OUTDATE+2,C'/'      YY/MM...
121          MVI     OUTDATE+5,C'/'      YY/MM/..
122          MVC     OUTYY,INJYY         YY/MM/DD
123          L       R14,SAVEDR14        RESTORE RETURN ADDRESS
124          BR      R14                 RETURN TO CALLER
125 ***************************************************************
126 * THIS ROUTINE EDITS THE JULIAN DATE SUPPLIED BY THE CALLER IN THE   *
127 * YY.DDD FORMAT.  IF THE INPUT DATE IS FOUND TO BE VALID, THE YEAR WILL*
128 * BE CONVERTED INTO BINARY AND STORED IN THE HALFWORD 'BINYEAR'.      *
129 * ON EXIT FROM THIS ROUTINE, THE CONDITION CODE IN THE PSW MUST BE    *
130 * CHECKED.  CONDITION CODE = 0 MEANS THAT THE DATE WAS FOUND TO BE    *
131 * VALID.  ANY OTHER VALUE MEANS THAT AN ERROR WAS DETECTED.  HENCE THE *
132 * FOLLOWING METHOD OF CALLING THIS ROUTINE IS RECOMMENDED:            *
133 *          BAL     R14,EDITJUL                                        *
134 *          BNE     ERROR2                                             *
135 ***************************************************************
136 EDITJUL  EQU     *
137          CLI     INJX,C'.'           CHECK FOR DECIMAL POINT
138          BNER    R14                 ERROR IF NOT EQUAL
139          TRT     INJYY,NTAB          TEST YEAR FOR NUMERICS
140          BNER    R14                 ERROR IF NOT NUMERIC
141          TRT     INJDDD,NTAB         TEST DAY FOR NUMERICS
142          BNER    R14                 ERROR IF NOT NUMERIC
143          PACK    DOUBLE,INJYY        PACK YEAR
144          CVB     R2,DOUBLE           CONVERT TO BINARY
145          STH     R2,BINYEAR          STORE YEAR
```

```
146          CLC   INJDDD,=C'001'    TEST FOR MINIMUM DAY
147          BLR   R14               ERROR IF LOW
148          CLC   INJDDD,=C'366'    TEST FOR MAXIMUM DAY
149          BHR   R14               ERROR IF HIGH
150          BL    VALIDJUL          OK IF LOW
151          N     R2,=F'3'          IS IT A LEAP YEAR?
152          BR    R14               OK IF YES, ERROR IF NO
153 VALIDJUL EQU   *
154          XR    R2,R2             SET CONDITION CODE TO ZERO
155          BR    R14               OK RETURN
156 *********************************
157 * WORK AREAS
158 *********************************
159 DOUBLE   DS    D                 GENERAL WORKAREA
160 WORK1    DS    D                 C'0YY.DDDX'
161 SYSDATE, DS    F                 X'00DDYYYF'
162 SAVEDR14 DS    A                 RETURN ADDRESS FOR FUNC03
163 JULDAY   DS    H                 JULIAN DAY IN THE BINARY FORMAT
164 JULTAB   DS    CL24              WILL CONTAIN EITHER JTN OR JTL
165 JTN      DC    H'0,31,59,90,120,151,181,212,243,273,304,334'
166 JTL      DC    H'0,31,60,91,121,152,182,213,244,274,305,335'
167 NTAB     DC    240X'1',10X'0',6X'1'
168 BINDAY   DS    H
169 BINMONTH DS    H
170 BINYEAR  DS    H
171          LTORG
172          END
***********************************************************************
```

Figure C.1. continued.

C.2 SUBPROGRAM HEXCOMP TO COMPRESS A NUMBER OF BYTES CONTAINING HEXADECIMAL CHARACTERS INTO HALF AS MANY BYTES

This subprogram is called using the CALL statement of COBOL or the CALL macro of Assembler. The calling program can be a COBOL or an Assembler program for execution in batch or under CICS command level.

Procedure for Installing Subprogram HEXCOMP

Step 1. Enter this subprogram shown in Figure C.2 in member HEXCOMP of a source PDS.

Step 2. Compile and link this subprogram using the JCL given in Section B.3 in Appendix B. This job will create load module HEXCOMP in your load library. This load library must be included under DDname SYSLIB of the job step that executes the linkage editor to link any program that invokes HEXCOMP using the CALL statement of COBOL or the CALL macro of Assembler.

Procedure for Using This Program

In a COBOL program, the following calling sequence must be used:

```
CALL'HEXCOMP'USING in-area, out-area, length, status-code
where   in-area     = input string of n bytes where n must be even.
        out-area    = output string of n/2 bytes.
        length      = length of output-string; must be defined as
                      full word binary, e.g., PIC S9(8) COMP SYNC.
        status-code = one-byte flag, set by HEXCOMP to indicate
                      result of processing. S = Success; B =
                      Failure, because input string contains an
                      invalid character.
```

See program BNUTL01 in Figure 2.8 for an example of how to call this subprogram.

C.3 SUBPROGRAM BNSUB01 TO EXPAND A NUMBER OF BYTES INTO TWICE AS MANY BYTES CONTAINING HEXADECIMAL CHARACTERS OR VICE VERSA

This program, shown in Figure C.3, is invoked by programs BNINFP2, BNINFP3, and BNINFP4 presented in Chapter 9. When you invoke this subprogram to translate a field of n bytes into another field that is twice as long, the input field can contain any character, whereas the output field will contain only hexadecimal characters which are 0 through 9, A, B, C, D, E, and F. This is called translating a smaller field into a larger field. On the other hand, you

```
***********************************************************************
 1  *          DATA SET HEXCOMP        AT LEVEL 006
 2  HEXCOMP   CSECT
 3  ***********************************************************************
 4  * UTILITY TO CONVERT A STRING OF BYTES CONTAINING HEX CHARACTERS ONLY
 5  * INTO HALF AS MANY BYTES WITH HEX DE-CONVERSION.
 6  *
 7  *     PARAMETERS PASSED TO THIS PROGRAM ARE AS FOLLOWS:
 8  *
 9  *        1 - STRING TO BE COMPRESSED (INPUT)
10  *        2 - OUTPUT STRING (SMALLER FIELD)
11  *        3 - LENGTH OF OUTPUT STRING (FULL-WD BINARY)
12  *        4 - ONE BYTE RETURN CODE (S= SUCCESS, B= BAD CHARACTER; FAILURE
13  *            DUE TO INPUT AREA CONTAINING INVALID HEX CHAR.
14  *
15  * THIS PGM MOVES A QUESTION MARK IN STATUS CODE BEFORE STARTING TO DO
16  * ANY COMPRESSION.
17  ***********************************************************************
18  * MACROS USED:
19  *   REGDEF
20  ***********************************************************************
21            COPY   REGDEF
22            B      28(R15)              BRANCH AROUND NEXT THREE CONSTANTS
23            DC     CL8'HEXCOMP'         CONSTANT
24            DC     CL8'YY/MM/DD'        DATE OF THIS ASSEMBLY
25            DC     CL8'CICSBOOK'        ANOTERH CONSTANT
26            STM    14,12,12(13)         SAVE R14,R15...R12
27            LR     R12,R15              LOAD R12 WITH ADDRESS OF THIS PGM
```

Figure C.2. Source code of Subprogram HEXCOMP

```
28          USING HEXCOMP,R12
29          ST    R13,SAVE+4      SAVE R13
30          LA    R13,SAVE        POINT R13 TO MY SAVE AREA
31          SR    R3,R3           CLEAR R3
32          L     R3,8(R1)        R3 POINTS TO AREA CONTAINING LENGTH
33          L     R3,0(R3)        R3 CONTAINS LENGTH OF SMALLER AREA
34          L     R4,4(R1)        R4 POINTS TO OUTPUT AREA (SMALLER FIELD)
35          L     R6,0(R1)        R6 POINTS TO INPUT AREA (LARGER FIELD)
36          L     R2,12(R1)       R2 POINTS TO ONE BYTE AREA WITH RET CODE
37          MVI   0(R2),C'?'      INITIALIZE STATUS CODE TO UNDETERMINED
38    LOOP  EQU   *
39          SR    R5,R5
40          MVI   0(R4),X'00'
41          BAL   R14,DETRANS
42          IC    R5,0(R4)        INSERT OUTPUT CHAR IN R5
43          SLL   R5,4            SHIFT LEFT BY 4 BITS
44          STC   R5,0(R4)        STORE R5 AT OUTPUT LOCATION
45          LA    R6,1(R6)        ADVANCE R6 BY 1
46          BAL   R14,DETRANS
47          LA    R4,1(R4)        ADVANCE R4
48          LA    R6,1(R6)        ADVANCE R6
49          BCT   R3,LOOP         LOOP BACK IF NOT EXHAUSTED
50          MVI   0(R2),C'S'      INDICATE SUCCESS TO CALLER
51          B     GETOUT
52 DETRANS  EQU   *
53 TEST0    CLI   0(R6),C'0'
54          BNE   TEST1
55          BR    14
56 TEST1    CLI   0(R6),C'1'
57          BNE   TEST2
```

```
58         OI    0(R4),X'01'
59         BR    14
60  TEST2  CLI   0(R6),C'2'
61         BNE   TEST3
62         OI    0(R4),X'02'
63         BR    14
64  TEST3  CLI   0(R6),C'3'
65         BNE   TEST4
66         OI    0(R4),X'03'
67         BR    14
68  TEST4  CLI   0(R6),C'4'
69         BNE   TEST5
70         OI    0(R4),X'04'
71         BR    14
72  TEST5  CLI   0(R6),C'5'
73         BNE   TEST6
74         OI    0(R4),X'05'
75         BR    14
76  TEST6  CLI   0(R6),C'6'
77         BNE   TEST7
78         OI    0(R4),X'06'
79         BR    14
80  TEST7  CLI   0(R6),C'7'
81         BNE   TEST8
82         OI    0(R4),X'07'
83         BR    14
84  TEST8  CLI   0(R6),C'8'
85         BNE   TEST9
```

Figure C.2. continued

```
 86           OI    0(R4),X'08'
 87           BR    14
 88   TEST9   CLI   0(R6),C'9'
 89           BNE   TEST10
 90           OI    0(R4),X'09'
 91           BR    14
 92   TEST10  CLI   0(R6),C'A'
 93           BNE   TEST11
 94           OI    0(R4),X'0A'
 95           BR    14
 96   TEST11  CLI   0(R6),C'B'
 97           BNE   TEST12
 98           OI    0(R4),X'0B'
 99           BR    14
100   TEST12  CLI   0(R6),C'C'
101           BNE   TEST13
102           OI    0(R4),X'0C'
103           BR    14
104   TEST13  CLI   0(R6),C'D'
105           BNE   TEST14
106           OI    0(R4),X'0D'
```

```
107                 BR      14
108     TEST14      CLI     0(R6),C'E'
109                 BNE     TEST15
110                 OI      0(R4),X'0E'
111                 BR      14
112     TEST15      CLI     0(R6),C'F'
113                 BNE     BADCHAR
114                 OI      0(R4),X'0F'
115                 BR      14
116     BADCHAR     EQU     *
117                 MVI     0(R2),C'B'
118     GETOUT      L       R13,SAVE+4      RESTORE R13
119                 LM      14,12,12(13)    RESTORE R14,R15...R12
120                 LA      R15,0           MOVE ZERO INTO R15
121                 BR      R14             RETURN TO CALLER
122     SAVE        DC      18F'0'
123                 END
```

****

Figure C.2. continued.

can also invoke this subprogram to translate a field of n bytes (where n is even) into a field that is half that long. In this case, the input field can have only hexadecimal characters, which are 0 through 9, A, B, C, D, E, and F, whereas the output field can have any character. This is called translating a larger field into a smaller field.

Procedure For Installing Subprogram BNSUB01

Step 1. Enter this program in member BNSUB01 of a source PDS.

Step 2. Compile and link program BNSUB01 using the JCL given in Section B.2 in Appendix B. This job will create load module BNSUB01 in your load library. This load library must be included under DDname DFHRPL in the CICS start-up procedure or job.

Step 3. Define the following in the CICS PPT:

```
PROGRAM     BNSUB01
GROUP       CICSBOOK
LANGUAGE    ASSEMBLER
```

Other parameters for BNSUB01 in the PPT should be the same as those for the sample program BNPROG1 given in Section 1.6

Procedure for Using This Program

In an Assembler language program, you can invoke this subprogram in this manner:

```
EXEC CICS LINK PROGRAM('BNSUB01') COMMAREA(COMMAREA) LENGTH(11)
```

The communication area passed to BNSUB01 is always of 11 bytes, aligned on a fullword, whose layout is as follows:

START POSITION	END POSITION	TYPE OF FIELD	LENGTH OF FIELD	CONTENT OF FIELD
1	4	Fullword	4	Address of input area
5	8	Fullword	4	Address of output area
9	10	Halfword	2	Length of smaller field in binary format
11	11	Character	1	Request type: A = Translate smaller field into larger field B = Translate larger field into smaller field

```
*****************************************************************************
 1          COPY  REGDEF
 2   EIBREG  EQU   11
 3   BNSUB01 DFHEIENT CODEREG=(9),DATAREG=10,EIBREG=11
 4   *=================================================================*
 5   * CONVERT A SMALL  FIELD INTO LARGE  FIELD, AND VICE VERSA. THE LARGE
 6   * FIELD CONTAINS PRINTABLE CHARACTERS (0-9,A,B,C,D,E,F) WHEREAS SMALL
 7   * FIELD CAN CONTAIN ANY VALUE (X'00' THRU X'FF')
 8   *=================================================================*
 9   * R1 WILL BE USED AS A WORK REGISTER.
10   * R3 WILL CONTROL NUMBER OF TIMES THE LOOP IS EXECUTED.
11   *    IT WILL CONTAIN LENGTH OF SMALLER FIELD.
12   *    (WILL BE DECREMENTED BY BCT INSTRUCTION)
13   * R4 WILL POINT TO THE CHARACTER BEING TRANSLATED IN THE INPUT AREA, IF
14   *    TRANSLATING SMALL TO BIG.
15   * R4 WILL POINT TO THE CHARACTER IN THE OUTPUT AREA IF
16   *    TRANSLATING BIG TO SMALL.
17   *    (WILL MOVE ONE CHAR AT A TIME TO THE RIGHT)
18   * R6 WILL POINT TO THE POSITION IN OUTPUT AREA, IF
19   *    TRANSLATING SMALL TO BIG.
20   * R6 WILL POINT TO THE POSITION IN INPUT  AREA, IF
21   *    TRANSLATING BIG TO SMALL.
22   *    (WILL MOVE ONE CHAR AT A TIME TO THE RIGHT)
23   *=================================================================*
24          L     R1,DFHEICAP        R1 POINTS TO COMM AREA.
25          CLI   10(R1),C'A'
26          BE    TRANSSTL           TRANSLATE SMALL TO LARGE
27          CLI   10(R1),C'B'
```

Figure C.3.   Source code of CICS program BNSUB01

```
28       BE    TRANSLTS
29       MVI   10(R1),C'F'
30 GETOUT  EXEC  CICS RETURN
31 TRANSSTL EQU   *
32       SR    R3,R3          CLEAR R3
33       LH    R3,8(R1)       LOAD LENGTH INTO R3
34       L     R4,0(R1)       R4 POINTS TO INPUT AREA
35       L     R6,4(R1)       R6 POINTS TO OUTPUT AREA
36 LOOP    EQU   *
37       SR    R5,R5          CLEAR R5
38       IC    R5,0(R4)       INSERT IN 5 ONE CHAR FROM INPUT AREA
39       SRL   R5,4           SHIFT RIGHT- FOUR BITS
40       BAL   14,TRANSLAT
41       IC    R5,0(R4)       FETCH ONE CHAR FROM INPUT INTO R5
42       SR    R1,R1          CLEAR R1
43       LA    R1,15(R1)      ADD 15 TO R1.
44       NR    R5,R1          CLEAR BITS 24-27 IN R5
45       LA    R6,1(R6)       ADVANCE R6 TO NEXT SLOT IN OUTPUT AREA
46       BAL   14,TRANSLAT
47       LA    R4,1(R4)       ADVANCE R4 TO NEXT SLOT IN INPUT AREA
48       LA    R6,1(R6)       ADVANCE R6 TO NEXT SLOT IN OUTPUT AREA
49 * THE FOLLOWING COMMAND CAN BE USEFUL IN DEBUGGING THRU CEDF.
50 *****   EXEC  CICS ADDRESS EIB(EIBREG)
51       BCT   R3,LOOP        BRANCH TO LOOP. IF NECESSARY
52       L     R1,DFHEICAP    R4 POINTS TO COMM AREA.
53       MVI   10(R1),C'S'    INDICATE SUCCESS TO CALLER
54       B     GETOUT         GET OUT OF HERE
55 TRANSLAT EQU   *
56 CHECK0  SR    R1,R1
57       CR    R5,R1
```

TRANSLATE LARGE TO SMALL

```
58              BNE    CHECK1
59              MVI    0(R6),C'0'
60              BR     14
61     CHECK1   LA     R1,1
62              CR     R5,R1
63              BNE    CHECK2
64              MVI    0(R6),C'1'
65              BR     14
66     CHECK2   LA     R1,2
67              CR     R5,R1
68              BNE    CHECK3
69              MVI    0(R6),C'2'
70              BR     14
71     CHECK3   LA     R1,3
72              CR     R5,R1
73              BNE    CHECK4
74              MVI    0(R6),C'3'
75              BR     14
76     CHECK4   LA     R1,4
77              CR     R5,R1
78              BNE    CHECK5
79              MVI    0(R6),C'4'
80              BR     14
81     CHECK5   LA     R1,5
82              CR     R5,R1
83              BNE    CHECK6
84              MVI    0(R6),C'5'
85              BR     14
```

Figure C.3. continued.

527

```
86   CHECK6   LA    R1,6
87            CR    R5,R1
88            BNE   CHECK7
89            MVI   0(R6),C'6'
90            BR    14
91   CHECK7   LA    R1,7
92            CR    R5,R1
93            BNE   CHECK8
94            MVI   0(R6),C'7'
95            BR    14
96   CHECK8   LA    R1,8
97            CR    R5,R1
98            BNE   CHECK9
99            MVI   0(R6),C'8'
100           BR    14
101  CHECK9   LA    R1,9
102           CR    R5,R1
103           BNE   CHECK10
104           MVI   0(R6),C'9'
105           BR    14
106  CHECK10  LA    R1,10
107           CR    R5,R1
108           BNE   CHECK11
109           MVI   0(R6),C'A'
110           BR    14
111  CHECK11  LA    R1,11
112           CR    R5,R1
113           BNE   CHECK12
114           MVI   0(R6),C'B'
115           BR    14
```

```
116   CHECK12   LA    R1,12
117             CR    R5,R1
118             BNE   CHECK13
119             MVI   0(R6),C'C'
120             BR    14
121   CHECK13   LA    R1,13
122             CR    R5,R1
123             BNE   CHECK14
124             MVI   0(R6),C'D'
125             BR    14
126   CHECK14   LA    R1,14
127             CR    R5,R1
128             BNE   CHECK15
129             MVI   0(R6),C'E'
130             BR    14
131   CHECK15   LA    R1,15
132             CR    R5,R1
133             BNE   ABEND1
134             MVI   0(R6),C'F'
135             BR    14
136   ABEND1    EQU   *
137             EXEC CICS ABEND ABCODE('BARY')
138   *--------------------------------------*
139   TRANSLTS  EQU   *
140             SR    R3,R3
141             LH    R3,8(R1)         LOAD LENGTH INTO R3
142             L     R4,4(R1)         R4 POINTS TO OUTPUT AREA
143             L     R6,0(R1)         R6 POINTS TO INPUT  AREA
```

Figure C.3. continued.

529

```
144  LOOP2    EQU   *
145           SR    R5,R5
146           MVI   0(R4),X'00'
147           BAL   R14,DETRANS
148           IC    R5,0(R4)
149           SLL   R5,4              SHIFT LEFT BY 4 BITS
150           STC   R5,0(R4)
151           LA    R6,1(R6)          ADVANCE R6 BY 1
152           BAL   R14,DETRANS
153           LA    R4,1(R4)
154           LA    R6,1(R6)
155           BCT   R3,LOOP2
156           L     R1,DFHEICAP       R4 POINTS TO COMM AREA.
157           MVI   10(R1),C'S'       INDICATE SUCCESS TO CALLER
158           B     GETOUT
159  DETRANS  EQU   *
160  TEST0    CLI   0(R6),C'0'
161           BNE   TEST1
162           BR    14
163  TEST1    CLI   0(R6),C'1'
164           BNE   TEST2
165           OI    0(R4),X'01'
166           BR    14
167  TEST2    CLI   0(R6),C'2'
168           BNE   TEST3
169           OI    0(R4),X'02'
170           BR    14
171  TEST3    CLI   0(R6),C'3'
172           BNE   TEST4
173           OI    0(R4),X'03'
```

```
174             BR    14
175   TEST4     CLI   0(R6),C'4'
176             BNE   TEST5
177             OI    0(R4),X'04'
178             BR    14
179   TEST5     CLI   0(R6),C'5'
180             BNE   TEST6
181             OI    0(R4),X'05'
182             BR    14
183   TEST6     CLI   0(R6),C'6'
184             BNE   TEST7
185             OI    0(R4),X'06'
186             BR    14
187   TEST7     CLI   0(R6),C'7'
188             BNE   TEST8
189             OI    0(R4),X'07'
190             BR    14
191   TEST8     CLI   0(R6),C'8'
192             BNE   TEST9
193             OI    0(R4),X'08'
194             BR    14
195   TEST9     CLI   0(R6),C'9'
196             BNE   TEST10
197             OI    0(R4),X'09'
198             BR    14
199   TEST10    CLI   0(R6),C'A'
200             BNE   TEST11
201             OI    0(R4),X'0A'
```

Figure C.3. continued.

531

```
202              BR    14
203    TEST11    CLI   0(R6),C'B'
204              BNE   TEST12
205              OI    0(R4),X'0B'
206              BR    14
207    TEST12    CLI   0(R6),C'C'
208              BNE   TEST13
209              OI    0(R4),X'0C'
210              BR    14
211    TEST13    CLI   0(R6),C'D'
212              BNE   TEST14
213              OI    0(R4),X'0D'
214              BR    14
215    TEST14    CLI   0(R6),C'E'
216              BNE   TEST15
217              OI    0(R4),X'0E'
218              BR    14
219    TEST15    CLI   0(R6),C'F'
220              BNE   ABEND2
221              OI    0(R4),X'0F'
222              BR    14
223    ABEND2    EQU   *
224              EXEC CICS ABEND ABCODE('HARY')
225              DFHEISTG
226              END
```

****

Figure C.3. continued.

The caller must place proper values in all four fields of the communication area. BNSUB01 will carry out the translation requested. It will read the input data from the location whose address is given in the first four bytes of the communication area. It will place the output data at the location whose address is specified in bytes 5 through 8 of the communication area. Before returning, BNSUB01 will place the following code in the 11th byte of the communication area:

F—Failure occurred while translating

S—Successful translating

The caller can test the return code to determine if any error was detected by the called subprogram. BNSUB01 will also cause abend of the program on one of the following user abend codes:

HARY—Larger field was being translated into a smaller field and one or more characters in the larger field were not in the set, 0 through 9, A, B, C, D, E, and F.

BARY—This indicates logic error in BNSUB01. This abend should not occur unless the program was not coded properly.

For examples of using this subprogram, see programs BNINFP2, BNINFP2, and BNINFP3 in Chapter 9, which link to it for both types of data translation.

C.4   SUBPROGRAM BNTRNSL TO CONVERT NON-PRINTABLE CHARACTERS IN ANY CALLER-SUPPLIED AREA INTO DOTS

This program is useful when you want to display on the terminal or print on a printer the content of a storage area that contains one or more non-displayable or non-printable characters. If you do not convert such non-displayable characters into a displayable character, such as a dot, an error will occur when the user receives the data on the terminal or when the data is printed on a printer.

Procedure for Installing Subprogram BNTRNSL

Step 1. Enter this program shown in Figure C.4 in member BNTRNSL of a source PDS.

Step 2. Compile and link program BNTRNSL using the JCL given in Section B.2 in Appendix B. This job will create load module BNTRNSL in your load library. This load library must be included under DDname DFHRPL in the CICS start-up procedure or job.

```
#--------------------------------------------------------------------
1   #
2   # PROGRAM NAME: BNTRNSL
3   # FUNCTION:     REPLACE ALL NON-PRINTABLE CHARACTERS IN THE
4   #              COMMUNICATION AREA SUPPLIED BY THE CALLER WITH DOTS.
5   #              THE LENGTH OF COMMUNICATION AREA MUST NOT BE GREATER THAN
6   #              256 BECAUSE THE LENGTH USED ON TR INSTRUCTION CAN NOT EXCEED
7   #              256. IF THE INCOMING COMMUNICATION AREA LENGTH IS GREATER
8   #              THAN 256, THIS PROGRAM WILL DISPLAY AN ERROR MESSAGE.
9   #--------------------------------------------------------------------
10          COPY  REGDEF
11  BNTRNSL DFHEIENT CODEREG=(9,10),DATAREG=11,EIBREG=12
12          LH    R3,EIBCALEN    LOAD R3 WITH COMM AREA LENGTH
13          LTR   R3,R3          DOES R3 CONTAIN ZERO
14          BZ    ERROR01        YES, THIS IS ERROR
15          CH    R3,=H'256'     CONTENT OF R3 MORE THAN 256?
16          BH    ERROR02        YES, BRANCH
17          SR    R1,R1          CLEAR R1
18          LA    R1,1           LOAD 1 INTO R1
19          SR    R3,R1          SUBTRACT 1 FROM R3
20          L     4,DFHEICAP     R4 POINTS TO INPUT AREA
21          EX    R3,VARTRNS
22          B     RETURN
23  VARTRNS TR    0(0,R4),TRTABLE    TRANSLATE ALL DATA IN COMM AREA
24  ERROR01 EQU   #
25          EXEC CICS SEND FROM(ERRMSG01) LENGTH(80) ERASE
26          EXEC CICS RECEIVE INTO(DATAIN) LENGTH(LEN160)
27          B     RETURN
28  ERROR02 EQU   #
29          EXEC CICS SEND FROM(ERRMSG02) LENGTH(80) ERASE
30          EXEC CICS RECEIVE INTO(DATAIN) LENGTH(LEN160)
31          B     RETURN
32  RETURN  EQU   #
```

```
33              EXEC CICS RETURN
34  *=================================================
35  LEN160   DC   H'160'
36  ERRMSG01 DC   CL40'NO COMM AREA PASSED TO PROGRAM BNTRNSL '
37           DC   CL40' NO ACTION TAKEN. '
38  ERRMSG02 DC   CL40'COMM AREA LENGTH MORE THAN 256. BNTRNSL '
39           DC   CL40' CAN NOT PERFORM TRANSLATION. '
40  ****************       0123456789ABCDEF
41  TRTABLE  DC   C'................'   00-0F
42           DC   C'................'   10-1F
43           DC   C'................'   20-2F
44           DC   C'................'   30-3F
45           DC   C' .<(+|.........'   40-4F
46  *** NOTE TWO AMPERSANDS TELL ASSEMBLE RO REPLACE THEM BY ONE ASSEMBLER.
47           DC   C'&&.........$*);-''  50-5F
48           DC   C'-/.........,%_>?'   60-6F
49           DC   C'........:#@.=''     70-7F
50           DC   C'.ABCDEFGHI......'   80-8F
51           DC   C'.JKLMNOPQR......'   90-9F
52           DC   C'..STUVWXYZ......'   A0-AF
53           DC   C'...............'    B0-BF
54           DC   C'.ABCDEFGHI......'   C0-CF
55           DC   C'.JKLMNOPQR......'   D0-DF
56           DC   C'..STUVWXYZ......'   E0-EF
57           DC   C'0123456789......'   F0-FF
58  *=================================================
59           DFHEISTG
60  DATAIN   DS   CL160
61           END
```

Figure C.4.   Source code of CICS program BNTRNSL

Step 3. Define the following in the CICS PPT:

```
PROGRAM    BNTRNSL
GROUP      CICSBOOK
LANGUAGE   ASSEMBLER
```

Other parameters for BNTRNSL in the PPT should be the same as those for the sample program BNPROG1 given in Section 1.6.

Procedure for Using This Program

To use this program, just LINK to it passing a communication area of n bytes where n must be one or greater, but less than 257. BNTRNSL will replace all non-printable and non-displayable characters in the communication area supplied by the caller with dots. This is an example of how to LINK to it in a COBOL program:

```
EXEC CICS LINK PROGRAM('BNTRNSL') COMMAREA(COMMAREA) LENGTH(n)
    END-EXEC.
```

But what do you do if the area you want to convert is larger than 256 bytes? Well, in a COBOL or Assembler program, you can always redefine that area as an area containing multiple fields, each of which contains less than 257 characters. Then you can LINK to BNTRNSL multiple times, passing it each of these fields in turn. At the end, all your data will have been converted.

See program BNVSVIEW in Figure 2.13 for an example of how to invoke this subprogram.

C.5 ASSEMBLER COPYLIB MEMBER REGDEF

This COPYLIB member is shown in Figure C.5. It consists of register equates. These equates allow us to code like this:

```
LA R1,6
```

rather than like this:

```
LA 1,6
```

The first way of coding makes the program easily readable. If an Assembler program is not readable, God help the programmer who might be trying to understand it.

```
***********************************************************************
 1    R0    EQU    0
 2    R1    EQU    1
 3    R2    EQU    2
 4    R3    EQU    3
 5    R4    EQU    4
 6    R5    EQU    5
 7    R6    EQU    6
 8    R7    EQU    7
 9    R8    EQU    8
10    R9    EQU    9
11    R10   EQU    10
12    R11   EQU    11
13    R12   EQU    12
14    R13   EQU    13
15    R14   EQU    14
16    R15   EQU    15
***********************************************************************
```

Figure C.5. Source code of assembler copybook REGDEF

Index